Intermediate Chinese Reader

Part I

INTERMEDIATE CHINESE READER

Part I

by John DeFrancis

WITH THE ASSISTANCE OF

Teng Chia-yee and Yung Chih-sheng

Published for Seton Hall University

by Yale University Press, New Haven and London

Printed in the United States of America by
The Murray Printing Co., Westford, Mass.

Library of Congress catalog card number: 67–24494
ISBN: 0–300–00065–0

This work was developed pursuant to a contract between the United States Office of Education and Seton Hall University and is published with permission of the United States Office of Education, Department of Health, Education, and Welfare.

16 15 14 13 12 11 10 9

To the Memory of

George A. Kennedy

Intermediate Chinese Reader

Contents of Part I

Acknowledgments xi
Preface xiii

UNIT I

Lesson 1 3
Lesson 2 43
Lesson 3 89
Lesson 4 135
Lesson 5 187
Lesson 6 243

UNIT II

Lesson 7 271
Lesson 8 321
Lesson 9 377
Lesson 10 424
Lesson 11 473
Lesson 12 519

UNIT III

Lesson 13 543
Lesson 14 591
Lesson 15 639

Contents of Part II

Lesson 16 691
Lesson 17 741
Lesson 18 790

UNIT IV

Lesson 19 815
Lesson 20 852
Lesson 21 896
Lesson 22 943
Lesson 23 986
Lesson 24 1036

UNIT V

Lesson 25 1056
Lesson 26 1095
Lesson 27 1137
Lesson 28 1179
Lesson 29 1221
Lesson 30 1265

Supplementary Lessons on Simplified Characters 1291
Stroke-Order Chart 1345
Summary Chart I. Characters Arranged by Lesson 1351
Summary Chart II. Characters Arranged by Number of Strokes 1352
Summary Chart III. Characters Arranged by Radical 1353
Summary Chart IV. Comparison of Sung and Ming Type Faces 1354
Summary Chart V. Comparison of Regular and Simplified Characters 1356
Summary Chart VI. Variant Forms of Characters 1357
Index 1359

ACKNOWLEDGMENTS

I wish to thank the following institutions and individuals for helping to make this book possible:

Office of Education, Department of Health, Education and Welfare, for a grant to compile the book.

Seton Hall University, for providing institutional support for my work.

Dr. John B. Tsu, Director of the Institute of Far Eastern Studies, Seton Hall University, for his constant concern to make available whatever assistance was needed at all stages of the work.

Mrs. Teng Chia-yee and Mr. Yung Chih-sheng, for their able and painstaking collaboration in writing the book.

Mr. Chao Chih-ch'ao, Mr. Chao Tze-yi, Mr. Frank F. K. Chang, Mr. Ma Kuang-heng, and Mrs. Pauline Chang, for suggesting many improvements.

My wife, for typing and other assistance in the preparation of the text.

John DeFrancis

Honolulu, Hawaii

PREFACE

The present work forms part of three closely integrated sets of texts in spoken and written Chinese prepared at Seton Hall University. The relationship among them can be seen from the following outline:

CONVERSATION SERIES

Transcription Version	Character Version
Beginning Chinese	Character Text for Beginning Chinese
Intermediate Chinese	Character Text for Intermediate Chinese
Advanced Chinese	Character Text for Advanced Chinese

READING SERIES

Beginning Chinese Reader
Intermediate Chinese Reader
Advanced Chinese Reader

The general approach in writing this text is the same as that in Beginning Chinese Reader. It is discussed in some detail in the introduction to that work and in my article "Why Johnny Can't Read Chinese."* Salient features include: (1) selection of characters on the basis of frequency; (2) provision of a large number of compounds and a large amount of reading matter relative to the number of characters; (3) inclusion of dialogue material in order to provide students with audiolingual support of what they read; (4) close correlation with Beginning Chinese, Advanced Chinese, and the character versions of these two texts.

The present volume contains 400 characters, some 2,500 compounds, and about 200,000 characters of running text. As in the case of Beginning Chinese Reader, the review lessons may be omitted if the remaining lessons have been thoroughly mastered without them, and the dialogues can be stud-

* Journal of the Chinese Language Teachers Association I,1 (February, 1966), 1-20.

ied or not depending upon whether it is desired to add oral mastery to passive command of the material. The same option exists in studying the related materials in Advanced Chinese and Character Text for Advanced Chinese. Concurrent study of these texts will add a certain amount of new material and, more importantly, will provide a vast amount of practice in speaking and reading with a limited vocabulary.

Of the thirty lessons in Intermediate Chinese Reader (ICR), the first six assume prior mastery of the contents of Beginning Chinese and Beginning Chinese Reader. The remaining lessons (7-30) are correlated with the first nine lessons of Advanced Chinese (AC) and Character Text for Advanced Chinese (CTAC) as follows:

ICR	AC and CTAC
7-8	1
9-12	2
13-15	3
16-19	4
20-22	5-6
23-25	7
26-27	8
28-30	9

Of the 400 characters in this text, 82 (mostly in the first five lessons) have been taken from Character Text for Beginning Chinese, and 312 have been taken from the first nine lessons of Character Text for Advanced Chinese. The large amount of overlap between the Readers and the Character Texts is also indicated by the fact that of the 494 characters in Character Text for Beginning Chinese, all but 42 occur in one or the other of the three Readers; of the 431 in the first nine lessons of Character Text for Advanced Chinese, all but 115 are used in Intermediate Chinese Reader; and of the 473 in lessons 10-24 of Character Text for Advanced Chinese, all but 152 have been selected for use in Advanced Chinese Reader. The characters rejected for use in the Readers in general include those of lesser frequency. With few exceptions the Readers can be said to include all and only characters of the highest frequency.

Besides emphasizing a careful selection of characters, the present text and its successor Advanced Chinese Reader seek to provide an adequate coverage of the grammatical constructions which may be encountered in modern Chinese. Toward this end we have undertaken a systematic search through the material contained in Professor Y. R. Chao's monumental A Grammar of Spoken Chinese, and have sought additional items in a wide variety of sources. As a result, when students finish Intermediate Chinese Reader and Advanced Chinese Reader, they should command not only the basic vocabulary but also most of the structures needed to read modern Chinese.

With respect to the arrangement of the material in this text, the twenty-five main lessons, that is, all but the review lessons and supplementary lessons, have the same basic subdivisions. These include the following:

New characters, combinations, and illustrative sentences
Dialogues
Narratives

Following the narratives are English translations of selected illustrative sentences, usually those of special importance or difficulty which have been singled out for translation to make sure that they are thoroughly understood by the student. In addition, there are occasional notes at the end of the lesson, and also some miscellaneous exercises, such as Excerpts from Actual Publications in lessons 1-17.

Each of the main lessons introduces sixteen new characters. These are presented first in handwritten form in large size. They are presented again in smaller size together with the transcription and definition. These are followed immediately by special combinations formed from the new characters and by sentences illustrating the use of the new characters and compounds.

All the material introduced in this book is presented according to a carefully worked-out schedule of repetition. Each combination is used at least once each in the illustrative sentences, dialogues, and narratives, and occurs once again for review purposes in the Unit-final lesson. All the 1,250 compounds introduced in Beginning Chinese Reader are reviewed at least once in the present text.

Single characters occur at least five times in the lesson of first occurrence—once each in the illustrative sentences, dialogues, and narratives, and twice more in exercises other than the dialogues. They reoccur a minimum of two times in the next lesson (here and below not counting possible occurrences in the dialogues), once after a gap of one lesson, once in the Unit-final lesson, and once each in the first half and second half of each succeeding Unit. All 400 characters are reviewed in Lesson 30. In addition, all 400 characters in Beginning Chinese Reader are used at least once in each of the six units. Adequate repetition has also been assured for the simplified characters introduced in both texts. As noted in Beginning Chinese Reader, the point in having so much repetition is not merely to acquire a recognition knowledge of the individual characters, which can be accomplished with far less repetition, but to achieve a more thorough mastery of the characters in a wide variety of combinations and contexts.

Such extensive use of the characters is necessary precisely because they are of high-frequency occurrence. As Dr. John B. Carroll has noted, "... it has been observed that in normal English there is a high correlation between the frequency of a word and the number of separate dictionary meanings associated with it."* The same is probably true of other languages; it is certainly true of Chinese. To study characters, particularly high-frequency characters, without studying them in a wide variety of combinations and contexts is to delude oneself as to how much one has accomplished.

* The Study of Language. (Cambridge: Harvard University Press, 1961)

UNIT I

第 一 課

1	2	3	4	5	6	7	8
啊	呀	吧	啦	哪	午	晨	刻

9	10	11	12	13	14	15	16
詞	辭	暖	汽	謝	您	她	它

1.0. 啊 **a** (final particle; see note 1)

1.1. 要考試了．你們怎麽還不念書啊？

1.2. 書啊、紙啊、本子啊，我都買了．

2.0. 呀 **ya** (final particle, used for a after palatal **i, ü, e, ua, uo**)

啊呀 **aya** Gosh! My!

2.1. 來呀！來吃飯了．

2.2. 啊呀！你怎麽這個樣子了？誰把你打了？

2.3. 我呀，我也不懂．(T)

3.0. 吧 **ba** (final particle; see Beginning Chinese, p. 20, note 7)

比方説吧 **bǐfang shuō ba** for example

比方 A 吧 **bǐfang A ba** take A, for example

3.1. 走吧！車已經來了．

3.2. 張先生對人太客氣了．比方説吧，要是你跟他一塊兒到飯館兒吃飯去都是他給錢.

3.3. 比方王先生吧，他也是主張不結婚的. (T)

4.0. 啦 **la** (final particle, fusion of **le**+**a**)

4.1. 我們學校要去南湖旅行. 因為我去過了，所以我不去啦.

5.0. 哪 **nǎ, něi, nǎi** which? how? (see note 2)

na (final particle formed by the linking of a syllable ending in **n** with a following particle **a**)

ne (final particle for a continued state or action, equivalent to 呢)

哪兒 **nǎr** where?

哪裏 **nǎlǐ** where?

5.1. 書店離這兒還很遠哪.

5.2. 張小姐是哪兒的人? 在哪個學校念書?

5.3. 你在哪裏買的紅紙?

5.4. 我昨天到張先生家去，他正在寫字哪.

6.0. 午 **wǔ*** noon

上午 **shàngwǔ** forenoon, morning

中午 **zhōngwǔ** noon

下午 **xiàwǔ** afternoon

正午 **zhèngwǔ** (exactly) noon

午飯 **wǔfàn** lunch

6.1. 正午就是白天十二點鐘的時候.

6.2. 他每天上午、下午都在學校，只有中午在家.

6.3 我每天中午離開學校，在外邊吃午飯.

7.0. 晨 **chén*** morning

早晨 **zǎochen** morning

晨報 **chénbào** morning newspaper

7.1. 我每天早晨起來，第一件事是看報紙. 我看的是上海晨報.

8.0 刻 **kē, kè** carve (wood, etc.)

kè quarter of an hour (M)

刻字 **kēzì** carve characters (VO)

木刻 **mùkē** woodcut, wood-engraving (either an engraved woodblock used as an ornament, or an illustration printed from a woodblock)

時刻 **shíkè*** (1) constantly; (2) time

時時刻刻(的) **shíshíkèkè(de)** constantly, every moment

8.1. 他喜歡用刀子刻東西，更喜歡刻字.

8.2. 有人給我一塊木刻說是元朝人刻的.

8.3. 他對我的好處我是時刻難忘. (W)(T)

8.4. 我在外國的時候，時時刻刻的都想回家.

8.5. 我剛回來，我到了家還沒有一刻鐘呢.

8.6. 北方木刻這本書是甚麽時候出版的？(T)

9.0. 詞 **cí** (1) phrase, word (of one or more syllables); (2) diction, wording (see note 3)

詞兒 **cér** word, phrase, expression

詞典 **cídiǎn** dictionary (of phrases)

名詞 **míngcí** (1) noun; (2) expression

連詞 **liáncí** conjunction

介詞 **jiècí** preposition, coverb

主詞 **zhǔcí** subject

借詞 **jiècí** loan-word

用詞(兒) **yòngcí(r)** (1) to use words (VO); (2) use of words, choice of words

9.1. 學中文要多認識字，同時更要多記住詞兒.

9.2. 我想買一本中文詞典. 不知道甚麽詞典最好.

9.3. 我念中文的時候，覺得名詞比連詞、介詞容易記.

9.4. 先生，請問你這個句子裏那個是主詞啊？

9.5. 在中國語文裏有些詞兒是外來語，也叫「借詞」.

9.6. 初學中國語文如果用詞兒用的不出錯，那就很不容易了.

10.0. 辭 **cí** (1) phrase, word (of one or more syllables); (2) diction, wording (see note 3)

辭兒 **cér** word, phrase, expression

辭典 **cídiǎn** dictionary (of phrases)

辭海 **Cíhǎi** (title of an outstanding Chinese dictionary)

10.1. 「辭」有的時候可以寫作「詞」.

10.2. 在中國語文裏「辭兒」和「詞兒」的意思是一樣的.

10.3. 中國有一本最好的辭典叫做辭海.

11.0. 暖 **nuǎn** warm

暖和 **nuǎnhuo** warm

11.1. 一到天暖的時候他就有病. (T)

11.2. 這個地方的天氣真好. 一年十二個月都是暖和的. (T)

12.0. 汽 **qì*** steam

汽車 **qìchē** motor vehicle, automobile

汽船 **qìchuán** motorboat

汽水 **qìshuǐ** aerated water, soda

12.1. 「汽」和「氣」這兩個字的用法不同. 比方說「汽車、汽船」的「汽」不能寫作「氣」.

12.2. 那個孩子天天要買汽水.

13.0. 謝 **xiè** (1) to thank; (2) (a surname)

謝謝 **xièxie** (1) to thank; (2) thank you, thanks

多謝 **duōxiè** Many thanks !

不謝 **búxiè** (1) not thank; (2) you're welcome, don't mention it

13.1. 昨天我看見謝先生了. 他說我給他兒子介紹的那個工作很好. 他要請我吃飯謝謝我.

13.2. 在有人對你說「謝謝」的時候, 你可以說「不謝不謝」.

14.0. 您 **nín** you (singular, polite)

14.1. 學生對先生說:"您隨便甚麽時候教我都可以". (T)

15.0. 她 **tā** she, her (see note 2)

她們 **tāmen** they, them (referring to girls and women)

15.1. 她是那個大學裏最好的學生.

15.2. 田先生有三個女兒. 她們都没結婚呢.

16.0. 它 **tā** it (see note 2)

16.1. 這是誰的東西? 請你把它拿走.

17.0. 他 **tā** them (used for inanimate things in object position)

他們 **tāmen** and the others, et al

17.1. 這些書對我們没有用. 最好把他給別人. (T)

17.2. 昨天早上邊先生他們到哪兒去了? (T)

18.0. 才 **cái** very (see also meanings given in Beginning Chinese Reader, Lesson 26).

才V不久 **cái V bùjiǔ** V'd a short while ago

一直到A才V **yìzhí dào A cái V** not V until A

只有V_1才V_2 **zhǐ yǒu V_1 cái V_2** only if V_1 then V_2

18.1. 張小姐長的才好看哪. (T)

18.2. 那本發音練習我才買了有一個星期. (T)

18.3. 您的小兒子念書了嗎?……沒有哪. 他才四歲. (T)

18.4. 華先生才來不久就走了. (T)

18.5. 我到湖北來才有五個月.

18.6. 他本來說上個月就來, 可是一直到今天才來了. (T)

18.7. 只有去工作才能生活. (T)

19.0. 部 **bù** (measure for automobiles; see also BCR, lesson 44)

19.1. 我才買的那部車, 才用了不到一千塊錢. (T)

20.0. 只有N V **zhǐ yǒu N V** only N does V

20.1. 中國飯我們五個人裏頭只有張先生喜歡吃. (T)

21.0. 一點(兒)也不V **yìdiǎn(r) yě bu V** not V at all, not at all V

有(一)點(兒) SV **yǒu(yi)diǎn(r) SV** somewhat SV

21.1. 我對中文一點兒也不會, 可是中國話我懂一點兒.

21.2. 老張這幾天有點兒不高興，因為他考的不好.

22.0. 難住 **nánzhù** baffle, stump (RV)
考住 **kǎozhù** baffle, stump (RV).
書本(兒) **shūběn(r)** a book

22.1. 那個學生問我書本以外的題目，把我給難住了.

22.2. 今天我把老路考住了. 我問他一個歷史問題，他一點兒也不會.

23.0. (該)多麽(的)SV/V **(gāi) duómo(de) SV/V** How SV/V!
多少的N **duōshǎode N** so many N

23.1. 今天的天氣該多麽暖和呀！(T)

23.2. 你看那些小孩子是多麽的高興！

23.3. 你説馬先生多麽有學問吧. 關於文學一方面的東西你問他甚麽也問不住他. (T)

23.4. 為了我要進那個大學，我父親想了多少的法子. (T)

24.0. 同音 **tóngyīn** have the same sound
同音字 **tóngyīnzì** homophonous characters
同音詞 **tóngyīncí** homophonous words

24.1. 中國字同音的很多，可是意思多半不同.

24.2.「近」和「進」是同音字，但是用法不一樣．一個是「遠近」的「近」，一個是「出來進去」的「進」．

24.3. 你們看這些句子裏，那兩個詞兒是同音詞？

25.0. 沒了 **méile** (1) not have any more; (2) be exhausted, be used up

25.1. 幾個孩子都到哪兒去了？怎麽都沒了？(T)

25.2. 謝先生從三歲就沒了父親．(T)

26.0. 這兒 **zhèr** here (see note 4)

那兒 **nèr** there (see note 4)

26.1. 你明天晚上到我這兒來吃晚飯好不好？

26.2. 你明天在家嗎？我想明天到你那兒去．

26.3. 明天晚上，是你到我這兒來，還是我到你那兒去，我們先説明白．(T)

27.0. 發表 **fābiǎo** make known, announce, publish

27.1. 聽説錢漢生先生要當第一小學的校長了，已經發表了沒有？

28.0. **V_1了就V_2** **V_1 le jiu V_2** V_2 after V_1

V_1了再V_2 **V_1 le zài V_2** V_2 after V_1

28.1. 昨天我請老王吃飯．他吃了飯就走啦．

連一分鐘都沒坐. (T)

28.2. 我們馬上就要吃飯啦. 你吃了飯再走. (T)

29.0. V (不/得)上來 **V (bu/de) shànglái** unable/able to V (up)

V (不/得)出來 **V (bu/de) chūlái** unable/able to V (out)

29.1. 中國字難極了. 我學了一個月連我的名字還寫不上來哪.

29.2. 王先生請我吃中國飯. 到了飯館兒, 王先生問我要吃甚麽. 我想了半天也說不出來.

29.3. 王先生那兩個女兒長的一樣. 我認不出來那個是姐姐那個是妹妹. (T)

30.0. 書報 **shūbào** books and journals

書房 **shūfáng** a study (room)

書面(兒) **shūmiàn(r)** (1) written form; (2) front cover of a book

書面談話 **shūmiàn tánhuà** written statement (read for writer by someone else)

30.1. 高先生書房裏的書報太多了.

30.2. 你看那本書書面兒上的畫兒多麽好看!

30.3. 王省長下了火車就發表了一個書面談話.

31.0. 古史 **gǔshǐ** ancient history

上古史 **shànggǔshǐ** history of early antiquity

中古史 **zhōnggǔshǐ** history of middle antiquity

近古史 **jìngǔshǐ** history of late antiquity

31.1. 他寫的古史一共有八册,兩册是上古史,兩册是中古史,四册是近古史.

32.0. 怎麽了? **zěnmole** Well? What's the matter?

怎麽也不/没 **zěnmo yě bù/méi** nohow, not at all

32.1. 怎麽了?為甚麽又不高興了?

32.2. 我的字怎麽也寫不好了.(T)

33.0. N算得了甚麽! **N suàndeliǎo shénmo!** What's N?, N's nothing

就算(是) **jiù suàn(shi)** even if

33.1. 算了,不要生氣了.這算得了甚麽!

33.2. 就算是你有錢在這兒也買不着那麽好的房子.

34.0. 天文(學) **tiānwén(xué)** astronomy

研究會 **yánjiuhuì** (1) research conference; (2) research institute

從早到晚 **cóng zǎo dào wǎn** from early to late, from morning to night

34.1. 張校長是研究天文的.

34.2. 這裏有一個天文學研究會,從早到晚都有人在那裏研究.

35.0. 男孩(兒) **nánhái(r)** (1) boy; (2) son

男孩子 **nánháizi** (1) boy; (2) son

女孩(兒) **nǚhái(r)** (1) girl; (2) daughter

女孩子 **nǚháizi** (1) girl; (2) daughter

35.1. 關先生他們有三個男孩兒兩個女孩兒.

35.2. 我那幾個男孩子跟女孩子念書都不怎麽用功. (T)

36.0. 父子 **fùzǐ** father and son

父女 **fùnǚ** father and daughter

母子 **mǔzǐ** mother and son

母女 **mǔnǚ** mother and daughter

36.1. 張老太太和他兒子，母子兩個人下月十八號到湖南去旅行. (T)

36.2. 昨天我們父子兩個去拜訪田先生，他沒見我們.

36.3. 田小姐很小就沒了母親，就是父女兩個人過日子.

36.4. 我們母女兩個有十五年沒見面了.

37.0. 中國城 **Zhōngguochéng** Chinatown

家人 **jiārén** (people in) a family

37.1. 昨天我跟家人一塊兒到中國城吃晚飯去了.

38.0. 多少 V 一點(兒) **duōshǎo V yidiǎn(r)** more or less V, somewhat V

38.1. 我念了五年的中文了，可以説多少懂得

一點兒了. (T)

39.0. 古人 **gǔrén** an ancient person, the ancients

古書 **gǔshū** ancient book(s)

從古(以)來 **cóng gǔ (yǐ) laí** from antiquity

39.1. 文言文是古人說的話嗎?

39.2. 你買那麽多古書作甚麽?

39.3. 這個學説是從古來就有的. (T)

40.0. (在) N 上説 **(zài) N shang shuō** it says in N

40.1. 今天我看報紙. 在報紙上説我們這兒的王縣長要發表當省長了. (T)

41.0. 看不起 **kànbuqǐ** look down on, despise

41.1. 你别看不起他. 他很有本事.

41.2. 我不論怎麽沒錢, 也不跟別人借錢. 我覺得有錢的人要是你一跟他借錢, 他就看不起你了. (T)

42.0. 文學史 **wénxuéshǐ** literary history, history of literature

往往(的) **wǎngwǎng (de)** often, frequently

42.1. 我寫那本文學史的時候往往的幾天不吃中飯.

43.0. V 下去 **V-xiaqu** (1) (go) down; (2) (RV ending meaning 'to continue V-ing')

有趣兒 **yǒuqù(r)** be interesting

43.1. 這個故事很有趣兒. 你再說下去呀.

44.0. 這樣一來 **zhèyàng yìlái** thus

道路 **dàolù** road (figurative)

44.1. 他在哪兒作事也不好好兒的作. 這樣一來, 将來一定没人用他了. (T)

44.2. 他現在開始走上一條很有希望的道路. (T)

45.0. 目前 **mùqián** at present

一時 **yìshí** (for) a moment, on the spur of the moment, momentary

45.1. 我雖然一直的都在找事, 可是目前一時找不到. 没有哪兒要找人. (T)

45.2. 他那本書一時寫不好. 我想他必得用一年以上的時間. (T)

46.0. 種出來 **zhòngchulai** raise (referring to plants) (RV)

46.1. 我們家吃水果不必拿錢買, 都是我們自己地裏種出來的.

47.0. 進錢 **jìnqián** receive money as income, earn money (VO)

飯錢 **fànqián** food money

47.1. 很奇怪他每月進錢不少, 怎麽有時候連飯錢都没有啊?

48.0. 早 **Zǎo!** Good morning!

早報 **zǎobào** morning newspaper

老早 **lǎozǎo** early, long since

記錄 **jìlù** (1) to record; (2) records, minutes

48.1. 白先生早．謝謝你給我那本書．……不謝不謝．

48.2. 馬少奇，你回來的時候給我帶一張中華早報可以嗎？

48.3. 馬初民，上次開會的記錄在哪兒？……在您那兒哪．我老早給您啦．(T)

49.0. 黑天 **hēitiān** (1) night-time; (2) get dark (VO)

49.1. 上星期老張説早晨就到我這兒來，可是一直到黑了天他也沒來．

49.2. 昨天謝小姐到我這兒來了，我們談的很有意思．黑了天她才走的．(T)

49.3. 你真忙啊！白天、黑天都做事啊．

50.0. 科目 **kēmu** course, subject (of study)

50.1. 我念的這些科目裏我覺得數學是比較難一點兒．

51.0. 日子久了 **rìzi jiǔle** a long time, after a long time

V久了 **V jiǔle** V for a long time

多久 **duōjiǔ** how long?

51.1. 我才到這兒的時候很想家. 後來日子久了我就不想了.

51.2. 要是我能在這兒住久了我也買一所兒房子.

51.3. 他本來中國話説的不錯了, 可是他不説中國話的日子太久了, 所以又都忘了.

52.0. 從 **N** 學來 **cóng N xuélai** learn from N

52.1. 我的語言學是從謝先生那兒學來的. (T)

Checklist

The following list includes all the items presented in the preceding pages. The material is arranged and numbered in the same sequence as presented. Check over the items and make sure that you know each one thoroughly before going on to the subsequent exercises.

1. 啊
2. 呀
   啊呀
3. 吧
   比方説吧
   比方 **A** 吧
4. 啦
5. 哪
   哪兒
   哪裏
6. 午
   上午
   中午
   下午
   正午
   午飯
7. 晨
   早晨
   晨報
8. 刻
   刻字
   木刻
   時刻
   時時刻刻的
9. 詞
   詞兒
   詞典
   名詞
   連詞
   介詞

主詞
借詞
用詞(兒)
10. 辭
辭兒
辭典
辭海
11. 暖
暖和
12. 汽
汽車
汽船
汽水
13. 謝
謝謝
多謝
不謝
14. 您
15. 她
她們
16. 它
17. 他
他們
18. 才
才V不久
一直到A才V
只有V_1才V_2
19. 部
20. 只有NV
21. 一點(兒)也不V
有(一)點(兒)SV
22. 難住
考住
書本兒
23. (該)多麽(的)
SV / V
多少的N
24. 同音
同音字
同音詞
25. 没了
26. 這兒
那兒
27. 發表
28. V_1了就V_2
V_1了再V_2
29. V(不/得)上來
V(不/得)出來
30. 書報
書房
書面(兒)
書面談話
31. 古史
上古史
中古史
近古史
32. 怎麽了?
怎麽也不/没
33. N算得了甚麽!
就算是
34. 天文(學)
研究會
從早到晚
35. 男孩(兒)
男孩子
女孩(兒)
女孩子
36. 父子
父女
母子
母女
37. 中國城
家人
38. 多少V一點(兒)
39. 古人
古書
從古(以)來
40. (在)N上說
41. 看不起
42. 文學史
往往(的)
43. 有趣(兒)
V下去
44. 這樣一來

道路	飯錢	49. 黑天
45. 目前	48. 早	50. 科目
一時	早報	51. 日子久了
46. 種出來	老早	V久了
47. 進錢	記錄	52. 從N學來

Exercise 1. Excerpts from Actual Publications

The following excerpts are taken from Act I, Scene III of Romeo and Juliet as translated by the dramatist Cáo Yú (Ts'ao Yü). The scene includes Lady Capulet (L), a Nurse (N), and Juliet (J).

L:我的女兒呢？她在哪兒？叫她來.

N:天哪，這孩子到哪兒去了？

J:是誰，誰在叫我？

N:你的母親.

J:我來了，您有事麽？

L:是這樣.——〔對用人:〕你先去一會，我們母女兩個要談談. 不，你還是回來…你知道我的女兒也到了年紀.

N:她有多少天，多少點鐘我都說得出…她沒有到十四歲…

L:够了，別說了，請你別往下說下去了…〔對她的女兒:〕好了，現在想想結婚這件大事吧.

Exercise 2. Dialogues

In the dialogues of this and subsequent lessons the various speakers will be designated by names composed of characters studied to date. A few characters, namely 白, 高, 毛, 華, 馬, 文, 美, 學, will be used specifically to designate persons who appear in Beginning, Intermediate, and Advanced Chinese. The persons so designated are as follows:

白：Vincent White

高：Mr. Gao, manager of the Three Friends Bookstore, or Mrs. Gao

毛：Mr. Mao, a clerk in the Three Friends Bookstore

華：Mr. (or Mrs.) Hua, at whose home Vincent lives during his stay in China

馬：Professor Ma, Vincent White's tutor at Far Eastern University

文：Vincent

美：Gao Meiying, daughter of Mr. and Mrs. Gao and a friend of Vincent's

學：Hua Xuexin, son of Mr. and Mrs. Hua and a friend of Vincent's

1. 謝：田小姐來了，你好啊？

田：我好，你好嗎？我們好久不見啦.

謝：可不是嗎！

田：這幾天天氣很暖和. 沒旅行去嗎？

謝：沒有，因為學校要考試了. 而且我還在一個機關裏做一點兒事. 每天從早到晚一點兒工夫也沒有. 這幾天老早就得起來念書.

田：你在哪兒做事啊？

謝：在中國文學研究會裏.

田：工作難不難？

謝：開始做有一點兒難. 做久了一點兒也不難. 比方說吧，他們每次開會他們研究的問題給他們記錄下來.

田：你做多久啦？

謝：我做了才有三個月.

田：你真有本事. 又念書又做事.

謝：哪兒啊. 我聽說你這學期不在那個學校念書了.

田：是的. 我對天文學沒興趣. 我想念文學，可是這個學校功課裏的科目主要的是科學，對文學不怎麽注重.

謝：研究天文也很有意思.

田：這是興趣的問題. 我從來就喜歡文學. 因為我父親是研究天文的，他一定讓我念天文學.

謝：你說的也對. 要是對它沒興趣就算是念下去也沒意思啊.

田：是啊.

2. 王：張子奇，府上看甚麽報啊？

張：晨報.

王：晨報早晨很早就有嗎？

張：不，往往十點多了才來．可是晨報很好，上面時常有很有趣兒的故事．今天報紙上説，萬先生要當省長了．他是你的朋友，你得給他道喜去呀！

王：政府還没發表呢．怎麽道喜？

張：萬先生才當了不久的縣長，是不是？

王：對了．他當縣長還不到兩年哪，就要當省長了.

張：他家人都在這兒嗎？

王：他太太跟一個女孩子在這兒．兩個男孩子在老家呢.

張：我聽説萬小姐很好看．我想請你…

王：怎麽啦？為甚麽不説下去哪？

張：你給我介紹介紹好不好？

王：你時時刻刻的想找女朋友．我弟弟跟你一樣，老想有一個女朋友．可是没有本事，怎麽也找不着.

張：我跟你弟弟一樣．就是你有本事，有那麽多女朋友．

王：明天我請萬小姐吃飯．你也來，你們就可以認識了．

張：謝謝你．甚麽時候？

王：中午十二點吃午飯好不好？

張：好．

3．邊：常先生早．

常：我跟您借的書怎麽没拿來呀？

邊：啊呀！對不起，我忘了．我來以前覺得有點事，可是一時怎麽也想不起來是甚麽事．明天早晨一定帶來．我還要問你，你借那麽多古書作甚麽？

常：我還想寫一本中國古代史．

邊：你上古史已經寫完了，還寫甚麽呢？

常：我想把中古史跟近古史都寫了．

邊：你甚麽時候開始寫？

常：目前我没工夫．我也不知道甚麽時候才能寫．我還忘了告訴你，昨天華思奇他們父子兩個人來了，跟我談的也是關於寫書的問題.

邊：華先生寫的那本中國文學史出版了没有？

常：老早出版了. 老華説他想寫一本詞典，他説他寫那本詞典的目的是要把詞兒的用法説明白，要讓人會用詞兒.

邊：華先生見了人就跟人家説“詞兒”，不是告訴人家甚麽叫主詞、連詞跟介詞，就是告訴人家應該怎麽用詞兒.

常：所以他的外號叫「詞典」哪.

邊：他寫詞典要用多少時候？

常：他説他得慢慢兒的寫，得三年以上的時間.

4. 路：田太太，您來了！怎麽拿這麽多水果來呀？真謝謝您.

田：這算的了甚麽！都是我們地裏種出來的.

路：今天田小姐怎麽沒來哪？

田：跟他父親，父女兩個人進城買東西去了．

路：田小姐今年多大了？

田：十九歲了．

路：定親事沒有？

田：沒有．

路：張老先生的兒子書念的很好，大學才畢業不久．

田：您給介紹介紹吧．

路：過幾天找個機會給他們兩個人介紹介紹．

田：好極了．多謝您．我現在要走了．

路：怎麽才來了就走呢．吃了午飯再走吧．

田：不．我家裏有不少的事哪．還有我妹妹他們才買了一部汽車，跟他女兒，母女兩個人今天從北部坐汽車到我那兒去，說正午就到．現在已經十點三刻了．我必得回家做飯去．

路：是啊．那麽再見了．謝謝您到這兒來看我．

田：不謝不謝．再見．

路：再見，再見．

5．簡：畢代遠下星期六你有事没有？要是没事我們一塊兒旅行去好不好？

畢：好啊．到哪兒去？

簡：我們過河到南山去．

畢：要不要再請幾個同學的？

簡：當然了．最好七八個人一塊兒去．

畢：要請誰呢？

簡：請老路跟錢小平，也請關文喜跟王始美小姐她們兩個人．

畢：關文喜不會去吧．她才去過不久．

簡：我們讓她再去一次．

畢：我們借老張的小汽船去好不好？

簡：好極了．我們早點兒去，四五點鐘就回來，不要黑了天才回來，我們吃的也不要買的太多．多少買一點兒，可是别忘了買汽水跟水果．

畢：好吧.

6. 白：常先生,「介詞」的意思我明白.「我跟他」的「跟」,「這個和那個」的「和」都是介詞. 我在一個書本兒上看見「借詞」是用「借東西」的「借」字. 這個「借詞」是甚麼意思呢？

常：「借詞」就是借來的詞，跟「外來語」的意思差不多.

白：在辭海裏没有這個詞兒.

常：辭海裏没有. 這是現在發明的辭兒. 最近編的辭典可能有.

白：我忘了在哪本書上看見過了.

常：你前幾天在中國城買的甚麼書？

白：我買了兩本書. 一本是中國文學史，一本是現代漢語.

常：我知道了，那是現代漢語上的. 我想起來了，以後你要是到中國城買書報甚麼的你到三民書店去買. 你就說我介紹的，價錢他們可以少算一點兒，因為那兒的經理是我的朋友.

常：好的. 謝謝您.

7. 萬：老紀，昨天晚上你請的客人都來了嗎？

紀：没有，我一共請了六個客人. 到下午六點鐘只有張子久和張太太來了.

萬：為甚麽都没來呢？

紀：不知道他們是真有事,是看不起我.

萬：我想一定是大家有事. 張子久結婚有三年了吧？

紀：差不多. 他們有一個男孩兒一個女孩兒了. 老張昨天很高興，吃了飯以後在我書房裏給我寫了兩張字畫兒.

萬：他字寫的很好，是不是？

紀：很好. 我們都寫不出來他那麽好的字.

8. 張：方先生來了，你好？

方：好，真對不起您. 上次您讓我刻字因為考試一直到現在才給您刻好.

張：你刻好了，謝謝你．刻的真好．是不是木刻比較難？

方：是的，比刻別的難一點兒．

張：你從哪兒學來的？

方：簡先生教我的．我從簡先生那兒學來的．

張：哪個簡先生？

方：簡法高先生．

張：我想起來了．今天早報上說他要到別處去了．

方：是，他要到東部去了．

9．張：我明天上午要到城外頭中華書店買書去．

簡：城裏頭有很多書店，為甚麽要到城外頭買書哪？

張：我想買的那部書只有中華書店才能買的到．

簡：原來是這麽一回事．可是路很遠，要用很多時候了．

張：三里路也不太遠，坐汽車一刻鐘就

到了.

簡：我想起來了，上次買書的錢我還沒給你哪.

張：算了，算了.

簡：你別客氣，這樣兒一來以後我不好意思讓你買書了.

10. 錢：老張，我有幾個詞兒不懂，請你告訴我好不好？

張：要是我知道我一定告訴你.

錢：甚麽是同音詞？

張：同音詞是兩個詞兒的意思不一樣可是同音. 比方「他們」、「她們」吧，就是同音詞.

錢：同音詞多不多？

張：這回你把我考住了，我一時說不上來.

錢：還有，「時刻」跟「時時刻刻的」有分別嗎？

張：意思一樣，可是「時刻」是寫的，「時時刻刻」是說的.

11\. 路：方太太，您上哪裏去？

方：我到城外頭看王太太去了.

路：他們近來怎麽樣？

方：別提了. 母子兩個人全病了. 兒子也沒去做工.

路：看大夫了沒有？

方：吃飯的飯錢都沒有，怎麽看大夫哪？

路：我們都是沒錢的人，雖然我們很關心他們，可是沒錢給他們. 母子都病了也沒有別的進錢的道路. 希望他們母子的病早些好了.

方：是的.

12\. 史：老邊，昨天老王把我給難住了.

邊：甚麽事啊？

史：我說我要進城，到三友書店去買書，他說讓我給他買一本書來. 我問他書名子. 他說不上來書名子，他說："你看書面兒上畫着一個古人，還有山水，就是我要買的那本書."

邊：我看從古以來到現在沒有買書看書

面上畫兒的. 都是說書名子.

Exercise 3. Narratives

1. 有一天早晨還不到六點鐘,我在路上走,天氣很暖和, 路上没有多少人. 有幾個學生,還有一些工人, 他們走的都很快. 我心裏想, 只有這些老早就出來的人,才知道甚麽是早晨.

2. 母女三個人在書房裏看書報. 母親看的是晨報, 大女孩子看中國文學史, 小女孩兒看的是畫報. 她們看了一會兒, 小女孩兒對她母親說:“我要汽水.” 她母親說:“那很容易, 可是你要用「汽水」的「汽」字說出兩樣東西來. 你說了我就給你買汽水.” 小女孩兒說“好”. 她正在想的時候, 那個大女孩子說:“妹妹說不上來啦!讓母親給考住啦!” 這個小的女孩兒說:“我想出來啦.—汽車、汽船.”

3. 高先生說:“我把張先生寫的中國上古史、中古史和近古史都看過了. 有人問我,看這麽多的書最少也要用兩三個星期吧！我告訴他，才用一個星期我就把它看完啦. 為甚麽看的這樣快呢？我是從早到晚時時刻刻的都看它呀.”

4. 有一個外國學生研究中國語法. 有人問他甚麽樣的詞兒是名詞. 他說:“書、馬、車等等都是名詞.”又問他甚麽是介詞和連詞. 他說:“「我跟你」的「跟」字是介詞.「所以」、「可是」都是連詞.”

5. 「詞」和「辭」是同音的字. 這兩個字在用的時候，有的時候没有分別. 比方說吧，「辭典」往往可以寫作「詞典」.

6. 今天中午在學校吃午飯的時候，我才坐下不久，就不想吃了. 有人問我:“怎麽啦？為甚麽不吃了呢？”我說:“我想起這次考試真把我難住了，我甚麽也寫不出來，所以午飯怎樣也吃不下去了.”有人說:“就算是考試一時没考好，也不應該不吃飯啊！算了，算了. 不要再想它啦. 吃飯吧！”

7. 我有一個男孩子，最喜歡用刀刻東西．到了哪裏就在哪裏刻字．有一天，我給他買了一塊木刻．他看見了很高興．他說：“木刻我會一點兒，可是刻的不好．我要刻的和這塊木刻一樣的好．”從那天起他就時時刻刻都離不開這塊木刻了．

8. 張先生喜歡研究天文，他是天文研究會的會長．他想寫一本天文學用詞的書．有人說這本書只有張先生寫才可以寫得好．

9. 從前中國人到了外國，往往喜歡住在一個地方．這樣一來，日子久了那個地方的人多半都是中國人了．大家就把那個地方叫做「中國城」．在美國的東部、西部有幾個大城都有中國城．

10. 張先生喜歡買古書．他說從這些書本兒裏可以知道古人的語言和生活，又可以知道甚麼東西是從古來就有的．

11. 有一個母親和她的一個六七歲的小男孩

兒在家裏吃飯. 母親説:"如果有人請我們母子兩個人吃飯, 在吃完飯的時候我們應該説甚麽?" 這個男孩兒説:"應該説「謝謝, 多謝, 多謝」."母親説:"對了. 你怎麽知道的呢?" 這個男孩兒説:"這是從您那兒學來的, 我常聽見您説的呀!" 母親又問他:"如果我們請别的人吃飯, 别的人吃完飯説「謝謝」我們是不是應該説「不謝, 不謝」呢?" 這個男孩兒説:"這我就説不上來了, 因為我家從來没請别人吃飯, 我没聽見您説過呀!"

12. 中國有一部編的很好的辭典, 名子叫辭海. 辭海的辭兒在十萬個以上, 裏面有不少「借詞」.「借詞」就是「外來語」.

13. 一個很老的水手要叫他的兒子也去做水手. 他對他的兒子説:"不做水手我們父子就没有生活的道路. 你為甚麽不做呢?" 他的兒子説:"我多少念了一點兒書, 不論哪個地方都可以找工作, 所以我不想當水手."

14. 我家只有一部車. 上午是我女兒開車去上學, 下午是我常用它. 有的時候我們父女兩個人都要用它, 我的女兒一點也不客氣, 就把車開走了. 她還對我說: “你看開車該多麽的有趣啊!”

15. 在今天的早報上説, 謝省長坐的飛機在今天上午八點鐘來到這裏, 可是一直到正午才來. 為甚麽晚了呢? 有人説是因為天氣不好, 又有人説是早報發表的時間錯了.

16. 我們吃的東西多半是從田裏種出來的, 所以我們吃東西的時候, 應該知道種田的人種出這些東西真不容易. 我們不要看不起種田的人啊!

17. 學校給我打電話説我去年在學校的紀錄都很好, 叫我把今年要念的科目用書面告訴他們. 我就給學校寫信説要念化學、數學跟天文學.

18. 今天上午在上語法課的時候, 馬先生告訴我們甚麽是主詞. 他說:"比方這個句子吧：「你有飯錢嗎？」「你」字就是主詞."

19. 有一天我請父親的朋友給我找工作. 他說:"啊呀！你來晚了. 要是前天來，這裏正要用人. 目前没有哪兒要用人啦. 多少的人要找事都找不着."

20. 我才打開書本兒要念書，有一位小姐來了. 她看我是要念書的樣子，她說:"我說幾句話就走."可是她一直說下去，說了兩個多鐘頭才走.

21. 有一個中國學生在美國的南部念書. 他說:"這個地方的天氣真奇怪，已經到了十二月還是很暖和."

22. 我正在王先生這兒坐着哪，弟弟打電話來了. 他說:"我甚麽時候兒到王先生哪兒啊？" 我說:"黑了天你再來."

23. 連先生對人很客氣，對人常常說「謝謝」. 他今天到我家裏來，進了門以後還不到一刻鐘就說了二十多次「謝謝」.

24. 高友文去跟張少奇借錢. 張少奇說:“我每個月進錢也不多,只能借給你一塊錢.”高友文生了氣說:“我雖然沒有錢,可是一塊錢算得了甚麽. 我不跟你借了.”

25. 今天早晨我去找張先生. 張先生的家人看見了我,對我說:“早.”我也說:“早,早.”我問他們張先生在家嗎?他們說老早就出去了.

Exercise 4. Illustrative Sentences (English)

The following sentences are translations of a selected number of the illustrative sentences in Chinese—those which are more difficult or more important and hence to be noted especially carefully. The English versions can be used both as a check on your understanding of the original Chinese sentences and as an exercise in translation from English to Chinese. The numbering follows that of the original sentences.

2.3. As for me, I don't understand either.

3.3. Take Mr. Wang, for example, he also advocates not getting married.

8.3. His kindnesses [lit. advantages] toward me I shall always remember [lit. hard to forget]. (W)

8.6. When was the book Northern Woodcuts published?

11.1. As soon as the weather [lit. day] gets warm he becomes sick.

11.2. The weather here is really nice. It's warm twelve months of the year.

14.1. The student said to the teacher; "You can teach me at any time you please."

17.1. These books are of no use to us. It would be best to give them to someone else.

17.2. Where did Mr. Bian and the others go yesterday morning?

18.1. Miss Chang is [lit. has grown] very pretty.

18.2. I bought that <u>Pronunciation Exercises</u> only a week ago.

18.3. Has your youngest son started in school? ··· No, he's just four years old.

18.4. Mr. Hua left a little while after arriving.

18.6. He originally said he was coming last month, but he didn't come until today.

18.7. Only if one works can one make a living.

19.1. I spent less than a thousand dollars on that car I just bought.

20.1. Among the five of us only Mr. Zhang likes to eat Chinese food.

23.1. How warm the weather is today!

23.3. [You say] how learned Mr. Ma is. No matter what you ask him concerning literature you can't stump him.

23.4. My father thought of so many schemes for getting me into that university.

25.1. Where have the [several] children gone? How come they're not around?

25.2. Mr. Xie lost his father when he was three years old.

26.3. Let's decide definitely [lit. say clearly] as to whether I go to your place or you come to mine tomorrow evening.

28.1. Yesterday I asked Wang to dinner. He left right after eating. He didn't stay [lit. sit] for even a minute.

28.2. We're going to eat right away. Have dinner and then go.

29.3. Mr. Wang's two daughters look identical. I can't tell which is the older and which the younger sister.

32.2. I can't write my characters well any more no matter how (I try).

35.2. None of my sons or daughters are particularly diligent in their studies.

36.1. Old Mrs. Zhang and her son [mother son two persons] are going on an excursion to Hunan on the 18th of next month.

38.1. I've studied Chinese for five years and [it can be said that] I more or less understand it.

39.3. This theory has been in existence since antiquity.

40.1. [In reading the paper today] the newspaper says it will be announced that our [here] District Magistrate Wang will be the provincial governor.

41.2. No matter how lacking in money I am I don't borrow from other people. I feel that as soon as you borrow money from a wealthy person he looks down on you.

44.1. Whenever he works, he doesn't work hard. This being so, in the future it's certain no one will employ him.

44.2. Now he has begun to take a road for which there is hope.

45.1. Although I've been looking for work continuously, I can't find any right now. Nowhere are they looking for people.

45.2. He can't finish writing that book soon [lit. one moment]. I think he will need more than a year's time.

48.3. Ma Chuwei, where are the minutes of the last meeting? ··· At your place there. I gave them to you long ago.

49.2. Yesterday Miss Xie came to my place here and we had a very interesting talk. She didn't leave until after dark.

52.1. I learned my linguistics from Mr. Xie.

Notes

1. The character 啊 **a** represents a particle which is spoken with several different intonations and has a number of different meanings. (For a detailed discussion see Y. R. Chao, A Grammar of Spoken Chinese, pp. 1079-1083.) Its chief functions are as a pause particle within a sentence

and as a final particle in commands, exclamations, questions, and sentences expressing a polite request or a presumption.

張先生啊，他也走了．"As for Mr. Zhang, he's gone too."

老張啊！走啊！ "Zhang! Let's go!"

他不走啊？ "He's not going, I take it?"

書啊、報啊、地圖啊，都買了． "I've bought everything—books, newspapers, maps."

2. In modern written Chinese the attempt is often made to provide distinctions in writing for elements which are pronounced the same but have different meanings or functions. One such case, noted in BCR lesson 25, involved the use of 得 instead of 的 in resultative verbs and adverbs of manner. The present lesson gives some further illustrations of such special usages. Thus, to represent **nǎ** "which? how?" the specialized form 哪 is often used in place of the less specialized 那, which might be read not only as **nǎ** but also as **nà** "that." Other examples include the replacement of the generalized 他 "he, she, it" by the more specialized forms 她 for "she" and 它 for "it."

3. The two forms 辭 and 詞 both have the pronunciation **cí** and the meaning "word, phrase," but the second is more widely used since it is easier to write. In a few cases, however, one or another form is preferred or mandatory. Thus the title of one of the foremost Chinese dictionaries can only be written as 辭海 **Cíhǎi**, literally "Sea of Phrases."

4. The place-words **zhèr** "here" and **nèr** "there" are used after substantives to indicate the location of the latter, as these cannot be used alone in this meaning. Thus English "Come to me" or "Come to my place" is expressed as **dào wǒ zhèr lai**. Similarly: **Tā zài Wáng Xiānsheng nèr** "He's at Mr. Wang's."

第 二 課

1	2	3	4	5	6	7	8
喝	茶	酒	湯	杯	碗	菜	肉

9	10	11	12	13	14	15	16
鷄	豬	燒	豆	腐	麵	李	油

1.0. 喝 **hē** to drink

he! Gosh! My!

1.1. 你要喝汽水嗎？我們有.

1.2. 我喝完了，謝謝你.

1.3. 喝！這兒怎麽這麽多人哪？

2.0. 茶 **chá** tea

茶館(兒) **cháguǎn(r)** teahouse

茶會 **cháhuì** tea party

茶話會 **cháhuàhuì** tea party

茶房 **cháfang** waiter, attendant (in a restaurant, hotel, train, etc.)

茶點 **chádiǎn** tea and pastries, refreshments, a light meal

喝茶 **hē chá** drink tea

紅茶 **hóng chá** black tea

2.1. 你知道中國甚麽時候開始有茶？

2.2. 真奇怪他出了飯館兒又到茶館兒去啦.

2.3. 大家要開一個茶會歡迎張先生.

2.4. 昨天在這個地方的中國同學開茶話會.

2.5. 飯館兒的茶房告訴我, 他們這兒的中國飯最好吃.

2.6. 我們學校每次開完了會, 都有一點兒茶點.

2.7. 我很喜歡喝茶. 茶裏頭我最喜歡喝的是紅茶.

2.8. 今天買紅茶我是為了請外國客人用. (T)

2.9. 明天的茶話會我想不必買點心了. 有茶就可以啦. (T)

3.0. 酒 **jiŭ** liquor, wine

酒錢 **jiŭqián** tip, gratuity

喝酒 **hē jiŭ** drink wine

3.1. 太太説:"家裏沒有酒了. 你要喝, 自己去買吧!"

3.2. 旅館的茶房給我拿東西, 我給了他一點兒酒錢."

3.3. 他在高興的時候要喝酒, 不高興的時候也要喝酒.

3.4. 你喝酒嗎？…我不會喝酒. (T)

4.0. 湯 **tāng** (1) soup; (2) (a surname)

高湯 **gāotāng** clear soup (usually served without charge)

喝湯 **hē tāng** drink soup

4.1. 今天的午飯沒有湯.

4.2. 在中國飯館裏有高湯. 高湯只有湯，沒有別的東西.

4.3. 外國人吃飯的時候先喝湯. 中國人吃飯的時候後喝湯.

4.4. 昨天我在一個茶話會上看見湯先生了.

5.0. 杯 **bēi** cup (M, N)

杯子 **bēizi** cup (N)

酒杯 **jiǔbēi** winecup

茶杯 **chábēi** teacup

5.1. 怎麽連一杯茶都不喝就要走了哪？(T)

5.2. 他家裏喝茶的杯子，有的是英國的，有的是中國的.

5.3. 他拿起酒杯來，話就多了. (T)

5.4. 這裏有三個人，只有兩個茶杯，怎麽喝茶呀？

6.0. 碗 **wǎn** a bowl (M, N)

飯碗 **fànwǎn** rice-bowl

湯碗 **tāngwǎn** soup-bowl

6.1. 那個孩子每次吃飯能吃三碗.

6.2. 有人說中國人用的飯碗比日本人用的飯碗大.

6.3. 我家那個大湯碗是元朝的.

7.0. 菜 **cài** (1) vegetable; (2) a dish (of food), a course

菜心 **càixīn** vegetable heart (tenderest part of a vegetable)

點菜 **diǎn cài** select courses from a menu (VO)

菜園子 **càiyuánzi** vegetable garden

菜單(兒) **càidān(r)** menu, bill of fare

西菜 **Xīcài** Western food

中菜 **Zhōngcài** Chinese food

生菜 **shēngcài** (1) raw vegetable; (2) lettuce

白菜 **báicài** cabbage

白菜湯 **báicài tāng** cabbage soup

7.1. 這種菜的菜心最好吃了.

7.2. 我到了中國飯館兒不會點菜.

7.3. 我家菜園子裏種的菜才多哪!

7.4. 這張菜單兒上的字, 你看是不是法文? (T)

7.5. 有的中國人喜歡吃西菜, 有的外國人喜歡吃中菜.

7.6. 這條船上吃的是法國菜，我很喜歡吃.

7.7. 你知道白菜和生菜有甚麽分別嗎？

7.8. 你要喝白菜湯呢，還是要喝高湯呢？

8.0. 肉 **ròu** meat

牛肉 **niúròu** beef

牛肉湯 **niúròu tāng** beef soup

牛肉菜心湯 **niúròu càixīn tāng** beef soup with hearts of vegetables

8.1. 中國人吃牛肉的比較少.

8.2. 這碗牛肉菜心湯只有牛肉，没有菜心，簡直是牛肉湯了.

9.0. 鷄 **jī** fowl, chicken

鷄肉 **jīròu** chicken meat

鷄湯 **jītāng** chicken soup

鷄叫 **jī jiào** cock crows (subject-verb)

jījiào cock-crow (N)

鷄子兒 **jīzǐ(r)** (chicken) egg

火鷄 **huǒjī** turkey

9.1. 鷄在早晨叫的聲音最好聽.

9.2. 他每天吃飯不吃別的,就吃一點兒鷄肉. (T)

9.3. 他病了. 甚麽也不想吃，就想喝鷄湯. (T)

9.4. 萬先生每天早飯吃兩個鷄子兒.

9.5. 每天早晨聽見鷄叫我就起來.

9.6. 美國人在甚麽日子吃火鷄，你知道嗎？

10.0. 豬 **zhū** pig

豬肉 **zhūròu** pork

10.1. 他只吃飯不作事，簡直的像一個豬.

10.2. 這個地方的豬肉貴不貴？

11.0. 燒 **shāo** (1) burn; (2) roast; (3) stew in soybean sauce

燒酒 **shāojiŭ** (a popular Chinese wine)

紅燒 **hóngshāo** red-cooked (See Beginning Chinese, p. 313, footnote)

發燒 **fāshāo** be feverish, have a fever (VO)

11.1. 他家的房子去年叫火燒了. (T)

11.2. 燒酒是中國一種酒的名子.

11.3. 那個中國飯館兒最好的菜是紅燒牛肉.

11.4. 王先生病了，有一點兒發燒.

12.0. 豆 **dòu*** beans, peas

豆子 **dòuzi** beans

大豆 **dàdòu** soybean

12.1. 這塊地裏種了很多的豆子.

12.2. 中國東北的大豆最出名.

13.0. 腐 **fŭ*** (1) decay; (2) decayed, rotten

腐化 **fŭhuà** corrupt

豆腐 **dòufu** beancurd

13.1. 那個政府太腐化了，所以人民都不喜歡它.

13.2. 豆腐是用大豆做的. 中國人多半喜歡吃.

14.0. 麵 **miàn** things made of wheat flour (e.g. noodles, spaghetti, dumplings, steamed bread)

麵條(兒) **miàntiáo(r)** noodles, spaghetti

14.1. 中國北方人喜歡吃麵，南方人多半拿麵做點心. (T)

14.2. 我最喜歡吃中國飯館做的麵條兒.

15.0. 李 **lǐ*** (1) a plum; (2) (a surname)

李子 **lǐzi** plum

行李 **xíngli** baggage

張三李四 **Zhāng Sān Lǐ Sì** anybody, Everyman

15.1. 那個人是不是李先生？

15.2. 美國李子又大又好吃.

15.3. 旅行的時候不要帶太多的行李.

15.4. 他家的園子好像公園一樣. 張三李四都可以進去. (T)

16.0. 油 **yóu** oil, fat, grease

油條 **yóutiáo** fritters of twisted dough

菜油 **càiyóu** vegetable oil

豬油 **zhūyóu** lard

汽油 **qìyóu** gasoline

豆油 **dòuyóu** bean oil (made from soybean)

16.1. 那個菜裏的油太多了. 我不喜歡吃.

16.2. 中國人吃早飯的時候, 有的人喜歡吃油條.

16.3. 中國人做菜有時候用菜油, 有時候用豬油. 但是菜油用的比較多.

16.4. 他的汽車每天要用很多汽油.

17.0. 好用 **hǎoyòng** good for use, suitable, easy to use

好事 **hǎoshì** a good thing

要好 **yàohǎo** friendly, cordial

17.1. 這部汽車很好用, 不會出毛病的.

17.2. 你知道這部車不好用, 為甚麽還要開哪?

17.3. 你女兒出國念書是好事啊. 你為甚麽不叫她去呀? (T)

17.4. 他們兩個人是很要好的朋友.

17.5. 我老早知道你那個表快不好用了. (T)

18.0. 少有 **shǎoyǒu** (1) rarely have; (2) rare

有力 **yǒulì** have power, be powerful

有意見 **yǒu yìjian** (1) have an idea; (2) have conflicting views

$N_1 N_2$是有(了) **N_1N_2 shi yǒule** N_1 has N_2, but…

$N_1 N_2$是V (了) **N_1N_2 shi Vle** N_1 has V'd N_2, but…

A 對於 B 有了認識 **A duìyu B yǒule rènshi** A became acquainted with B

18.1. 像這樣暖和的天氣近來很少有.

18.2. 先生對學生說:"寫中國字必得要有力."(T)

18.3. 他們兩個人有了意見啦.(T)

18.4. 張先生汽車是有了,可是他不會開.(T)

18.5. 文太太要買飯碗,她讓文先生去買.他碗是買了,可是他買錯了,買了一個湯碗.

18.6. 那個國家的人民近來對於民主政治有了認識.(T)

19.0. V過 **Vguo** (1) surpass (as RV ending); (2) past, away (as postverb)

開過(來/去) **kāiguo(lai/qu)** drive over(to), drive past (RV)

用不着 **yòngbuzháo** not necessary to

19.1. 得了!得了!我不跟你說了.我說不過你.(T)

19.2. 這是一點兒小事.你用不着謝我呀.

19.3. 我在這兒等你.你把車開過來.(T)

20.0. 來 **lái** cause to come, have come, bring

回 **huí** cause to return, send back

要來 **yào lái** want to come

yàolai to order, ask for (in a restaurant)

來信 **láixìn** (1) send a letter (VO); (2) letter received, inward correspondence

回信 **huíxìn** (1) answer a letter (VO); (2) an answering letter

去信 **qùxìn** send a letter (VO)

20.1. 再來一碗吧. (T)

20.2. 昨天晚上我跟老張去吃飯館兒. 剛跟茶房把菜單兒要來, 有人給他打電話, 他沒吃就走了. (T)

20.3. 我家給我來信了, 叫我好好兒念書. (T)

20.4. 她給我來信, 我還沒給她寫回信呢.

20.5. 姐姐給我來電報, 問我去不去日本? 我馬上回他的電報說不去.

20.6. 我有半年沒給家裏去信了.

20.7. 有一個學校請我去教書, 問我能去不能去, 叫我回他們電報. (T)

21.0. 過 **guò** (1) pass (of time); (2) after (followed by expression of time)

近年 **jìnnián** recent years

近年以來 **jìnnián yǐlái** in recent years

近 TW (以) 來 **jìn TW (yǐ) lái** during the past TW

21.1. 日子過的真快. 今天星期六, 明天又是星期了. (T)

21.2. 再過三個月我就中學畢業了. (T)

21.3. 近年以來外國人學中文的比以前多了.

21.4. 近十年來中國對於科學上也有了表現. (T)

22.0. 一半天 **yíbàntiān** in a day or two

大半天 **dàbàntiān** a long time

22.1. 校長說一半天要和我談談.

22.2. 我在學校等了大半天也沒有一個人來.

23.0. 不上 **búshàng** (1) not ascend; (2) less than

V到不能再V **V dào bù néng zài V** V until impossible to V any more

SV到不能再SV **SV dào bù néng zài SV** couldn't be more SV

23.1. 他學中文不上一年就會了一千多字了.

23.2. 昨天我寫的字太多了,寫到不能再寫了.

23.3. 華先生那個人太好了,好到不能再好了.

24.0. 一姓 **yíxìng** one surname, same surname

24.1. 我們是一姓的人. 他姓李, 我也姓李.

25.0. 國內 **guónèi** in one's own country (i. e. not abroad)

國外 **guówài** abroad

口外 **kǒuwài** beyond the Great Wall

25.1. 在國內念書的時候我們是同學.

25.2. 弟弟給家裏來信說他在國外很好, 不久

就要回國了. (T)

25.3. 長城以外的地方叫做「口外」. 口外的人口比較少.

26.0. 方 fāng square

四方的 sìfāngde square

(平)方里 (píng) fānglǐ square lǐ

方英里 fāng Yīnglǐ English square mile

英方里 Yīng fānglǐ English square mile

方塊 fāngkuài square block

方塊字 fāngkuàizì Chinese characters

26.1. 馬家的菜園子是個四方的.

26.2. 這塊地一共有多少平方里？…有一百方里.

26.3. 先生, 「方英里」跟「英方里」一樣嗎？…是一樣的, 有兩種說法.

26.4. 中國每一個字都是方塊的, 所以也叫做「方塊字」.

27.0. 口語 kǒuyǔ spoken language

口試 kǒushì (1) an oral examination; (2) take an oral examination

27.1. 「口語」就是日常所說的話, 是語言學裏時常用的詞兒.

27.2. 你考大學的時候經過口試了嗎？(T)

28.0. 吃水 **chī shuǐ** (1) drink water; (2) use water (as a drink or as part of food.) (Note: <u>chī</u> is widely used in place of <u>hē</u> "drink" in non-Pekingese dialects, as in <u>chī chá</u> "drink tea," <u>chī jiǔ</u> "drink wine," etc.)

重大 **zhòngdà** great, heavy important

28.1. 那個地方吃水是一個重大的問題.

29.0. 大起來 **dàqilai** grow up

29.1. 那個孩子還小, 不知道念書. 等他大起來就知道了. (T)

30.0. 讓出 **ràngchu** yield, give up

30.1. 他們說那所兒房子在一個月以後可以讓出來.

31.0. 共同 **gòngtóng** joint, collective, general, united, common

作用 **zuòyong** (1) activities, action, work; (2) function, use, purpose

31.1. 他說這話是為大家共同的好處, 沒有甚麽別的作用. (T)

32.0. 年輕 **niánqīng** young (of people)

32.1. 我們兩個人都是三十歲, 可是看起來他比我年輕.

33.0. 正寫 **zhèngxiě** (1) be in the act of writing; (2) write regular characters (i.e. not abbreviated or grass characters)

33.1. 先生，這個字正寫我會，簡寫我不會.

34.0. 常用 **chángyòng** (1) use generally; (2) commonly used, common; (3) common use, general usage

34.1. 你有沒有國語常用詞表這本書？(T)

35.0. 打聽 **dǎting** inquire, ask (about) (coverb: **gēn**)

35.1. 我跟您打聽一件事，您可以告訴我嗎？(T)

36.0. 隨着 **suízhe** following (CV)

36.1. 我隨着大家走進了公園.

37.0. (在)(沒)V以前 **(zài) (méi) V yǐqián** before V-ing

37.1. 在沒走以前我要把話說明白了.(T)

38.0. 外國語 **wàiguoyǔ** foreign language

38.1. 考大學必得會第二外國語.(T)

39.0. 去到 **qùdao** go to

39.1. 昨天我想看電影兒，可是我去到電影兒院票已經賣完了.

40.0. 請教 **qǐngjiào** ask instructions, consult, seek (your) guidance

40.1. 關於中文這方面以後我得常跟您請教.(T)

41.0. 幾時 **jǐshí** (1) at what time, when; (2) at some time or other, sometime

41.1. 你幾時有工夫，我們一塊兒去吃法國菜去好不好？

42.0. 對的 **duìde** Right！

42.1. 往公園去走這條路對不對？…對的.

43.0. 出價錢 **chū jiàqian** offer a price, make an offer

43.1. 誰出價錢多就賣給誰. (T)

44.0. 起名字 **qǐ míngzi** give a name to (coverb: **gěi**)

起外號(兒) **qǐ wàihào(r)** give a nickname to (coverb: **gěi**)

44.1. 湯先生生了個兒子，讓我給起個名字. (T)

44.2. 謝力夫老是給人家起外號兒. 因為王小平走路走的快, 他給他起個外號兒叫「小汽車」.

45.0. 間 **jiān** (measure for rooms in a house)

45.1. 昨天你看的那所兒房子一共有幾間？…一共有五間房子.

46.0. A 拿 B 當 C **A ná B dāng C** A takes B as C; A considers B as C; A mistakes B for C

A 拿 B 當 C 一樣 **A ná B dāng C yíyàng** A looks upon B the same as C; A considers B to be the same as C

A 拿 B 當 C V **A ná B dāng C V** A V's B as(if it were) C

46.1. 昨天上課的時候我把書拿錯了. 我拿歷

史當國文啦. 結果跟王力夫兩個人看一本國文.

46.2. 張理明的父親拿我當他兒子一樣.

46.3. 北方人拿麵當飯吃. 南方人拿麵當點心吃. (T)

47.0. (N) 這(麽)一 V (N) **zhè (mo) yī V** such V-ing (by N), (in view of) N's V-ing

47.1. 我父親這一病用了很多錢. (T)

47.2. 你跟我這麽一說話我把字都寫錯啦. (T)

47.3. 這麽一說你很有希望跟她結婚啦. (T)

Checklist

1. 喝
2. 茶
   茶館(兒)
   茶會
   茶話會
   茶房
   茶點
   喝茶
   紅茶
3. 酒
   酒錢
   喝酒
4. 湯
   高湯
   喝湯
5. 杯
   杯子
   酒杯
   茶杯
6. 碗
   飯碗
   湯碗
7. 菜
   菜心
   點菜
   菜園子
   菜單(兒)
   西菜
   中菜
   生菜
   白菜
   白菜湯
8. 肉
   牛肉
   牛肉湯
   牛肉菜心湯
9. 鷄
   鷄肉
   鷄湯
   鷄叫
   鷄子兒
   火鷄
10. 豬
   豬肉
11. 燒
   燒酒
   紅燒
   發燒

12. 豆
豆子
大豆
13. 腐
腐化
豆腐
14. 麵
麵條(兒)
15. 李
李子
行李
張三李四
16. 油
油條
菜油
豬油
汽油
豆油
17. 好用
好事
要好
18. 少有
有力
有意見
N_1N_2是有(了)
N_1N_2是V(了)
A對於B有了認識
19. 過
開過(來/去)
用不着
20. 來
回
要來
來信
回信
去信
21. 過
近年以來
近 TW (以)來
22. 一半天
大半天
23. 不上
V到不能再V
SV到不能再SV
24. 一姓
25. 國內
國外
口外
26. 方
四方
方里
方英里
英方里
方塊
方塊字
27. 口語
口試
28. 吃水
重大
29. 大起來
30. 讓出
31. 共同
作用
32. 年輕
33. 正寫
34. 常用
35. 打聽
36. 隨着
37. (在)沒V以前
38. 外國語
39. 去到
40. 請教
41. 幾時
42. 對的
43. 出價錢
44. 起名字
起外號(兒)
45. 間
46. A拿B當C
A拿B當C一樣
A拿B當C V
47. (N)這(麽)一V

Exercise 1. Practice in Reading Chinese Menus

菜 單

湯

1. 牛肉湯……………………一元
2. 鷄　湯……………………一元
3. 白菜湯……………………五毛
4. 牛肉白菜湯………………一元
5. 白菜豆腐湯………………五毛
6. 牛肉菜心湯………………一元
7. 牛肉白菜豆腐湯……一元五
8. 豬肉白菜湯………………一元

菜

9. 紅燒魚………………三元二
10. 紅燒鷄………………二元四
11. 紅燒牛肉……………三元二
12. 紅燒豬肉……………二元八
13. 紅燒大魚頭……………三元
14. 牛肉豆腐……………一元四
15. 紅燒豆腐………………一元
16. 家常豆腐……………一元五
17. 菜心牛肉……………一元五

麵

18. 牛肉湯麵……………一元四
19. 菜心湯麵……………一元二
20. 紅燒牛肉麵…………一元八
21. 紅燒鷄麵……………一元六

飯

22. 白　飯……………………一毛

點心

23. 油　條…………………一毛五

Exercise 2. Excerpts from Actual Publications

The following excerpts are from the play Fragrant Rice, written in 1931 by **Hóng Shēn** (Hung Shen), one of China's leading dramatists.

1.「你們是來做甚麽的？」…「我們是來喝茶的」.

2. 我們…都是種田的，可是種田人實在没有法子可以活了！

3. 你們田裏種出來的，你們自己怎麽也吃不完.

4. 現在人過日子，不論家裏有没有，吃要吃好的，…用要用好的！

5. 你幾時買的這種東西？…為甚麽我問你，你不説話？

6.「價錢呢？」…「自然自然，我出的價錢要比別人高些.」

7. 有的地方，…多得没人要；有的地方，…好些人没有東西吃.

8. 在十月初，大家是多麽的高興，做了多少的打算.

9. 為甚麽我們田裏種出這樣多，我們自己吃得這樣少？

10. 是男是女？(高興得話都說不上來)男—男—男—的！(大喜)是男的！

Exercise 3. Dialogues

1. 學：文山，明天是星期，我父親、母親他們都不在家吃飯，我們兩個人吃點兒甚麽？

文：隨便，你說吧.

學：明天我自己做.

文：你做的了嗎？

學：試試看哪. 我做兩個菜一個湯.

文：太多了吧！簡單一點兒.

學：不多. 我做一個紅燒豬肉，一個紅燒豆腐，做一個菜心鷄湯.

文：好極了.

學：可是不一定好吃啊，因為我是頭一次做. 你在美國做過飯沒有？

文：我做過幾次. 我想過幾天我做一次美國菜請你.

學：西菜我一點兒也不會. 幾時得跟你請教.

文：西菜比中菜容易．不像中菜得有經驗．

學：也不簡單．要是不學也是不會．

2．張：李太太，這兒有賣碗的嗎？

李：你要買嗎，張太太？

張：是的．我的飯碗、杯子甚麽的都没帶來．在我没到這兒來以前我都把他賣了．因為我是坐飛機來的，不能帶太多的行李．

李：我跟你一塊兒去買．

張：那太好了．多謝你．

李：別客氣．你都買甚麽呢？

張：我想買一個大湯碗，買幾個飯碗，還要買幾個茶杯跟酒杯．

李：張先生喝酒嗎？

張：不，他不喝酒．平常用不着，我是為了有時候請客用．

李：是啊．

3．姐：妹妹，回來了．怎麽樣，這個學校容易考不容易考？

妹：這個學校難考極了．我們今天去到那兒先口試，而且口試很難，問的問題有很多我說不上來，我想我考不上．

姐：我想你能考上．

妹：就算考上了，可能上課的時候也跟不上．我差點兒忘了，剛才我從學校回來的時候，在路上看見馬老太太了，她說他們菜園子裏種的生菜跟白菜長的大極了．她說一半天叫弟弟到她那兒去拿．

姐：不行啊！弟弟這幾天有點兒發燒，不能去呀．這麽着，明天我們兩個人去拿去．

4．中國人：李先生，你開始對中文有興趣，是在甚麽時候？

外國人：我在美國念中學的時候，對中文就有了認識．

中國人：你在美國怎麽會有機會對中文有了認識哪？

外國人：我有一個要好的朋友，有一次給我介紹了一位中國朋友．這位中國朋友當時就給我起了一個中國名字，而且把我的中文名字寫在一張紙上．我一看這種方塊字我很喜歡．從這個時候我就學中國話．我考大學拿中文當第二外國語．

中國人：你中國話説的不錯．請你寫幾個中國字我看看，好不好？

外國人：我寫的不怎麽好．…

中國人：寫的好極了．你看這幾個字寫的多麽有力呀．你常用中文寫東西嗎？

外國人：最近没有．在過去的幾年裏，我常用中文給中國朋友寫信．

中國人：近年以來，有很多外國人能看中文，同時也能寫中文．

外國人：對的．好些人對中國文化有興趣．

5．邊：湯明理，你到哪兒去？

湯：我打電報去.

邊：給誰打電報啊？

湯：今天早晨接到西南中學來信，説叫我到他們哪兒教書去．我不想去，所以我回他們電報.

邊：用不着打電報啊．他們給你來信你回信就可以了.

湯：信上寫着是讓我回他們電報啊.

邊：這兒打電報可是很貴呀.

湯：我聽説往國内打用不了多少錢．往國外打就貴了.

6．謝：李先生，一會兒下課以後你有事没有？

李：没甚麽事.

謝：我們一塊兒去吃中飯．我請你吃一個中國小館兒.

李：你老請我．今天我請你吧.

謝：别客氣．我們簡單一點兒吃．今天我請客，可是你點菜，試試你能不能看中國菜單兒.

李： 大概我把所有的湯都得要來了.

謝： 這是怎麽回事？

李： 你不知道這個故事嗎？你聽我告訴你．有一個外國人到中國飯館兒去請客，看中國菜單他看不懂．他把菜單兒上所有的湯都點了．茶房很奇怪，就問他："您幾位都喜歡喝湯嗎？"他没明白茶房的意思．他説："喜歡，喜歡．你來湯好了．"等到菜一來了，没別的，都是湯：高湯、牛肉湯、白菜湯、牛肉菜心湯、鷄子兒豆腐湯.

謝： 你可不會的.

7. 湯： 老李，我跟你打聽一個人，不知道你認識不認識？

李： 誰呀？

湯： 跟你是一姓，也姓李，叫李更生.

李： 我認識他．你問他作甚麽？

湯： 我這幾天正在找房子．有人介紹説他的房子多，可以讓出來一間給我住.

李：你可別跟他住在一塊兒．他的生活很腐化.每天下午一兩點鐘才起來.天天在外邊兒喝酒,他拿酒當水喝,鷄叫了才回家.

湯：這個人有多大歲數？

李：很年輕，還不到三十歲哪.

湯：這麽年輕為甚麽要這麽樣子？

李：原因是因為他跟他的女朋友有意見了，他女朋友不理他了.

8. 方：老湯你是個外國人，你喜歡吃麵條兒不喜歡？

湯：喜歡吃．是中國飯我都喜歡吃.

方：還有一種東西你吃過沒有？

湯：甚麽東西？

方：油條.

湯：沒吃過.是甚麽做的,是菜還是飯？

方：是麵做的．不是菜也不是飯，算是點心.

湯：油條一定也用油啦？

方：是，多半是用菜油．說菜油我想起來了，是不是外國人不吃豬油？

湯：不是不吃，吃的比較少．不像中國人吃的那麽多．中國人除了吃豬油、菜油以外，還吃甚麽油？

方：也有吃豆油的．

湯：是不是東北人吃豆油？

方：是的，因為那兒出豆子．

湯：聽說東北大豆很出名，每年出口很多．

方：不錯．從前我們這兒的大豆都是東北來的．近幾年來不是了，都是吃美國大豆了．

9．路：老紀，我告訴你一件事．李漢生跟張小姐要結婚了．

紀：好事啊．甚麽時候？

路：日子還沒定呢，因為他們給張小姐的母親去信說他們要結婚，她母親回他們的電報說結婚的日期等她母親到這兒再定．

紀：她母親從哪兒來呀？

路：從口外來，他們家住在張家口的北邊兒.

紀：李漢生本來沒錢. 他這一結婚不是要用很多錢嗎？

路：我想他用不了很多錢. 他說他結婚那天不請人吃飯，只是茶點.

紀：要是喝茶、吃點心就用不了很多錢了.

10. 萬：毛小平，昨天你到那兒去啦？我到你家叫了大半天的門也沒人開.

毛：是麽？真對不起. 昨天有一位美國老太太請我到他家去吃飯，所以我不在家.

萬：美國老太太請你吃飯，一定是吃西菜啦？

毛：吃的火鷄. 她告訴我，說他一共請八個中國學生吃飯，她說就吃鷄. 等我到他那兒一看. 喝！不得了！是一個大火鷄. 這個火鷄大到不能再大啦，我們八個人拿鷄肉當飯吃了．那位老太太還買了很多李子，還有一些別的水果．我們大家連一個都沒吃．

萬：你們昨天晚上一定喝酒啦．外國人請客吃飯以前一定每人先來一杯酒．

毛：昨天老太太那兒有酒，可是誰也沒喝．她想我們是中國人，她買了很多燒酒，可是我們幾個人誰也不能喝燒酒．

萬：這位老太太對你們真好啊．

毛：可不是嗎．她平常很關心我們，拿我們幾個人當兒女一樣．要是她做了甚麽好吃的東西，一定打電話讓我們去．

11. 馬：王漢生，你那個錄音機還好用不好用了？

王：老早不好用了．怎麽？你要錄音嗎？

馬：是，我想你那個也快不好用了．隨便張三李四跟你借，你就借給人家．

最近我也想買一個.

王：應該買一個. 你學語言學，對你很有用.

馬：前兩天我在賣錄音機的地方看見一個，樣子很好看，是一個小四方的. 我很喜歡，我想買，可是價錢太貴了.

王：多少錢？

馬：他們要三百塊錢. 我讓他們少算點兒. 他們說叫我出個價錢.

12. 謝：我們明天到西山去，可是那兒沒水喝呀. 最好在家裏頭把水喝好了，要不然一天喝不着水.

湯：我們不會帶水去嗎？

謝：水那麽重怎麽帶呀？

湯：我想說不定一路上也有小茶館兒.

13. 學生：先生請問您「方英里」跟「英方里」是不是一樣的意思？

先生：意思是一樣，是兩種說法. 現在我問你們啦. 「方里」和「方英里」有甚麽不同？

學生：「方里」是中國里.「方英里」是英國里.

先生：對啦. 現在還有幾個生詞兒，我先念一次你們聽，然後你們隨着我共同念兩次.

14. 湯：馬初民，明天歡迎校長回國那個茶話會是幾點鐘開呀？

馬：明天下午三點鐘.

湯：不知道五點鐘完的了完不了？

馬：誰知道哪？要是校長高興了跟我們多談一點兒，時間就要長了. 而且這次的茶會點心買的很多. 吃點心也要用很多時候.

湯：聽說茶就有好幾種是嗎？

馬：沒有. 就有紅茶，可是有汽水.

15. 簡：李先生，您近來有甚麽著作嗎？

李：我最近沒寫甚麽，只是給晨報寫社論了.

簡：晨報的社論原來是您寫的？

李：是，我沒用真名字，所以你不知道是我寫的.

簡：前天您寫的關於吃水問題您的意見太好了. 希望政府注意您的意見.

李：我想一個老百姓在報紙上發表一點兒意見沒多大作用. 政府不會注意的.

簡：可是近來這裏吃水是一個重大的問題呀.

李：政府也是正在想法子啦.

簡：政府那方面法子想是想了，可是只是說了，也不見他們實行.

16. 萬：錢先生，你這幾天在家做甚麽哪？

錢：我天天寫中國字.

萬：你真用功.

錢：不是用功啊. 你看我們大家同時一塊兒學中文跟寫字，別人都寫的比我好. 比方我們兩個人吧，我就寫不過你.

萬：我寫的雖然比你快，可是正寫的字

你寫的比我好的多.

錢：我寫的也不行.

萬：說實在的，方塊字真是不容易寫. 外國人寫中國字像中國人寫的那麽好的實在少有.

17. 邊：萬太太，您上哪兒去？

萬：我買菜去. 您哪？

邊：我給我那個小女兒買書去.

萬：您那麽多的兒女每月一定要用很多錢啦.

邊：可不是嗎！真不得了. 孩子們慢慢兒的大起來啦，用錢的地方太多了. 您一會兒買完了菜還到別的地方去嗎？

萬：我不到別的地方去. 買完了菜就回家.

邊：那麽您在這兒等等. 我把車開過來，您坐我的車回去吧.

萬：好極了. 謝謝您. 有車可方便多啦.

邊：方便是方便啦，可是每月算起來汽

油錢不少.

萬: 您府上還是那個老用人嗎?

邊: 他走了. 我現在也沒用用人. 要是有甚麽事了, 我就去找我們後邊兒住的那個老頭兒, 完了事隨便給他一點兒酒錢.

18. 張: 聽説那個外國人學寫字學了不上一年的工夫, 就寫的很好啦.

華: 他不但字寫的好, 他能用中文寫論文.

張: 他學問是有, 可是中國話説的可不好. 他説話多半兒不是口語, 好像念書.

華: 那是他學的時候沒注意甚麽是口語甚麽是寫的.

Exercise 4. Narratives

1. 有幾個外國人, 有的中國話説的很好, 有的多少會一點兒. 有一天中午他們去到中國飯館兒吃午飯. 他們跟茶房把菜單兒要來, 看了大半天也沒點菜. 茶房問他們喝不喝酒. 他們說不喝酒. 問他們吃甚麽. 一個人說要吃麵條兒, 一個人說要吃鷄, 要紅燒的. 還有一個不大會說中國話的說要吃牛, 也要紅燒的. 茶房說:“是紅燒牛肉吧?”他說:“對的, 對的.”

2. 豆腐和油條都是中國人常吃的東西. 豆腐是大豆做的. 很多人在吃飯的時候拿豆腐當菜吃. 油條是麵做的. 多半是在早晨拿它當點心吃.

3. 我小的時候母親教我識字. 她拿很多四方的小方塊紙, 在每一個方塊紙上寫一個字叫我念. 不上三個月我就認識四百多個字啦.

4. 我有一個很要好的同學, 昨天病了, 有一點兒發燒. 他想喝湯, 我問他:“鷄湯好不好?” 他說:“鷄湯油太多, 我不想喝. 我要喝白菜湯.”

5. 每天早晨我聽見鷄叫就起來念書. 母親說:"就算是用功也用不着這麽早啊!"我說:"有很多功課要是不多用點兒功可能我跟不上, 所以我必得老早就得起來."

6. 有一個中國人在國內的時候喜歡吃西菜, 特別喜歡吃法國菜. 後來他到了國外很少有中國菜吃, 可是他又喜歡吃中菜了.

7. 學校裏最近來了一位教外國語的王先生. 因為他很年輕, 在没上課以前有些學生有點兒看不起他. 昨天星期一王先生用兩種外國語對學生演說, 又拿出來一本他編的大辭典. 這樣一來學生對於王先生有了認識, 都對他客氣起來了.

8. 有一個朋友給我來信, 跟我打聽我們學校裏有一個姓李的中國學生, 念書怎麽樣? 我給他回信說:"姓李這一姓的人在這裏有好幾個. 你打聽的那個姓李的? 叫甚麽名字啊?"

9. 我到茶館兒喝茶. 我一看没有坐的地方,

我正要走，有一個人說："我已經喝好了. 我馬上就走. 你坐在這兒吧."

10. 老張問我："明天開茶話會買不買點心？" 我說："應該買一點兒." 老李說："茶話會有茶就可以，不一定茶點都有. 以前開了幾次會，都是只喝茶，沒有點心，這次也不必買啦！"

11. 我家房子後邊兒有一個菜園子，種了不少的白菜、豆子甚麽的. 有時候我們從菜園子裏拿來一些生菜的菜心，在吃飯的時候大家都喜歡吃. 母親說："常吃生菜容易生病，以後要少吃."

12. 有一次我到一個地方去旅行，到了以後我先找旅館. 到了一個旅館，他們那兒所有的房子都有客人，沒房子住了. 我正要走的時候，有一個客人說："我可以讓出一間房子，可是那間房子有點兒不大暖和." 我說："只要有房子住就行. 暖和不暖和都可以. 多謝你讓出來." 我就叫茶房把我的行李拿到那間房子裏去. 我給茶房兩塊錢酒錢. 茶房說:“謝謝您給我這麽多的酒錢.”

13. 有一個國家近年以來政治上很腐化. 政府的人常用種種法子, 時時刻刻的想怎麽樣跟人民要錢, 人民就共同給政府去信, 說希望政府不用這些人. 不知道他們寫的信有沒有作用?

14. 有一個地方雖然離海很近, 可是當地人的吃水從來就有問題. 近三年來, 人口比以前多了, 吃水更是一個重大的問題了.

15. 有一個外國人剛到了中國, 他隨着一個姓湯的中國朋友去買茶杯、酒杯還有飯碗和湯碗甚麽的. 買完了以後湯先生對他說:“杯子、碗是買了, 是不是還要買吃的哪?” 他說:“要買. 我得買麵條兒、肉跟水果. 這也得請教您到哪兒買.”湯先生說:“這一帶都有.”

16. 張校長是東北人，最近從中國來到美國. 這幾天都有人請他吃飯，或者是開茶會歡迎他. 今天晚上我請他在家裏吃飯. 我和我內人都知道他不吃豬肉，同時他近來有病，大夫說最好他多吃水果跟鷄子兒，肉裏頭只能吃鷄肉. 所以我內人做菜的時候連豬油也沒用，只用菜油跟豆油. 我內人就做了一個紅燒鷄、紅燒豆腐，白菜湯. 我們買了很多水果. 他最喜歡吃李子. 現在雖然李子很難買，可是我們也買到了.

17. 汽車用的汽油有很多種. 哪種好用哪種不好用很難分別. 有人說價錢貴的汽油一定好用，可是也有人說價錢不貴的汽油也不一定不好用.

18. 有一個人到中國飯館兒去吃飯. 茶房給他菜單兒請他點菜. 他說:“我不要菜，只要一碗飯和一個湯.”茶房說:“這裏的牛肉湯和牛肉菜心湯都很好.”他說:“我都不要，我要高湯.”

19. 有一個人最喜歡喝酒. 他簡直的拿酒當水. 有一天他喝多了, 他說:“我覺得最有趣兒的是每天喝幾杯酒. 今天酒是喝了,可是明天呢?…明天再說明天的吧!今天先喝今天的.”

20. 有人問我:“方里、英方里、方英里有甚麽不同?” 我告訴他:“方里是中國里. 英方里和方英里是一樣的意思, 都是英國里. 三中國里是一英里, 九方里是一英方里.”

21. 我有一個外國朋友學寫中國字. 他說:“中國字真不容易寫. 我已經寫過三個多月了, 還是寫不好.”我告訴他:“中國字是方的, 所以叫方塊字, 是很不容易寫. 寫的時候最要注意的是有力, 不能輕輕的寫. 還有中國字有簡寫的有正寫的,應當先學正寫的,然後再學簡寫的.”

22. 我弟弟最喜歡開快車. 在他開車的時候只要是前邊兒有車, 他一定從後邊開過去. 我告訴他:"開快車不是好事, 早晚要出事的."

23. 我跟老王我們本來是要好的朋友. 我們兩個人住在一塊兒, 每天都是在一塊兒吃飯. 我最喜歡吃豬肉, 而且喜歡吃紅燒的. 每次吃飯要是有紅燒肉, 我就吃的比他吃的多, 都是吃到不能再吃了, 才不吃. 日子久了, 老王就有點兒不高興了, 他想兩個人一樣出錢, 我吃的多, 他吃的少. 有一天他跟我說, 以後吃菜要公平一點兒. 他這麽一說, 我很不好意思, 從這個時候起大家沒有以前那麽要好了.

24. 一個從外國回來的中國人說:"外國的汽車太多了. 不論張三李四多半都有車, 都會開車. 因為從小就常坐汽車, 所以大起來就很容易學會開車啦."

25. 有一本小說是用文言寫的. 我看了它以後覺得用的詞兒不太好. 有人問我怎麽

樣不好？我説:“小説裏寫一個沒念過書的孩子，這個孩子所説的話都是文言，不是常用的口語．我不知道那個孩子怎麽會説出那樣的話來？”

26. 我到北京來考大學，父親母親都很關心我能不能考上，所以前天母親從湖南家裏來電報，問我考上沒考上，叫我馬上回她的電報．同時父親正在日本旅行，昨天也來電報問我．今天必得回他們電報告訴他們我已經考上了．

27. 文山：

昨天我給你打了好幾個電話，你都不在家．這個星期六你有工夫到我們家來嗎？我母親説請你到我們家吃晚飯，希望你早一點兒來．昨天路太太給了我們一些她從老家帶來的中國紅茶．我母親説你是外國人，一定喜歡喝紅茶．我們四點鐘吃點心喝茶．同時我父親也好久不見你了，希望和你談談．還有，上次你讓我畫的畫兒過一半天一定畫好給你．

問
好

美英 十月三日晨

28. 父母親：

我離開家差不多有一個月啦．才到這裏的時候，每天很想家．這幾天認識的人多了，也有了好幾個比較要好的同學了．大家在一塊兒談談或者在外面走走，好的多啦．學校前幾天對我們外國學生有一個口試，很難．有好幾個問題我都沒聽懂．

我住在離學校不遠一個外國太太的家裏．這位太太好極了．她有四個兒女，拿我也當他的兒女一樣．每天早晨我跟她的四個孩子一塊兒吃早點．午飯、晚飯我在學校吃．前幾天他們家裏吃火鷄，她一定叫我回去吃晚飯．她大兒子跟我一樣年紀，今年也十七歲了．我們兩個人說，看誰吃的最多．結果我吃的雖然很多，還是吃不過他．晚飯以後有茶、水果、點心甚麽的. 正在喝茶吃水果的時候, 這位太太還給了我一本英文小辭典. 我高興極了. 我正想買這麽一本辭典哪.

我在這兒很好, 一定好好兒的用功念書. 同時希望父親不要像以前那麽喜歡喝燒酒, 以後少喝一點兒. 別的下次再報告你們兩位老人家. 問
好

兒先念上 十二・一.

Exercise 5. Illustrative Sentences (English)

2.8. I'm buying black tea today for some foreign guests [lit. for using in order to invite foreign guests].

2.9. We don't need to buy pastries for tomorrow's tea party.

3.4. Do you drink ? ··· No, I don't [lit. can't drink].

5.1. What, you're leaving without even having a cup of tea ?

5.3. Whenever he drinks [lit. picks up wine-glass] he becomes too talkative.

7.4. Look, aren't the words on the menu in French ?

9.2. Each day [in eating] he doesn't eat anything but a bit of chicken [meat].

9.3. He's sick. He doesn't want to eat anything but just wants to have some chicken soup.

11.1. His house burned down [by a fire] last year.

14.1. Northern Chinese like to eat things made of flour. Most Southerners take these as snacks.

15.4. His family's garden is like a public park. Anybody can go in.

17.3. It's a good thing for your daughter to go abroad to study. Why don't you let her go?

17.5. I knew long ago that that watch of yours would soon be of no use [lit. not be good to use].

18.2. The teacher told the students: "In writing Chinese characters one should bear down [lit. have strength]."

18.3. The two of them had a difference of opinion.

18.4. Mr. Zhang has a car, to be sure, but he doesn't know how to drive it.

18.6. The people of that country have recently become acquainted with democratic politics.

19.1. O.K.! O.K.! I won't talk to you any more. I can't out-talk you.

19.3. I'll wait for you here. Drive the car over.

20.1. How about another bowl (of soup or rice)?

20.2. Yesterday evening Zhang and I went to eat in a restaurant. Just as we asked the waiter to bring the menu, someone called Zhang on the phone, and he left without eating.

20.3. My family sent me a letter telling me to study hard.

20.7. A school has invited me to go and teach (there). They asked if I could go or not, and requested that I wire them an answer.

21.1. The days pass very quickly. Today (is) Saturday, and tomorrow is Sunday again.

21.2. After three more months I'll graduate from middle school.

21.4. During the past ten years China has also become outstanding in science.

25.2. My younger brother sent a letter to the family saying he's fine abroad and will return home [lit. to country] before long.

27.2. When you took the exams for college were you subjected to [lit. experienced] an oral examination?

29.1. That child is still young and doesn't know (that he should) study. He'll realize it when he grows up.

31.1. His saying this was for the common good. There was no other purpose.

34.1. Do you have the book List of Commonly Used Words in the National Language ?

35.1. I'd like to ask you something. Could you tell me ?

37.1. Before leaving I want to clear up that matter [lit. speak the words clearly].

38.1. In taking the exams for college one must know a second foreign language.

40.1. Regarding matters of the Chinese language hereafter I must constantly seek your guidance.

43.1. I'll sell it to whoever offers the highest price.

44.1. Mr. Tang has acquired a son and has asked me to think up a name for him.

46.3. Northerners eat noodles as the staple [lit. rice]. Southerners eat it as a delicacy.

47.1. My father's being sick took a lot of money.

47.2. Your talking to me has made me write all the characters wrong.

47.3. From what you say you have high hopes of marrying her.

第 三 課

1	2	3	4	5	6	7	8
筆	聽	師	授	封	放	假	祝

9	10	11	12	13	14	15	16
遇	拼	概	接	情	附	緊	敢

1.0. 筆	**bǐ**	writing instrument (pen, pencil, etc.)
毛筆	**máobǐ**	Chinese writing brush
筆記	**bǐjì**	notes (academic)
寫筆記	**xiě bǐjì**	take notes
作筆記	**zuò bǐjì**	take notes
筆記本(兒)	**bǐjìběn(r)**	notebook
筆試	**bǐshì**	written examination
筆名(兒)	**bǐmíng(r)**	pen-name
筆力	**bǐlì**	vigor of strokes in writing
主筆	**zhǔbǐ**	editor
(筆)畫	**(bǐ)huá, (bǐ)huà**	strokes (in writing Chinese characters)

1.1. 從前寫中國字都用毛筆，連寫筆記都用毛筆.

1.2. 念書好的學生多半喜歡作筆記.

1.3. 這個本子可以做筆記本兒.(T)

1.4. 考大學的時候，筆試以後還有口試.

1.5. 他在報上發表的小說用的是筆名. (T)

1.6. 他寫的中國字很有筆力.

1.7. 他是上海晨報的主筆.

1.8. 中國字筆畫最多是多少畫，你知道嗎？

2.0. 聰 **cōng*** clever, intelligent

聰明 **cōngming** clever, intelligent

2.1. 他念書比誰都聰明. (T)

3.0. 師 **shī*** teacher

老師 **lǎoshī** teacher (also used as title)

大師 **dàshī** great teacher, great scholar

師母 **shīmǔ** wife of a **lǎoshī** (also used as title)

3.1. 老師對學生說："你們要注意「見上」、「見下」跟「見甚麽甚麽條」這幾個詞兒，因為這是在字典上常用的." (T)

3.2. 他的中國學問特別好，所以大家都叫他是「大師」.

3.3. 老師的太太是師母. 比如張老師的太太吧，一定得叫她「張師母」.

4.0. 授 **shòu*** give

教授 **jiàoshòu** (1) professor (also used as title); (2) teach

教授法 **jiàoshòufǎ** teaching method

4.1. 祝教授真可以説是中國文學大師.

4.2. 現在的教授法注重學生自己研究.

4.3. 我跟張教授學着了不少的東西. (T)

4.4. 學生們都喜歡謝教授. 他人又和氣, 而且他學問也好. (T)

4.5. 我這點兒本事是從萬教授那兒得來的. (T)

4.6. 聽說學校下學期請王大文先生教授我們語言學.

5.0. 封 **fēng** (measure for letters)

封面(兒) **fēngmiàn(r)** front cover of a book

信封(兒) **xìnfēng(r)** envelope

5.1. 老王給我來一封信説明天請我喝酒.

5.2. 那本畫報的封面很好看, 可是内容不太好.

5.3. 我寫完了信才知道沒有信封.

6.0. 放 **fàng** (1) let go, release; (2) place, put

放下 **fàngxia** (1) put down; (2) discard

放心 **fàngxīn** rest assured, be easy in one's mind (VO)

放心得下 **fàngxīndexià** able to be easy in one's mind (RV)

放在一邊(兒) **fàngzai yìbiān(r)** put to one side, put aside

放在心裏 **fàngzai xīnli** bear in mind

放在心上 **fàngzai xīnshang** (1) bear in mind; (2) keep anxiously in one's thoughts

放學 **fàngxué** let out school, release from school (VO)

放牛 **fàng niú** tend cows

放牛的 **fàngniúde** a cowherd

6.1. 你把那碗紅燒豬肉放在甚麼地方啦？

6.2. 他聽見有人來了就把手裏拿的刀放下了.

6.3. 我想去是想去，不知道他們放我過去不放我過去.… 你放心吧！他們一定放你過去. (T)

6.4. 他兒子在外國念書，他老是放心不下.

6.5. 那個孩子從來不念書. 他放學以後就把書放在一邊兒.

6.6. 我跟他說了好幾次啦，可是他沒把那件事放在心裏.

6.7. 這是一件小事. 你不要老把它放在心上.

6.8. 我兒子到了英國這麼久，連一封信都沒來過. 我怎麼能放心得下哪？

6.9. 他雖然是個放牛的，可是他不喜歡放牛，他喜歡念書.

7.0. 假 **jià** vacation, holiday

jiǎ false

告假	**gàojià**	ask for leave (VO)
請假	**qǐngjià**	ask for leave (VO)
放假	**fàngjià**	have a vacation (VO)
病假	**bìngjià**	sick-leave
年假	**niánjià**	New Year's vacation
假話	**jiǎhuà**	falsehood, lie
假名(兒)	**jiǎmíng(r)**	a false name
假如	**jiǎrú**	if, supposing, granted that
假定	**jiǎdìng**	(1) hypothesize; (2) hypothesis, supposition; (3) supposing, if

7.1. 過年的時候我們有幾天假？…去年的年假是三天，聽說今年只放一天.

7.2. 希望你不要時常告假.

7.3. 明天是學校紀念日. 放假一天.

7.4. 因為先生請假了，所以今天上午不上課.

7.5. 他說他病了，昨天請了一天病假. 那是假的. 他一點病也沒有.

7.6. 你怎麽知道他說的是假話呢？

7.7. 他旅行的時候在旅館寫的名字都是假名.

7.8. 假如她是我的女朋友，我一定不讓她喝酒.

7.9. 假定在星期天開會，大家能來不能來？

8.0. 祝 **zhù** (1) wish (someone well, etc.); (2) (a surname)

8.1. 祝你一路平安.

9.0. 遇 **yù*** meet with

遇見 **yùjian** meet with, run across (RV)

遇着 **yùzhao** meet with, run across (RV)

9.1. 好久没看見祝小姐啦. 没想到今天在路上遇見她了.

9.2. 你在山上遇着甚麽啦?

10.0. 拼 **pīn** (1) to piece together; (2) to spell; (3) spelling; (4) to risk

拼音 **pīnyīn** (1) spelling (in general); (2) mainland China system of transcription

拼音法 **pīnyīnfǎ** (way of) spelling

拼音化 **pīnyīnhuà** alphabetize

漢語拼音 **Hànyǔ Pīnyīn** Chinese Phonetic Alphabet (mainland China system of transcription)

拼字 **pīn zì** to spell words (VO)

拼法 **pīnfǎ** (way of) spelling

拼起來 **pīnqilai** piece together (by spelling or otherwise)

10.1. 把幾個字母字拼在一塊兒就叫做拼音.

10.2. 有人説中國字假如拼音化就容易學了.

10.3. 那本漢語課本是用漢語拼音寫的.

10.4. 你如果學過拼音法就會拼字了.

10.5. 這個漢字的音是怎樣拼法? 是用幾個字母拼起來的?

10.6. 他主張用拼音寫大方言不寫小方言（地點方言）.（T）

11.0. 概 **gài*** in general

大概 **dàgài** (1) in general; (2) general outline; (3) probably

一概 **yígài** all, the whole (of), altogether

概要 **gàiyào** essentials (used in book titles)

概念 **gàiniàn** concept, idea

概論 **gàilùn** summary, general survey

11.1. 那件事我大概知道一點兒.

11.2. 那件事我只知道一個大概.

11.3. 明天那個茶話會我大概不能去因為我有事.

11.4. 用豬油做的菜他一概不吃.

11.5. 中國歷史概要是誰寫的？

11.6. 「原子」是怎麽一回事，我連一點兒概念也没有.

11.7. 在那本語法裏前邊寫的是概論，後邊寫的是怎麽樣用詞兒和怎麽樣做句子.

12.0. 接 **jiē** (1) to join; (2) to receive (guest, messages, etc.)

接到 **jiēdao** receive (RV)

接見 **jiējiàn** receive in an official visit

接頭 **jiētóu** contact (N/V), consult together

接近　　**jiējìn**　(1) adjoin;　(2) be adjoining, near to, close

間接(的)　**jiànjiē(de)**　indirect(ly)

直接(的)　**zhíjiē(de)**　direct(ly)

接着　　**jiēzhe**　(1) be joined;　(2) continue to (followed by a verb);　(3) connectedly, right after

jiēzháo　meet, receive (mail, plane, people, etc.)(RV)

12.1. 你開車接王先生去.

12.2. 這封信你甚麽時候接到的?

12.3. 昨天省長接見我, 他告訴我那件事沒有人和他接頭.

12.4. 小考過了還不到一個月接着就是大考.

12.5. 他沒直接跟我請假, 他是讓別人間接告訴我的.

12.6. 張校長坐飛機來的時候, 我去接他. 因為我去晚了沒接着.

12.7. 弟弟問我:"到哪裏去?" 我說:"我到車站去接人去."

12.8. 高先生明天坐船來. 我們要不要去接船哪?

12.9. 他念了上一半兒了. 下一半兒你接着念. (T)

13.0. 情　　**qíng***　(1) emotion, feeling;　(2) condition

人情　**rénqíng**　(1) human feelings;　(2) kindness, favor

事情 **shìqing** matter, affair, business, event

13.1. 他的老朋友沒錢吃飯.跟他借錢他不借,他一點人情也沒有.

13.2. 老王的事情你知道嗎?…我不知道啊.甚麽事情?

14.0. 附 **fù** enclose (in a letter), attach to

附近 **fùjìn** near to, neighboring

附錄 **fùlù** append; appendix

14.1. 他給我寫的信裏附了一張給我弟弟的信.(T)

14.2. 學校附近沒有中國飯館兒.

14.3. 文先生編的中國古代史上有一個附錄是"中國歷代大事年表."

15.0. 緊 **jǐn** (1) tight; (2) urgent; (3) close, near

要緊 **yàojǐn** be important, be necessary, to matter

緊要 **jǐnyào** important, urgent

那不要緊 **nà bú yàojǐn** that doesn't matter, that's nothing, never mind

緊張 **jǐnzhāng** be tense

緊接着 **jǐn jiēzhe** immediately after, right after (MA)

15.1. 他叫我在十天以内把這本書寫完. 日子太緊了, 怎麽能寫完呢? (T)

15.2. 這是緊要的電報. 你怎麽不早點兒告訴

我呢？

15.3. 我這幾天緊的不得了．哪兒有錢看電影呢？(T)

15.4. 他才到外國老想家．… 那不要緊．過一些日子他就不想家了．

15.5. 飛機雖然有點小毛病可是不要緊，請大家不要緊張．

15.6. 我們年假放完了以後，緊接着就要考試．(T)

16.0. 敢 **gǎn** dare

不敢當 **bùgǎndāng** Thank you, I don't deserve (your compliment)

16.1. 你敢在黑天的時候在大山裏走路嗎？

16.2. 馬老師說："明天我到你家來看你．" 我說："不敢當，還是我到您的府上來吧．"

17.0. 跟在 N 後頭 **gēnzai N hòutou** follow behind N

一 V 就(是)(V) X **yī V jiu(shi) (V) X** to V to X extent (implying excess)

一 M 不如一 M **yī M bùrú yī M** one M is worse than another, be worse one M after another

NU－SV－M－(N) **(e.g. yí dà zhāng zhǐ** "a big sheet of paper")

17.1. 小學生們跟在先生後頭走進了公園．

17.2. 校長演說，一說就是三個鐘頭．

17.3. 他喝酒，一喝就喝十幾杯.

17.4. 他的事業從前很好，現在一天不如一天了.

17.5. 他寫的這幾本書一本不如一本.

17.6. 我就喝了一小杯酒，可是他喝到不能再喝啦.

18.0. 知道 V **zhīdao V** know enough to, have sense to

不知(道) V **bùzhī(dào) V** not know enough to, not have sense to

18.1. 從前念書我不知用功. 現在我知道啦.

19.0. 先後 **xiānhòu** (1) before and after, first and last; (2) at various times; (3) successive(ly); (4) succession

先前 **xiānqián** former(ly)

提前 **tíqián** update, advance, move an event to a time earlier than originally planned

19.1. 他們兩個人不是同時來的，是先後來的.

19.2. 教我中文的老師有兩位. 先前的姓李，現在的姓王.

19.3. 原來說是六點鐘開會. 現在提前一點鐘，要在五點鐘開會了.

19.4. 聽說我們今年的年假要提前放一天. (T)

20.0. 對內 **duìnèi** internal(ly)

對外 **duìwài** external(ly), foreign

20.1. 那個政府對內對外都想不出一個最好的方法來.

21.0. 平地 **píngdì** a plain, flat surface, level ground
太平 **tàipíng** (1) peace; (2) peaceful
安定 **àndìng** (1) pacify; (2) settled, peaceful; (3) peace

21.1. 山下邊有一塊平地. 這塊平地就是我家的菜園子.

21.2. 一個老年人說:"從前太平的時候我們生活很安定."

22.0. 上文 **shàngwén** preceding text, text above
下文 **xiàwén** following text, text below

22.1. 看書如果遇見不懂的地方看看上文跟下文, 有時候就能够懂得了.

23.0. 晚間 **wǎnjiān** (in the) evening
公開 **gōngkāi** (open to the) public, open, unrestrained
要點 **yàodiǎn** essential point

23.1. 昨天晚間他對大家公開發表的意見, 好像没把要點說出來. (T)

24.0. 家政 **jiāzhèng** household management, home economics
理想 **lǐxiǎng** ideal (N/SV)

24.1. 有人說一個理想的太太主要的是他得懂得家政.

25.0. 多年 **duōnián** (1) many years; (2) for many years, for a long time, long-standing, long-time

看上去 **kànshangqu** (1) consider; (2) seemingly, in appearance (MA)

25.1. 我多年没回國了. 現在回到國內, 一看比從前好多了.

25.2. 萬太太是我多年的朋友. 雖然十年没見了, 還是那麽年輕. 今年已經四十多了, 看上去好像二十幾歲.

26.0. 票子 **piàozi** paper bill

(在)地下 **(zài) dìxia** on the ground

26.1. 在地下有一張票子. 是誰的?

27.0. 口氣 **kǒuqì** tone of voice, expression

27.1. 聽他説話的口氣他是有一點兒不高興了.

28.0. 前次 **qiáncì** previous time, previously

甚麽道理 **shénmo dàolǐ?** Why? What's the idea?

28.1. 你前次説可以, 這次又説不行, 這是甚麽道理?

29.0. (就)像 **(jiu) xiàng** (1) be like; (2) for example, such as; (3) take for example

29.1. 有的人雖然没念過很多書, 可是他的學問很好. 像祝先生吧, 他只念過五年書.

29.2. 中國字，一個字往往有兩個念法. 就像長城的「長」也就是校長的「長」.

29.3. 姐姐，要是你出去請你給我帶一個本子來，就像你那個一樣的.

30.0. 跟着 **gēnzhe** (1) follow (TV); (2) following along with (CV)

緊跟着 **jǐn gēnzhe** follow(ing) close behind

30.1. 放年假的時候弟弟老跟着我，叫我帶他看電影去.

30.2. 電影院門前的人一個緊跟着一個來買票. (T)

31.0. 從N V起 **cóng N V qǐ** start V-ing from N, take up N first

31.1. 政府近來做了很多事. 從學校說起吧，我們這一帶就有六個小學校. (T)

32.0. 再說 **zài shuō** (1) say again; (2) take up again (not necessarily involving actual speech; (3) moreover

32.1. 老師，我沒懂. 請您再說一次.

32.2. 我今年不想出國，明年再說.

32.3. 明天開會我不去，因為我的主張大家都不同意，再說我還有病，所以我一定不去.

33.0. 道 **dào** (measure for walls, streams, topics, etc.)

33.1. 中國北部有一道很長的城叫做萬里長城.

33.2. 你們考試中文的時候，先生出了幾道題目？…就出了三道題，可是我一道也不會.(T)

34.0. 處理 **chùlǐ, chǔlǐ** manage, handle, dispose of, make a disposition

V(有)X **V (yǒu) X** to V to such-and-such an extent

結論 **jiélùn** conclusion

34.1. 為了處理那件事情開會已經有七天了，還沒得到一個結論呢.

34.2. 李教授那本白話文學史一共寫了有二十多萬字.

35.0. 甚麽(N)嗎？ **shénmo (N) ma**？ What N？ (see note 1)

S好(了) **S hǎo (le)** It is good that S; It would be best if S

35.1. 你有甚麽心事嗎？跟我説好了.

35.2. 事太多了. 我不知道先做甚麽好了.(T)

35.3. 他開車開的太快. 不叫他開車好.(T)

36.0. 心得 **xīndé** a gain, attainment

從頭 **cóngtóu** (1) from (the) head; (2) from the beginning

36.1. 我念了一年的中文一點兒心得也没有. 我想從頭再念一次.

37.0. 得N(V) **děi N (V)** requires (that) N (V) (see note 2)

37.1. 買那部大辭典得三百塊錢. 我可買不起. (T)

Checklist

1. 筆
   毛筆
   筆記
   寫筆記
   作筆記
   筆記本(兒)
   筆試
   筆名(兒)
   筆力
   主筆
   (筆)畫
2. 聰
   聰明
3. 師
   老師
   大師
   師母
4. 授
   教授
   教授法
5. 封
   封面
   信封兒
6. 放
   放下
   放心
   放心得下
   放在一邊(兒)
   放在心裏
   放在心上
   放學
   放牛
   放牛的
7. 假
   告假
   請假
   放假
   病假
   年假
   假話
   假名(兒)
   假如
   假定
8. 祝
9. 遇
   遇見
   遇着
10. 拼
    拼音
    拼音法
    拼音化
    漢語拼音
    拼字
    拼法
    拼起來
11. 概
    大概
    一概
    概要
    概念
    概論
12. 接
    接到
    接見
    接頭
    接近

間接(的)
直接(的)
接着
13. 情
人情
事情
14. 附
附近
附錄
15. 緊
要緊
緊要
那不要緊
緊張
緊接着
16. 敢
不敢當
17. 跟在N後頭
一V就(是)(V) X
一M不如一M

NU-SV-M-(N)
18. 知道V
不知(道)V
19. 先後
先前
提前
20. 對內
對外
21. 平地
太平
安定
22. 上文
下文
23. 晚間
公開
要點
24. 家政
理想
25. 多年

看上去
26. 票子
(在)地下
27. 口氣
28. 前次
甚麽道理
29. (就)像
30. 跟着
緊跟着
31. 從NV起
32. 再説
33. 道
34. 處理
V(有)X
結論
35. 甚麽(N)嗎
S好(了)
36. 心得
從頭
37. 得N(V)

Exercise 1. Excerpts from Actual Publications

The following excerpts are taken from **Xiàndài Hànyǔ** (Contemporary Chinese), compiled by the Department of Chinese Language and Literature at Peking University. (Peking, 1963)

1. 文字是書面的語言. … 有了文字, 語言的作用更大了.

2. 北京話是地點方言(小方言).

3. 漢字已經有三千多年的歷史了.

4. 過去漢字沒有能走上拼音的道路.

5. 先談同音詞問題. 漢語同音詞比較多.

6. 在沒有實行拼音化以前, 我們還離不開漢字.

7. 常用的漢字不過四五千.

8. 漢語的借詞有的是從外國語言中借來的.

9. 這些詞都是我們直接從日語中借來的.

10. 要知道詞是甚麽, 最好先從字說起.

11. 要注意的是有些字有的時候是詞, 有的時候不是.

12. "他她宅"是書面上的分別.

13. "他哪兒都到過"也可以說"哪兒他都到過."

14. 連詞的數目比較多.

15. 文言裏的“所以”跟現代語裏的“所以”用法不一樣.

Exercise 2. Dialogues

1. 白：馬教授，兩個星期沒見啦. 您跟馬師母都好嗎？

馬：我們都好. 放這幾天假你都作甚麽啦？

白：給家裏跟朋友們寫了幾封信，到高家去了兩次，還有一位英國同學他先前也是您的學生，請我到他家去吃一次飯.

馬：你説的那位英國同學，是不是錢初民？

白：是.

馬：他毛筆字寫的很好，寫的很有筆力.

白：是的，他聰明極了. 不但漢字寫的好，還會畫中國畫兒哪.

馬：我知道他會畫畫兒，可是我沒看見過.

白：我那兒有他一張畫兒，下次我帶來

您看看.

馬：日子過的真快，兩個星期的假很快的就過去啦.

白：再上兩個星期的課緊跟着又放年假啦.

馬：是啊. 聽説今年的年假還要提前放兩天.

2. 祝：張太太，你到哪兒去？

張：我到王太太家去. 你到哪兒去，祝太太？

祝：我就在這附近買點兒東西. 聽説王先生最近又沒事了.

張：可不是嗎！這幾年裏頭他們的生活老也沒安定過.

祝：怎麽王先生的工作老是不長呢？

張：他為了病老請假，所以在甚麽地方做事都不會長的. 説起來也沒法子，人口多，進錢少，不够吃，當然要有病啦.

祝：他們那幾個孩子都知道用功，將來

他們有希望.

張：將來是將來呀. 目前的生活這麽難. 就像前天吧，那個最小的兒子要錢買書. 王太太拿不出錢來給孩子. 孩子當然不知道父母的難處啦. 那個孩子就跟在他母親後頭要錢. 你說作母親的心裏多麽的難過.

祝：是啊.

3. 先生：請你們先把書放在一邊兒，我先問你們問題.

學生：好的.

先生：這個字你們認識吧？

學生：筆.

先生：對了. 請你們用「筆」字說詞兒.

學生：毛筆、筆記、寫筆記、作筆記、筆試、筆名、主筆、筆畫.

先生：我很高興你們雖然念中文没有好久，可是每一位同學都很有心得.

4. 師：這幾天我跟你們在一塊兒研究你們認為這種教授法怎麽樣？

生：老師這個法子好極啦.

師：好，我們以後就用這個法子. 我們今天的功課都學完了，還有十五分鐘才下課哪. 你們有甚麽問題或者對別的事情都可以隨便發表意見.

生：老師，我有一個問題. 對漢語拼音化您的意見怎麽樣？

師：很難説. 我認為它的好處是，假如把字母跟拼法學會了以後，就是没念過書的人，也能把他要説的話用拼音法寫出來. 它的短處是，要是多少年以後我們研究學問遇着問題要看古書，所有的古書一概不會看了.

生：我也聽人説過，拼音不是真正的中國字. 漢字要是用拼音字母拼起來，那就不是漢字啦. 您説這話對嗎？

師：這是每個人的看法不同.

生：老師，學漢語拼音難不難？如果字母都會，只是學用字母拼音大概要多少時候？

師：這個不敢説．要是你很聰明當然學得快．

生：希望以後我們跟您學一點兒漢語拼音．

師：好的，我們從明天起就學．請你們明天上課的時候每人帶一本筆記本兒來．我們試試看要是有興趣學下去，再買拼音的漢語課本兒．

生：好的．

師：還有甚麽問題嗎？

生：「直接」跟「間接」怎麽用？

師：我説個比方：那件事情我是間接請王先生告訴李先生的，不是我自己直接跟李先生説的．… 現在時候到了．有問題我們明天再説啦．

生：老師，明天見．

師：明天見．

5. 湯：老邊，昨天我在路上遇見祝先生了．他説下星期他到上海去．

邊：啊呀！他要走啦，我們兩個人有很

多事情，他走了我跟誰去接頭哪？

湯：他告訴我了，他說他走了以後所有的事讓王經理接着跟你談.

邊：他去多久？

湯：他每次一去就是兩三個月.

邊：聽說他的生意都不怎麽理想.

湯：都不行.

邊：他又有錢，又會做生意，這是甚麽道理呢？

湯：誰知道哪？

6. 王：老田，你有信封兒沒有？借我一個.我往家裏寫信，沒信封兒啦.

田：有有.你這幾天好像有心事？

王：前天接到我姐姐來信說我母親又病啦.她信上雖然寫着現在好些了，可是我天天不放心.本來想告兩天假回去看看，可是前次她病了我已經請了一次假了.

田：你母親是甚麽病啊？

王：她是多年的老病啦.平常看上去一

點兒也不像有病．要是病一來了就不得了．幾天不吃不喝．連大夫也説不來她是甚麽毛病．

田：我想老毛病不要緊．我父親就有這種老病，他現在已經七十多啦．

王：我母親可不同．她近來給我來信常提到她自己一天不如一天，所以我一接到家裏的信我就天天放心不下．

7．紀：老邊，我們三年不見啦．你和你太太都好嗎？

邊：好．你這三年裏也很好吧？

紀：好．我在船上剛才還想呢，這麽早你一定不會來接我的．還有，我信上寫着是早上九點鐘船到這兒．你怎麽知道提前了呢？

邊：昨天晚上一個朋友告訴我的．他説這條船今天到的早，六七點鐘就可以到了．我怕接不着你．早上四點鐘我就起來啦．

紀：你起來那麽早作甚麽呀？

邊：因為從我家到這兒還得過一道河哪．過河要用半個鐘頭的時間．

邊：你在這三年裏頭學問一定研究的不錯啦．

紀：我才去的那年，老有病常請病假．這兩年來實在學着了一點東西．我們那位國文老師學問好極了．人家都叫他是張大師．我跟他得到了不少的學問．

邊：李美英小姐你常看見她嗎？

紀：我跟她不常見面．他是學家政的．

邊：我想起一件事來，很對不起．去年你來信說要買文字學概要，所有的書店我都去啦，都沒有這本書．

紀：後來我買到啦．我寫信給日本一個朋友，在日本買到了．我寫信請你定的旅館離這兒遠不遠？

邊：不很遠，就在這條路上．對了，我們先到旅館看看．你先把行李放下，然後到我家去吃飯談談．

紀：你同你太太對我這麽客氣真是不敢當.

邊：老朋友別客氣.

8. 錢：老王，張力子的女朋友真好看.

王：你看見過？

錢：沒有．昨天他拿了一本小說，封面上是一個很好看的小姐，他說是他女朋友.

王：你別聽他的．他老說假話．那是一個電影女明星，王美如.

錢：他說姓張，是張文喜小姐.

王：他是跟你說個假名兒．你怎麽連那麽有名的女明星都看不出來呢.

9. 湯：老謝，你聽我告訴你一件事.

謝：甚麽事啊？

湯：我寫了好幾封信給張漢生，大概先後寫了有十封信，請他給我找一個工作．昨天我去看他．我一提到這件事，聽他的口氣他就沒把我的事放在心上.

謝：你不必生氣. 他不但不把別人的事放在心裏，而且他連一點兒人情也不懂. 你看我跟他是老朋友啦. 我父親母親從很遠的地方來，他都沒到我這兒來看看兩位老人家.

湯：我以後也不理他了.

謝：我想起來啦，關於找工作的事你去找李先生好了. 請他給你想法子. 他人又和氣，而且他朋友也多.

10. 先生：現在我給你們說一個故事.

學生：好.

先生：在明朝初年的時候有一個很有學問而且畫兒也畫的很好的人. 他小的時候念書很知道用功. 才十歲就沒父親啦. 母子兩個人生活很不容易. 有一天他放學回來，他母親對他說："孩子啊，我家沒錢，你不可能再念書啦. 有人找放牛的，你去給人家放牛去吧."

學生：十歲的小孩兒怎麽會放牛哪？

先生：没法子．從這個時候開始，他就給人家放牛了．

學生：老師，您説他是很有學問的人．他給人家放牛，那兒有機會念書啊？

先生：他一邊兒放牛，一邊兒看書．他的學問是這樣兒得來的．有一次牛在河邊兒喝水，他站在那邊兒看山水．他心裏想古人説「人在圖畫中」真是一點兒也不錯．他就想畫下來．

學生：他怎麽畫呢？

先生：你們聽我説呀．他就找一塊平地拿一小張紙放在地下，就畫起來啦．他的畫兒是這樣兒畫出來的．

11. 生：老師，我不論看甚麽書，老是覺得没甚麽心得．看完了以後都忘了，一點兒也得不到．

師：看書有看書的方法．我們從看文學書上説起．拿起一本書來，必得從頭兒慢慢兒看下去．如果有不明白的句子，或是不懂的詞兒，看看上文跟下文，要多用一點兒思想.

生：如果還是不懂呢？

師：假定哪個句子或者哪個詞兒還是不懂，再看字典，這一本書完全都明白了，再研究這本書所說的要點是甚麽，你就都明白了，都懂了．說來説去還是那個結論，看書要用思想才有心得.

12. 李：紀初民，昨天我買了一本中國文學概論，書後面有附錄，上面有一個詞兒是「概念」. 這個詞兒我不大懂.

紀：概念是心理學上的名詞.

李：我還有幾個詞兒得請問你．你現在有事没有？

紀：我没事.

李：「晚間」是説的還是寫的？

紀：是寫的，口語上都是用「晚上」.

李：「接見」和「見面」是一樣的意思嗎？

紀：不．假如你有事去見省長，他見你就用「接見」.

李：「緊要」跟「緊張」有甚麽分別？

紀：「緊要」是「重要」的意思．比如「那件事情很緊要」．「緊張」是「他們的工作很緊張」，「你不要那麽緊張」．

13. 簡：李先生，對不起我明天請一天假，事情得你多做一點兒啦．

李：別客氣，那不要緊．你明天請假有甚麽事嗎？

簡：我去接船．我父母跟我姐姐，他們明天從老家到這兒啦．

李：聽説那兒王省長對行政上不怎麽好，是不是？

簡：我父母他們到這兒來就是這個原因．從他當省長以來東西就貴起來啦．

李：是．我看報紙上説，那兒的東西近來貴的不得了．

簡：大事小事他都處理的不好．他很不民主．在政治上有很多事情他不公開．

14. 常：我們還有一星期就放假啦．

萬：放完了假緊接着就考試.

常：我不喜歡這樣兒放假. 我說最好是先考試然後再放假.

萬：像這樣兒放了假跟着就考試，在放假這幾天心裏頭老是有一件事.

常：可不是嗎！

15. 邊：昨天我看報上說，那個國家的老百姓沒有一天過太平日子的. 本國裏頭，不是你打我就是我打你.

路：那個國家真是不行，對內對外都沒有好法子.

邊：比如他們的票子吧，今天一塊錢可以吃一碗麵，明天同樣的一碗麵，就得一塊二啦.

Exercise 3. Narratives

1. 研究學問的人多半喜歡寫筆記. 筆記是把看過書裏的要點和自己的心得記下來. 中國明朝有一位學者，他從小的時候念書就作筆記，記了三十多年. 他的筆記本有三十二部．這些筆記本後來是一部最有名的書，書名叫做日知錄．

2．中國元朝的時候，有一個很有學問又會畫畫的人．他小的時候就喜歡念書．因為家裏没有錢，就去給人家放牛．可是他這個放牛的和別的放牛的不一樣．別人只是放牛，他一面放牛一面念書和練習畫畫兒，所以後來他是一個很有學問而且很有名的畫家．

3．錢先生是教我中文的老師．他教我不到兩年，我學會了漢語拼音，我認識有一千中國字，還能用中國字寫簡單的信．近來他教我用毛筆寫字，先教我怎樣拿筆，又教我怎樣用筆才有筆力．今天他對我說："在我教的學生裏你是最聰明的，所以你的中文功課樣樣都好．"我說："不是我聰明，是您的教授法好．"

4．田先生是我多年的朋友．他太太是學家政的，她把家裏的事情樣樣全處理的很好. 大家都說田先生有一個最好的太太, 有一個最好的家. 田先生說:“理想的家, 這話實在不敢當. 不過我覺得太太懂得家政真是家裏最要緊的一件事.”

5. 有一個人買了一部汽車, 他想自己開車. 有人告訴他在這個地方開車先要經過政府考試, 考試的時候不但要看你開車好不好, 還要經過一次筆試. 筆試的題目不太難, 考的都是關於開車應當知道的事情, 只要大概寫的對了就可以考上了.

6. 有一個美國學生, 中文很好, 中國字也寫的好. 有一天是美國一個紀念日, 他用兩大張紅紙寫了十個中國字. 在頭一張紅紙上寫的是「祝美國萬歲」. 在第二張紅紙上寫的是「望天下太平」. 教他中文的先生看見了說:“不但字寫的很有筆力, 而且句子作的也很有意思.”

7. 錢先生有兩個兒子. 大兒子從小就知道念書, 後來書念的很好. 小兒子小時候雖然不知道念書，可是後來書念的比大兒子還好．錢先生說：“小孩子開始不知道念書那不要緊．最要緊的是大了以後，如果不知道念書那就沒希望了．”

8．湯先生和我在一個大學念書．湯先生有一個中學同學，王先生，也要到這裏來．王先生先後給湯先生來了兩封信說是坐船來，叫他去接船．今天湯先生對我說：“老王今天下午到，我去接飛機去．”我說：“王先生不是坐船來嗎？你為甚麼不去接船，要去接飛機呢？”湯先生說：“我是到船上接飛機去．”我聽見這句話，我更不明白了．後來湯先生告訴我：“老王在中學的時候有一個外號叫「飛機」，所以我說去接飛機．”

9．從前在北京一個大學裏有一個姓關的學生很用功．他從來不告假．就是有病還是去上課也不請病假．他念到第四年差幾天就要畢業的時候，他病了，病的連路都不能走了．他還是要上課，一定不請假，可是不能走路怎能上課呢？這時候，教這門功課的教授知道了，來對他說：“你不要上課,也用不着請假．我請假好了．”這位教授就真的沒給學生上課，這個學生就有了念四年大學沒請過假的最好的紀錄．

10. 弟弟問我：“你到火車站接人去接着了沒有？”我說：“沒接着．”弟弟接着說．“我早就知道你接不着，因為你走了以後，那個人來電話,是從別的地方來的電話,說今天不能來了．我問他甚麽時候來，他說：“以後再說吧．”

11. 我家附近有一條小河．我記得我小的時候常跟着父親到河邊去．河的這一邊都是平地，有很多菜園子．河的那一邊有些山．那些山看上去不算高，可是我們從來沒上去過,只是在河這邊遠遠的看,覺得那裏有山有水很好看．現在我離開家有很多年了,不知道甚麽時候能回家,再跟着父親到河邊去看看山水．

12. 田先生是大學教授也是大華報的主筆.他對國家大事常在報上發表意見，用的都是筆名.他的學生問他，為甚麼不用真的姓名.他說:“你們都很聰明.我想，就是我不說，你們也能知道我為甚麼要用筆名.”

13. 中國字每一個字有多少筆畫，有的字很容易看出來.比方說「人」字是兩畫，「三」字是三畫，一看就知道了.可是有的字不大容易看.就像「嗎」字吧，有人說是十三畫，有人說是十二畫.

14. 今天我接到一封信，信封的左角上有「緊要」兩個字.我心裏想這信裏一定有要緊的事，我就很緊張的看這封信.看完以後原來是王小姐請我在年假的時候到他家裏過年.我說:“這算甚麼要緊的事呢!”可是我這句話剛說完，緊跟着我就想明白了，她信裏的口氣不只是請我去過年，大概前次我對她提出的結婚…有希望了.怪不得她在信封上寫着「緊要」

兩個字呢.

15. 簡先生是中國一位有名的學者. 大家都叫他是簡大師. 有一年他到外國的大學教書, 他的太太—人家都叫她是簡師母—也一起去了. 這位簡師母到了外國, 天天緊跟着簡先生. 她說:"簡先生年紀大了, 他走路的時候不知道小心. 我雖然時常告訴他要小心, 他把我的話也不放在心上. 他每次一個人出來, 我就放心不下, 所以我必得跟着他, 我才放心."

16. 有一個小學生每天放學回家就把書放在一邊兒不知道用功. 有一天他回家才要把書放下, 他的母親說:"你把書放在這裏, 你想做甚麽去? 你書念的一天不如一天, 你把我和你父親說的話一概不放在心裏. 從今天起每天晚間都要在家用功, 不能出去了."

17. 李先生不喜歡請客, 可是人家請他的時候, 他們全家都去, 一去就是七八口兒.

有一天他太太對他說：“我們老吃人家，從來也不請客，我們找一個放假的日子也請請客好不好？”李先生說：“不必吧．一請客就得三塊五塊錢．”他太太說：“你太不懂人情啦．吃人家不是鷄就是魚．要是你不想多用錢，我們就是做幾碗湯麵或是白菜豆腐哪，也得請請人家呀．”

18. 我買了一本漢語拼音法．這本書前邊是概論，中間是說用字母拼字是怎樣的拼法，後邊就是用拼音寫的會話和短句子．最後是附錄，是把兩千多常用的漢字都用字母寫出來，為的是一看就知道那一個漢字是用那幾個字母拼起來的．

19. 謝先生正寫中國地理概要．他要看看中國地圖，可是他有一張中華大地圖不見了．他說：“奇怪，這是甚麼道理？剛才我還看了呢，怎麽會不見了呢？”他太太說：“你看，那不是在地下嗎？”

20. 有一個外國人最喜歡吃中國菜．有一天去到一個中國飯館. 茶房給他拿來菜單. 他看看菜單，要了一杯酒、一個紅燒牛肉還有家常豆腐，又要了一碗麵和一杯茶. 茶房問他，茶是要先來還是後來. 他說:“酒和菜先來. 喝完酒吃完菜就來麵，茶跟在麵的後頭來.”

21. 有人問我:“初級漢語課本封面上的畫是誰畫的？畫的是甚麼地方的山水？” 我告訴他:“那是一位馬小姐畫的，畫的是西湖. 西湖的山水是中國最有名的. 你看這張畫裏遠遠的山，來往的船，人在船上，路在湖邊，真是好看極了.”

22. 我正在看書，老田來了. 我問他:“你來有甚麼事嗎？” 他說:“我們開會的日子本來是後天，現在提前一天要在明天開了.”我說:“好吧.”他就走了. 在他走了以後，我又拿起書來看，可是先前我看到甚麼地方，我找不着了，我只好又從頭看起.

23. 一個國家如果國內讓人民的生活不安定，

國外又有很多的問題,政府對內對外都想不出好的法子來.這個國家就一定沒有希望了.

24. 有一個孩子時常說假話.他母親告訴他:"一個人不可以說假話.假如說了假話,人家早晚會知道的.要是人家知道他是說假話的人,將來他就是說的話是真的,人家也不信了."

25. 有一個外國人能看中文報紙.有人對他說:"你的中文一定很好,所以能看中文報."他說:"報上所有的字,我不都認得.有時遇着不認得的字,就看看上文再看看下文,多半就可以知道是甚麽意思啦."

26. 昨天我到出版社去拜訪大方先生接頭一件事情.到那兒一問,出版社裏的人說:"我們這裏沒有大方這個人哪."我說了半天他們說:"大概是毛力子先生吧.你說的那個名字是他的筆名.那是一個假名兒."

27. 我有一個很要好的朋友，來跟我借錢.他說馬上要用一百或者五十塊錢.我說：“我正有一張一百塊錢的票子.”那位朋友說：“那麽你就借給我五十好啦.”

28. 我很喜歡研究文學，可是父親叫我念科學，更希望我研究原子能.我說：“我對原子能連一點概念都沒有，怎麽能研究呢？我想我還是研究文學.”

29. 在政府裏工作的人應當時常跟人民接近，才可以多知道人民的意見.可是有的時候要是你去見政府裏的人，他們有時候接見，有的時候不接見.不接見的原因或者因為他們事情太多，沒有時間吧！

30. 有一次在大考以前，老王問我：“這次考國文要出幾道題？”我說：“我不知道.”老王說：“我知道，要出四道題.”我說：“你怎麽知道的呢？是不是先生直接告訴你的呢？”老王說：“不是.我是間接聽說的.”

31. 我最喜歡鷄，所以我家裏有很多鷄．每天早晨我聽見鷄叫，我就起來．先給他們東西吃，緊接着就給他們水喝．我看着這些鷄吃着、喝着、走來走去，我越看越覺得有意思．

32. 有一個不大聰明的孩子，他母親叫他去買酒和油．她知道她的孩子去買兩樣東西一定記不住，就給他兩個碗，叫他用左手拿一個碗，用右手拿一個碗．同時告訴他把酒放在左手的碗裏，油放在右手的碗裏．她想這樣一來，就能記住是買兩樣東西了．這個孩子就去買去了．過了一會兒，他回來了，甚麽也沒買．他母親問他："怎麽甚麽也沒買呢？" 他說："我記不住是酒放在哪個碗裏，油放在哪一個碗裏了．"

33. 有一次我弟弟說坐飛機來看我，我去接飛機．可是那個飛機弟弟沒來．我遇見一個朋友他是坐那個飛機來的．他看見了說："謝謝你來接我．"我當時有點兒不知道説甚麽好了．要是我説我不是來接他的，有點兒不好意思．可是我又不能説假話，説是來接他的．後來我還是説了實話，説我是來接我弟弟的．

34. 有一個學會每年開會一次．今年開會在要開完的時候，研究下次開會的日期和地點．研究了很多時間没有結論．後來會長説：“我們假定還是在這個日子這個地點，大家的意見怎麽樣？”大家都説：“可以．”

Exercise 4. Illustrative Sentences (English)

1.3. That booklet can be used as a notebook.

1.5. (The name) he used in the story which he published in the newspaper was a pen-name.

2.1. He's brighter than anyone else in his studies.

3.1. The teacher said to the students: "You must note the terms 'see above,' 'see below,' and 'see such-and-such column,' as they are frequently used in dictionaries."

4.3. I learned quite a few things from Professor Zhang.

4.4. All the students like Professor Xie. He's easy to get along with [as a person] and he's also very learned.

4.5. What little ability I have was acquired from Professor Wan.

6.3. I'd like to go, to be sure, but I don't know whether they will let me go or not.··· Don't worry, they'll surely let you go.

10.6. He advocates using **pīnyīn** to write the main dialects but not the lesser dialects (the local dialects).

12.9. He's read the first [lit. upper] half. You go on reading the second half.

14.1. In the letter that he wrote to me he enclosed a letter for my younger brother.

15.1. He asked me to finish writing this book within ten days. The time's too short [lit. tight]. How can I finish writing it (in that time)?

15.3. I've been very strapped for money the past few days. Where would I have the money to see a movie?

15.6. Right after our New Year's vacation is over we'll have exams.

19.4. I hear that our New Year's vacation this year is going to be advanced a day.

23.1. In the views which he publicly expressed yesterday evening, it seems that he didn't come out with the essential points.

30.2. The people in front of [the door of] the theater are coming one right after the other to buy tickets.

31.1. The government has recently done many things. To start with schools, in this area alone there are six elementary schools.

33.2. When you had the exam in Chinese how many questions did the teacher give? ··· He gave out only three, but I couldn't manage even one.

35.2. I have too much to do. I don't know what it would be best to do first.

35.3. He drives too fast. It would be best not to let him drive.

37.1. It'll take $300 to buy that dictionary. I certainly can't afford it.

Notes

1. The use of the particles 嗎 and 啊 after a sentence containing a question word softens the effect of the question:

   你有甚麽事? This is a blunt way of asking "What do you have to do?"

你有甚麽事啊？ This suggests "I take it you have something to do, and would like to know what it is if you don't mind telling me."

你有甚麽事嗎？ This has much the same effect as the preceding sentence.

The first sentence might be said with a tone of displeasure that the person spoken to has something else to do. The other two sentences contain no such feeling but show friendly concern and interest.

2. The verb 得 **děi** and related verbs besides being used as auxiliaries are also used before nominal expressions or sentences:

做這件事得三天. **Zuò zhèijiàn shì děi sāntiān.** "Doing this job will require three days."

這件事得我自己做. **Zhèijiàn shì děi wǒ zìjǐ zuò.** "This job requires that I do it myself."

我的名字寫了. 該你了. **Wǒde míngzi xiě le. Gāi nǐ le.** "I've written my name. It's your turn."

第 四 課

1	2	3	4	5	6	7	8
色	顏	怕	恐	忙	幫	助	費

9	10	11	12	13	14	15	16
累	煩	麻	送	玩	笑	收	拾

1.0. 色 **sè*** color

黑色 **hēisè** black (color)

白色 **báisè** white (color)

紅色 **hóngsè** red (color)

面色 **miànsè** complexion, facial expression

特色 **tèsè** (special or distinctive) feature

起色 **qǐsè** improvement (in health, market, etc.)

出色 **chūsè** outstanding, striking

1.1. 他的車是黑色的，我的車是白色的.

1.2. 有的人喜歡紅色，有的人不喜歡.

1.3. 你看他的面色很難看，好像是有病了.

1.4. 他們家的孩子都能喝酒，這可以說是他們家的特色.

1.5. 他的病没甚麽起色了.

1.6. 在這些女人裏最出色的是<u>王</u>太太.

2.0. 顏 **yán*** (1) color; (2) (a surname)

顏色 **yánse** color, pigment

帶顏色的 **dàiyánsede** having color, colored

2.1. 你要買甚麼顏色的紙？

2.2. 我要買一張帶顏色的地圖.

3.0. 怕 **pà** (1) be afraid, fear; (2) fear that, be afraid that

怕太太 **pà tàitai** be afraid of one's wife, be henpecked

怕甚麼？ **pà shénmo?** What are you afraid of? Don't be afraid! What's there to be afraid of?

可怕 **kěpà** frightening, fearful

3.1. 我的書不怕看，就怕別人看我的書往上記記號兒.(T)

3.2. 我們這裏有一個怕太太會. 你怕不怕太太？你是會員不是？

3.3. 你父親不在這裏你怕甚麼？(T)

3.4. 老顏老說可怕的故事. 昨天晚上他又說了一個可怕的故事.

3.5. 你為甚麼怕你妹妹？妹妹怕甚麼？(T)

4.0. 恐 **kǒng*** be afraid, fear

恐怕 **kǒngpà** (1) be afraid that; (2) probably, perhaps

4.1. 他說的話，恐怕是假話吧！

5.0. 忙 **máng** busy

別忙 **bié máng** don't be in such a hurry

不要忙 **bú yào máng** don't be in such a hurry

忙甚麽？ **máng shénma**？ What's your hurry？

忙得過來 **mángdeguòlái** able to finish (despite being rushed)

忙着V(呢) **mángzhe V (ne)** (1) be busy V-ing; (2) be in a hurry to V

5.1. 我今天太忙了．中午連吃飯的時間都沒有．

5.2. 你別忙．等他看完了一定給你看．

5.3. 你不要忙．火車還有半點鐘才開呢．

5.4. 你忙甚麽？慢慢兒的吃好不好？

5.5. 要做的事情太多了，我簡直的忙不過來．

5.6. 他忙着去接飛機，連午飯都沒吃．

6.0. 幫 **bāng** to help

幫手 **bāngshǒu** a helper

幫工 **bānggōng** (1) assist (VO); (2) helper

幫工的 **bānggōngde** helper

幫忙 **bāngmáng** to help (VO)

幫N(的)忙 **bāng N(de) máng** help N

6.1. 大家都沒錢，誰也幫不了誰．(T)

6.2. 他是我很好的一個幫手．

6.3. 他沒錢念書．他給人家幫工．

6.4. 我是一個幫工的，工錢每月少得很．

6.5. 你能不能給我幫忙？(T)

6.6. 這件事我自己能做.不用別人幫我的忙.

7.0. 助 **zhù*** to help

幫助 **bāngzhu** to help

助手 **zhùshǒu** an assistant

助理 **zhùlǐ** (1) to assist; (2) an assistant

7.1. 做事要自己去做，不要希望別人幫助.

7.2. 他是<u>王</u>先生的助手．他助理<u>王</u>先生有十五年啦.

8.0. 費 **fèi** (1) expend, spend; (2) expenses; (3) (a surname)

費事 **fèishì** require effort, be troublesome (VO)

費心 **fèixīn** (1) expend (mental) effort (with human subject); (2) require effort (with inanimate subject); (3) thank you for your trouble

費力 **fèilì** expend (physical) effort (VO)

學費 **xuéfèi** tuition

車費 **chēfèi** transportation costs (by car, train, or other **chē**)

船費 **chuánfèi** transportation costs by boat

旅費 **lǚfèi** travelling expenses

小費 **xiǎofèi** a tip

8.1. 我這次去旅行費了很多時候，而且費了很多錢，結果是一點意思也沒有.(T)

8.2. 你說一句話也費不了甚麼事．你為甚麼不說呢？(T)

8.3. 甚麽事都得我自己想．我太費心了．

8.4. 那個學校的學費太貴了．每一個學生一年得兩千多塊錢．

8.5. 我每天到學校，一來一去要用兩塊多錢的車費呢．(T)

8.6. 從美國到中國的船費要多少錢你知道嗎？

8.7. 費更生先生出國的旅費是政府給他的．

8.8. 在飯館兒吃飯一定要給小費嗎？

8.9. 我費了心費了力幫他那麽大的忙，他連個謝字都沒跟我說．(T)

9.0. 累 **lèi** (1) tired; (2) tiring; (3) implicate, involve; (4) (also used as postverb)

連累 **liánlei** implicate, involve

累病了 **lèibìngle** ill from overwork

9.1. 我今天工作了十二小時，我太累了．

9.2. 我的工作很累．不論大事小事都是我一個人做．

9.3. 你每天都這麽累我看你不久就要累病了．

9.4. 那不是他的錯，是別人連累了他．

9.5. 我今天寫了一天的字，把我寫累了．(T)

10.0. 煩 **fán** (1) troublesome, annoying, vexatious, vexing; (2) to bother; (3) (feel) vexed

煩心 **fánxīn** (1) troublesome, vexatious; (2) vexed, annoyed

心煩 **xīnfán** (1) troublesome, vexatious; (2) vexed, annoyed

煩難 **fánnán** troublesome and difficult

10.1. 我現在心裏煩得很, 我要出去走走.

10.2. 你天天不高興, 有甚麽事叫你煩心呢?

10.3. 他說他現在心煩, 念不下去書.

10.4. 你有甚麽煩難的問題都要對我說.

11.0. 麻 **má** (1) hemp; (2) numb, insensitive; (3) (a surname)

發麻 **fāmá** became numb (VO)

麻煩 **máfan** (1) troublesome; (2) trouble (N/V)

找麻煩 **zhǎo máfan** find fault, look for trouble, make trouble

麻將 **májiàng** mahjong

打麻將 **dǎ májiàng** play mahjong

麻子 **mázi** (1) pock-marks; (2) a pock-marked person

11.1. 你知道中國甚麽地方出麻?

11.2. 我字一寫多了手就發麻. 我現在手又麻了. (T)

11.3. 我每天都吃小館兒. 我覺得天天做飯吃太麻煩了.

11.4. 誰敢來找麻煩, 我就對誰不客氣了.

11.5. <u>麻文遠</u>每天甚麽也不做. 不是喝酒就是打麻將.

11.6. 顏大力有麻子，人家都叫他是顏大麻子．(T)

12.0 送 **sòng** (1) send; (2) see off; (3) present with, give

送給 **sònggei** give (to), present (to)

不送 **bú sòng** (1) not send; (2) not see off

別送 **bié sòng** (1) don't send; (2) don't see off

送上 **sòngshang** send (to a superior)

送信 **sòng xìn** send a letter

送信的 **sòngxìnde** (1) letter-carrier, postman; (2) messenger

送客 **sòng kè** see off, escort a visitor to the door

送人 **sòng rén** (1) present (something) to someone; (2) see a person off

送行 **sòngxíng** give a farewell party

送回 **sònghuí** send back

12.1. 我叫你給出版社送的東西你送出去了沒有？(T)

12.2. 我去看老田，他要送我到門外，我說："我常來，別送別送．"

12.3. 我在信裏寫："現在把我近來畫的畫兒送上一張請你看看．"

12.4. 弟弟問我上那兒去，我說："我去送信．"

12.5. 他在回國以前把他的書都送人了．… 送給誰了？(T)

12.6. 在客人走的時候我們應該送客.

12.7. 我女朋友寫給我的信，怎麽還沒有接到呢？一定是送信的送錯了，送到別人家去了.

12.8. 王先生要到外國去. 這幾天有很多朋友請他吃飯，給他送行.

12.9. 這本書當然你可以拿去看，可是看完了得給我送回來.

13.0. 玩 **wán*** (1) to play; (2) curio, antique

玩兒 **wár** play (at), amuse oneself, have a good time

古玩 **gǔwán** curio, antique

玩意兒 **wányìr** toy, plaything

好玩(兒) **hǎowán(r)** (1) amusing, pleasurable; (2) amused, pleased

13.1. 這幾天放假你玩兒的很高興吧.

13.2. 那一條路上都是賣古玩的.

13.3. 他從中國帶來了很多小孩子的玩意兒.

13.4. 我坐船到英國去. 在船上好玩極了.

13.5. 我本來不想玩兒麻將. 因為他們三個人要玩兒把我給叫去了. (T)

13.6. 他從到這兒就沒好好兒的念過書，天天玩兒. (T)

14.0. 笑 **xiào** smile, laugh (at)

笑話 **xiàohua** (1) a joke; (2) laugh at, ridicule

出笑話 **chū xiàohua** cause laughter (by doing or saying something wrong)

可笑 **kěxiào** laughable, funny

玩笑 **wánxiào** a joke

開玩笑 **kāi wánxiào** play a joke (on)

14.1. 他說的笑話，多半沒有人笑.

14.2. 外國人吃中國飯時常出笑話.

14.3. 昨天我看的電影太可笑了.

14.4. 你說要找女朋友，是真話還是玩笑？要是真的我就給你介紹一個.

14.5. 你說的是真的，還是開玩笑呢？

14.6. 他說的故事雖然太長了，可是很可笑.大家一直聽到完. (T)

15.0. 收 **shōu** receive, collect

收到 **shōudao** receive

收起來 **shōuqilai** put away, keep safely

收條 **shōutiáo** a receipt

收工 **shōugōng** stop work (VO)

收回 **shōuhuí** take back

收錢 **shōu qián** receive money

收下 **shōuxia** accept, take

15.1. 今天來的信是誰收的？(T)

15.2. 我現在出去．要是收到王先生的信請你給我收起來．

15.3. 請你在收到那些書以後，寫一個收條．

15.4. 我們每天上午九點開始工作，下午五點收工．

15.5. 在那個圖書館借書，借一個星期他們就要收回．

15.6. 書店的人對我說："這本書是送給你的，不收錢．"

15.7. 弟弟，要是送信的來送信，你把信收下．

16.0. 拾 **shí** pick up

拾起來 **shíqilai** pick up

收拾 **shōushi** (1) gather together, tidy up, clean up; (2) make ready, put in order, fix

16.1. 請你把地下的紙都拾起來．

16.2. 你把行李收拾收拾．我們這就要上船了．

17.0. 口頭(兒) **kǒutóu(r)** oral(ly), verbal(ly), by word of mouth, in words

口頭(兒)上 **kǒutóu(r)shang** orally

17.1. 他口頭兒說不收錢，可是我給他錢他也收了．

17.2. 那件事情我沒給他寫信，我口頭上告訴他的.

18.0. 出發 **chūfā** start out, depart

出發點 **chūfādiǎn** starting point

發行 **fāxíng** (1) to issue; (2) publish

18.1. 我們這次旅行，是在這個星期天早上九點鐘從學校出發.

18.2. 「出發點」就是開始走出去的地點.

18.3. 那種票子是甚麽時候發行的？

19.0. 古國 **gǔguó** an ancient country

國名 **guómíng** name of a country

19.1. 東方有一個古國，國名是中國.

20.0. 國土 **guótǔ** national territory, territory of a country

本土 **běntǔ** one's native land

要想 **yàoxiǎng** (1) would like to; (2) if one would like to, if one intends to

20.1. 長城以外的地方也是中國的國土.

20.2. 有人要想到別的地方去，有人不想離開本土.

20.3. 要想念大學一定得用功.

21.0. 水路 **shuǐlù** waterway, water route

早期 **zǎoqī** (at) an early period

所員 **suǒyuán** member of a <u>**suǒ**</u>

館員 **guǎnyuán** member of a library staff

21.1. 從北京到上海可以坐火車去，也可以從水路坐船去.

21.2. 地理研究所的所長、所員都是北京大學早期畢業的.(T)

21.3. 那個圖書館所有的館員都是女的.(T)

22.0. 人生 **rénshēng** human life, man's life

22.1. 人生太短了，也不過是一百年左右.

23.0. 請來 **qǐng lái** (1) invite to come; (2) please come

V了(一)V **Vle(yi)V** V for a while, V'd for a while

就是了 **jiù shìle** and that's that, and that'll be that

治法 **zhìfǎ** way of curing

23.1. 我病了請來了一位大夫給我看.他看了一看說："你病的治法是少吃點兒就是了."

24.0. (在)TW 有的(N) **(zài) TW yǒu de (N)** (N) which existed at such-and-a time

原有的(N) **yuányǒude (N)** (N) which existed originally, the original (N)

功課表 **gōngke biǎo** course schedule

編定 **biāndìng** compile

24.1. 古時有的字跟現在的不一樣.(T)

24.2. 這個功課表編定以後原有的就不用了.

24.3. 這本書是才買的，還是舊有的？(T)

25.0. 論理(學) **lùnlǐ(xué)** (study of) logic

著手 **zhuóshǒu** start, put one's hand to

25.1. 他想寫一本論理學.現在還沒着手寫呢.

26.0. 帶有 **dàiyǒu** contain, have

26.1. 聽他説話的口氣帶有不高興的樣子.(T)

27.0. 有**V**的 **yǒu V de** (1) there are some that V; (2) there is some to be V'd

27.1. 中華大辭典這裏有賣的沒有?

27.2. 有吃的沒有?…沒甚麽吃的啦.就有一點兒麵啦.(T)

27.3. 有人説古時候就有白話文.…是,也有這樣説的.(T)

28.0. 快活 **kuàihuó** happy

28.1. 我一天不看書就覺着不快活.

29.0. 處處 **chùchù** everywhere

29.1. 這部汽車太老了,差不多處處都有毛病.

30.0. 年號 **niánhào** reign-title (see note 1)

30.1. 那件古玩上的年號是不是漢朝?

31.0. 早點 **zǎodiǎn** breakfast

31.1. 他每天的早點不是紅燒豬肉麵就是紅燒牛肉麵.

32.0. **V N_1 用的 (N_2)** **V N_1 yòng de (N_2)** (N_2) used to V N_1; (N_2) used for V-ing N_1

32.1. 他叫我寫大字. 我沒有寫大字用的筆, 怎麽寫哪?

33.0. 差別 **chābié** difference

33.1. 我在放假的日子也一樣工作, 所以跟不放假沒有甚麽差別.

34.0. 原理 **yuánlǐ** (1) actual facts; (2) basic principle; (3) theory

34.1. 原子能的原理你知道嗎?

35.0. 老弟 **Lǎodì** (Old) Youngest (see note 2)

35.1. 我有四個弟弟. 我叫最小的弟弟是「老弟」.

36.0. 女子 **nǚzǐ*** woman, girl

36.1. 她和她的二姐、四妹都在女子中學念書.

37.0. 連 N 在內 **lián N zài nèi** (1) include N; (2) including N

37.1. 我們這次到西部去旅行, 連不連費大小姐在內呀? (T)

37.2. 我們這次考中文連寫字在內嗎?

38.0. 分(兒) **fēn(r)** grade, mark

打…分(兒) **dǎ…fēn(r)** get a grade of …, give a grade of …

38.1. 我們國文先生給的分兒很少. 最高分兒

是八十五分兒.

38.2. 我用毛筆寫的漢字先生打了八十分.

39.0. 筆 **bǐ** (measure for sums of money)

39.1. 我大兒子一定要到外國去念科學. 你説我那兒有這筆錢呢? (T)

40.0. (也)不見得 **(yě) bújiànde** not likely, hardly

40.1. 他的工作雖然很累, 但是他的病也不見得是累的. (T)

40.2. 你為甚麽不喜歡那個工作, 是不是太累呀?…累也不見得. 主要的是我對那種工作没興趣. (T)

41.0. 才一 **cáiyī** just as, just when, when first

41.1. 我才一學中國話的時候覺得很難.

42.0. $\mathbf{N_1}$家住在$\mathbf{N_2}$ **$\mathbf{N_1}$ jiā jùzai $\mathbf{N_2}$** N_1 lives at N_2

42.1. 我家就住在學校附近.

43.0. 連**V**都不**V** **lián V dōu bù V** not even V

43.1. 他考的不好是應該的. 考試以前書他連看都不看. (T)

44.0. 好意 **hǎoyì** good idea, good intention, friendly feeling

44.1. 他説的話是好意, 你為甚麽要生氣哪?

45.0. 日子長了 **rìzi chángle** (after) a long time

45.1. 學語言要常說，日子長了就會說的很自然了.

46.0. **V_1V_1看** **V_1V_1 kàn** V and see, try and V, try V-ing

46.1. 這個紅燒豬肉你吃吃看. 如果喜歡吃，多多兒吃點兒. (T)

Checklist

1. 色
   黑色
   白色
   紅色
   面色
   特色
   起色
   出色
2. 顏
   顏色
   帶顏色的
3. 怕
   怕太太
   怕甚麽？
   可怕
4. 恐
   恐怕
5. 忙
   別忙
   不要忙
   忙甚麽？
   忙得過來
   忙着 V (ne)
6. 幫
   幫手
   幫工
   幫工的
   幫忙
   幫 N (的) 忙
7. 助
   幫助
   助手
   助理
8. 費
   費事
   費心
   費力
   學費
   車費
   船費
   旅費
   小費
9. 累
   連累
   累病了
10. 煩
   煩心
   心煩
   煩難
11. 麻
   發麻
   麻煩
   找麻煩
   麻將
   打麻將
   麻子
12. 送
   不送
   別送
   送上
   送信
   送信的
   送給
   送客
   送人
   送行
   送回
13. 玩

玩兒
古玩
玩意兒
好玩(兒)
14. 笑
笑話
出笑話
可笑
玩笑
開玩笑
15. 收
收到
收起來
收條
收工
收回
收錢
收下
16. 拾
拾起來
收拾
17. 口頭(兒)
口頭(兒)上
18. 出發
出發點
發行
19. 古國
國名
20. 國土
本土
要想
21. 水路
早期
所員
館員
22. 人生
23. 請來
V了(一)V
就是了
治法
24. (在)TW有的(N)
原有的(N)
功課表
編定
25. 論理(學)
着手
26. 帶有
27. 有V的
28. 快活
29. 處處
30. 年號
31. 早點
32. V N_1用的(N_2)
33. 差別
34. 原理
35. 老弟
36. 女子
37. 連N在內
38. 分(兒)
打…分(兒)
39. 筆
40. (也)不見得
41. 才一
42. N_1家住在N_2
43. 連V都不V
44. 好意
45. 日子長了
46. V_1V_1看

Exercise 1. Practice on Nominal Predicates (see note 3)

1. 我們是三個男孩兒一個女孩兒. 我們三

個男孩兒一個女孩兒.

2. 我們有三個男孩兒一個女孩兒. 我們三個男孩兒一個女孩兒.

3. 藍先生是河南人. 藍先生河南人.

4. 這個字典賣三塊五. 這個字典三塊五.

5. 今天是星期一. 今天星期一.

6. 謝先生是好人. 謝先生好人.

7. 北京是好地方. 北京好地方.

8. 我是中午到的. 我中午到的.

9. 這個治法是好治法. 這個治法好治法.

10. 她就有十五歲. 她就十五歲.

11. 王老師是一直從學校回家的. 王老師一直從學校回家的.

12. 他中國話是會說的. 他中國話會說的.

13. 十點鐘上國文. 十點鐘國文.

14. 他簡直的是累病了的. 他簡直的累病了的.

15. 我的老弟是很聰明的. 我的老弟很聰明的.

Exercise 2. Excerpts from Actual Publications: Practice on Reading Entries in Chinese Dictionaries

The following excerpts consist of entries in **Hànyǔ Cídiǎn** (Dictionary of Chinese) [Peking, 1957], which was originally published in 1937 under the title **Guóyǔ Cídiǎn** (Dictionary of the National Language). The defined terms (enclosed in parentheses) and the definitions include some items which have not previously been introduced but should be clear from the context. You do not need to memorize these items, but make sure you understand them and can read through the list quickly.

1. (本意)原來意思
2. (四部)見四部書條
3. (拜客)拜望人
4. (白話)口語
5. (白魚)魚名
6. (半道兒)半路
7. (所長)見上
8. (幫助)幫忙
9. (表面)外面
10. (不能不)不得不
11. (不會)不能
12. (不知道)不知
13. (不日)不久
14. (學友)同學
15. (賣不了)不能賣出
16. (出外)離家遠行
17. (發言) 1. 出語 2. 發表意見
18. (打票)買票
19. (打電報)發電報
20. (大多數)極多數
21. (定親)定婚
22. (太古)上古時代
23. (天天)每日
24. (聽不得)不可聽, 不必聽
25. (內部)裏面部分
26. (難得)少有, 不易得
27. (難聽)不好聽
28. (年紀)年數
29. (年來)近年以來, 一年以來

30. (女生)女學生
31. (口外)長城以外
32. (看不得)不可看，不必看，不好看
33. (上半天)上午
34. (詞典)同辭典
35. (書目)圖書目錄
36. (冊子)本子
37. (一路)同行一路，如“我和你一路走”
38. (一回)一次
39. (一時)短時間內
40. (刀魚)魚名

Exercise 3. Dialogues

1. 費：老紀，你這幾天好像有甚麽心事.

紀：別提了. 我這些日子心煩得很.

費：為甚麽？

紀：我弟弟病了這麽久，看了好幾個大夫，病也沒甚麽起色. 昨天張大夫告訴我，他的病很不容易治.

費：這位小老弟年紀這麽輕，怎麽得了這種病呢？

紀：我這個弟弟呀，他的病完全是累的. 他不但功課忙，而且他的工作也太累了.

費：他又念書又作工是太累了. 他不會少作一點兒事嗎？

紀：因為我家没錢，我們都不可能念大學．可是他一定要念大學．他這幾年的學費都是他自己作事得來的．我是一個圖書館的館員，每月錢不多，我也幫不了他的忙．

費：老弟在那兒作事啊？

紀：在謝先生出版社給謝先生當助手，助理謝先生．

費：老弟每天作甚麽事呢？

紀：他幫助謝先生處理出版社所有的事情．

費：謝先生的助手就是老弟一個人嗎？

紀：就是他一個人．忙極了．處處得費力．天天人家工人都收工啦，他還得做，有時候簡直的忙不過來．我弟弟常常中午不吃飯．你説日子長了怎麽不病？

2. 李：顏力子，人家都説你會説笑話．你説個笑話好不好？

顏：我現在想不出笑話來．我説一個故

事，可是不一定可笑.

李：好.

顏：從前有一個人想給他兒子定親事，他就請人家幫忙給介紹. 有一天來了一個人就跟他說:“你們不是要給你兒子定親事嗎？現在有一個很好的機會. 有一位姓麻的，家裏有一個麻小姐，年歲和你兒子差不多，又有本事人長的又出色. 如果你們兩家定了親事，那太好了.”這家信了那個人的話,就定了這門親事了. 等到結婚那天一看，那位小姐有麻子，原來是個大麻子.

李：這不麻煩了嗎？

顏：是啊. 這個人對那位介紹人說:“你說麻小姐很出色，原來出色的是有麻子，你以前為甚麽不告訴我們她有麻子啊？”那位介紹人說:“我說過了是一位麻小姐呀.”

3. 祝：費老師早. 真不敢當，您來看我.

您吃早點了没有？

費：吃過啦．行李都收拾好了没有？

祝：差不多啦．我東西不多,容易收拾．

費：星期六晚上到我家吃晚飯我給你送行．

祝：您別客氣啦．又得讓師母費事．我從到這兒這幾年裏頭，您跟費師母兩位費心的地方太多啦．

費：這是應該的．你是我的學生，而且我跟你父親又是多年的老朋友．你買的幾等船票？

祝：二等的．我本來想買三等的，可是都賣完了，所以買二等的．這條船的船費比較貴一點兒．聽說這條客船特別好．

費：是．以前有的客船都没有這條好．

祝：本來我父親來信說叫我坐飛機回去．我想坐船走水路有意思．坐船可以看看每一個地方的山水．

費：我到那兒去也喜歡坐船．你這次回

去你父親有了一個好幫手．

祝：不見得．

費：前幾天我還收到你父親的信．他信上說近來心煩的很，因為你弟弟不大聽話．

祝：我二弟書念的不怎麽好，不知道用功，所以父親常生氣．

費：現在還小．慢慢兒的大了就知道用功啦．好了，我走了．星期六早點兒來．

祝：好的，謝謝您．

費：別送，別送．星期六見．

祝：星期六見．

4．師：請你們大家把書收起來．

生：是．

師：你們聽着啊．我說幾個生詞兒，你們用它說出句子來．比如我說「年號」，你們就用「年號」說一個句子．我說「出發點」，你們就拿「出發點」說．我說「原理」，你們就用「原理」

說. 明白吧?

生: 明白了.

師: 好, 現在我們開始:「出笑話」.

生: “你吃外國飯小心一點兒, 別出笑話.”

師: 好極了. 打一百分兒.「帶顏色的」.

生: “茶是帶顏色的, 水不是帶顏色的,”

師: 好.「玩意兒」.

生: “小孩子没有不喜歡玩兒玩意兒的.”

師: 好極啦. 我真高興, 詞兒你們都會, 而且用的那麽自然. 好. 現在你們問我.

生:「帶有」.

師: “他今天帶有不高興的樣子”. 「帶有」不是口語, 是寫的. 口語是「帶着」.

生:「着手」.

師: “費教授正在着手編寫一本論理學.”「着手」是寫的, 就是「正在開始作」的意思.

生：「送回」

師："從圖書館借的書，昨天已經送回圖書館."「送回」是寫的，口語是「送回去」. 好. 今天是星期五，我出一個題目你們作文兒，下星期給我.

生：老師，甚麽題目？

師：「我最快活的一天」. 還有十個詞兒你們用這些詞兒作短句子.

生：老師，作幾個短句子？

師：隨便. 現在你們看着詞表，我念你們記記號兒.

生：好.

師：早期、國土、本土、古國、編定、特色、發行、國名、找麻煩、原有的，一共十個. 要是有不會用的現在可以問.

生：都會了.

師：時候到了. 我們下課.

生：老師，星期一見.

師：星期一見.

5. 湯：老謝，你怕太太都出了名了. 誰都知道你怕太太.

謝：別開玩笑了. 太太怕甚麽？我才不怕她哪. 說他怕我還差不多.

湯：你怕就說怕，那有甚麽呢？有一位有名的學者，他自己就說他怕太太. 他還發表一個怕太太理論.

謝：他的理論是甚麽？

湯：那位學者說才一結婚的時候太太又年輕又好看，當然得怕他. 等到她老了的時候，一看了她老的那個樣子更是可怕.

謝：我太太是中年. 他不年輕也不老，所以我不怕她.

湯：恐怕你說的話不對吧.

謝：怎麽不對？

湯：昨天我到你家去的時候，你太太正要打你，一看見我進去了，她就沒打你.

謝：她那是跟我開玩笑哪.

6. 生：請問老師「送上」是甚麽意思？

師：「送上」就是「送給」客氣的說法就是了.

生：「口頭上」跟「口頭」一樣嗎？

師：一樣，没差別.

生：「好玩兒」跟「玩意兒」呢？

師：不同.「好玩兒」是「有意思」.「玩意兒」是小孩子玩兒的東西. 還有別的問題嗎？

生：没有啦.

師：我們從明天開始，放年假一星期. 希望你們大家在放假的期間玩兒的很快活. 還有，我們放假以後開學就不是現在這個功課表啦. 在開學的頭一天你們到學校來看一看，每天甚麽時間，上甚麽課，最好用筆記下來.

7. 麻：老費，好久不見了. 你這些日子都忙甚麽呢？

費：没忙甚麽. 這些日子煩心的事太多

了.

麻：甚麽事啊？

費：不是我母親來信說我弟弟給人家幫工累病了，就是說我父親天天喝酒打麻將，再不然就說她要想和父親離婚了. 她離婚這話當然不是真的了. 可是我看了這種信，心裏就煩.

麻：古人有兩句話意思就是一個人不如意的事情常常有，能跟別人說的只有兩三件. 人生就是這麽一回事.

費：還有，不是縣政府叫我到西北去嗎？本來說旅費是縣政府給，前天他們又說是先借給我，將來到四個月以後，縣政府還要把這筆錢收回. 這也是個煩難的問題.

麻：這個不應該，不是你要去的，是他們要你去的.

費：是啊.

8. 錢：謝力夫，我近來右手老發麻. 不知道是甚麽原故.

謝：你大概是累的吧.

錢：我的工作一點兒也不累呀. 每天就是收收錢寫寫收條.

謝：你沒找大夫看嗎？

錢：前天找了一個大夫看了一看. 他說沒甚麽治法，慢慢兒會好的.

謝：我認識一個大夫，讓他給你看看. 不過他住的地方很遠，你一來一去車費不少，你看一次得二十塊錢.

錢：連不連車費在内？

謝：在内，在内.

錢：那不算多了. 他能治這種病嗎？

謝：我們研究所有一位所員手發麻就是他給治好的. 好. 我走了.

錢：別忙. 我還有話跟你說哪.

謝：我先送信去一會兒再來.

錢：好. 我不送你了？

謝：不送，不送. 回頭見.

9. 生：老師早.

師：早. 你們昨天下課以前寫的句子我

看過了，錯兒都不多．每一個人最少也有八十分兒．昨天那課書的生詞兒有甚麽問題没有？

生：「女子」是説的還是寫的？

師：是寫的，要是説話都是説「女人」或是「女的」．

生：「面色」怎麽用？

師：“他大概是病了．你看他的面色多麽難看．”還有别的問題嗎？

生：没有啦．

師：好，現在我問你們啦．請你們先把書收起來．這張紙是甚麽顏色的？

生：是黑色的．

師：這張呢？

生：是白色的．

師：請你們用「紅色」這個詞兒説一個句子．

生：“那條小汽船是紅色的．”

師：請用「出發」説一句話．

生：“明天我們旅行去幾點鐘出發呀？”

師：好極了.「拾起來」這個詞兒你們明白它的意思嗎？

生：明白.“你把地下那本書拾起來.”

師：對了.我現在問你們一個問題.中國在甚麼時候有的紙？

生：中國在東漢的時候發明的紙.

10. 費：怎麼好些日子不見你呀？近來忙甚麼哪？

謝：我忙着考試哪.我好幾天沒出去了.你近來怎麼樣？

費：別提了.老張在我那兒住着呢，事也找不着.我這麼沒錢，他還天天吃我.把我連累的有時候連坐車的錢都沒有.

謝：你也幫他找找事啊.

費：我幫他找了，他不去呀.前天我在一個飯館兒給他找到了一個事情.我想有吃的有住的不是很好嗎？他說就有小費沒工錢他不做.我對他真沒法子.

11. 李：我想買點兒東西送人．你說我買甚麽好呢？

張：那個人喜歡甚麽呢？

李：他喜歡古玩．

張：我有個朋友家裏有很多古玩，現在沒錢啦，家裏正在賣古玩呢，天天有很多人去看．

李：走．我們去看看去．

張：不要忙．聽說他們原來定的價錢太高了．現在又請來一位懂古玩的人，把價錢再定一次．等他們定好了價錢我們再去吧．

李：對了．

12. 妹：姐姐，你回來了．車站送客的人多不多？

姐：人多的不得了．接人送人的很多．送信的來過了嗎？

妹：來過了，可是没有你的信．姐姐，今天我們到那兒玩兒去呀？

姐：看電影兒去好不好？

妹：好．我們到中華去看，聽說中華電影兒院演的那部電影兒可笑極了．

姐：好啊．

13. 顏：老李，好久不見．你今天怎麽有工夫到我這兒來哪？

李：我一來是看看你，二來是為了幫別人忙到你這兒來．昨天你那個工人張笑千去找我，他知道我跟你是老朋友，他讓我跟你說說，每月多給他一點兒工錢．

顏：他要那麽多錢作甚麽？

李：你是有錢的，不知道沒錢的難處．他是個幫工的，天天從很遠的走到這兒來．如果坐車就沒錢吃飯啦．

顏：他家住在那兒啊？

李：他家住在北城外頭．

顏：他請你來跟我說你對他說甚麽？

李：我說我對顏經理說說看，或者顏經理連理都不理，因為我沒有那麽大的面子．

顏：你真對張笑千這麼說的嗎？
李：我是這麼說的.
顏：好，別讓你沒面子. 下月起每月多給他十塊錢.

14. 謝：湯小姐明天生日了，我想送他一點兒東西，又怕她不收.
費：你送她東西是好意，我想她一定收下的.
謝：要是她不收呢？
費：你再送去呀.

Exercise 4. Narratives

1. 有一家只有母子兩個人. 母親常有病，孩子才十幾歲也找不到甚麼工作. 他們簡直是沒法子生活了. 有一天在他們附近住的王先生給這個孩子找了一個工作. 緊接着這個孩子的母親的病也好了. 這個孩子的母親說:“要不是王先生幫我們，恐怕我們早就活不下去了. 我們應該去謝謝王先生.” 他們母子兩個人就去見王先生．這個孩子的母親對王先生説:“多謝您費心給我孩子找事，我們母子才能生活．”王先生説:“這算不了甚麽．我給孩子找事不過是説一句話介紹介紹．説一句話也不費力．”

2．張先生家住在王先生家附近．他們兩個人都怕太太，可是在口頭上都説不怕．有一天張先生來到王先生家説:“今天我在家裏和太太生氣了，所以我出來走走．”王先生説:“不要説大話了，你還敢和太太生氣？恐怕又是太太要打你，所以你走出來了．你太怕太太了．要是我呀，我就不能這樣怕她．她要打我我就打她．”這話剛説出來，王太太聽見了就緊接着問王先生:“你再説一次，要是你，你要怎麽樣？”王先生説:“要是我…她要打我，我連出來都不敢出來，就在家叫她打．”

3．有一個外國人喜歡寫中國字，更喜歡給別人寫字畫，可是他寫的不大好，所以沒人請他寫. 有一天來了一個朋友手裏拿着一張畫畫兒用的紙. 他以為人家來請他在紙上寫字呢. 他就拿起筆來要寫. 他的朋友說:“謝謝你…” 他說:“寫幾個字一點兒也不麻煩, 用不着說謝謝呀.” 他的朋友說:“我不是謝謝你給我寫字, 我是恐怕你在這張紙上寫字, 所以我說謝謝你別在我這張紙上寫呀.”

4. 有一個人喜歡喝酒, 有人問他為甚麽要喝酒? 他說:“我遇着心煩的事, 就想要喝酒. 近來我的兒子到外國去了, 我很想他, 心煩得很, 所以我天天喝酒. 等到我兒子回來以後, 我就不喝了.” 後來他的兒子回來了, 他還是天天喝酒. 有人問他為甚麽還喝呢? 他說:“兒子回來了我快活極了. 有這樣高興的事為甚麽我不喝酒哪?”

5. 姐姐叫弟弟去買三張帶顏色的紙, 弟弟問都要甚麽顏色的. 姐姐說:“要一張紅色的、一張黑色的, 還要一張…” 姐姐正在想弟弟說:“要不要白色的？” 姐姐說:“白色的我有. 你可以隨便買一張別的顏色的吧.”

6. 有一個人喜歡打麻將, 可是他打的不大好, 常常出笑話, 每次打完麻將, 都是拿出錢來給別人. 他說:“我現在還是學習時期, 所以打的不大好. 將來畢了業打的就好了.”有人問他甚麽時候畢業？他說:“我也希望快畢業, 不然這學費可真不少啊！” 有人問他:“怎麽打麻將還有學費呢？” 他說:“每次打完給人家的錢不就是學費嗎？等到我學習好了不給人錢了, 也就是我不給學費的時候, 那就是畢業了.”

7. 張先生用很少的錢買了一件古玩. 有人說是明朝的, 有人說大概是元代的, 還有人說是假的. 有一天張先生請來了一位懂得古玩的給看一看. 這個人看完了說:“這件古玩上頭刻有年號, 這年號是漢朝早期時候的, 也就是漢初的時候的.”

他又告訴張先生:"別人隨便説的話你不要聽. 你把它好好的收起來就是了."

8. 你為甚麽叫我「別忙, 別忙」?
你知道現在是一個甚麽時代?
人家都是「一日千里」的往前進.
你為甚麽還説「不要忙, 不要忙」?

9. 王先生是一個女子中學的教員. 他對學生都很好, 不但關心她們的功課, 就是她們有甚麽煩難的問題, 他也常給她們幫忙. 有一次有一個學生家裏沒有錢, 拿不出來學費. 王先生就給她拿. 大家都説他是一個好老師. 可是也有人説: "王先生這樣對這個學生雖然是一種好意, 可是這種好意是不是帶有別的作用呢?" 王先生聽見了這些話很生氣. 他説:"我做事的出發點就是要幫助沒錢的學生念書. 怎麽會還有別的作用呢!"

10. 王教授病了. 他是累病的. 他又教書又寫書, 太累了. 日子長了怎能不累病了呢！在他沒病以前，有一天我去看他．他說："我正寫一本論理學現在已經把目錄編定了．你看一看這個目錄就知道我這本書有甚麽特色了."我說："我先不看這本書有甚麽特色．我先告訴你，我見了你以後覺得你的面色沒有從前那麽好．上次我看見你，你的面色是紅紅的．是不是太累了？小心累病了．寫書忙甚麽呢，為甚麽一定要忙着寫呢！" 他說："不要緊，累不着，也病不了．前幾天我的右手雖然有點發麻，可是我想不見得就是病，是寫字寫多了．這幾天完全好了."他說這話以後還沒有三天，就有人來給我送信，說王教授病了．

11. 在我們同事裏，老李的年紀最大．他時常不客氣的叫我是老弟．有一天老李對我說："老弟，你的歲數也不小了，應該有一個女朋友了．我給你介紹一位小姐．她在女子中學念書．人很聰明，長的又出色．一半天我先介紹你們見見面，好不好？”我說：“好吧.”過了幾天老李介紹我跟這位小姐見面了. 見面的第二天老李問我：“這位小姐怎麽樣？”我說：“你太開玩笑了.為甚麽給我介紹一個大麻子？”

12. 高太太病了有很多日子了，不論用甚麽治法都治不好. 前些日子，高先生請來一位外國大夫來給她治. 治了還不到十天，她的病就有一點兒起色了. 高先生說：“還是外國大夫有本事. 才一着手病就好啦.”

13. 有一個人最喜歡旅行，只要是放假的日子他就去旅行，所以他每年用了很多旅費. 有人問他：“你費了這麽多的船費、車費去旅行，你一定覺得旅行是最有意思的. 可是你在每次旅行的時候，是不是也覺得是麻煩的事呢？”他說：“只有一件事麻煩得很，吃飯館兒住旅館連叫汽車在内…處處要給小費. 給少了他們不高興，給多了也不好.應該給多少呢？

這雖然是一件小事，可是它是最麻煩的事.”

14. 有一個朋友叫我給他找工作. 我說:“我弟弟現在在政府裏作事. 他的工作是收錢. 他忙的不得了，正要找一個助手. 我介紹你去做他的幫手吧.” 這個朋友說:“收錢的工作我怕.”我問他:“你怕甚麽？”他說:“我怕收錯了連累了你弟弟.”我說:“我弟弟不一定叫你收錢，也許就叫你寫寫收條. 他原有的助手就是幫他寫收條的.”

15. 從前我是給人家幫工的. 做幫工的可真不容易. 上午八點鐘就開始工作，下午五點鐘才收工. 工作的時候必得隨着人家的意思，不然人家是不高興的. 後來我不給人家幫工了，自己做買賣. 買賣雖然很小，可是不必看人家的面色啦.

16. 從前我給王經理當助理的時候，大事小事他都叫我做. 他有甚麽煩難問題也常和我研究. 他說:“你就是我的左右手.”後來王經理的事業越來越大了. 大家都說:“王經理真有本事.”王經理說:“不是我有本事. 我有一位有本事的助理.”

17. 我有一個好朋友, 有一天來跟我借錢. 我問他:“要借多少?”他說:“要借兩千.”我說:“你借這筆錢一定有要緊的用處, 能不能告訴我做甚麼用呢?”他說:“我當然有要緊的用處, 可是我得先問你能不能借. 我再告訴你做甚麼用.”我說:“能借.”他說:“我告訴你吧, 我不是要借錢, 我是跟你開玩笑.”

18. 祝先生和一個很有錢的女人結了婚. 這個女人的年歲比祝先生大的多. 有人說:“祝先生這麽年輕, 為甚麽和一個比他老的女人結婚呢?”有人說:“你這個人真不聰明. 只要有了錢有了票子, 為甚麽還要看票子發行的日期呢?”

19. 今天我到王先生家去看王先生, 他不在家. 他的太太說:"王先生這幾天不常在家, 因為有一件事, 是別人連累了他. 近來常有人來找麻煩, 他對這種煩心的事不想和找麻煩的人見面, 所以他不常在家."

20. 今天早晨收到我大姐一封從日本來的信. 當時我正在吃早點, 我就一面吃早點, 一面看這封信. 信裏是這樣寫的:

二妹:

好久沒給你寫信了. 你好吧! 我現在告訴你一件有趣的事情. 前幾天我在電車站遇見了王美心, 她從前是我們中學的同學. 她不是個麻子嗎? 大概你還記得. 這回我們在外國見了面大家都很高興. 她說她已經跟一個姓方的結了婚, 她就給我介紹站在她後面的人, 說:"這就是我的先生—方先生."我一看方先生, 我差一點兒要笑出來. 原來方先生也是一個大麻子, 而且他們兩個人長的一樣, 沒有多大差別…
我看到這裏，笑得我連早點都吃不下去了.

21. 我是一個送信的. 有人說這種工作沒有意思，可是我的看法就不同了. 我認為工作沒有沒意思的，只是怎樣看法了. 每天把幾百幾千封信，都經過我的手送出去，送給人家. 這種工作完全是為了別人，不是為了自己. 你怎能說這種工作沒意思呢？

22. 有人認為人生不過一百年，不論在那一方面說都應該好好兒的去做一點兒事情. 也有人認為百年是很短的一個時間，應該找最快活的事情.

23. 有五個人在一塊兒說笑話，每人說一個. 有四個人已經說完了大家都笑的不得了. 到了第五個人說笑話了，他說："有一個古國國名是甚麽我忘了，只知道這個古國國土很大. 國王喜歡聽笑話. 每次有人給他說笑話他就送給一塊土地. 有人對國王說:“不要再聽笑話了. 要是再聽下去將來可能連住的地方都沒有了. 國王聽了那個人的話以後,就不聽笑話了.”這個說笑話的說到這裏, 大家覺得沒甚麽可笑的, 大家就誰也沒笑. 這個時候說笑話的人很大的聲音說:“怎麽別人說笑話你們都笑, 可是我說笑話你們都不笑呢?” 他說完這句話, 大家覺得這真是可笑就大笑起來了.

24. 謝老師:

聽說您明天要到外國去, 本來想請您吃飯給您送行. 可是知道您太忙, 沒有時間,所以就沒法子請您吃飯了. 現在送上一些水果, 這些水果是有人才從我的老家帶來的. 在外國或者沒有賣的, 請您收下. 祝

一路平安! 學生 大文上 一月七日

25. 從前中國人有一句常說的話, 這句話的大意是說:“東西如果離開了本土它的價

錢就貴了.要是一個人,如果離開本土就不如在本土好了.”這句話在從前看來是很有道理的,在現在看來是不是有道理?請你想想看!

26. 在客人要走的時候,我們一定要送客,可是客人多半說:“別送別送,”我們是不是就不送了呢?這要看是甚麼客人.對應當客氣的人,還是要送.對不必客氣的人就不用送了.還有,如果是常來的客人也不必送.

27. 我有一個很好玩的玩意兒.有一個同學要拿去玩兒.我說:“明天我一定把這個玩意兒送到府上,可是你玩兒幾天以後,千萬把它再給我,因為我也喜歡玩兒.”

28. 有一個科學研究所的所長,為了研究原子的原理,叫研究所的一個所員到圖書館去借一本書.圖書館的館員說:“現在這種書只能在這裏看,不能借出去.以前借出去的,沒人送回圖書館,也沒法子收回，所以現在不能借了.”

29. 老王正在收拾行李，我去幫忙. 我看見地下有一張功課表，我就給他拾起來. 他說:“這張功課表沒用了.”我說:“沒用也不要放在地下呀！”他說:“地下現在有的東西都是沒用的，我都不要了，你不必拾起來了.”我說:“還有幾本拼音的書呢.”他說:“你真給我找麻煩. 拼音的書也是不要的. 你這種幫忙是越幫越忙啊！”

30. 田先生兒女很多. 有一天他的大兒子說:“今天天氣很暖和，我們應當從水路到上海去旅行.”田先生說:“你不要老想旅行. 你看你大姐、二姐、三妹和二弟都在做功課呢.”這個大兒子說:“他們這樣用功也不見得功課都能打一百分. 我雖然現在不做功課也不見得我的分兒比他們少.”田先生一聽兒子的話，覺得很有道理，就讓兒子女兒們大家一塊兒去旅行. 他們走的時候已經很晚了，下午兩點鐘才出發.

Exercise 5. Illustrative Sentences (English)

3.1. I have no objections to my books being read, I just object [lit. fear] to [other] people making marks when they read my books.

3.3. Since your father isn't here what are you afraid of?

3.5. Why are you afraid of your younger sister? What's there to be afraid about in a younger sister?

6.1. No one has any money. No one can help any one else.

6.5. Can you help me?

8.1. This trip took a lot of my time and money, but [lit. the result was that] it wasn't at all interesting.

8.2. It won't require any effort on your part to put in a word. Why not do so?

8.5. On my daily trips to school, a round trip fare costs over two dollars.

8.9. I put in a lot of thought and effort to help him, and he didn't even say a word of thanks.

9.5. I wrote characters all day today. I got tired from writing.

11.2. As soon as I write a lot of characters my hand gets numb. Now my hand has gotten numb again.

11.6. Yan Dali is pock-marked. People call him Big-Pocks Yan.

12.1. Did you send to the press the things I asked you to?

12.5. He gave away all his books before he returned to his own country. ··· Who did he give them to?

13.5. Originally I had no intention of playing mahjong. Because the three of them wanted to play they called me over.

13.6. Since coming here he hasn't studied hard, he's played every day.

14.6. Although the story he told was too long, it was very funny. Everyone listened right to the end.

15.1. Who took in the mail that came today?

21.2. The director and members of the Geography Research Institute are all oldtime graduates of Peking University.

21.3. The whole staff of that library consists of women.

24.1. The writing which existed in ancient times is different from that of today.

24.3. Did you just now buy this book, or have you had it for a long time?

26.1. From his tone of voice he seems to be displeased.

27.2. Is there anything to eat? ··· There isn't anything much to eat. There's just a few noodles.

27.3. Some people say that even in olden times there was vernacular literature. ··· Yes, there are also those who say so.

37.1. On our present trip to the west, is the eldest Miss Fei included?

39.1. My eldest son insists on going abroad to study science. Where, pray tell, would I find the money?

40.1. Although his work is tiring, it isn't likely that his illness is due to being (over-)tired.

40.2. Why don't you like that work? Is it too tiring? ··· It's hardly tiring. The main reason is I'm not interested in that kind of work.

43.1. That he did badly on his exams was inevitable. Before the exams he didn't even look at a book.

46.1. Try this red-cooked pork. If you like it, have a lot more.

Notes

1. Beginning in the Han Dynasty, Chinese emperors adopted the practice of designating their reigns by special **niánhào** "reign-titles" such as Great Beginning, Forever Flourishing, and so on. These reign-titles were the basis of Chinese historical chronology. Thus reference might be made to "third year of the Great Beginning." Such references are sometimes clear from the context, but when this is lacking it is often

difficult to determine what dynasty or emperor is being referred to. The problem is complicated by the fact that from Han to Yuan the emperors frequently divided their reigns into several reign-periods each with its own reign-title.

2. As noted in Beginning Chinese Reader (pp. 508-509), children in a family are often referred to by designations indicating their serial order:

males		females	
老大	"Eldest Brother"	大姐	"Eldest Sister"
老二	"Second Brother"	二姐	"Second [Elder] Sister"
老三	"Third Brother"	三姐	"Third [Elder] Sister"

If there are both brothers and sisters in a family, each sex is generally enumerated separately but both are sometimes counted together. Thus 三姐 might refer to a female who has (1) two older brothers and no older sisters; (2) one older brother and one older sister; (3) two older sisters regardless of whether or not there are any older brothers.

The designations for females apply to persons older than the person speaking or being spoken to. Younger sisters are referred to by number plus 妹 "Younger Sister." Thus the third of four sisters is referred to by her two older sisters as 三妹 "Third Younger Sister" and by her younger sister as 三姐 "Third Elder Sister."

The previously mentioned designations for brothers can be used regardless of the serial rank of the person speaking or being spoken to. In addition there are special forms for designating younger brothers. Thus if I am the third of four brothers, I am referred to as 老三 "Old Third," and I (or a person speaking to me) would refer to my oldest brother as 老大 "Old Eldest," to my next older brother as 老二 "Old Second," and to my younger brother as either 老四 "Old Fourth" or 四弟 "Fourth Younger Brother" or 老弟 "Old Youngest." The latter is also used for the youngest brother regardless of the number of brothers in the family.

3. While most Chinese sentences contain verbs, as in the patterns SVO (subject-verb-object), SV (subject-verb), and VO (verb-object), some sentences occur without verbs, i.e. have nominal predicates. This is especially common when the nominal predicate consists of a phrase ending in the subordinating particle **de.** (See Advanced Chinese, lesson 2, note 1). Some sentences can only occur with nominal predicates. In other cases the form with nominal predicate is preferred over a possible form containing a verb. Many sentences with nominal predicates can be considered variants of sentences containing a verb—most commonly **shì** "is" (see especially Beginning Chinese, p. 152 note 2, p. 219 note 9, p. 268 note 13), but sometimes some other verb. Note carefully the following pairs;

1a. **Wǒ shi jīntian kànjian ta de.** "I saw him today"

1b. **Wǒ jīntian kànjian ta de.** (same meaning as preceding)

2a. **Wǒmen shi liǎngge nánháizi sānge nǚháizi .** "We are two boys and three girls" (spoken by children in reference to themselves)

2b. **Wǒmen liǎngge nánháizi sānge nǚháizi** (same meaning as preceding)

3a. **Wǒmen yǒu liǎngge nánháizi sāngge nǚháizi.** "We have two boys and three girls" (spoken by parents in reference to their children)

3b. **Wǒmen liǎngge nánháizi sāngge nǚháizi .** (same meaning as preceding)

Thus sentences 2b and 3b are identical in form but different in meaning. The exact meaning can of course be determined only by the context. For practice on nominal predicates, see Exercise 1, which consists of pairs of sentences having the same meaning but providing a contrast between verbal and nominal predicates.

第 五 課

1	2	3	4	5	6	7	8
掛	剩	猜	勞	亮	準	永	藍

9	10	11	12	13	14	15	16
廣	州	媽	廳	市	場	片	其

1.0 掛 **guà** hang, suspend

掛上 **guàshang** hang up

掛起來 **guàqilai** hang up

掛畫 **guà huà** hang up a picture

掛念 **guànian** worry, be anxious

掛心 **guàxīn** worry, be anxious (about) (that)

掛在心上 **guàzai xīnshang** keep anxiously in one's thoughts, fret about

掛號 **guàhào** to register (VO)

掛號信 **guàhàoxìn** registered letter, registered mail

1.1. 這張畫是誰掛的？為甚麽要把它掛上哪？

1.2. 請你把這張地圖掛起來.

1.3. 他在房子裏掛畫呢？

1.4. 我給父親寫信說我在外國很好，請他不要掛念.

1.5. 你不必掛心你兒子的功課，他一定知道用功的.

1.6. 那件事情沒有甚麽大問題. 你不要老掛在心上. (T)

1.7. 在這個地方，如果去看病，必得先掛號. (T)

1.8. 你是那天收到的謝先生那封掛號信？(T)

2.0. 剩 **shèng** (1) have as remainder; (2) leave behind, be left (behind)

剩飯 **shèng fàn** (1) leave food (uneaten); left-over food

剩錢 **shèng qián** (1) have money left over; (2) balance, money remaining

剩下 **shèngxia** (1) have left over; (2) be left over

有剩 **yǒushèng** there is a remainder, have something left over

2.1. 碗裏的湯是誰剩的？

2.2. 我不吃人家的剩飯.

2.3. 我作工做了一年，也沒剩錢.

2.4. 我們剩下的菜給要飯的吃吧？

2.5. 那本書賣八毛錢. 你拿一塊錢去買，還有剩.

2.6. 這次旅行用的錢太多了. 你帶的一百塊錢還剩多少？

2.7. 那杯酒他喝了一半剩了一半.

3.0. 猜 **cāi** guess

猜想 **cāixiǎng** conjecture, guess

猜猜看 **cāicai kàn** guess, see if you can guess

猜算 **cāisuàn** (1) conjecture; (2) anticipate

猜着 **cāizháo** guess correctly, succeed in guessing (RV)

3.1. 這些字你猜是誰寫的?

3.2. 我的猜想,那件事情他還沒着手處理呢. (T)

3.3. 你猜猜看張小姐有多大歲數.

3.4. 你猜算猜算, 我們每月過日子要用多少錢?

3.5. 他說我就有一塊錢. 真叫他猜着了. (T)

4.0. 勞 **láo*** (1) toil (V/N); (2) (a surname)

勞工 **láogōng** labor (N)

勞工日 **láogōngrì** Labor Day

勞心 **láoxīn** to labor with the mind, do mental work

勞力 **láolì** (1) do physical work; (2) physical work

4.1. 從前中國人到外國去的多半是作勞工.

4.2. 哪一天是勞工日, 你知道嗎?

4.3. 寫書的人是勞心的,種田的人是勞力的.

4.4. 他的生活好他是用勞力得到的. (T)

4.5. 這裏的勞工問題很是一個問題. (T)

5.0. 亮 **liàng** (1) bright; (2) light, illumination

月亮 **yuèliang** moon

天亮 **tiānliàng** (1) dawn, daylight; (2) dawn, become daylight (subject-verb)

5.1. 我每天早晨天還沒亮的時候就起來.

5.2. 我在外國的時候一看見月亮就想家.

5.3. 今天早晨天一亮就有人來叫門.

5.4. 在黑天的時候人人希望天亮.

6.0. 準 **zhǔn** (1) accurate, precise (e.g. of schedules, timepieces, predictions); (2) certainty; (3) standard*

準對 **zhǔnduì** quite correct, exactly right

準的 **zhǔnde** (1) accurate, precise; (2) really, definitely

水準 **shuǐzhǔn** standard, level

生活水準 **shēnghuó shuǐzhǔn** standard of living

沒準兒 **méi zhǔnr** (1) can't be counted on, unreliable; (2) there is no telling, perhaps

6.1. 你說你明天五點鐘來, 是不是準五點鐘來?

6.2. 你跟我走吧. 我走這條路準對, 不會錯的.

6.3. 你借我的錢那天給我?…明天.…準的?…準的.

6.4. 他們做出來的東西不够水準. (T)

6.5. 美國人的生活水準比英國人高.

6.6. 前天你買的表走的準不準？

6.7. 這幾天我太忙了. 明天那個會我都没準兒去不去哪.

6.8. 你别聽他的, 他説的話是没準兒的.(T)

7.0. 永 **yǒng*** perpetual(ly), forever

永遠 **yǒngyuǎn** forever, eternal(ly), perpetual(ly)

永久 **yǒngjiǔ** forever, eternal(ly), perpetual(ly)

7.1. 那個孩子從他母親打了他以後, 永不説大話了.

7.2. 勞老師説的話我永遠忘不了.

7.3. 不要就看目前, 應當有一個永久的打算.

7.4. 不論那個國家的人民都希望永久和平. (T)

8.0. 藍 **lán** (1) blue; (2) (a surname)

藍色 **lánsè** blue (color)

8.1. 這兩張紙一張是藍的, 一張是紅的.

8.2. 大海裏的水是藍色的.

9.0. 廣 **guǎng** broad, wide, extensive

廣東 **Guǎngdōng** (1) Kwangtung (Province); (2) Canton

廣西 **Guǎnxī** Kwangsi (Province)

廣告 **guǎnggào** advertisement, notice

廣告部 **guǎnggào bù** advertising department

9.1. 中國在元朝的時候國土最廣.（W）

9.2. 廣東和廣西是中國的兩個省.

9.3. 我看見報上的廣告才知道那本書出版了.

9.4. 他在廣東晨報廣告部工作.

9.5. 廣東省在中國的南部.

10.0. 州 **zhōu** (1) sub-prefecture (in China); (2) state (in the United States)

州政府 **zhōu zhèngfǔ** state government (in the United States)

廣州 **Guǎngzhōu** Canton

貴州 **Guìzhōu** Kweichow (Province)

10.1. 從前中國每一個省裏分好幾個州.

10.2. 美國每一個州裏的政府叫做州政府.

10.3.「廣州」是廣東省的省城.「貴州」是中國一個省的名子.

11.0. 媽 **mā** (1) ma, mother; (2) (used after surnames of married maidservants)

媽媽 **māma** mamma, mother

老媽子 **lǎomāzi** maidservant

11.1. 媽，我從早上到現在還沒吃飯呢.

11.2. 我告訴你的話，你不要告訴你媽媽.

11.3. 他有一個七十多歲的老媽媽.

11.4. 從前北京的老媽子差不多都是河北省三

河縣人.(T)

11.5. 王媽有個兒子也在我家幫工.

12.0. 廳 **tīng** (1) hall, room; (2) living room or dining room (when contrasted with **fáng** 房 "bedroom, study, kitchen, etc.") (N or M)

飯廳 **fàntīng** dining room, dining hall

客廳 **kètīng** living room, reception room

12.1. 我想在這兒找一所兒房子, 要兩房一廳的.(T)

12.2. 你猜誰在飯廳吃飯呢?

12.3. 李先生在客廳裏坐着喝茶呢.

13.0. 市 **shì** (1) market, fair; (2) municipality, city

菜市 **càishì** food market

市上 **shìshang** on the market

市面 **shìmiàn** state of the market, state of trade

黑市 **hēishì** black market

都市 **dūshì** metropolis, city

城市 **chéngshì** city, urban center

市民 **shìmín** city people, inhabitants of a city

市政 **shìzhèng** municipal administration

市長 **shìzhǎng** mayor

13.1. 市和州有甚麽分别, 你知道嗎?

13.2. 今天菜市没有賣豆腐的.

13.3. 這些白菜是我自己種的,不是在市上買的.

13.4. 現在市面不大好，生意很難做.

13.5. 市上買不到肉. 我買的是黑市肉，所以價錢很貴.

13.6. 我是種田的，我不喜歡都市的生活.

13.7. 近年來很多種田的人都到城市裏去做工人了.

13.8. 他不住在這兒，所以他不是這個市的市民.

13.9. 他當了市長以後，市政比從前好多了.

14.0. 場 **chǎng** (1) place, field, yard; (2) (measure for occurrences)

市場 **shìchǎng** a market

東安市場 **Dōngān Shìchǎng** a famous market in Peking near **Dōngān** Gate

場面 **chǎngmiàn** staging (of a drama, event, etc.)

場所 **chǎngsuǒ** a place, location

在場 **zài chǎng** be in the act, be on the spot, be at a place, be present

飛機場 **fēijīchǎng** airport

菜場 **càichǎng** food market

14.1. 他昨天先看了一場電影兒，然後又跟朋友們打麻將. (T)

14.2. 這個地方雖然不大，可是市場不少.

14.3. 北京有一個東安市場，你去過嗎？

14.4. 他家很有錢．他結婚的時候場面很大．

14.5. 你是個學生．像這種場所不應該常來．

14.6. 他打人的時候我沒在場，我沒看見．

14.7. 她走的時候我幫她收拾行李，還送她到飛機場．

14.8. 菜場裏有賣菜的，也有賣鷄的，還有賣魚的、賣肉的．

14.9. 前些日子他病了一場，所以現在他的面色還不大好呢．

15.0. 片	**piān***	movie
	piàn*	slice, strip (M)
肉片(兒)	**ròupiàn(r)**	meat slices, sliced meat
名片(兒)	**míngpiàn(r)**	a calling card
片子	**piānzi**	a movie (M: **bù**)
	piànzi	a calling card (M: **zhāng**)
明信片(兒)	**míngxìnpiàn(r)**	post-card
片面	**piànmiàn**	unilateral, one-sided, prejudiced
一片好心	**yípiàn hǎoxīn**	a kind heart, a good intention

15.1. 這是猪肉片兒還是牛肉片兒？

15.2. 我去看王先生他不在家．我在我的名片上寫了幾個字，放在他家了．(T)

15.3. 您是張先生嗎？…是，我是張大文．啊呀！我忘了帶片子了．

15.4. 現在大華電影兒院演的那部片子很好．你可以看看去．

15.5. 我收到姐姐給我來的明信片，知道她已經到了日本了．

15.6. 你說她要和你結婚，恐怕那是你片面的想法吧．

15.7. 你幫助他是你一片好心．他怎能不知道呢！(T)

16.0. 其 **qí** his, her, its, their (W)

其實 **qíshí** in fact, as a matter of fact, actually, really

其後 **qíhòu** after this, afterwards, thereafter

其中 **qízhōng** in the midst, in it, among them

16.1. 大家都以為他是老師，其實他是學生．

16.2. 我就知道他叫人家打了，其後的事我就不知道了．(T)

16.3. 學校有三百多學生，其中有五十多是女的．

17.0. V為 **V wéi** V to, V into, V as

17.1. 中國分為多少省，你知道嗎？

18.0. V_1好V_2 **V_1 hǎo V_2** to V_1 in order to V_2, to V_1 the better to V_2

18.1. 我們快吃飯，好去看電影去.

19.0. 還 **hái** rather, somewhat (AD) (see also BCR, lesson 9)

huán to return (TV)

19.1. 現在給你幫工的這個人怎麽樣？…還好. (T)

19.2. 我今天吃了早點,得先到圖書館去還書.

19.3. 他去年從我這裏借去一本書，現在還沒還給我呢.

20.0. 我 **wǒ** we, us, our (W)

我國 **wǒ guó** our country (W)

20.1. 我國人民知識水準是不是比以前高了？

21.0. 他 **tā** other (W)

其他 **qítā** other

21.1. 我就認識這幾個字. 其他的字我都不認識.

22.0. 次 **cì** (1) inferior in quality; (2) second, vice-, sub-

次(一)等 **cì(yì)děng** second quality, second grade

次要 **cìyào** be of secondary importance, secondary, subordinate

次長 **cìzhǎng** deputy minister, vice-minister

其次 **qícì** next, secondly

又其次 **yòuqícì** third, thirdly

22.1. 我買東西喜歡買好的，不喜歡買次的.

22.2. 我不要這麽好的燒酒，我要次一等的．你們有沒有？

22.3. 我能不能看書還是次要．我主要的是想先把中國話說好．

22.4. 他父親從前當過內政部的次長．

22.5. 我們三個人走路，老王在前，其次是我，又其次是我弟弟．

23.0. 不(是) A 就(是) B 要不然(是) C **bú (shi) A jiù (shi) B yào-burán (shi) C** either A or B or C

先 V_1 再 V_2 **xiān V_1 zài V_2** first V_1 and then V_2

不但 V_1 也 V_2 **búdàn V_1 yě V_2** not only V_1 but also V_2

不但 V_1 還 V_2 **búdàn V_1 hái V_2** not only V_1 but also V_2

經過 V_1 就 V_2 **jīngguo V_1 jiù V_2** after V_1 then V_2

23.1. 我們吃的太好了．不是鷄就是肉要不然就是魚．

23.2. 一個人做事要先做了再說，不要先說了再做．

23.3. 藍媽的兒子不但種田，也念書．

23.4. 他家不但有汽車還有汽船．

23.5. 我的病經過麻大夫看了就慢慢兒的好了．

24.0. 懂事 **dǒngshì** understand (things)

家事 **jiāshì** family matters

24.1. 他是一個不懂事的孩子，不要跟他生那麽大的氣.

24.2. 他的家事都是他的太太作主.

25.0. 麻州 **Mázhōu** Massachusetts

麻省 **Máshěng** Massachusetts

25.1. 「麻州」又叫「麻省」. 美國最老的大學就在那兒.

26.0. 一連(着) **yìlián(zhe)** in succession, successively, without interruption

就(是)連 **jiù(shi) lián** even

26.1. 我一連幾十天沒寫信了. 就連家信也沒寫.

26.2. 今天生意不會好的. 我想就是連一塊錢也賣不了. (T)

27.0. 特有的 **tèyǒude** special(ly possessed)

特出 **tèchū** special, distinctive

館子 **guǎnzi** restaurant, inn, tavern

27.1. 這個菜是這個館子特有的.

27.2. 在科學一方面他是一個特出的人才.

28.0. 發電 **fādiàn** generate electricity, produce electricity (VO)

28.1. 現在可以用原子能發電了.

29.0. 言語 **yányu** to speak
yányǔ (1) speech; (2) linguistics (now obsolete, replaced by 語言)

不言不語 **bùyán bùyǔ** not speak, remain silent, not utter a word

29.1. 我跟你說了半天的話，你怎麽不言語呢？

29.2. 他一個人不言不語的把事都做了.(T)

30.0. 親近 **qīnjìn** intimate, close, friendly

30.1. 他跟誰都不好，只有和我還比較親近一些.(T)

31.0. 還不V(嗎)? **hái bù V (ma)?** How come you still haven't V'd? Why not V? You should V

31.1. 你那張畫兒他給你十塊錢你還不賣嗎？

32.0. 美人 **měirén** a beautiful woman

32.1. 田小姐長的很好看. 人人都說他是一個美人.(T)

33.0. 不知(道)怎麽的 **bùzhī (dào) zěnmode** I don't know why, for some unknown reason

今後 **jīnhòu** from now on, hereafter

有問題 **yǒu wèntí** (1) have a question; (2) be in question, be in doubt, be a problem, be questionable

33.1. 他的家裏不知怎麽的不給他錢了. 今後他的學費和他的生活都有問題了.

33.2. 張大文的母親給他寫信. 信上頭一句話

是"大文兒，只要你能考上大學，學費沒有問題的."(T)

34.0. 必定(得) **bìdìng (děi)** bound to, sure to, must

想念 **xiǎng niàn** plan to study (followed by reference to a subject of study)

xiǎngniàn think of with affection or concern (followed by reference to a person)

34.1. 我離家很久家裏的人必定很想念我.

34.2. 王先生病了好幾天了.我必定得去看他.

34.3. 我在大學的時候,本來是想念社會學的.

35.0. 點(兒) **diǎn(r)** a dot

35.1. 「黑」字和「馬」字的下邊都有四個點兒.

36.0. 重心 **zhòngxīn** center of gravity, key point

全面 **quánmiàn** (1) all aspects, every side; (2) full-scale, all-out, thorough-going

36.1. 那個研究生現在研究的重心是原子能.

36.2. 這次全市的工人都不工作了，是一個全面的問題.(T)

37.0. 男男女女 **nánnán nǚnǚ** men and women

老老少少 **lǎolǎo shàoshào** the old and the young

大大小小 **dàdà xiǎoxiǎo** the old and the young

37.1. 車站上的人太多了. 男男女女老老少少都在那裏等着上火車呢.

37.2. 那個外國人一家大大小小都喜歡吃中菜.

38.0. 除了…才 **chúle…cái** only if…then (see note at end of lesson)
再…也 **zài…yě** no matter how…still

38.1. 除了你介紹我才能到市政府作事.

38.2. 我的中國話再學也學不好了.

39.0. (必)得 N (V)	**(bì) děi** N (V)	it takes N (to V), it is necessary for N (to V), it is up to N (to V)
(應)該(是) N (V)	**(yīng) gāi (shi) N (V)**	
應當(是) N (V)	**yīngdāng (shi) N (V)**	

39.1. 你到那個大學工作必得馬先生給你寫一封介紹信.

39.2. 老湯, 你天天吃人家, 這次該你請客了. (T)

39.3. 這件事情不應該你去, 應該張先生去.

39.4. 考試用的本子是應當學校給, 還是我們自己買呢?

39.5. 現在該是校長跟我們說話了.

39.6. 這次上菜市買菜去, 該我了還是該你了? (T)

39.7. 你幫我這麽大的忙, 太不好意思了. … 老朋友這是應該. (T)

40.0. 跑馬 **pǎomǎ** race a horse, do horse-racing
跑馬場 **pǎomǎchǎng** race-track

40.1. 昨天我們幾個人大家一塊兒到跑馬場去看跑馬的.(T)

41.0. 住家 **zhùjiā** reside, live

對着 **duìzhe** face toward, be facing

41.1. 這個地方前面對着大湖後面有小山, 是住家最理想的一個地方.

42.0. 為難 **wéinán** (1) be in a dilemma, be in a difficult position; (2) make trouble for

42.1. 他為了這件事情很為難.

43.0. 廣大 **guǎngdà** broad, extensive (W)

43.1. 我們中國有廣大的土地.

44.0. 就 **N** **jiù N** only N (see Advanced Chinese, lesson 7, note 2)

44.1. 我們幾個人裏就馬廣平字寫的好.

45.0. 意思(就)是說 **yìsi (jiù) shi shuō** to mean, that is to say, i.e.

45.1. 甚麼叫漢語拼音化呢?意思就是說把中文用拼音寫出來.

45.2. 我的意思是說他可以不去, 不是我不叫他去.(T)

46.0. V_1 還不算還 V_2 **V_1 hái búsuàn hái V_2** besides V_1 also V_2, not only V_1 but also V_2

46.1. 他們那個孩子一到人家家裏就要吃東西.

吃了還不算而且走的時候還要拿着.

Checklist

1. 掛
   掛上
   掛起來
   掛畫
   掛念
   掛心
   掛在心上
   掛號
   掛號信
2. 剩
   剩飯
   剩錢
   剩下
   有剩
3. 猜
   猜想
   猜猜看
   猜算
   猜着
4. 勞
   勞工
   勞工日
   勞心
   勞力
5. 亮
   月亮
   天亮
6. 準
   準對
   準的
   水準
   生活水準
   沒準兒
7. 永
   永遠
   永久
8. 藍
   藍色
9. 廣
   廣東
   廣西
   廣告
   廣告部
10. 州
    州政府
    廣州
    貴州
11. 媽
    媽媽
    老媽子
12. 廳
    飯廳
    客廳
13. 市
    菜市
    市上
    市面
    黑市
    都市
    城市
    市民
    市政
    市長
14. 場
    市場
    東安市場
    場面
    場所
    在場
    飛機場
    菜場
15. 片
    肉片兒
    名片兒
    片子
    明信片(兒)
    片面
    一片好心
16. 其
    其實
    其後
    其中
17. V 為
18. V_1 好 V_2
19. 還
20. 我
    我國
21. 他
    其他
22. 次
    次(一)等
    次要
    次長
    其次
    又其次

23. 不(是)A就(是)B要不然(是)C
先V_1再V_2
不但V_1也V_2
不但V_1還V_2
經過V_1就V_2
24. 懂事
家事
25. 麻省
麻州
26. 一連(着)
就(是)連
27. 特有的
特出
館子
28. 發電
29. 言語
不言不語
30. 親近
31. 還不V(嗎)?
32. 美人
33. 不知怎麽的
今後
有問題
34. 必定(得)
想念
35. 點(兒)
36. 重心
全面
37. 男男女女
老老少少
大大小小
38. 除了…才
再…也
39. (必)得N(V)
(應)該(是)N(V)
應當(是)N(V)
40. 跑馬
跑馬場
41. 住家
對着
42. 為難
43. 廣大
44. 就N
45. 意思(就)是說
46. V_1還不算還V_2

Exercise 1. Practice in Reading Compound Sentences

(see note at end of lesson)

1. 如果你到廣告部就必得坐車去.
你到廣告部必得坐車去.

2. 就是你猜一百次也猜不着
你猜一百次也猜不着.

3. 今年湖南大水的時候你在那兒嗎?

今年湖南大水你在那兒嗎？

4. 我雖然學了兩年的刻字還是刻的不好.
我學了兩年的刻字還是刻的不好.

5. 謝教授因為今天病了，所以我們今天沒上課.
謝教授今天病了,所以我們今天沒上課.

6. 只要你掛號了就一定收的到.
你掛號了一定收的到.

7. 雖然市場離我家很近我也不常去.
市場離我家很近我也不常去.

8. 他不但能看中文書報而且也能寫中國字.
他能看中文書報而且也能寫中國字.

9. 除了他幫助我我才能寫那本書.
他幫助我我才能寫那本書.

10. 我每天天一亮就念書.
我每天天亮就念書.

11. 我剛到研究會就開會了.
我到研究會就開會了.

12. 我兒子我不論怎麽想念他他也不來信.
我兒子我怎麽想念他他也不來信.

13. 他不論怎麽没錢也要到國外去念書.
他怎麽没錢也要到國外去念書.

14. 別的菜我都能做，紅燒肉我再做也做不好了.
別的菜我都能做，紅燒肉我做也做不好了.

15. 我今天早晨才天亮就起來了.
我今天早晨天亮就起來了.

Exercise 2. Excerpts from Actual Publications

The following excerpts are taken from the novel Spring, by Bā Jīn (Pa Chin)

1. 二姐快九點鐘了，你們還没有起來.

2. 她心裏有點緊張，猜不到母親要談甚麽事情.

3. 房裏的客人都是他見過的.

4. "你自己的意思怎樣？"

"我沒意見,我父親的主張大概不會錯."

5. "媽媽真的不會再來看我們嗎?"
"我不是對你說過媽媽到天上去了嗎?她在天上很快活."
"你也想媽媽, 我也想媽媽, 她在天上很快活, 為甚麼不回來看看我們?"

6. 這是我自己的事. 我不怕. 我自己有主張!

7. 你年紀輕. ... 你不應該時常去想那些不快活的事情.

8. 這不是能力的問題. ... 要說能力不够, 我們大家都是能力不够.

9. 我不敢再往後面想.

10. 我不要活了, 我不要活了. ... 三妹, 我不要活, 我實在活不下去了. ... 做人真沒有意思.

11. 事情過了, 也不必再提了.

12. 二小姐, ... 是不是有甚麼心事? 可不可以告訴我？讓我看看我可不可以給你幫忙.

13. 我也很想念你們,我也時常想來看你們.你們怎麽不到我們家裏去呢？

14. 他近來不如意的事太多了.

15. 你放心，只要我能够，一定盡力給他幫忙.

16. “她明天一定來”
“怎麽今天不來？”
“她今天有點事情.…她明天也可以住一天.”

17. 不要再提這件事情了.

18. “你還可以做你自己高興做的事.”
“你説我可以做自己高興做的事情,這也不見得.我想做的事情真多.”

19. 以後的日子我簡直不敢想.我怕我活不到多久.

20. 我不要聽你這種話！…你…一點人情也

不懂.

Exercise 3. Dialogues

1. 勞: 老藍聽說你太太要從貴州來了?

藍: 是的, 大概下月就到了. 我這幾天累的不得了, 天天没事就得出去找房子. 到現在也没找到呢.

勞: 你打算在那兒找房子? 找甚麽樣兒的房子?

藍: 因為我還有兩個孩子, 最理想的是兩房一個廳的房子, 而且還得房錢不貴的, 地點要離小學校跟菜場近一點兒的.

勞: 離我那兒不遠有一所房子, 就對着公園, 離菜市跟中心小學都很近. 可是有兩個廳. 一個是飯廳一個是客廳.

藍: 也可以. 就是房錢不知道怎麽樣?

勞: 房東是我的一個朋友. 要是你住我想跟他去說說, 讓他把房錢少算點兒, 我想一定可以的.

藍：好極了．謝謝你．我家這次來了要費很多錢．我在大學這幾年每個月我都可以剩下幾個錢．將來有了家這兒的生活水準高，我看以後每月不但不剩錢，够了就是好事．我還有一件事，得請勞太太幫忙找一個老媽子．

勞：那是小事，沒有問題的．

2. 姐：弟弟，不要玩兒了．我們現在先念一個鐘頭的書，要不然一會兒媽媽回來了要生氣了．

弟：大姐，國文有很多詞兒我不懂．

姐：我告訴你呀．

弟：「今後」是甚麽意思？

姐：就是「從今以後」．

弟：「其後」呢？

姐：就是「以後」．

弟：「其他」？

姐：就是「別的」．

弟：大姐你的表準不準？

姐：作甚麽？你又要玩兒去．你都會了嗎？

弟：都會了．

姐：把書放下，我現在問你．廣東、廣西都在那兒？

弟：都在中國的南邊兒．

姐：廣東省跟廣州有甚麽分別？

弟：廣州是廣東省的一個市．

姐：你用「我國」說一句話．

弟：“我國土地廣大．”

姐：日本的政治重心在那兒？

弟：在東京．

姐：「全面」怎麽用？

弟：“這是一個全面的問題，不是那一部分的事情．”

姐：「片面」呢？

弟：“你不要只聽他片面的．”

姐：「特出」怎麽用？

弟：我們學校的張大文在數學方面他是一個特出的人才．「其次、又其次」

我不會用.

姐：比如“這次我們學校考試最高分兒的是勞廣方，其次是田思聰，又其次是費永和.”

弟：「永遠」和「永久」有分別沒有？

姐：沒有多大的分別，差不多.

3. 湯：費廣平謝謝你來接我.

費：老朋友應該的.

湯：日子過得真快. 我離家快三年了.

費：是啊. 你記得你走的那天我們兩個人在飛機場附近那個小館子吃的紅燒肉、白菜肉片兒湯？

湯：記得.

費：你這兩三年在美國怎麽樣？

湯：很好. 不過我才一到那兒的時候病了一場.

費：你怎麽會病了呢？

湯：奇怪. 不知怎麽的就生病了.

費：美國大學的水準怎麽樣？

湯：很高. 我才去的時候，簡直的跟不

上.那個時候我真用功了.我天天天一亮就起來念.後來慢慢兒的才跟上了.

費:你後來才到麻州的是不是?

湯:是.我一去的時候是在西部一個大學,念了一年就到麻省去了.

費:你這次回來打算住多久?

湯:我打算住三個星期就回去.這次回來主要的是看我的老媽媽.我很想念她老人家.年紀太大了.我在外國天天掛念着她一個人在家裏.

費:前些日子我和我內人去看了老太太一次.她老人家説他很好,就是有一件掛心的事,關心你一個人在外頭的生活.

湯:作父母的就是這個樣子,老是把兒女掛在心上.其實我在美國生活很好.

費:聽説中國學生一到了美國就會做飯了.

湯：是啊．我現在也會做了．因為在外面吃太貴了，而且天天跑出去吃飯館兒也太費時間．

費：你飯做的怎麽樣？

湯：我沒做飯的天才．我就會紅燒．天天不是紅燒魚，就是紅燒鷄．有時請外國朋友吃吃，他們說我做的還不錯．

費：要到出口了．你還有別的行李嗎？

湯：沒有．就手裏這點兒．

費：那麽我送你去．一半天我請你到我家去吃飯，那個時候我們再好好兒談．

湯：不敢當．我明天到府上看你和你太太去．

4. 麻：藍永和你借我的錢日子這麽久了，還不還我嗎？

藍：我老早就想還你這筆錢，可是想不出法子來．你看我們一家老老少少大大小小幾口人，就我一個人做小買賣生活，而且現在市面也不好，有時候就連一塊錢也賣不了.

麻：那你說甚麽時候還我好呢？

藍：從下月起我每月還您五塊錢.

麻：你準還嗎？

藍：準的，準的.

5. 李：謝先生你來了，真不敢當．應該我們先去看你去.

謝：老朋友別客氣.

李：怎麽樣，在外國這兩年學了不少的東西吧？

謝：學是學了一些，可是我覺得還是不够.

李：你這次回來打算住多久？

謝：我打算在家住兩個月就回去．你還是在市政府嗎？

李：我還是在市政府.

謝：還是祝市長是不是？

李：是的.

謝：他當市長當了很久啊.

李：祝市長在這兒幾年，市政很好，所以市民都很喜歡他．

謝：我們這個城是個大城市，市長很不容易作，是一種很勞心的工作．

李：是啊．前幾天為了勞工問題還有市場上的黑市問題，市長天天晚上開會，一連着有三個晚上都開到天亮．

謝：你在市政府還是以前那種工作嗎？

李：還是．我的工作一點兒也不累，每天没有多少事情．

謝：我也認為你的工作不錯．在市政府有多少人工作？

李：不少．男男女女有三百多人．

謝：如果到市政府去工作，怎麽樣才可以進去？

李：經過市長考試就可以進去．

謝：是不是大學畢業就可以？

李：分為兩部分．一部分是大學畢業的就可以，一部分不但要大學畢業也必定得對社會工作有點兒經驗的．

6. 子：媽媽！我這碗飯太多了．我吃不了了．

母：你天天剩飯這是不應該的．你要知道種田的人每天多麽的不容易．天一亮就得起來到地裏去工作．人家勞力得到的，你吃還不算而且還剩下．

子：李媽天天給我飯都是一大碗．她還說叫我多多兒的吃．我每次都吃不了．

母：你不能怪李媽呀．李媽喜歡你，她是一片好心，希望你多吃，長的又高又大．

7. 顏：湯教授，您掛的這張畫兒是北京嗎？

湯：是的．那是在我要離開北京的時候，一個學生的父親是個畫家，他送給我的．

顏：北京那個地方很好，是不是？

湯：我真喜歡那個地方，實在好．

顏：聽說到過中國的外國人，你要問他

南京、北京、廣東、廣西這些地方其中那個地方最好，他一定告訴你，他喜歡北京.

湯：這是實在的.北京雖然是個大都市，可是它跟別的城市不同.

顏：聽說北京城有五百年了.

湯：差不多了.是從明朝有的.

顏：聽說在北京住家是最理想的.

湯：也是學生念書最好的地方.

顏：東安市場您去過嗎？

湯：去過.那是學生們常去的場所.學生們一到了星期六，多數都是到東安市場去.那裏頭不但有吃的，有玩兒的，還有賣日用的東西.我有好幾張在北京買的明信片兒.你下次再來我拿給你看看.

顏：好.我要走了.

湯：忙甚麼？再談一會兒.

顏：談了好久了.我該走了.再見湯教授.

湯：再見．有工夫來啊．

8．田：老邊，今天晚上那個會你去不去呀？

邊：沒準兒．我把書先念了再說．要是有時間我就去．

田：明天是勞工日放假呀．你明天不念書不行嗎？看你的樣子好像有心事？

邊：你看出來我有心事了？那我就告訴你吧．前天接到我父親來了一封信．我一看是掛號的就知道一定家裏有要緊的事，要不然不會來掛號信．信裏說，我母親病了一個多月了，家事都是父親做，意思就是說他太累了．還說我弟弟不懂事，不好好兒念書，老出去看電影兒，出去的時候連言語都不言語．

田：離家這麽遠你也沒法子幫助你父親．

邊：可不是，沒法子，就希望母親病好了好幫助父親．

田：我還忘了．上次你讓我買那本書還剩了五毛錢，現在還給你．

邊：還有剩呢．我還以為不够呢．我也忘了問你．

9．張：李亮平，昨天你去看電影兒，片子好不好？

李：不好，沒甚麽意思．就是最後還不錯．是在跑馬場看跑馬的，場面很大，有好幾萬人．你上那兒去了，昨天？

張：我昨天哪，你猜猜看．

李：你看藍小姐去了．

張：沒有．

李：那我就猜不着了．

張：我到大華日報廣告部給他們畫廣告上的畫兒去了．

李：廣告上的畫兒一定是美人了．

張：其實我畫不好美人，他們一定叫我畫．

李：你給藍小姐畫的那張美人不錯呀．

張：你怎麽看見了？

李：有一天我到她家去，藍小姐正在掛

畫兒呢. 等她掛上了我一看原來是你畫的.

張：畫的那麽難看她還掛起來了.

10. 謝：老費，今天十五了，晚上你到我那兒去，我們在院子裏一邊兒吃點心談天兒，一邊兒看月亮. 我家才來這老媽子，她說她會做北方點心. 今天讓她做了我們試試看.

費：你這個老媽子事做的怎麽樣？

謝：不錯. 每天不言不語的把事都做了. 早上六點鐘就到市上把菜買回來. 而且人也很聰明. 不論叫她買多少樣東西，買回來準對，一點兒也不會錯的.

11. 方：昨天田聰到我這兒來了，我没在家. 他給我內人一張名片兒，上面寫了幾個字，說今天下午還來，和我有緊要的事談.

錢：他大概還是為了發電那個問題.

方：為了發電這件事我很為難. 我們發

的電，我們自己剛够用．目前要是幫助他們，這件事情很是一個問題．在我們幾個朋友裏，你跟他比較親近．最好談這件事情的時候，有你在場．

錢：好的．他來了我們大家談談．

12. 生：老師早．

師：同學們早．你們這次的考試都很好．就是有的同學，在考試的時候太緊張．比如馬廣平吧，他把自己的姓「馬」字的四個點兒沒寫．還有一位同學「然而」的「然」也忘了寫點兒．原因都是太緊張了．

生：老師，不知怎麽的，一考試我們心裏就怕的不得了．

師：怕甚麽？

生：說不上來是怕甚麽，又緊張又怕．

師：以後不要怕也不要緊張，要小心，不要寫錯字．好．昨天的都會了嗎？

生：有的會，有的不會．

師：不會的你們先問.
生：美國有幾個州政府？
師：我問你們美國有幾個州？
生：美國有五十州.
師：當然有五十個州政府了.
生：中國的省是不是跟美國的州一樣？
師：在行政上是一樣,就是名子的不同.
生：老師,「猜算、猜想」意思是不是一樣？
師：差不多.
生：「藍色」的「藍」也是姓嗎？
師：是. 百家姓上有這個姓. 好，把書收起來，我問你們問題.

Exercise 4. Narratives

1. 我家附近有一條河. 來往過河的人必得坐船. 有一天早晨我坐船過河，船上的人很多. 有工人，有做買賣的，有種田的，還有上學校去的先生和學生. 坐在我左邊的是一位老年人，看起來是一個有學問的．我們就說起話來了，說到船上有這麽多的人．他問我：“船上這些人都是做甚麽的，你能看得出來嗎？”我說：“這麽多的人我怎麽能每一個人都看出來他們是做甚麽的呢？”我緊接着就問他：“您能看得出來嗎？”他笑了一笑說：“我看只有兩種人．”我說：“不只兩種人吧？”他說：“是兩種．只有兩種人，一種是勞力的人，一種是勞心的人．”

2．我小的時候很喜歡看月亮．有月亮的晚上就在院子裏看．有時候先看見一個大紅月亮從東邊的小山上慢慢的上來，越上越高，越高越小，越小越亮．一直上到天上，真是亮極了．我心裏也快活極了．要不是媽媽來叫我，我必定看到第二天的天亮．後來我長大了，去念中學．中學在城裏離家很遠，我不得不住在學校裏．遇着有月亮的晚上，我還是在院子裏看．可是我一看到月亮就想起了媽媽．有時候想，是不是媽媽也正在想念着我呢？後來我到了外國，離家更遠，簡直是沒有跟我親近的人．我時常想媽媽．去年家裏來信說，媽媽病了一場．最近一連幾個月不知道怎麽的家裏不來信了．就連最喜歡給我寫信的姐姐也不給我寫信了．昨天晚上，天上的月亮亮得很．我一個人又在院子裏看，一邊兒看着月亮一邊兒心裏掛念着媽媽．一邊看一邊想，我對着月亮說："啊！月亮你老是在天上？你永遠在天上？可是我的媽媽…？"說到這裏我不能再說下去了．

3. 父親叫我和弟弟收拾客廳也叫我們掛畫兒．我本來已經把畫兒掛上了．弟弟說："畫兒應該我掛．你把它拿下來．" 我只好拿下來，讓他再掛起來．

4. 母親對孩子說："你每天吃飯的時候千萬要把你碗裏的飯都吃完，不要剩飯，因為剩下的飯是沒人喜歡吃的．"正說到這裏外面來了一個要飯的說："我好幾天沒吃飯了．你們有剩飯甚麽的給我一碗吃吧！”孩子說：“您聽，那個人跟我們要剩飯吃呢.”

5. 一個不聰明的小學生帶着吃的東西去上學. 到了學校，同學們問他，帶的甚麽吃的？他說：“你們猜猜看. 誰要猜着，我就把帶的水果給他一半.”有一個學生說：“你帶的一定是水果.”這個小學生說：“你怎麽知道的呢？”那個學生說：“你想想，是不是自已先說了？”他想了半天才說：“可不是嗎. 怪不得你一猜就猜着了.”

6. 有一個地方生活水準雖然不高，可是多數人家都用老媽子. 有錢的人家用的更多. 其中有做飯的老媽子，她每天不但要做飯還要去買菜. 在早晨的菜場裏常有幾個老媽子在一塊兒說話. 不是說主人給的工錢少就是說主人對他們不客氣，要不然就說天一亮就起來一天忙到晚. 有人說：“早晨的菜市是老媽子開會最好的場所.”

7. 在北京住家是很好的一個地方. 我家從前就住在北京東城. 我記得我們附近有一個東安市場. 這個市場有很多年的歷史了. 市場裏地方很大, 賣甚麽的都有. 還有不少茶館、飯館. 我還記得我在北京大學念書的時候, 到了星期天必定到東安市場去. 到了市場裏, 先到書店看看書然後在市場裏走一走. 走累了, 就到茶館裏喝喝茶. 一面喝茶一面往外面看. 男男女女, 老老少少都很高興的走來走去. 有的時候看見一家的大大小小走進了飯館. 有的時候看見年輕的人帶着女朋友又説又笑. 我喝完了茶多半到飯館吃點東西. 我最喜歡吃一個小館子做的肉片兒湯麵, 我一吃就是兩三碗. 這樣在市場玩了一天也用不了多少錢. 要是帶一塊錢去還會有剩呢.

8. 有一個外國人在中國有很多年了. 我問他:"你到過甚麽地方?" 他説:"我到過廣東、廣西, 還去過貴州. 我在廣州住的最久.”我問他:“這些地方有甚麽最出名的東西，你知道嗎？”他說:“貴州出的酒最好．廣西的山水最有名．廣州沒有甚麽出名的，可是中國人有一句話是「吃在廣州」．這句話的意思是說吃的東西在廣州最出名，所以在外國的中國館子多半是廣東菜呀！”

9．一個喜歡都市生活的人說:“我喜歡都市．這裏有電，有水，有汽車．買東西甚麽的都很方便.”有人說:“如果有一天不發電了，水也沒有了，車也不開了，市上全面都有問題了．那時候你說方便不方便？”

10．從前的社會很看不起勞工．其實勞工在社會上是最有用的人．沒有勞工，甚麽也做不了．現代國家知道勞工的重要，不但關心他們的生活，也提高了他們在社會上的地位．每年有一天是勞工日，就是注重勞工的意思．

11. 前幾天我去看電影．電影片子是甚麽名子我不記得了，我就記得這個電影的場面很大．開始是有一個很大的飛機場，有很多飛機在天上飛來飛去的．其次就是一個城裏有大火，把城裏所有的房子都燒了．又其次是男男女女老老少少都往城外跑．我説這個電影的場面大是大了，可是有甚麽意思呢？這種電影還是不看好．

12. 有兩個人都在外國念書．一個人最喜歡給家裏寫信，天天寫信還不算而且還是掛號的．他説："不是掛號信恐怕送不到．家裏的人接着我的信就不掛念我啦．"一個人從來不給家裏寫信．有人問他為甚麽連一封信也不寫呢？他説："我家裏甚麽人也没有，没有人掛心我．我給誰寫信呢？"

13. 姐姐帶着兩個弟弟在外國念書．老家裏只有他們的母親．還有姐姐的一個要好的男朋友，常去看他們的母親．姐姐弟弟在外國都很想家. 兩個弟弟想家就說想家, 姐姐可就不是這樣了. 她想家的時候就一個人不言不語的坐着. 有一天姐姐又一個人坐着不言語了. 一個弟弟說:“我猜姐姐又是想起老家她的那位男朋友了.” 又一個弟弟說:“你猜的不準對. 不要隨便猜想.” 那個弟弟又說:“不是我隨便來猜想, 也不是說玩笑. 上次姐姐叫我猜算有多少日子回家, 就可以看見「他們」了. 「他們」當然是有男朋友在內呀!”

14. 有一天李先生要和張先生去吃飯, 李先生說:“我們下午六點鐘都要到飯館.” 張先生知道李先生一定來的晚, 就問李先生:“你說的下午六點鐘是不是準的?” 李先生說:“準的, 準的. 要是誰來的晚, 就叫誰請客.” 他們說完了話, 李先生就到圖書館去看書. 看了也不知多少時候, 他看累了. 天也快黑了, 李先生到了飯館. 在要進飯館門的時候, 他想起來看看手表.一看剛好是六點鐘.他心裏想:"這次我六點鐘到了飯館一點兒也没晚.這次該是張先生請客了."可是他才一進了飯館,就看見張先生已經來了.不但來了而且問他:"你怎麽又來晚了?得你請客了吧?"李先生説:"怎麽着?你説我又來晚了,請你先看看我的手表是幾點鐘?"張先生看了看又説:"你的表準不準?"他説:"準的很.我的表没有問題的.你看現在不是正六點嗎?"張先生説:"你再看看"他又看了看.還聽了聽這個表走的聲音.聽完了他説:"原來是這個表不走了.還是應當我請."

15. 有一個城市自從連市長來了以後,市政越來越好.很多人説:"連市長是一個有能力的市長."可是也有人説:"市政雖然比從前好了,但是多數市民的生活比從前難了,市面的買賣都不怎麽好,所以當市長的不應當只注意一方面,應當注意到全面."

16. 有一個外國人和一個中國人他們兩個人坐船到一個地方去. 船正在大海裏走, 他們在船邊往外看. 外國人說:“船走在海裏甚麽也看不見, 太没意思了.”中國人說:“你再看看, 下面是藍色的海, 上邊是藍色的天. 海離天本來是很遠, 可是你往遠遠的地方看, 海和天是分不開了. 而且他們很和平的在一塊兒, 永久不分開了. 這是一張很有意思的圖畫. 你能不能把這張圖畫的意思用中文說出來?”那個外國人想了想說:“海天一色, 永久和平.”

17. 老張跟我在跑馬場看跑馬. 在没跑以前, 老張問我:“你猜那些馬那個跑的最快?”我說:“我看那個紅色的馬又高又大, 一定跑的最快.”老張說:“你只看馬的外表, 那是没準兒的. 別的馬雖然不高不大可是不一定跑不快.”後來馬開始跑了, 結果跑第一的是白馬, 那個又高又大的紅馬跑在最後頭.

18. 王永生是一個著名的大夫. 他看病很有經驗. 每天忙得很. 讓他看病的人很多. 都是先掛號再看病, 先掛號的先看, 後掛號的後看. 有一天有一個女人送一個老年人來看病. 這個老年人好像病的很重. 那個女人正要給老年人掛號, 那些已經掛號的人說:"我們讓這位老人先去看吧. 要是經過掛號就得等着."那個送老年人的女人說:"謝謝大家的一片好心."

19. 我雖然喜歡看報, 可是我最不喜歡看報上的廣告. 有時候幾張紙上都是廣告, 我真不想看報了. 有人說:"報館的廣告部就恐怕廣告少."我說:"我們看報的, 就怕的是廣告多."

20. 我和我的太太正在飯廳裏吃早點, 王媽拿進來一張名片. 我一看名片上的名字, 是我不認識的人. 給我太太看, 她也不認得. 我對王媽說:"請這位客人先到客廳坐一坐吧."我到了客廳見着這位客人, 他說他是我弟弟的朋友, 從前弟弟没出國的時候，他到這裏來過，現在他沒有工作，希望幫助他給他介紹一個工作．我說，我試試看，看看有沒有機會．我請他把住的地方寫下來．他走了以後，我太太說:“你聽他片面說的話就信了．你怎麽知道他是不是弟弟的朋友，你就幫助他呢？”

21. 有一個外國人學寫中國字．他說中國字和英文的寫法是差不多的．有人聽了這句話覺得很奇怪，對他說:“中國字和英文的寫法差的太遠了，你為甚麽說差不多呢？”他說:“是差不多．比方說：英文字是從左往右寫的，中國字每一個字的寫法多半也是從左往右寫．就像「顏色」的「顏」、「麻煩」的「煩」還有「計、油」…等等的字，所有一個字分為左右兩部分的，不是先寫左邊的，然後再寫右邊的嗎？”

22. 有一個小學生作文，作文的題目是「生活」．他開始就寫:“我國雖然土地廣大，可是人民生活水準比其他國家差的太遠了. 有的人連吃飯都很為難. 今後應當把水準提高."其後他接着又寫:"生活用的東西都得到黑市去買, 這還算是一個現代的國家嗎?" 他作文的意思很好, 句子也很明白.

23. 費大文念中學的時候就是特出的一個好學生. 他還差一年才畢業, 因為他的功課太好了, 經過校長的介紹他就到美國麻省去念書. 他的母親很不放心, 有一天給他來一個明信片上面寫:

大文兒:

你到大學以後, 功課跟得上嗎?…

他回信說:"我在這裏很好, 功課也跟得上. 家裏有很多家事就您一個人做. 請您不要再把我念書的事情掛在心上."很多人說:"這個孩子不但書念得好, 而且也很懂事."

24. 藍廣平是在美國學政治的. 畢業以後就在州政府作事. 有一天他從州政府出來,

看見州政府門口兒有幾部黑色大汽車. 這幾部汽車特別大. 他往汽車裏一看, 汽車裏都有電話. 後來他問別人這都是誰的車, 人家告訴他這都是市長特有的車, 因為今天州政府開會, 幾位市長都到州政府來了.

25. 從前國家政治的重心在國王. 只要國王想做甚麽或者是不想做甚麽, 不論有道理和没道理都得隨着國王的意思去做或者是不做. 現在國家的政治重心在人民. 多數人民想做甚麽就做甚麽, 不要做甚麽就不做甚麽. 中國古人有一句話是「民為貴」就是人民是國家重心的意思.

26. 有一個國王因為喜歡一個美人把國家都不要了. 有人説:“這個國王太不聰明了. 為甚麽為了一個美人就不要國家了呢?”可是也有人説:“這個國王是最聰明的. 他想要甚麽就要甚麽, 只要能得到他想要的, 別的他都可以不要. 在他的看法國家有甚麽了不起? 就是美人是人生最難得的. 所以他不要國家, 他要美人.”

27. 在一個十字路口有兩部汽車出事了. 這兩部汽車的開車的都說他自己有理, 是別人的錯, 所以就出了事. 他們說了半天也沒有結論. 這時候來了一個人問他們:“在出事的時候有人看見嗎？” 他們都說:“沒有人在場, 沒有人看見.”這個人說:“要是沒有人在場, 你們說的都是片面的話. 我看你們算了吧！”

28. 有一個很有錢的母親要讓她兒子到外國去旅行可以多得一點知識. 兒子說:“我不想去.”母親問他為甚麽不去. 他說:“恐怕用的旅費太多, 所以我不想去.”他母親說:“多多的給你旅費, 你還不去嗎？” 他說:“那就沒有問題了, 我可以剩一點兒錢.”

29. 有一個母親教給他兒子認中國字. 有一天教他一個「馬」字. 她恐怕他記不住, 就告訴他:“「馬」字有四個點兒. 要先記住有四個點就容易想起是「馬」字了.”過了幾天，這個孩子對他母親説:“我看見一個字有四個點兒，我就想起是「馬」字了，可是這個字和「馬」字不一樣. 這個字好像有一把刀，您看看！” 他母親看了看説:“這是「魚」字.”

30. 有人借了錢就想法子還，有人借去錢永遠不想還. 要是這兩個人來跟你借錢，你借給誰呢？我説:“我想借給那個不想還的人，因為他借了不還就不好意思再來借啦.”

Exercise 5. Illustrative Sentences (English)

1.6. There's no great problem about that matter. You shouldn't worry about it all the time.

1.7. In this locality if you go see a doctor you have to register first.

1.8. What day did you receive that registered letter from Mr. Xie?

3.2. It's my guess that he hasn't yet started to take care of that matter.

3.5. He said I had only a dollar. He certainly guessed right.

4.4. As to his having a good life, he got it by working hard.

4.5. The labor problem here is quite a problem.

6.4. The things they produce are not up to standard.

6.8. Don't listen to what he says. You can't count on what he says.

7.4. The people in every country hope for lasting peace.

11.4. In the past the maidservants in Peking were almost all natives of Sanhe District in Hopei Province.

12.1. I'd like to find a house here, one with a living room-dining room and two other rooms.

14.1. Yesterday he first saw a movie and then played mahjong with friends.

15.2. I went to see Mr. Wang, but he wasn't at home. I wrote a few words on my calling card and left it at his home.

15.7. Your helping him was due to your kind-heartedness. How can he help but realize it?

16.2. I know only that he was beaten up by someone. What happened afterwards I don't know.

19.1. How's the man who's helping you now? … Quite good.

26.2. Business today isn't likely to be any good. I suppose we won't even be able to sell a dollar's worth.

29.2. He did all the work himself without saying a word.

30.1. He's on bad terms with everyone. Only with me is he a little friendly.

32.1. Miss Tian is very good-looking. Everyone says she's a beauty.

33.2. Zhang Dawen's mother wrote him a letter. The first words of the letter were: "Son Dawen, if only you can pass the exams to enter college, tuition will present no problem."

36.2. This time the workers throughout the city have stopped work. It's a city-wide [lit. total] problem.

39.2. Tang, you're always eating off other people. This time it's up to you to be host.

39.6. This time is it my turn or yours to go to the market to buy food?

39.7. I'm very embarrassed that you help me so much.…(We're) old friends, and I should (help you)

40.1. Yesterday we [few people] all went to the race-track together to see the horse-racing.

45.2. I mean to say that he doesn't have to go, not that I want him not to go.

Notes

The semantic connection between two sentences or two verbal phrases in a compound sentence is sometimes indicated by expressions equivalent to English "after …", "…but", "if … then", "although … yet", "because … therefore". Often, however, there is no such clear marker, and only the context can make the relationship clear. When the sentence connectors do occur, they may be found in either the first sentence, or the second, or in both. Thus, if we let C stand for a sentence-connector, there are the following possible occurrences between two sentences:

C…C

C…

…C

…

It often happens that the same compound sentence can be written with or without sentence-connectors. Omissions of these connectors occur most frequently in the first sentence. Some of the most common connectors which we have studied so far are given below. Note the frequent occurrence of 就 and 也 in the second sentence with different expressions in the first sentence. Thus 就 occurs in compound sentences the first part of which might contain expressions meaning variously "if" or "only if" or "even if" or "as soon as" or "just as." Besides being used as sentence-connectors, **jiù** and **yě** also occur with their usual adverbial meanings. As a result of the heavy semantic load on these expressions, sentences in which they occur are sometimes ambiguous out of context, especially if there is no sentence-connector in the first sentence. Thus the sentence

他不去我也不去

might mean either "If he doesn't go, I won't go either" or "Even if he doesn't go I won't go", depending on whether **yàoshi** "if" or **jiùshi** "even if" is understood at the beginning. (In speech the two meanings would be distinguished by different stress and intonation patterns.) Practice in reading compound sentences with and without sentence-connectors is given in Exercise 1, using some of the following connectors which have been studied so far:

雖然…可是	although … yet
雖然…但是	although … yet
雖然…也	although … yet
因為…所以	because … therefore
要是…就	if … then
要……就	if … then
如果…就	if … then
假如…就	if … then
只要…就	only if … then
除了…就	only if … then
除了…才	only if … then
一…就	as soon as … then
剛…就	just as … then
才…就	just as … then
就是…也	even if … still
不論…也	no matter … still
再…也	no matter how … still
不但…而且	not only … but also
…的時候	when

第六課

Exercise 1. Review of Single Characters

The eighty characters studied in this unit are listed below in scrambled order. Run through the list as fast as you can, giving the pronunciation and meaning of each character.

1. 酒	11. 肉	21. 市	31. 拾	41. 費	51. 永	61. 啊	71. 您
2. 忙	12. 掛	22. 場	32. 州	42. 午	52. 吧	62. 刻	72. 她
3. 汽	13. 聰	23. 收	33. 媽	43. 累	53. 杯	63. 燒	73. 謝
4. 笑	14. 勞	24. 色	34. 放	44. 詞	54. 師	64. 顏	74. 猜
5. 呀	15. 碗	25. 其	35. 油	45. 緊	55. 接	65. 藍	75. 恐
6. 剩	16. 腐	26. 豆	36. 筆	46. 封	56. 晨	66. 幫	76. 菜
7. 湯	17. 亮	27. 怕	37. 煩	47. 情	57. 拼	67. 助	77. 概
8. 豬	18. 授	28. 假	38. 麻	48. 玩	58. 暖	68. 祝	78. 鷄
9. 啦	19. 敢	29. 麵	39. 廳	49. 送	59. 遇	69. 喝	79. 哪
10. 片	20. 辭	30. 附	40. 準	50. 廣	60. 李	70. 它	80. 茶

Exercise 2. Distinguishing Partially Similar Combinations

Practice pronouncing and translating the following groups of combinations which you have already studied (either in the present text or in *Beginning Chinese Reader*) until you can run through them swiftly without being thrown off by the changes in meaning, pronunciation, or function which some characters acquire when used in different positions or when compounded with different characters. Be careful. In order to sharpen your understanding and test your mastery, traps have been set deliberately by including in some groups one or more terms which at first glance look like the others but which are actually quite different.

A. Same Character in Initial Position

1	2	3	4	5	6	7
要來	好吃	國王	上船	麻省	一生	口頭
要好	好玩	國內	上午	麻子	一概	口語
要是	好意	國文	上半	麻將	一連	口試
要點	好事	國外	上古	麻煩	一時	口外
要飯	好用	國名	上課	麻州	一點	口氣
要價	好的	國土	上下			

8	9	10	11	12	13	14
放下	不行	廣東	下課	汽車	主人	中文
放心	不謝	廣大	下午	汽油	主詞	中午
放牛	不錯	廣州	下山	汽水	主編	中外
放學	不上	廣告	下月	汽船	主筆	中山
放假	不送	廣西				

15	16	17	18	19	20	21
正好	早飯	古國	發麻	大意	吃飯	出錯兒
正寫	早點	古史	發行	大概	吃水	出笑話
正在	早晨	古玩	發電	大豆	吃湯	出發點
正午	早期	古書	發燒	大師	吃茶	出價錢

22	23	24	25	26	27	28
有意思	開玩笑	對外	老弟	作事	有力	名字
有意見	開汽車	對內	老早	作用	有剩	名人
有趣兒	開八字	對的	老家	作家	有趣	名詞
有問題	開單子	對着				

29	30	31	32	33	34	35
請來	平常	水平	市民	時候	送信	收工
請教	平地	水準	市政	時間	送客	收下
請客	平等	水路	市長	時刻	送給	收拾

36	37	38	39	40	41	42
少數	喝茶	回家	可笑	高中	旅行	多謝
少有	喝酒	回信	可怕	高湯	旅費	多年
少年	喝湯	回來	可是	高興	旅館	多麽

43	44	45	46	47	48	49
常用	研究所	女孩兒	打電話	放在心上	我國	太多
常識	研究會	女朋友	打麻將	放在心裏	我的	太平
常年	研究院	女孩子	打這兒	放心得下		

50	51	52	53	54	55	56
生日	男孩	年輕	目前	木刻	用人	永遠
生菜	男女	年號	目次	木船	用詞	永久

57	58	59	60	61	62	63
連累	介詞	教書	客廳	紅茶	火車	告訴
連詞	介紹	教授	客家	紅燒	火雞	告假

64	65	66	67	68	69	70
貴姓	飯館	豆子	打算	幫助	別送	菜園子
貴州	飯碗	豆腐	打聽	幫忙	別的	菜單兒

71	72	73	74	75	76
掛起來	緊接着	教法文	起名字	同音字	日子長了
掛號信	緊跟着	教授法	起外號	同音詞	日子久了

B. Same Character in Final Position

1	2	3	4	5	6	7
白色	館子	小心	場面	隨着	論理	重要
黑色	女子	掛心	裏面	忙着	道理	主要
顏色	杯子	菜心	封面	跟着	原理	次要
紅色	母子	中心	書面	遇着	代理	還要
出色	豆子	重心	全面	接着	地理	概要
藍色	父子	費心	片面	猜着	助理	
特色	票子	勞心	市面			

8	9	10	11	12	13	14
中文	飯錢	以後	收起來	文字	菜油	菜市
天文	剩錢	其後	拾起來	刻字	豬油	城市
上文	酒錢	然後	大起來	漢字	汽油	黑市
下文	收錢	先後	拼起來	拼字	豆油	都市
論文	進錢	今後	掛起來			

15	16	17	18	19	20	21
家人	美女	水力	説話	幫工	學費	哪兒
古人	母女	筆力	笑話	手工	車費	詞兒
送人	兒女	費力	白話	收工	船費	辭兒
美人	父女	勞力	假話	勞工	小費	玩兒

22	23	24	25	26	27	28
平等	不到	辭典	編定	白菜	上古史	難住
次等	去到	字典	安定	中菜	中古史	考住
等等	接到	古典	必定	西菜	近古史	拿住
頭等	收到	詞典	假定	點菜	文學史	

29	30	31	32	33	34	35
第一	內政	錄音	收下	旅行	來信	麵條
才一	家政	同音	剩下	送行	不信	油條
萬一	行政	發音	放下	發行	去信	收條

36	37	38	39	40	41	42
國土	鷄湯	老實	助手	一時	懂事	掛上
本土	高湯	其實	水手	幾時	家事	市上
地土	喝湯	事實	幫手	小時	費事	送上

43	44	45	46	47	48	49
假如	牛肉	先前	想念	筆名	理論	附錄
不如	鷄肉	目前	掛念	假名	概論	記錄
比如	豬肉	提前	概念	出名	不論	目錄

50	51	52	53	54	55	56
請假	接近	腐化	送回	年號	開會	上海
病假	附近	文化	四回	外號	茶會	辭海
年假	親近	開化	收回	掛號	不會	北海

57	58	59	60	61	62	63
地方	菜場	酒杯	晨報	試試看	方英里	天文學
四方	市場	茶杯	書報	猜猜看	英方里	念文學
比方	在場	一杯	早報	吃吃看	平方里	論理學

64	65	66	67	68	69	70
送信的	初中	姓張	館員	理想	玩笑	飯碗
幫工的	其中	緊張	所員	猜想	可笑	湯碗
放牛的						

71	72	73	74	75	76	77
不同	裏頭	飯廳	打算	人生	學説	事情
共同	接頭	客廳	猜算	先生	再説	人情

78	79	80	81	82	83	84
可怕	肉片	幫忙	天亮	一連	水路	離開
恐怕	名片	別忙	月亮	就連	道路	公開

85	86	87	88	89	90	91
喝酒	看見	筆記	暖和	掛畫	生活	吃飯
燒酒	遇見	日記	説和	筆畫	快活	午飯

92	93	94	95	96	97	98
書房	拼法	中大	茶點	讓出	目次	發表
茶房	治法	重大	早點	特出	前次	手表

99	100	101	102	103	104	105
牛肉湯	寫筆記	同音字	一半天	等一等	男孩子	父母
白菜湯	作筆記	方塊字	大半天	次一等	女孩子	師母

106	107	108	109	110	111	112
大刀會	王太太	外國語	州政府	教授法	怕甚麽	飯館兒
茶話會	怕太太	外來語	市政府	拼音法	忙甚麽	茶館兒

113	114	115	116	117
內政部	跑馬場	放在心上	他不出來	從中國來
廣告部	飛機場	掛在心上	看不出來	從古以來

C. Same Character in Different Positions

1	2	3	4	5	6	7
片子	場所	其他	晚間	直接	科目	茶點
子音	所以	他們	間接	接見	目錄	點菜

8	9	10	11	12	13	14
心煩	借詞	有剩	哪裏	毛筆	聰明	準對
煩難	詞典	剩飯	裏頭	筆試	明天	對門

15	16	17	18	19	20	21
說起	一帶	送信	封面	連累	行李	差別
起色	帶有	信封	面色	累病	李子	別忙

22	23	24	25	26	27	28
暖和	書本	隨着	拿住	分為	跑馬	出發
和氣	本土	着手	住家	為難	馬來	發電

D. Reversibles

1	2	3	4	5	6
天黑	煩心	想要	要緊	語言	外國
黑天	心煩	要想	緊要	言語	國外

Exercise 3. Partition Problems

One of the main problems in reading Chinese is knowing how to divide up a sequence of characters into meaningful groups, that is, knowing how characters relate to each other. In this exercise attention is drawn to partition problems involving sequences of identical characters. It often happens that the characters in such a sequence form a combination. At times, however, they do not, in which case the line of partition comes between the characters. Read through the following sentences and make sure you know when to read two identical characters together and when not to do so. To make things a little more difficult for you, we have, as is frequently the case in Chinese publications, omitted the underline under proper names.

1. 人人都說湯太太太好了.
2. 我吃得太多了. 我可吃不了了.
3. 費廣平在大學學文學.
4. 今天天氣很好. 我們出去玩玩兒.
5. 我天天天一亮準起來.
6. 謝謝謝先生到這兒來幫我的忙.
7. 天上的月亮亮極了.
8. 這三張張先生畫的畫兒張張都很難看.
9. 要學好好多東西才可以到那裏作事.
10. 今天公園裏處處都是人.
11. 他說他要到別的地方去了, 因為這裏的東西太貴, 他月月不够用.
12. 他們姐妹四個人人人書都念的那麽好.
13. 謝大夫今天真忙. 你看看病的人有多少.
14. 他做的菜不好吃, 樣樣都剩下了.
15. 我們得快快兒的走, 要不然今天到不了了.

16. 日本本來人口很少.

17. 這幾天天天天氣這麽暖和.

18. 你不要和和我有意見的那幾個人作朋友.

19. 我要說說說假話的人.

20. 我想請請請我吃過飯的幾個朋友.

Exercise 4. Dialogues and Narratives

1. 從前我在北京念書的時候, 離我們學校不遠有一個東安市場. 那是一個平民化的市場. 它不但有賣東西的, 還有玩兒的地方, 所以不論老老少少、大大小小都喜歡到東安市場去. 學生們更喜歡這個地方. 裏面有吃的有玩兒的. 東安市場的東西都不貴, 所以人們一到了那裏多少都買一點兒東西.

2. 昨天是中國人過年. 我下課以後就到中國城去看看. 到了中國城路上人很多, 做買賣的都開着門做買賣沒放假. 在路上遇見一位中國朋友，勞先生．那個時候正是十二點鐘，是吃午飯的時候．勞先生請我到一個廣東館子去吃中飯．到了飯館兒以後，勞先生問我喝酒不喝，要是我喝酒呢，我們就要一個喝酒的菜．我説我不會喝酒，所以就要了吃飯的菜——一個菜心鷄片、一個家常豆腐跟牛肉菜心湯．菜做得不錯．我們吃的一點兒也沒剩．吃完了一算，連小費在内不過才四塊錢．

3. 我寫的這本中國的文學，在沒出版以前很多朋友關心我而且幫助我．有的告訴我書裏面的錯兒，有的關心這本書出版以後它的結果怎麽樣？我自己呢，也怕寫的不好，對於研究中國文學的朋友沒有甚麽幫助，所以也很費了一些力．為了寫這本書這次我對寫作又有了一些經驗．這本書在出版以前第一個要謝謝顏教授．他對我幫助很多．同時也要謝謝中心出版社這方面的朋友，他們説準在十二月把這本書出版．其次也要謝謝我的學生麻思聰和勞思亮．在我寫書的期間，他們從早到晚都幫我的忙，往往的晚上十點鐘他們才走．也要謝謝藍美英跟祝小平小姐，她們也幫了我不少的忙．書面上的畫兒就是她們畫的，也在這裏謝謝她們．

這本書一共用了三十萬字．在編寫一方面分為四部分．一是概論，二是古文法和今文法的分別，三是明代的文學，四是從五四到現在的文學．希望看了這本書的人對於這本書有甚麽意見請直接寫信告訴我．謝謝．

4．日子過得真快．我離開家已經三年了．在這三年裏常常想家，想念我的母親，原因是家裏只有母親一個人．記得我六歲的那一年，不知怎麽的父親就病了，没有好多日子我就是一個没有父親的孩子了．從那個時候開始，母親不但作母親的事，而且連父親的事也要作，意思就是說母親不但得作家事，也得到外面去工作，好得一點兒錢．我那個時候年紀小不懂事，母親不論怎麽忙不過來，我也不幫助母親．有一年在我十歲生日的時候，母親到市場去買東西，叫我跟她去．一到了市場看見市場裏有很多賣玩意兒的，我跟母親說要買一個玩意兒．母親說：“孩子啊，我們那兒有錢買玩意兒哪？”我不知道母親的難處．我很不高興，等母親把東西買好了以後說讓我幫他拿一點兒，我說：“東西太重了，我拿不了．”母親說：“你拿起來試試看不很重．”我拿了一拿我說：“媽不行．”其實東西一點兒也不重，我拿的了．因為母親不給我買玩意兒我不高興給她拿東西．那次不但沒幫母親，而且給她找了麻煩．因為我跟在母親後頭，而且離她很遠，母親手裏拿了很多東西還得一邊兒走着一邊兒回頭看我．想起來那次實在對不起母親．

5．昨天在報上看見市長發表了一個書面談話，内容當然都是關於市政問題了．他先說了幾句客氣話，然後就說關於買賣東西有黑市的問題．他說希望所有的市民都幫助市政府以後不再有黑市．他又說近年以來人民的生活水準越來越高，可是學校的功課水準沒有以前那麽高了．

6．我弟弟今天已經十一歲了，對於念書一點興趣也沒有．每次放學回家把書本兒放在一邊兒就出去玩兒，一玩就是幾個鐘頭．前幾天學校裏的藍老師給我父親來了一封信，把我弟弟在學校不知用功的情形都寫給我父親了．信上說他上課的時候不但不寫筆記就連寫筆記的筆記本兒都沒有．你想我父親接到這封信是多麽的生氣？等到他回來父親說他，你猜他說甚麽？他說:“父親，聰明的孩子都是把功課記在心裏頭，不必用筆記本兒．記在心裏頭是永遠忘不了的．”父親說:“就算是當時記住了，可是日子久了會忘了的. 如果記在本子上永遠不會忘的.”父親越說越生氣, 要打他. 他才對父親說:“您不要生氣了. 您是一片好心, 希望我作一個好孩子. 我以後聽您的話, 不敢讓您生氣就是了.”

7. 二月十六日. 今天是星期六. 天氣很好. 白天在家裏看了一天的書. 下午三點多了媽媽說:“大文, 你念了一天的書了, 應該出去走走.”我聽了媽的話就出去了. 遇見李思聰. 他家就住在我家附近. 我們兩個人走到中山路, 到大華電影院門口兒, 看見男男女女很多人在那裏買票. 我想片子一定不錯. 我們兩個人就看了一場電影兒. 回來的時候買了幾張明信片兒. 將來給外國朋友寫信的時候, 就用明信片兒寫. 到家一看, 媽媽已經把晚飯做好了. 今天媽媽做的是我最喜歡吃的菜——紅燒鷄跟紅燒魚, 還有菜心鷄子兒豆腐湯. 菜心好吃極了, 是媽媽自己在地裏種出來的. 吃着飯我給媽媽說電影故事. 她老人家聽的很高興. 這就是我今天一天的生活.

8. 廣平：

接到你的信我高興極了. 近來因為我忙着寫那本漢語拼音字典, 所以連寫信的時間都沒有. 你問我關於漢語拼音化我的意見怎麽様. 我認為那是很好的方法. 過去我們中國人有很多人不念書, 原因是因為原有的中國字很不容易記. 要是認識了幾百個方塊字也不見得能寫信、看書、看報. 要是從拼音學來當然開始也有一點兒難了, 可是要是把二十六個字母學會, 就能寫能看了. 你是學古文學的, 我想你一定認為我説的話不對.

祝

好　　文遠　二月十二日

9. 昨天是勞工日放假, 我們幾個要好的同學大家一塊兒到我們這一州的一個小城去旅行. 我們説好走路去不坐車, 要是没有本事走路的不要去. 老李的女朋友湯小姐也要跟我們去．出城以後走了沒有一里路，湯小姐說她累了，走不了了．只好找一個地方讓她坐一會兒．我說：“跟女孩子出門真麻煩．”她聽了我的話很不高興．她說我看不起她了．後來老李跟我說，和小姐在一塊兒說話處處要小心，時時刻刻要注意．我跟老李說：“要是女人都這個樣子，我可不要女朋友了．我想走這麼一會兒一點兒也不會累的，用不着坐着．”老李說：“得了，得了！你別說了．她聽見更生氣了．”我們到了那兒以後大家在一個飯館吃了東西，下午四點鐘坐了一部汽車回來了．要不是她怕累我們回來也是走路．

10. 張先生告訴我這張畫兒是一張古畫兒．我對中國畫兒很有興趣．中國從古來就有很有名的畫家和很好的畫兒．以前很多人不怎麼注意中國畫兒．近幾十年來大家都注意研究中國畫兒．畫中國畫兒有一種特有的方法．我希望有機會也學一點兒中國畫兒.

11. 中國在過去的幾十年裏，勞工問題是一個很大的問題. 比方說吧，過去中國的工人每天工作的時間必得十二個鐘頭，可是工錢給得少到不能再少. 這樣一來勞工問題跟着就發生了. 比方上海吧，它是全中國工人最多的地方，聽說在民國二十二年那一年中國十八省裏發生勞工問題的地方一共有八百多處，只是上海這一個地方就有五百多處. 現在中國有一個紀念日是五月三十日，那也是因為勞工發生的. 以後工人有了知識也有了政治思想，他們就有了工會. 工人第一次全國勞工大會是在廣州，時間是民國十一年. 民國十七年以後工人工作的時間就都是八個鐘頭了，工人的工錢也提高了.

12. 昨天是星期日. 因為我起來晚了，等我起來一看老李跟老費他們兩個人都没了，就剩我一個人了. 我走到飯廳一看有一大碗牛肉麵．我把那一大碗麵都吃了．麵吃完了以後我想，一個人在家念書好呢，還是去看電影好呢？正在這個時候聽見門口兒有人叫門．我出去開門一看，原來是祝教授來了．我對祝教授說：“祝老師，我應當看您去，您到我這兒來真不敢當．”祝教授說：“別客氣．我來看看你，同時也讓你幫忙．”我和祝教授一邊兒談着一邊兒就走到我那間書房裏．坐下以後祝教授接着說：“一個大學請我寫一部中國語法理論．口頭上他們很早就跟我說過幾次了．前天那個大學的遠東學院院長又給我來信，說希望我告訴他們甚麽時候可以開始寫這本書．本來我是打算先出版一本小册子中國古文法．經過院長這麽一來信問我，我就得先寫語法理論了．目前我的學生裏就你是研究語言學的，而且你比別人也有時間．這部書在時間上說，寫下去得兩年的工夫．只有你能幫助我．”我對祝教授說：

“我對語言學多少懂一點兒.我願意幫你忙.”我這麽一說祝教授很高興，他一定要請我出去吃飯.我說:“我才吃了不久，您自己去吃吧.”他說他也吃過了.他接着跟我說那部書大概要四十萬字.從甚麽是語言學寫起，讓人對語言學有一個概念，其次再說中國文法和外國文法的不同，這樣子寫下去.我對祝教授說:“這種關於語法的書不太多.這本書很有用的.”祝教授很高興.他坐了有三個鐘頭才走.今天簡直是上了三個鐘頭的語言學.

13. 張思聰的家裏本來很有錢，而且也有很多古書古畫甚麽的.從他父親過去以後，他天天玩麻將喝酒，也不念書也不做事，家裏的錢都用完了.沒法子了.開始先賣房子賣地，後來把家裏有的古書古畫都賣了.前天我在路上看見他簡直的跟要飯的一樣了.

14. 我家門前有一道河，河裏有小船來來去去的.昨天我和我姐姐還有幾個同學的，在河裏坐小船看山水很有意思.

15. 我對中文有了認識是在初中念書的時候.因為教我念歷史的老師他到過中國，上課的時候他常對我們說，中國有幾千年的歷史，中國文學怎麽好，中國地方怎麽大.等到高中一第一學期開學的時候，我一看功課表上有中文這一科，我高興極了.從那個時候我就開始學中文了.

16. 謝：啊呀，老費來了.怎麽好久沒來呢？

費：這些日子老出門兒.市長不是叫我到上海就是叫我到南京，要不然就是叫我到湖北，到處跑.前天我才從南京回來的.

謝：這麽一回事.來先喝一點茶再談.

費：好的.其實不應該我去，應當是一位張先生去.可是那位張先生不去.

謝：甚麽道理他不去呢？

費：因為他有一位老母親常生病.他不放心，所以他不想往遠的地方去.

謝：這次你回來最近還到別的地方去嗎？
費：大概在一個月裏頭不會的.
謝：好極了.我們可以在一塊兒玩幾天.你今天在我這兒吃飯吧，我們多談一會兒.
費：不.我一會兒就走.我還有事呢.我們下次再談.我差點兒忘了，你有畫地圖用的帶顏色的筆沒有？
謝：有.
費：借我用一用，下次我來就還你.
謝：我沒有用.你不必還我了.
費：謝謝你.
謝：別客氣.
費：再見.
謝：再見.

17. 生：老師，這次考試我打多少分？
師：你打八十分兒.今天的功課都會了嗎？
生：國文跟歷史都會了.可是這本國文上有的字跟上冊的不同.比方「然

而」的「然」字下頭不是四個點兒.

師：那是簡寫的．這本書上是讓你們學習簡寫的字．還有甚麽問題，還有不會的嗎？

生：還有兩個字我寫不上來.

師：甚麽字？

生：「藍顏色」的「藍」跟「客廳」的「廳」.

師：你們現在注意我寫給你們看．… 在地下那個本子是誰的？

生：是我的.

18. 湯：小祝怎麽了？為甚麽這幾天不高興？

祝：我這次考的太次了.

湯：那算得了甚麽！下次用功啊.

祝：你不知道我的事．我父親給我學費念大學是有個條件的．考試的分數不好是不給學費的.

湯：你不會作事嗎？

祝：是啊，我考的不好只有作事才能念下去．可是找事很難．昨天有人介紹我到電影院去賣票．這種工作你說我去好還是不去好呢？

湯：其實不論甚麽工作都是一樣的．如果你實在不喜歡去賣票呢，你先不要忙．昨天聽我父親說父親的書店裏要找一個人幫忙．如果你想去我介紹你去．

祝：我就喜歡書店的工作．那好極了．你介紹我去吧．

湯：好的．

19. 李：張媽，你是那兒的人？

張：我是河南人．

李：你幫工幫了多少年？

張：十幾年了，太太．

李：聽說以前你家裏很好，是不是？

張：是的．以前我家是個大地主．後來不行了，日子一天不如一天，只好出來給人家當老媽子了．

李：是啊！你在我這兒呢，就跟在你家裏一樣．你就拿我這兒當你自己家一樣．我的兒女多，你多幫助我作一點兒事就是了. 你有甚麽難處就告訴我.

20. 藍: 老麻的歷史又考一百分兒.
顏: 當然了. 他每天拿歷史當小説看. 當然考一百分兒了.
藍: 他以外, 其次是誰考得最好?
顏: 當然是你了. 除了你以外又其次就是勞思聰.

21. 謝: 邊太太您到那兒去?
邊: 我到城外頭藍先生家去.
謝: 他們近來好嗎?
邊: 很好.
謝: 他們那所兒房子那麽大就兩個人住.
邊: 是啊. 他們房子跟錢是有了, 就是没兒子. 藍先生最喜歡我那個孩子. 他們簡直的拿他當兒子.
謝: 你的兒子也真好, 用功還不算還那麽懂事.
邊: 也不怎麽懂事. 就是念書知道用功.

22. 應: 錢小姐, 路不好走. 你先在這兒等一等，我把車開過來.

錢：你的車在那兒呢？

應：就在菜場對面兒.

錢：得等多少時候啊？

應：不過五六分鐘吧.

23. 田：你的生活這麽不好，你為甚麽不去找找邊先生請他幫幫你的忙呢？

方：我跟人家没甚麽來往. 我不好意思去找人家.

田：他人好極了，好到不能再好了. 你去找他，他一定能幫你的忙.

方：我不打算麻煩別人，我想還是我自己來想辦法吧！

24. 廣平：

今天早上到你府上去拜訪，可是你不在家. 現在寫一封信給你. 李放教授前天從西部來了. 他在這裏一個星期就回去. 我們在這個星期六下午六點鐘，請他在華北飯店吃晚飯，然後到我家去，大家在一塊兒談談，也可以說是開一個歡迎晚會. 我想你一定要來的. 在你來以前希望你先打一個電話給我. 我的電話是四九三六八二.

祝

好 思聰 二月八日

UNIT II

第七課

1	2	3	4	5	6	7	8
成	贊	達	講	感	温	續	繼

9	10	11	12	13	14	15	16
許	努	專	形	況	决	孔	各

1.0. 成 **chéng** (1) succeed, achieve; (2) be all right, All right! That will do! (3) complete; (4) into, as (as postverb); (5) all, the whole

不成 **bùchéng** (1) not succeed; (2) That won't do! That won't work!

完成 **wánchéng** (1) to complete; (2) completion

分成 **fēnchéng** divide into

成分 **chéngfèn** element, constituent part

成功 **chénggōng** (1) finish, succeed; (2) finished, successful; (3) success

成就 **chéngjiù** achievement, accomplishment

成為 **chéngwéi** become

成語 **chéngyǔ** set phrase, idiom

成人 **chéngrén** become a man, become an adult (VO)

成年 **chéngnián** (1) come of age; (2) mature, adult; (3) all the time

成家 **chéngjiā** establish a family, marry (VO)

成見 **chéngjiàn** preconception, prejudice, fixed idea

成都 **Chéngdū** Chengtu (capital of Szechuan Province)

成了 **chéngle** (1) (successfully) completed; (2) That's fine, That'll do

1.1. 他前幾天請人在政府裏給他找工作，成了沒有？…還沒成呢.(T)

1.2. 王先生寫的那本書，再有一個月就可以完成了.(T)

1.3. 請你把這碗飯分成兩碗.

1.4. 水的成分是甚麽，你知道嗎？

1.5. 在事業上有成就的人就是成功的人.

1.6. 這句話因為人人常說所以成為成語了.

1.7. 他已經成人，應該成家了.

1.8. 成年的人多半有成見.

1.9. 我們下月到成都去成不成？…不成，不成！(T)

2.0. 贊 **zàn*** approve

贊美 **zànměi** to praise

贊成 **zànchéng** approve, agree to a proposition, second

贊同 **zàntóng** concur (in), agree, approve

2.1. 他畫的畫真好，人人贊美.

2.2. 我主張去看電影. 老王說："我贊成."

2.3. 「贊同」就是「贊成」和「同意」的意思.

3.0. 達 **dá*** attain, reach

達成 **dáchéng** achieve, succeed, obtain

發達 **fādá** prosperous, well-developed, flourishing

達到 **dádào** attain, reach, arrive at

3.1. 聽說他到外國去為的是研究原子能. 現在他達成他的目的了沒有?

3.2. 他的生意越來越發達.

3.3. 他想和王小姐結婚, 已經達到目的了.

4.0. 講 **jiǎng** (1) talk; (2) say (central and southern usage); (3) explain; (4) lecture

N 怎麽講? **N zěnmo jiǎng**? How is N to be explained? What's the explanation for N? What does N mean?

講學 **jiǎngxué** give lectures (on academic topics) (VO)

聽講 **tīngjiǎng** attend a lecture (VO)

講題 **jiǎngtí** lecture topic

主講 **zhǔjiǎng** lecture (on), have the responsibility for a lecture

主講(的)人 **zhǔjiǎng(de) rén** lecturer

講定 **jiǎngdìng** agree on, settle

講明 **jiǎngmíng** explain, expound

講明白 **jiǎngmíngbai** explain clearly, state clearly (RV)

講師 **jiǎngshī** lecturer (especially as an academic rank)

講好 **jiǎnghǎo** (1) agree (on)(RV); (2) finish speaking

講書 **jiǎng shū** teach, explain a lesson (VO)

講話 **jiǎnghuà** (1) converse, talk; (2) conversation (VO)

講演 **jiǎngyǎn** lecture (N/VO)

演講 **yǎnjiǎng** lecture (N/VO)

演講詞 **yǎnjiǎngcí** text of a lecture

4.1. 你聽誰講的我要去美國？

4.2. 這個字怎麽講？

4.3. 馬先生在美國講學，主講「中國文學」. 聽講的人很多.

4.4. 今天高先生在大學講演，講題是「怎樣學習中文」.

4.5. 主講的人是遠東大學的研究教授田先生. 本來已經跟他講好了，可是到時候他不講了.(T)

4.6. 給學生講書能講明白就算是好講師.

4.7. 昨天已經講明，他講話以後把演講詞給我. 今天他不給我了.

4.8. 這兩千字我和他講定了一定要在今天寫完.(T)

4.9. 今天校長演了講以後還有茶點哪.

5.0. 感 **gǎn*** (1) to affect, to move (emotionally); (2) to feel; (3) emotion, feeling

感謝 **gǎnxiè** (1) grateful to, grateful for; (2) appreciative

感覺 **gǎnjué** (1) to feel; (2) feeling, sentiment, affection

感情 **gǎnqíng** emotion, feeling, sentiment, affection

感想 **gǎnxiǎng** impression

感到 **gǎndào** reach (conclusion, feeling, opinion)

5.1. 那件事能够成功，我很感謝王先生的幫忙.(T)

5.2. 昨天我感覺右手發麻，所以我去看大夫.

5.3. 他們從結婚以後，感情越來越不好.

5.4. 你看完了這本小說有甚麽感想？

5.5. 我感到人生没有意思.

6.0. 温 **wēn** (1) to review (lessons); (2) warm

温暖 **wēnnuǎn** warm (figurative)

温習 **wēnxi** review, go over again

温和 **wēnhé** temperate

温水 **wēnshuǐ** warm water

温書 **wēnshū** review a lesson (VO)

温帶 **wēndài** temperate zone

6.1. 我很喜歡我這個温暖的家.

6.2. 昨天的功課我還没温習呢.

6.3. 這裏的天氣很好，氣候很温和.

6.4. 我每天早晨起來先喝一杯温水.

6.5. 母親叫孩子温書.孩子說:"我已經温了".

6.6. 中國大部分在北温帶.

7.0. 續 **xù*** continue

接續 **jiēxù** continue, carry on

續假 **xùjià** extend a vacation (VO)

7.1. 剛才我說的話還沒說完,就有人進來了,我沒往下說. 現在人走了, 我接續往下說.

7.2. 他已經續了三次的假了. 又要續假. 以後再續不續了? (T)

8.0. 繼 **jì*** continue

繼續 **jìxu** (1) continue, succeed; (2) continuously, unbroken

8.1. 那本小說我才看了一半, 我還要繼續往下看.

9.0. 許 **xǔ** (1) permit; (2) perhaps; (3) (a surname)

也許 **yěxǔ** perhaps, maybe

許可 **xǔkě** (1) permit, allow, sanction; (2) approval, permission

許多 **xǔduō** (1) quite a few, very much; (2) many things

許久 **xǔjiǔ** a long time

應許 **yīngxǔ** (1) to promise; (2) a promise

9.1. 這個跑馬場許不許小孩子進去?

9.2. 明天開會我也許去, 也許不去.

9.3. 沒有政府的許可不能出國.

9.4. 許多的人都說他許久不喝酒了.

9.5. 你應許給我畫一張畫兒, 甚麽時候給我畫呀?

10.0. 努 **nǔ*** exert, strive

努力 **nǔlì** (1) endeavor; (2) put forth effort, exert oneself

10.1. 只要努力工作，將來一定成功．(T)

11.0. 專 **zhuān** (1) concentrated, attentive, specialized; (2) special (ly)

專門 **zhuānmén** special(ly), specialized

專有 **zhuānyǒu** (1) have exclusively; (2) exclusively possessed

專用 **zhuānyòng** (1) use exclusively; (2) used exclusively (for)

專說 **zhuānshuō** make particular allusion to, talk of nothing but

專科 **zhuānkē** special course of study

專家 **zhuānjiā** a specialist, an expert

專一 **zhuānyī** be devoted to one thing, specialize

專心 **zhuānxīn** concentrate mentally

專題 **zhuāntí** special topic

11.1. 那個外國人專門研究中文．

11.2. 父親有一本字典，弟弟拿去了．他誰也不給用．他說是他專有的．

11.3. 我家有三部車．其中有一部是父親專用的．

11.4. 許希達專說別人不好，不說自己不好．

11.5. 她是教家政的專科教員．(T)

11.6. 他專門研究原子能．有人說他是原子能專家．

11.7. 研究學問要專一. 不然甚麽也研究不成功. (T)

11.8. 他家的孩子很多. 他在家寫書同時還要看孩子, 所以他没法子專心寫書.

11.9. 遠東大學常有「專題講話」, 講的多半是關於中國文化一方面的. (T)

12.0. 形 **xíng*** shape
形容 **xíngróng** to describe
形容詞 **xíngróngcí** adjective
形成 **xíngchéng** (1) to form, result in; (2) formation
形像 **xíngxiàng** appearance, figure, form, likeness
情形 **qíngxing** condition, situation, circumstances
看情形 **kàn qíngxing** (1) look at the situation; (2) depending on the situation

12.1. 那個女人太美了. 用甚麽形容詞也形容不出來她的美. (T)

12.2. 從前在外國的中國人多半喜歡住在一個地方. 慢慢的那個地方就形成了一個中國城.

12.3. 我已經寫信把我在學校的情形告訴母親了.

12.4. 你看她的形像, 真不像一個女人.

12.5. 明天開會我是不是講話，看情形再說. (T)

13.0. 况 **kuàng*** (1) moreover; (2) situation, circumstance, state

况且 **kuàngqiě** furthermore, moreover, besides

近况 **jìnkuàng** recent affairs, recent situation

情况 **qíngkuàng** circumstances

概况 **gàikuàng** a survey (W)

現况 **xiànkuàng** current situation, present state

13.1. 只要是認識他的人都去幫他的忙. 况且你是他的同學，怎能不去呢？(T)

13.2. 他的近况不大好，所以他的孩子没上學.

13.3. 張先生的情况一天不如一天了.

13.4. 「概况」就是「大概的情况」. 比方說「中國概况」就是「中國大概的情况」.

13.5. 老王的現况比從前好多了，所以他常去旅行.

14.0. 决 **jué*** decide

决不 **jué bù** decidedly not, definitely not, on no account

决意 **juéyì** determine, decide

决定 **juédìng** (1) decide upon, decide to; (2) fixed, certain; (3) decision

决心 **juéxīn** (1) resolve; (2) resolution, determination, decisiveness

下决心 **xià juéxīn** decide, make a decision

14.1. 我的現况雖然不好，可是我决不希望別人幫助.

14.2. 有人告訴他喝酒沒有甚麽好處，他就决意不喝了.

14.3. 今年年假我回不回家現在還沒决定.

14.4. 王小姐不理我. 我也下决心不理她了.

15.0. 孔 **kǒng** (a surname)

孔夫子 **Kǒngfūzǐ** Confucius, Master Kong

孔子 **Kǒngzǐ** Confucius, Master Kong

15.1. 孔子在老子以前還是在老子以後，你知道嗎？

15.2. 孔夫子就是孔老師的意思.

16.0. 各 **gè** each, the various

各V一M **gè V yì M** V one each of M

各有不同 **gè yǒu bùtóng** each different

各處 **gèchù** every place, everywhere, various places

各個 **gègè** each and every, all the…s

各方面 **gèfāngmiàn** (from) all sides, (from) every viewpoint

各種 **gèzhǒng** all kinds (of), every kind (of), each kind (of), various kinds (of)

各樣 **gèyàng** all sorts (of), every sort (of), each sort (of), various sorts (of)

各人 **gèrén** each person

各國 **gèguó** each nation

各位 **gèwèi** you (ladies and gentlemen) (used especially in lectures)

各V各的(N) **gè V gède (N)** each V's one's own (N)

16.1. 這種字典很好. 我和姐姐各買了一本. (T)

16.2. 各國的大學, 各有不同.

16.3. 圖書館裏有各種各樣的地圖.

16.4. 他們家裏各個人都是那麽聰明.

16.5. 為了給他找工作, 我到各處跟各方面説好話.

16.6. 校長對學生講話:"大家在這裏研究學問, 各人的家裏都希望各位有些成就." (T)

16.7. 今天中午我們三個人一塊兒去吃飯館兒, 各吃各的. 誰也没請客. (T)

17.0. 本校 **běnxiào** our school, this school (W)

17.1. 校長對學生説:"本校有八十多年的歷史."

18.0. N有V的 **N yǒu V de** (1) N has something to V; (2) with regard to N, some V

18.1. 只要是我有吃的, 我一定叫你也有吃的. (T)

18.2. 中學生們有喜歡寫筆記的, 有不喜歡寫筆記的. (T)

19.0. 才S_1就/又S_2 **cái S_1 jiù/yòu S_2** after S_1 then S_2, S_2 right after S_1 (see Advanced Chinese, lesson 1, note 2)

19.1. 他才來了就走了. (T)

19.2. 那個孩子老吃東西. 你看他才吃了現在又吃.

20.0. S_1才S_2 **S_1 cái S_2** S_1 and only then S_2 (see Advanced Chinese, lesson 1, note 3)

為了 **wèile** in order to, for

為了V_1才V_2 **wèile V_1 cái V_2** to V_2 in order to V_1

20.1. 他在這裏吃了飯才到學校去的.

20.2. 他是為了研究論理學才到這兒來念書.

21.0. 等(到/着)…再/才V **děng(dao/zhe)…zài/cái** to V after …

21.1. 今天的晚飯得等媽媽回來才吃呢.

21.2. 請你在這裏等我. 等到八點鐘我不來再走. (T)

21.3. 所有的事情, 等着院長從南京回來再說. (T)

22.0. 要是…的時候 **yàoshi…de shíhou** if and when

22.1. 你要是給王先生寫信的時候說我問他好.

23.0. 生字 **shēngzì** new character, new word, (new) vocabulary

生字表 **shēngzì biǎo** vocabulary (list)

生詞(兒) **shēngcí(r)** new word, (new) vocabulary

生詞表 **shēngcí biǎo** word list, vocabulary (list)

23.1. 我把今天要念的生字先寫一張生字表.

23.2. 這張生詞表上的生詞一共有多少個?

24.0. 分子 **fènzǐ** element, person (M)

知識分子 **zhīshi fènzǐ** intellectual(s), intelligentsia

24.1. 我是這個國家的國民一分子，所以我很關心國家的事.

24.2. 有學問的人是知識分子. 知識分子不一定都有學問.

25.0. 學識 **xuéshi** knowledge

25.1. 他雖然沒念過大學，可是他的學識比念過大學的都好.

26.0. 事前 **shìqián** before an event, beforehand

26.1. 張先生明天結婚，我們事前誰也不知道.

26.2. 昨天我們去旅行. 事前是老許做的飯，我做的菜. (T)

27.0. 安南 **Ānnán** Annam

27.1. 安南就是現在的越南. 它在中國的南邊.

28.0. 不過(是) Q 的樣子 **búguò (shi) Q de yàngzi** (seems to be) merely (some quantity)

28.1. 他那本書一共寫了不過三萬多字的樣子. (T)

29.0. 也不/没V_1就V_2 **yě bù/méi V_1 jiù V_2** V_2 without V_1

再V_1(就)V_2 **zài V_1 (jiù) V_2** if continue to V_1, then V_2

(要是) TW(以後)/(的時候)再V_1就V_2 **(yàoshi) TW (yǐhòu)/(de shíhou) zài V_1 jiù V_2** if after/at TW V_1 then V_2

29.1. 你說老温多没道理. 我那本字典他也不問問我就拿走了. (T)

29.2. 我得温書了. 再不温書我考不好了. (T)

29.3. 要是五點鐘再去買菜就買不到了. (T)

30.0. 單字 **dānzì** single character, single word

認字 **rènzì** learn characters, know characters

30.1. 開始念中文的時候必得先認字. 把每一個單字認識了以後再學詞兒.

30.2. 先生, 我問您一個生字. 「讓出」的「讓」跟「讓他去」的「讓」是一個字嗎? (T)

31.0. 報名 **bàomíng** enroll, register, sign up (VO)

31.1. 昨天到中心小學給我兒子報名去了.

32.0. 短文 **duǎnwén** short piece of writing, short essay

32.1. 他寫的那個短文雖然不到一百個字, 他把當時的情形形容的好像你看見了一樣.

32.2. 他寫東西太慢了. 寫了一個很短的短文用了三個鐘頭的工夫. (T)

33.0. 大聲(兒) **dàshēng(r)** loud voice

33.1. 請你大聲兒點兒說. 我聽不見. (T)

33.2. 他大聲的叫:"快來吧!" (T)

34.0. 問話 **wènhuà** (1) pose questions (VO); question (N)

34.1. 昨天校長問話問的很簡單.

Checklist

1. 成
   不成
   完成
   分成
   成分
   成功
   成就
   成為
   成語
   成人
   成年
   成家
   成見
   成都
   成了
2. 贊
   贊美
   贊成
   贊同
3. 達
   達成
   發達
   達到
4. 講
   N 怎麽講?
   講學
   聽講
   講題
   主講
   主講(的)人
   講定
   講明
   講明白
   講師
   講好
   講書
   講話
   講演
   演講
   演講詞
5. 感
   感謝
   感覺
   感情
   感想
   感到
6. 温
   温暖
   温習
   温和
   温水
   温書
   温帶
7. 續
   接續
   續假
8. 繼
   繼續
9. 許
   也許
   許可
   許多
   許久
   應許
10. 努
    努力
11. 專
    專門
    專有
    專用
    專說
    專科

專家
專一
專心
專題
12. 形
形容
形容詞
形成
形像
情形
看情形
13. 況
況且
近況
情況
概況
現況
14. 決
決不
決意
決定
決心
下決心
15. 孔
孔夫子
孔子
16. 各
各 V 一 M
各有不同
各處
各個
各方面
各種
各樣
各人
各國
各位
各 V 各的(N)
17. 本校
18. N有 V 的
19. 才S_1就/又S_2
20. S_1才S_2
為了
為了V_1才V_2
21. 等(到/着)…再/才 V
22. 要是…的時候
23. 生字
生字表
生詞(兒)
生詞表
24. 分子
知識分子
25. 學識
26. 事前
27. 安南
28. 不過(是) Q 的樣子
29. 也不/沒V_1就V_2
再V_1(就)V_2
(要是) TW(以後)/(的時候)
再V_1就V_2
30. 單字
認字
31. 報名
32. 短文
33. 大聲兒
34. 問話

Exercise 1. Practice on the Topic-Comment Construction

(see note 1)

1. <u>謝</u>教授年紀很輕, 可是學問很好.

2. 許達成說三友書店生意不錯.

3. 這本市政概況字不多, 不過是幾千個字的樣子.

4. 中國地大人多. 專說上海市吧, 就有幾百萬人.

5. 各個人都知道孔先生心好.

6. 今天的講話主講人是溫達開.

7. 我們這裏水大, 不能種田.

8. 許希達生活不錯.

9. 孔長望兒女多. 專說學費, 每月要用九百多塊錢.

10. 東北土地好, 地裏出的各種各樣的東西都不少.

Exercise 2. Excerpts from Actual Publications

The following excerpts are taken from a novel by Lao She which has been translated into English by Ida Pruitt under the title Yellow Storm. It deals with the occupation of Peking by the Japanese in 1937.

1. 「我得走!」

「走？上哪兒？」
「上哪兒都好.」
「對！…不過，也別太忙吧？…你還差一年才能畢業！」

2.「進去說，老三！」錢先生一邊關門，一邊說.

3.「你知道嗎？我的老二今天回來啦！」
「在哪兒呢？我看看他！」
「又走啦！又走啦！…他說不再回來了！」

4.「我該走了吧？」
「到上海去？」
「是呀！」
「怎麽走呢？…日本人能輕易放你過去？我不放心！」

5.「你別忙啊！」
「等！等！等！老是等！等到那一天？」

6. 中國還能打得過日本嗎？外國人都說，大概有三個月…事情就完了.」

7.「你得走！」

「走？…我没地方去！這是我的家.」

8.「有工夫没有？我有兩句話跟你談談！」

9.「我先回家一會兒…馬上就回來.」
「好！我等着你！」

10.「你…明天早晨走！」
「明…」老三…説不上話來.… 半天他才問出來:「帶甚麽東西呢？」
「啊？」
「我説，我帶甚麽東西？」
「就拿着點錢吧！…」他還有千言萬語，…可是他已經不能再説出甚麽來.

11.「我們都應當離開北平，可是中學和大學不同.…學生們的能力不够.…老師們，能走的請走.」

12. 他站住，想馬上回去，但是，回去又有甚麽用呢？

13.「今天不走．明天吃碗…麵再出城！」

14. 你們二位老人家先喝點酒吧？」

15. 「錢太太！…我是來幫忙的．有甚麽事情你說就是了！」…「你也在這兒幫忙哪？有甚麽我可以作的事沒有？」

Exercise 3. Dialogues

1. 溫：孔達成，你去過成都沒有？

孔：去過．在一九三七那年我們全家就到成都去了，因為華西大學請我父親去講學．

溫：華西大學是一個很有名的大學．

孔：那個大學不錯．這兒有好幾位很有名的小兒科大夫，就是華西大學畢業的．我大一就在那兒念的．後來因為我們家要回到上海去，父親的意思想讓我在華西繼續的念下去，可是母親決意不許我一個人在成都念書．她說我沒成人，是個小孩子，那兒能一個人在外面念書．

2. 費：顏教授這次到這兒來講演，我們應該開一個歡迎會歡迎他，可是不知道他在這兒幾天？

湯：上星期他給我來了一封信．他信上說，可能到演講那天他才來，講完了就走．最後他又說，他也許想法子能在這兒住兩三天．他說來了以後看情形，事前不敢說一定．

費：那麽我們的歡迎會怎麽決定日期呢？

湯：我想這麽着．我們給他寫一封信去，讓他現在就决定在這兒住幾天．跟他講定，他講演的第二天我們開會歡迎他．你說好不好？

費：對了．這個法子好，要是他來了的時候再決定日期就太晚了．

湯：是啊．

費：顏教授這次到學校來講演的講題是甚麽？

湯：我也不知道．學校專題講演題目表上有，可是我没看．他是語言學專家，一定是講語文一方面的題目．

費：顏教授的學識真好．聽說各處請他

講演的很多.

湯：是的. 有一次他說，他又得教書又得寫書，還得到處去講演，他真忙不過來了.

3. 李：老許，你年紀不小了，你怎麽不成家呢？

許：我在這兩三年以內決不成家. 等到事業有點兒成就再談這個問題.

李：你的意思是事業成功才結婚？

許：對了.

李：你的看法我不贊成. 我感到一個人要是有了一個溫暖的家，他的事業更容易成功.

許：我的感覺跟你不同. 要是有了一個家，你的心就不可能專一在事業上努力了.

李：你的看法我不贊同.

許：各人有各人的看法. 老李，你年紀這麽輕，為甚麽問我這個話. 大概你想結婚吧？

4. 方：聽説許達本的近況很不好.

錢：是的. 他才結婚的時候，生活還過得去. 生了孩子以後生活就不如從前了. 況且這裏的東西也越來越貴.

方：老許在大學裏當講師，每月可以拿到多少錢？

錢：也不過是四五百塊錢的樣子.

方：聽説他明年不在這兒了.

錢：我也聽説. 我又聽説他口頭上跟校長説要走，校長沒許可，同時也應許給他想法子. 可是他决心要走了. 我想他一定走的.

方：他甚麽時候走呢？

錢：他把這學期教完了才走.

方：我想老許一定走不了，因為每次校長對學生講話的演講詞兒都是老許寫的.

錢：學生們也很歡迎他，因為他講書講的好.

5. 李：老張怎麽好幾天沒看見你了？

張：我這幾天太忙了，忙得連飯都沒工夫吃.

李：忙甚麽呢？

張：市長讓我在這幾天以内把過去一年的市政概况寫出來，報告政府．要是專心寫這個還可以，同時還得作許多别的事情.

李：你這麽忙沒時間去看溫小姐了.

張：是啊！等着概况寫完了再説了.

李：你們甚麽時候結婚呢？

張：雖然我們兩個人感情很好，可是我們兩個人不可能結婚.

李：這話怎麽講？

張：她父母不喜歡我，對我有成見.

李：為甚麽？

張：他們看不起我，説我沒學問．將來沒甚麽希望.

李：你努力一定能達到目的.

6．湯：老費，怎麽樣，這幾天好一點兒了嗎？

費：好多了．從昨天起想吃東西了．我下星期一上課去了．

湯：忙甚麽？再續兩天假完全好了再上課去．

費：再不上課將來功課就跟不上了．昨天學校的專題講話，主講人是誰？

湯：是工業專科學校<u>張</u>校長主講的，因為他才從外國訪問回來．

費：他講的一定都是各國的工業的情形了．

湯：是．他講的是「近來西方國家工業的情況」．他講的大意是西方國家輕工業和重工業發達的情形．

費：聽講的同學多不多？

湯：不少．不但我們本校的同學，也有工業學校不少的學生．

7. 應：昨天你們到那兒去了？我叫門叫了許久也沒人開．

温：對不起，昨天我們到北河去了．你是幾點鐘來的？

應：我九點鐘.

溫：你有甚麽事嗎？

應：没甚麽事，就是想跟你談談我的將來.

溫：怎麽，你不想做現在的工作了嗎？

應：我不想長做下去. 雖然現況是不錯了，可是我不是這種工作的專門人才. 對於將來没多大希望.

溫：這是各個人的看法不同. 各有各的看法. 我的看法現在找事不容易. 作下去慢慢兒就有了經驗了. 從實在的工作經驗上成為一個專門人才也是一樣啊.

8\. 師：昨天的生詞表上的生字跟生詞兒你們都會了嗎？

生：生字都會了，還有幾個生詞兒不會. 老師，安南是那兒啊？

師：安南就是現在的越南.

生：「接續」就是「繼續」的意思嗎？

師：是.

生：「各有不同」這個詞兒怎麼用？

師："對那件事各有不同的說法，或各有不同的看法."

生：「講明白」跟「講明」意思一樣不一樣？

師：「講明白」可以當作「講明」用. 但是「講明」不能當作「講明白」用. 比如"老師把生字表上的生字都給我們講明白了."不能說"老師把生字表上的生字都給我們講明了.""我們兩個人先講明白是你請客，還是我請客"也可以說"我們兩個人先講明，是你請客還是我請客."還有甚麼問題？

生：「講好」跟「講明」一樣的意思嗎？

師：一樣."今天是誰請客我們先講好."

生：老師，「溫暖、溫和」都是形容詞嗎？

師：都是形容詞.

生：「溫帶」就是「南溫帶北溫帶」的意思.

師：我們這裏是北溫帶. 溫帶是地理上

專有的名詞．還有問題嗎？

生：沒有了．

師：好．現在我們溫習溫習以前的．

9．湯：我離開這裏不到三年的工夫．各方面看來都跟以前不同了．

謝：是啊，比方這條公路吧．你在這兒的時候就沒有．這條公路是去年才完成的．政府專為這條公路用了幾百萬．

湯：有了這條公路，方便的多了．

謝：是啊．

10．孔：這個書店是才有的嗎？我以前到這兒來沒有這個書店．

溫：是今年七月開的．是一位張先生開的．他過去老想做買賣，可是他是一個知識分子，別的買賣沒他可做的，只好開書店．

孔：他們書多不多？

溫：現在書不多．在九月開學的時候很多．都讓學生買去了．他們主要的書是各種教科書.

孔：我想麻煩你一件事.我想買一本書,可是我那兒沒有賣的.

温：甚麽書？

孔：中國漢語語法講話. 要是有，你給我買一本.

温：要是上下兩册呢？

孔：各買一本. 請你再看看有没有專門是成語的書也要一本.

温：好的.

11. 師：各位同學，現在我先跟你們説幾句話，然後我們再上課.

生：是.

師：在過去我的教學法是讓你們先學習生詞兒然後再認字. 我覺得這個方法不大好.我想從下星期一起,我們先認單字，然後再研究詞兒. 不知道大家的意思怎麽樣？

生：好，我們贊成.

師：還有. 上次考試的時候，好幾位同

學把字多數都寫錯了. 請你們以後温習的時候, 先把生字和生詞兒都會了, 再温習課文. 這一點請你們多注意. 還有, 你們問問題要大聲兒説, 要不然我聽不見. 好. 現在我們上課. 你們有問題嗎?

生: 老師, 在第三個短文裏的「成分」這個詞兒我不大懂.

師:「成分」是化學上的專用名詞. 比如“水的成分是甚麽?”

生:「形像」呢?

師:「形像」就是形容東西的樣子. 比如“他畫的牛的形像好像豬.”

生:「形成」怎麽用?

師: “大山大海是自然形成的.”「分成」你們明白它的意思吧?

生: 明白. “把一大張紙分成四小張.”

師: 用得好. 還有甚麽不懂的?

生:「贊美」就是説人和東西好的意思嗎?

師: 贊美人跟贊美東西都可以. 比如“王

小姐長的真好看人人贊美.”“温太太做的菜好吃極了. 吃過的都很贊美.”還有甚麽問題嗎？

生：沒有甚麽問題了. 老師，我有個弟弟下學期要到我們學校來念書.

師：好啊. 你給他報名了嗎？

生：沒有.

師：你先去給他報個名去.

12. 先生：現在我們談談孔子. 你知道孔子是那兒的人，他生在甚麽時候？

學生：孔子是山東人. 他生在紀元前五百五十一年.

先生：孔子是怎麽樣兒一個人？

學生：他是一位大思想家、文學家，也是政治家.

先生：對了. 中國文化的形成都是因為他的思想.

學生：先生，談到孔子有時候也説孔夫子，是甚麽意思？

先生：「夫子」就是「老師」的意思. 你看

四書上孔子的學生提到孔子的時候都是「夫子」.

學生：請問您，英文版孔夫子這本書有賣的沒有？因為那本書上專說孔子的事情，我想買一本.

先生：我想一定有．我想起來了．等張放來了，你可以讓他去買．他父親是書店經理.

學生：好的.

先生：從明天起我們放假了.

學生：是的．在這一學期裏，我很感謝您，我得到了不少的知識.

先生：這都是因為你聰明又用功得到的結果.

13. 女：媽，您回來了.

母：回來了．弟弟呢？

女：他才回來就走了.大概是玩兒去了.

母：這孩子真讓我生氣．也不念書就玩兒去.

女：也許去買玩意兒去了.

母：他各樣玩意兒都有，怎麽還買玩意兒呢？

14. 許：温太太，您好？老温在家嗎？

温：不在家．

許：到那兒去了？

温：他去看一位朋友．你大概也認識，田少奇田先生．

許：我認識．他以前的生活情况不大好．不知近來怎麽樣了？

温：田先生現在有事了．他們生活還可以．您請坐喝杯茶吧．

許：不坐了．我還有事呢．老温回來您告訴他就說我來看他．

温：好．謝謝您．再見了．我不送您了．

許：不送，不送．再見．

15. 太太：回來了．你喝茶吧！

先生：不要茶，給我一杯温水得了．

太太：剛才許先生來看你．

先生：老許來了．他坐了多久？

太太：没坐下．才來了就走了．

先生: 他沒說甚麽嗎?

太太: 他就說來看看你.

先生: 我知道了. 他給學生月報上寫了點兒東西, 一定是寫好了讓我看看.

太太: 他寫的題目是甚麽?

先生: "過去一年的感想."

Exercise 4. Narratives

1. 有一個外國人會說中國話. 他從前沒到過中國, 最近在中國旅行. 他走了很多地方. 每到一個地方, 多半常和知識分子接近. 他也喜歡和工人、買賣人、種田的人隨便談談. 他說: "我想多知道中國各處各方面的情形." 有一天有一個地方的中文學會開會歡迎他, 也請他講講在中國旅行的感想, 還希望他能用中國話來講演. 他聽說要讓他用中國話講話, 他心裏想: "這裏都是中國人, 又有許多學者、專家. 我要是用中國話講的時候, 恐怕要出笑話. 我就決意不講吧." 可是大家一定請他講，他沒法子就講了．他說：

“各位朋友，我很感謝各位的好意，叫我在這裏講話．我更感謝的是叫我用中國話來講話．我是第一次來到中國．我的中國話說的不大好．一個頭一次到中國的外國人，而且又是一個不大會說中國話的外國人，現在要在中國的學者、專家的面前來講中國話，這真好像是「在孔夫子的門前賣字啊！」”

他剛說到這裏，大家都笑了．有人說：

“他說的真好．想不到他會用中國人常說的成語，而且用的十分好．這真不容易呀！”

2. 人人都希望自己的事業能有成就，也就是人人都希望自己的事業成功．可是要怎樣才能成功呢？有人說：“走到成功的路就有一條．這條路就是「努力」．只有努力，努力，繼續的努力，才是達到成功最近最好的路．”

3. 有一天張思聰和我們在一塊兒談天兒，說到從前他母親要給他定親事的故事．他說他母親的思想很古老．他在十四歲的那一年，他的母親就讓他和一個比他年紀大了很多的女孩子定親事結婚．他的父親對他母親說："我們的兒子還沒成人，為甚麽這麽早就讓他成家呢？"他的母親說："我們家裏沒有多少人，我又時常有病，不能做家裏的事，看情形也許我活不了幾年了．兒子要是成了家可以有人幫助我做家裏的事，我也放心了．"他的父親說："結婚是人生的大事，不能因為現在家裏沒有人幫你做事，就讓兒子結婚．況且兒子還沒成年，和那個女孩子又不認識，又沒有甚麽感情，怎麽能叫他們結婚呢？你的說法我不贊成．我決不叫他現在就結婚．"他說他父母兩個人各說各的道理．說了有兩個鐘頭也沒結果．後來他母親想想也對，就沒給他定這個親事．

4. 有一個外國大學請了一位中國學者來講學. 講明是主講「中國文字學」，期間是半年. 這位中國學者在這半年裏把文字學只講了一半. 聽講的人都是研究中國語文的，都說他講的很好，希望他接續講下去. 他只好繼續講了半年，達成他來講學的目的. 後來這個大學把這次的講演詞出版了，成為一部很有名的書.

5. 有一個喜歡喝酒的人說:“我現在感覺喝酒沒有甚麽好處. 我從明天起就不喝了.” 可是到了第二天他還是繼續的喝. 有人問他:“你不是說了不喝酒了嗎？為甚麽還繼續喝呢？” 他說:“今天再喝一天，明天就不喝了.”又到明天，他還是喝，他還是說明天就不喝了. 有人告訴他:“你再沒有决心，你的酒要永久喝下去了. 你應當下决心從今天起就不喝酒，不要等明天了.”

6. 我和弟弟都在中學念書. 每天放學我們回到家裏我就温習功課，弟弟就去玩兒.

我問弟弟："你為甚麼天天不温書呢？要是在考試的時候再温書就晚了."弟弟說：我在學校老師講書的時候，我就用心聽.我都聽會了，用不着回家温書了."

7. 成都在中國的西部，是一個大城市. 從前我在成都念大學的時候，當地有不少大學. 各大學的學生下課以後，或者是遇着放假的日子，去的地方各有不同. 有的人喜歡在公園喝茶，有的人時常到城外看山水. 還有人看電影，吃飯館兒. 我是最喜歡吃飯館兒的. 為甚麼我最喜歡吃飯館兒呢？因為成都的飯館都有他們特別的菜. 比方說有一個飯館兒紅燒豆腐很出名，有一個飯館兒牛肉麵最好，還有專門賣點心的，做出各種各樣的點心都很好吃. 這些飯館兒有的在早晨生意好，有的在中午和晚上客人特別多. 有時候客人太多沒有地方坐，還得等着，等到先來的客人走了再吃. 這樣一來，飯館兒的生意越來愈發達，吃飯館兒的人也越來越多.

8. 有一個同學從外國給我來一封信，問我馬教授近來的情況．我回信告訴他："馬教授的近況比從前好的多．他現在是本校的研究教授，專心研究各國的語法．從前他要寫的幾本書最近都已經完成．他每天在他那個溫暖的家裏看看書，和家裏的人説説笑笑.他那種快活的樣子，我用甚麽形容詞也形容不出來."

9. 孔子是中國古時候很有學識的人．他的學生有三千人，其中的好學生有七十二個人．有一天孔子對幾個好學生説："你們各人説説將來想做甚麽事？" 有一個學生,也没用心想一想,緊接着就説："假如有一個小國在兩個大國的中間，這兩個大國時常都要打它，它國裏的人民連吃的東西都没有，這個小國國内、國外的問題太多了．可是要是我去治這個小國，在三年以内一定把它治理的很好."他説完這些話以為孔子一定要説他的理想很好．可是孔子聽了以後，只是笑了一笑．後來有人問孔子，當時為甚麽笑了呢？孔子説：“這個學生連説話都不能讓別人先説，所以我笑了一笑．”

10. 先生對學生説：“「成分」這個詞兒怎麽講，我已經給你們講明白了．現在還有甚麽問題要問嗎？”一個學生説：“我有一個問題．人的成分是不是都一樣？”先生説：“你們大家先自己想想，看看誰能説出來？”很多學生都説：“人的成分都是一樣．”先生説：“你們説的雖然不錯，可是這個問題要分成兩方面來説．一方面是從化學上説．人的成分當然都是一樣．可是有的國家近來還從別的方面來看，那就是從政治方面來看，人的成分就不都是一樣了．比方説，有兩個學生去考大學．他們在報名的時候要寫家裏的現況．一個學生家裏是種田的，沒有錢．一個學生家裏是做買賣的，很有錢．這個大學看這兩個學生的成分就有很大的差別了."

11. 有一個美國人會說日本話，日本字他也認識．有人問他："你用甚麼法子學的日本字呢？"他說："我學的法子很簡單．我先學生字、生詞．用一個小本子寫上生字表和生詞表．不論在甚麼時候只要我没有別的事我就把這個小本子拿出來念．日子久了，我會的生字、生詞就多了."

12. 我們學校每個月都有一次講演．主講的人多半是專家，講題也是專門的，所以我們叫這個講演是「專題講話」．明天又要有專題講話了．聽說要講的是越南的問題．越南就是從前的安南．很多同學對這個問題都很注意，所以事前多半買一張越南地圖．我也買了一張，可是我才買來就不見了．我看老王正看一張地圖，我就問他："你看的是不是我的地圖？"老王說："你忘了嗎？方才買地圖的時候我們幾個人各買一張，我看這張就是我自己買的.”我說:“我們為了聽講演才買越南地圖現在我的地圖不見了. 你的地圖要是看完了，可以讓我看看嗎？”他說:“當然可以.”

13. 我問李先生，近來為甚麽不常到學生中心去了呢. 他說:“學生中心本來是專門給學生用的. 從前去的都是學生，所以我很喜歡去. 現在去學生中心的，甚麽分子都有，我怕有麻煩，所以我不敢去了.”

14. 老馬是一個和我最好的同學. 我們在學校每年都住在一個房子裏. 兩個人有時候念書，有時候説説笑笑，我們感到這樣在學校的生活很有意思. 去年放假在收拾行李要走的時候，我們講好在今年開學的前一天我們一定都先到學校來為的是可以想法子還住在一個房子. 可是到了時候，他沒來. 過了幾天他叫人送來了一封信説他的家裏不許他再念書了，他決定不念了. 我看完了信，心裏難過的簡直是没法子形容出來.

15. 一種東西有一種東西的形像. 我們看見了東西的形像, 才可以知道它是一個甚麽東西. 比方說這裏有一把刀子, 我們怎樣知道是一把刀子呢？必得看見刀子的形像才知道這是一把刀子.

16. 祝先生在一個專科學校念書. 畢業的時候不過二十二三歲的樣子, 就在一個大學當講師. 他才到大學的時候, 多半是教一年級的學生. 後來他不上課了, 天天幫助一個教授做研究工作. 他說:“一個人如果專一研究一種學問, 日子久了, 多少能有一些心得, 比教書好的多呀！”

17. 有一個人專說別人不喜歡聽的話. 有人問他:“你為甚麽專說人家不喜歡聽的話呢？” 他說:“人家喜歡聽的話不一定是有用的話. 人家不喜歡聽的話, 也許就是最有用的好話.”

18. 有一個地方有一個國王不許人民出國.

如果有人要出國，必得經國王問話．國王親口許他出國才可以出國．可是問來問去結果都是不許出國．有一天問話問到一個人，想不到許他出國了．大家不知道是怎麽一回事．後來有人說："那個人的名字叫許可．國王第一次叫他的名字的時候，他没聽見，國王又大聲的叫了兩次「許可許可！」．當時給國王做事的人以為國王說的是許可許可出國了，就叫這個人出國了．"

19. 有一個小學生練習作文．事前先生告訴他，作文要能把實在的事情寫出來就是最好的作文．這個小學生想了一會兒，拿筆就寫："我住的地方是温帶，天氣很温和．有時候就連河裏的水也是温水．"先生看見了說："河裏的水怎麽能是温水呢？這就是離開事實了．"

20. 我在圖書館的門口看見張先生了．我問他："你一個人在這裏做甚麽呢？"他說："我有一個朋友讓我在這裏等他，等他來了就坐他的車一塊兒去吃晚飯. 我在這裏已經等了許久了. 不知道要等到甚麽時候他才來呢."

21. 廣生先生：

本校要出版一本小冊子，內容寫的是本校概況. 在這本小冊子的前面，希望本校教授把教學情形寫幾句話. 如果先生贊同，就請寫一個短文，我們是十分感謝的. 祝

近安

李明 二月七日

22. 許先生寫了一本書，內容本來不大好，可是他喜歡別人說他寫的好. 有一天他家裏來了兩個朋友. 他問他們："這本書寫的怎麽樣？" 他們說："寫的太好了." 後來許先生對別人說："有兩個朋友贊美這本書說是寫的太好了." 有人說："他那個朋友，一個是去跟他借錢的，一個是請他給找事的."

23. 孔先生家裏有一部車要賣給我. 價錢已

經講好，又講定在今天我給他錢，他給我車．今天我去給他錢，他說：“這部車不賣了．因為這部車從前是我父親專用的，我父親不賣．”我問他：“事前你問過你父親沒有？”孔先生說：“問是問過了，父親應許了，可是今天父親一定不賣了，我也沒法子呀！”

24. 高文遠本來是一個好學生，後來他時常請假．他請假的時候是先請一兩天病假，然後就說病沒好必得續假．這樣一來，他就不常上課，常和一些不喜歡念書的在一塊兒玩．日子久了，他就形成一個最不好的學生了．

25. 有一個小孩子不很聰明．他的父親教他認字，就是在每一個方塊兒紙上寫一個單字，叫他認．有一天寫了一個「一」字，告訴他：“這個字念「一」，很容易記，不要忘了．”第二天，他父親又在一張大的紙上用筆寫一個大一點兒的「一」字，問這個孩子念甚麼？這個孩子想了半天說不認識. 他父親說:"這是昨天教你念的那個「一」字, 怎麽才念的就忘了."這個孩子說:"昨天念的「一」字很小, 怎麽一天的工夫就長這麽大了. 我以為不是一個字呢."

26. 有兩個外國學生要學簡寫的中國字. 有人告訴他們:"近來專有一本書, 裏面全是簡寫的字. 你們應當各買一本看看."有一個人說:"我們就買一本就可以了. 我有看的他也有看的了."

27. 有些外國人說學中文很難, 因為中文不是拼音文字, 它是方塊字, 這些方塊字的發音必得有人來教. 又因為有些方塊字的筆畫太多, 很難寫. 我告訴他們, 現在中國文字的情況比以前不同了, 因為中國現在已經有漢語拼音, 而且許多難寫的漢字已經簡化, 所以現在外國人學中文方便多了.

28. 費先生叫我給他畫一張畫, 要帶顏色的. 我說:"這幾天我畫了很多畫, 太累了,必得多等幾天，才能給你好好的畫一張.”他說：“中國人有一句成語，「好飯不怕晚」. 你晚幾天給我畫也可以.”

Exercise 5. Illustrative Sentences (English)

1.1. A few days ago he requested people to find a job for him in the government. Did he suceed ? ··· Not yet.

1.2. The book that Mr. Wang is writing can be completed in another month.

1.9. Will it be all right to go to Chengtu next month ? ··· No, it won't !

4.5. The lecturer was (supposed to be) the Mr. Tian who is a research professor at Far Eastern University. We had originally reached an agreement with him (on this), but when the time came he refused to lecture.

4.8. He and I agreed that the writing of these two thousand characters must absolutely be finished today.

5.1. I'm very grateful for Mr. Wang's help in having been able to succeed in that matter.

7.2. He's already extended his vacation three times. He wants to extend it again. Will he extend it still again later on ?

10.1. If only you work hard you will certainly succeed in the future.

11.5. She's a specialist teacher in home economics.

11.7. In doing scholarly research one must be devoted to one thing. Otherwise one can't succeed in studying anything.

11.9. Far Eastern University often has Special Lectures, most of which deal with aspects of Chinese culture.

12.1. That woman is so beautiful. There are no adjectives to describe her beauty.

12.5. Whether or not I'll lecture tomorrow at the meeting depends on the situation [lit. look at the situation and then say].

13.1. Everyone who knows him has gone to help him. Besides, you're a fellow student of his, so how come you don't go?

16.1. This is an excellent dictionary. My sister and I each bought a copy.

16.6. The principal lectured the students: "You are all here to acquire knowledge. Your families hope that each of you will accomplish something."

16.7. At noon today the three of us went Dutch treat in a restaurant. No one played host.

18.1. As long as I have something to eat, I'll certainly see to it that you also have something to eat.

18.2. Some middle school students like to take notes, some don't.

19.1. He came and then left immediately.

21.2. Wait for me here. Wait until eight and leave then if I don't come.

21.3. We'll take up everything after the director returns from Nanking.

26.2. We took a trip yesterday. Before (we went) Xu cooked the rice and I cooked the (other) dishes.

28.1. His writing for that book amounted in all to 30,000-odd characters.

29.1. How unprincipled Wen is. He took away that dictionary of mine without even asking me.

29.2. I must review now. If I don't review I won't be able to do well on the exam.

29.3. If you wait until five o'clock to go buy food you won't be able to buy any.

30.2. Teacher, I'd like to ask you about a new character. Are the **ròng** of "give up" and the **ràng** of "Let him go" the same [lit. one] character?

32.2. He writes [things] too slowly. It took him three hours to write a very short essay.

33.1. Please speak a little more loudly, I can't hear.

33.2. He called in a loud voice: "Come quickly!"

Notes

1. In the Topic-Comment construction (see <u>Beginning Chinese,</u> p. 218, note

8) it is sometimes possible to have between the noun which functions as the topic and the verb which functions as the comment still another noun which functions either as another topic or as the grammatical subject of the verb. Sometimes this subject-verb cluster is so closely tied together as to form a sort of noun-verb predicate:

Wáng Xiānsheng xīn hǎo. "Mr. Wang is kind-hearted" [lit. "(As for) Mr. Wang, the heart is good."]

Sān Yǒu Shūdiàn shēngyi búcuò. "Business isn't bad at the Three Friends Bookstore."

In some cases it is possible to insert the subordinating particle **de** between the Topic and the Subject, but very often the sentence normally lacks the particle.

2. If a sentence contains both a question-word and question particle, the former has a meaning of indefiniteness:

   Tā shuō ma ? "Did he speak ?"

   Tā shuō shénmo ? "What did he say ?"

   Tā shuō shénmo ma ? "Did he say anything ?"

3. In referring to persons the repetition of a surname after the surname and given name adds a touch of informality:

   Wáng Dàwén Xiānsheng "Mr. Wang Dawen" (formal)

   Wáng Dàwén Wáng Xiānsheng "Mr. Wang Dawen" (less formal)

第八課

1	2	3	4	5	6	7	8
參	加	翻	譯	舉	例	滿	足

9	10	11	12	13	14	15	16
求	青	清	楚	程	職	術	樂

1.0. 參 **cān*** take part in

參考 **cānkǎo** (1) consult, refer to, examine into, compare; (2) a reference, something to consult

參考書 **cānkǎo shū** a reference work

參看 **cānkàn** inspect

1.1. 寫論文應當多找幾本書參考參考.

1.2. 我寫那本書的時候,我看了很多參考書.

1.3. 你不但要參考這些書, 也應當參看別的書.

1.4. 我的意見你們可以作一個參考. (T)

2.0. 加 **jiā** add

加重 **jiāzhòng** add weight, emphasize

加意 **jiāyì** give special attention to

加多 **jiāduō** increase more and more

加州 **Jiāzhōu** California

加拿大 **Jiānadà** Canada

參加 **cānjiā** participate, join in

更加 **gèngjiā** still more

2.1. 這部車已經坐了五個人．再加一個人能坐的下嗎？

2.2. 如果說："不是<u>張</u>先生來了，是<u>張</u>太太來了．"「太太」這個詞兒要加重了說．

2.3. 我說中國話的時候，雖然加意小心可是還出錯兒．

2.4. 我們機關裏的<u>王</u>先生走了，所以我的工作近來加多了．

2.5. 加州大學在美國的西部．

2.6. 他到加拿大參加一個學會的年會．

2.7. 他對工作本來很努力．聽說要多給他工錢，他更加努力了．(T)

3.0. 翻 **fān** (1) turn over; (2) translate

翻車 **fān chē** overturn a car (VO)

翻書 **fān shū** (1) leaf through a book; (2) translate a book (VO)

翻成 **fānchéng** translate into

翻過來 **fānguolai** (1) turn over; (2) translate (RV)

3.1. 快來吧！有人說河裏有一條小船翻了．

3.2. 高先生昨天開車在一條小路上翻車了.

3.3. 温老先生没事就到書店裏去翻書.

3.4. 謝先生的中文、英文都好. 他翻了很多書. 最近他又要翻一本英文書.

3.5. 你把這個英文句子翻成中文.

3.7. 你把地圖翻過來, 看看那一面. (T)

4.0. 譯 **yì** translate

翻譯 **fānyì** (1) translate, interpret; (2) translator, interpreter

翻譯員 **fānyiyuán** translator, interpreter

譯音 **yìyīn** (1) transliterate; (2) transliteration

譯意 **yìyì** translate the meaning

譯成 **yìchéng** translate into

4.1. 他是英國人, 不會説中國話. 他跟中國人説話都是我給他翻譯.

4.2. 那個翻譯員的英文、中文都很好. 他翻的東西不會錯的.

4.3. 外國地名翻成中文, 有的是譯音的, 有的是譯意的. 比方「加拿大」是譯音,「紅海」是譯意.

4.4. 請你把這些句子都譯成中文.

4.5. 請你讓才考進來的那位翻譯員把這些英

文譯成中文.(T)

5.0. 舉 jǔ lift (up high), raise; (2) elect

舉起來 jǔqilai raise up

舉手 jǔshǒu raise one's hand (VO)

舉行 jǔxíng (1) put into operation; (2) convene, hold, take place

5.1. 大家都舉他做代表.

5.2. 這個問題誰贊成誰舉手. 你不贊成為甚麽也把手舉起來了呢?

5.3. 貴校甚麽時候舉行歡迎家長茶話會?(T)

6.0. 例 lì example

例子 lìzi example

作例子 zuò lìzi make an example

舉例子 jǔ lìzi give an example

舉例 jǔlì give an example (W)

例句 lìjù illustrative sentence (W)

例外 lìwài (1) an exception; (2) exceptional, unusual

例如 lìrú for example, thus

定例 dìnglì fixed rule, fixed habit

前例 qiánlì a precedent

先例 xiānlì a precedent

6.1. 王先生講語法的時候, 一定講好多個例子.

6.2. 他不會寫字, 可以叫別人給他寫. 你是會寫字的. 你不能拿他作例子.

6.3. 你舉例子的時候不要舉的太多. 舉一個就可以了. (T)

6.4. 他們一家人都喜歡喝酒. 他是例外.

6.5. 學「生字」和「生詞」的時候要注意書裏的例句.

6.6. 「例如」是「就像」的意思.

6.7. 他每到星期天就去東安市場, 成了定例了. (T)

6.8. 這種事在歷史上沒有前例, 在各國也沒有先例.

6.9. 我拿「翻書」作例子. (T)

7.0. 滿 **mǎn** (1) whole*; (2) satisfied*; (3) full

N_1(的)N_2滿了 **N_1 (de) N_2 mǎnle** N_1 is full of N_2

滿地 **mǎndì** the whole ground, all over the ground

滿意 **mǎnyì** (1) satisfied; (2) satisfactory

N_1滿是N_2 **N_1 mǎn shi N_2** N_1 is full of N_2

滿N_1是N_2 **mǎn N_1 shi N_2** N_1 is full of N_2

7.1. 那個碗裏的水滿了. (T)

7.2. 那條路上滿地都是水, 沒法子走了.

7.3. 他天天努力工作, 我很滿意.

7.4. 滿城的人都説這個城的市政太不好了. (T)

7.5. 出了甚麽事了，路上滿是人？(T)

7.6. 那本書字很少. 滿書是畫兒，所以小孩子很喜歡看.

8.0. 足 **zú** (1) fully*; (2) sufficient, enough; (3) satisfied*

滿足 **mǎnzú** (1) to satisfy; (2) satisfied, contented; (3) satisfactory; (4) full, completed

知足 **zhīzú** be content(ed), satisfied

不足 **bùzú** (1) not satisfied; (2) not enough, deficient; (3) not quite, less than

心滿意足 **xīn-mǎn-yì-zú** perfectly satisfied

人心不足 **rén xīn bùzú** [the heart of] man is never satisfied

8.1. 他的希望沒有滿足的時候. (T)

8.2. 知足的人，心裏是常快活的. 不知足的人，永久沒有快活.

8.3. 他在加州不足一年又到加拿大去了.

8.4. 他的目的已經達到了. 他心滿意足了.

8.5. 沒有錢的人希望有錢. 已經有了錢以後，希望有更多的錢. 這就是人心不足.

9.0. 求 **qiú** beg, beseech

求學 **qiúxué** to study, seek information

求人 **qiúrén** ask help of people (VO)

9.1. 一個人求人幫忙是一時的,不能常求人.(T)

9.2. 求學的時候最好是不結婚.

10.0. 青 **qīng** (1) blue-green; (2) black (Peking dialect); (3) dark blue; (4) young

青海 **Qīnghǎi** Chinghai, Kokonor

青茶 **qīng chá** green tea

青年 **qīngnián** young person(s), youth(s)

青年會 **Qīngniánhuì** Y.M.C.A.

10.1. 青是藍顏色的, 可是北京人叫黑的也是青的.

10.2. 青海是中國的一個省, 在中國的西部.

10.3. 我喜歡喝紅茶, 他喜歡喝青茶.

10.4. 青年會是青年人常去的地方. 有男青年會, 也有女青年會.

11.0. 清 **qīng** (1) clear; (2) pure, uncorrupted; (3) Ch'ing dynasty (1644-1911)

清代 **Qīng Dài** Ch'ing dynasty

清朝 **Qīng Cháo** Ch'ing dynasty

清史 **Qīng shǐ** history of the Ch'ing dynasty

清華大學 **Qīnghuá Dàxué** Tsinghua University

11.1. 河裏的水很清, 可以看見魚了.

11.2. 在中華民國以前的那個朝代是清朝, 也叫清代.

11.3. 清朝的歷史叫做清史.

11.4. 清華大學是中國一個有名的大學.

12.0. 楚 **chǔ*** (1) clear; (2) (name of an ancient state)

清楚 **qīngchu** clear, lucid (also used as RV ending)

記不清楚 **jìbuqīngchu** unable to remember clearly, have no clear recollection

楚國 **Chǔ Guó** Kingdom of Ch'u

12.1. 他連說話都說不清楚. 怎能寫小說呢? (T)

12.2. 高先生的生日是那一天, 我記不清楚了.

12.3. 中國古時候有一個楚國, 就在現在湖南省、湖北省一帶地方.

13.0. 程 **chéng*** (1) journey; (2) a period, a spell; (3) (a surname)

工程 **gōngcheng** construction work, engineering

工程學 **gōngchengxué** engineering (as an academic subject)

工程師 **gōngchengshī** an engineer

課程 **kècheng** curriculum, courses

課程表 **kècheng biǎo** course schedule

過程 **guòcheng** a process, a course, a stage (in time)

13.1. 中國從古時候就注意治水的工程.

13.2. 程先生從前是念工程學的. 現在是一個

有名的工程師.

13.3. 這個大學課程的水準比別的大學高多了.

13.4. 這張課程表是去年用的.今年没有用了.

13.5. 做酒的過程你知道嗎?

13.6. 人的一生只有很短幾十年的過程,應該好好兒的做一點兒事.(T)

14.0. 職 **zhí*** office, duty

職業 **zhíyè** occupation, profession, vocation

職業學校 **zhíyè xuéxiào** vocational school

職員 **zhíyuán** official, functionary, workers, staff (non-teaching)

教職員 **jiàozhiyuán** staff-member (teaching and non-teaching)

14.1. 做工、做買賣、教書、種地都是一種職業.你喜歡那種職業呢?

14.2. 他没有職業.天天在家裏幫他太太做家裏的事.(T)

14.3. 職業學校的課程都是注重實用的.

14.4. 我們學校一共有教職員三十多人.其中有五個職員,别的都是教員.(T)

15.0. 術 **shù*** skill, technique

美術 **měishù** fine arts

算術 **suànshù** arithmetic

學術 **xuéshù** learning, scholarship

術語 **shùyǔ** technical term

15.1. 我弟弟能畫畫兒.他說他將來研究美術.

15.2. 他在小學裏教算術. 他說教小學生的算術很不容易.

15.3. 那個學校要請教算術的教員, 請你給老王注意注意.(T)

15.4. 在學術上專用的詞兒叫做術語.

15.5. 今天上算術的時候他們都不會. 先生把我叫出來給他們講.(T)

15.6. 我們學校每星期二有一個學術講演會.(T)

15.7. 我算算術的時候, 我不喜歡別人跟我說話.(T)

16.0. 樂 **lè** happy

yuè* (1) music; (2) (a surname)

快樂 **kuàilè** happy

樂事 **lèshì** pleasures, joys

樂意 **lèyì** (1) willing; (2) willingly

音樂 **yīnyuè** music

音樂家 **yīnyuejiā** musician

音樂會 **yīnyuehuì** a concert

16.1. 我有許多年沒回家了. 今年回到家裏,

父親、母親看見我都樂了.

16.2. 樂奇清說:"寫書是我最快樂的事."

16.3. 人生最大的樂事是有一個溫暖的家.

16.4. 你要做你不樂意做的事情.

16.5. 因為我喜歡音樂, 所以我常跟音樂家有來往.

16.6. 昨天女青年會有一個音樂會, 參加的人都是學生.

16.7. 昨天聽音樂的人很多, 在表演的前半個鐘頭人就都滿了. (T)

17.0. V滿 **Vmǎn** (1) V to the full; (2) V to the extent of …, V a full … (followed by an expression of quantity)

V够 **Vgòu** (1) enough; (2) V to the extent of …, V a full … (followed by an expression of quantity)

V足 **Vzú** V to the extent of …, V a full … (followed by an expression of quantity)

17.1. 離講演的時間還有一個鐘頭, 聽講的人已經坐滿了. (T)

17.2. 他在這個學校還沒念滿一學期呢, 他又到別的學校去了. (T)

17.3. 這幾天天天吃魚我真吃够了.

17.4. 要在那個學校念書, 必得考够八十分才

可以進去。(T)

17.5. 看病没錢，買菜没錢，這樣兒的日子我過够了。(T)

17.6. 我們學校是念足了一百三十五個學分兒才能畢業。(T)

18.0. 來 **lái** (RV ending; see note 1)

18.1. 廣東話我説不來。(T)

18.2. 我中國飯吃的來可是中國酒我喝不來。(T)

18.3. 所有的朋友裏我和程楚生最談得來。(T)

19.0. 只 **zhǐ** only (used also before a nominal expression; in translation, an appropriate verb is to be understood from the context)

只不過 **zhǐ búguò** only, no more than

只能 **zhǐ néng** (1) can only, the only alternative is; (2) if only, only if (often used in the first clause with **cái** "then" in the second)

只有 **zhǐ yǒu** (1) have only (followed by a nominal expression); (2) can only, must; (3) if only, only if (often used in the first clause with **cái** "then" in the second)

19.1. 你説他只有一個女朋友。我看他不只一個吧！

19.2. 他只不過念了三年中文，只能看白話小說.

19.3. 我只能晚上作工得點兒錢，才念得了大學. (T)

19.4. 要想你的中文學好了，只有努力. (T)

19.5. 只有你幫助我，才能完成那件事. (T)

20.0. 處 **chù, chǔ** get along with, get along together

20.1. 老張對人最客氣. 他最會處人，甚麽人都處得來.

21.0. 隨N的便 **suí Nde biàn** follow N's convenience, as N pleases (see note 4)

隨N的意思 **suí Nde yìsi** follow N's idea

隨N好了 **suí N hǎole** do what N likes

21.1. 我們開會他不想參加就隨他的便吧. (T)

21.2. 大家都主張不去，只有隨大家的意思.

21.3. 旅行去，還是看電影兒去，隨他好了. (T)

21.4. 他不聽你的，你就隨他的便好了. (T)

22.0. 哪兒(啊) **nǎr(a)** (1) where ?; (2) Not at all! That's not so! You flatter me! (see note 2)

哪裏(呀) **nǎlǐ(ya)** (1) where ?; (2) Not at all! That's not so! You flatter me!

哪兒的話哪! **nǎrde huà ne!** Nonsense! Not at all! That's not so! You flatter me!

22.1. 他説要請我看電影兒去. 我那兒有時間看電影兒啊?

22.2. 我這一點兒學問都是從您那兒學來的.
…哪裏! (T)

22.3. 我對張先生説:"你太幫忙了, 我太感謝了."張先生説:"哪兒的話哪. 我們多少年的老朋友, 應該的."

23.0. 經(過)…以後 **jīng(guo)…yǐhòu** after…
經…後 **jīng…hòu** after … (written style)

23.1. 他的英文經考試以後才知道不太好.

23.2. 那本書經翻成中文後, 看的人更多了.

23.3. 經過那次第九十六次火車翻車以後他説甚麽也不坐火車了. (T)

24.0. 生出(來) **shēngchu(lai)** (1) bear, produce; (2) be born
一生 **yìshēng** whole life(time)

24.1. 他生出來以後, 家裏就没有錢. 後來他的一生都是過着没有錢的生活. (T)

25.0. 談到 **tándào** (1) speak of, mention, discuss; (2) speaking of …
談起 **tánqǐ** to mention
從今 **cóngjīn** henceforth, from today

25.1. 談到結婚她就不高興, 從今以後不要談起了.

26.0. 高等 **gāoděng** superior rank

中等 **zhōngděng** middle rank

下等 **xiàděng** lower rank

初等小學 **chūděng xiǎoxué** lower elementary achool

高等小學 **gāoděng xiǎoxué** higher elementary school

26.1. 他說他的工作是下等職業. 我說職業沒有高等、下等的分別.

26.2. 他不是一個很有錢的人家, 也不是沒有錢的人家, 是一個中等人家.

26.3. 初等小學就是初小. 高等小學就是高小.

27.0. 再SV也沒有了 **zài SV yě méiyǒule** couldn't be more SV, there's none more SV

27.1. 老實說他來了就跟我借錢, 他不來再好也沒有了.

28.0. 有V的必要 **yǒu V de bìyào** have need to V

意識 **yìshi** consciousness

28.1. 有人要把現代青年的意識翻成中文. 我說:"這本書有翻成中文的必要."

29.0. 輕易 **qīngyì** lightly, unconcernedly, recklessly

29.1. 要不是為了生活，怎能輕易離開家呢.(T)

30.0. 這(麽)(樣)V 法 **zhèn(mo)(yàng) Vfǎ, zèn(mo)(yàng) Vfǎ** this way of V-ing

怎(麽)(樣)V 法 **zěn(mo)(yàng) Vfǎ** how V

算法 **suànfǎ** way of calculating, method of figuring

30.1. 我是這麽樣看法：人的一生也不過是六七十年，應該過的快樂一點兒.

30.2. 老張，第五道算術題目怎麽樣算法，你會嗎？(T)

30.3. 關於現在這個政治問題，你是怎麽一個想法？(T)

31.0. 方才 **fāngcái** (1) just a moment ago; (2) then and only then

這就 **zhèjiù** (1) this (then); (2) at once, immediately

講法 **jiǎngfǎ** way of speaking, way of explaining, explanation

31.1. 方才大家都說，請你決定. 這就要看你是怎樣講法了.(T)

31.2. 你別忙，我這就來.(T)

32.0. 在N面前 **zài N miànqián** in front of N, before N

32.1. 他不敢在你面前說那種話.

33.0. 來着 **láizhe** (past continuative suffix, added at the end of a sentence)

33.1. 昨天我給你打電話的時候，你作甚麽來

着？…我作功課表來着．(T)

34.0. 找(N)來 **zhǎo (N) lai** ask (N) to come, invite (N) to come (i.e. seek out and have come)

34.1. 你找音樂教員田美英小姐來．

35.0. 明明(的) **míngmíng (de)** clearly, obviously, evidently, doubtless

35.1. 那幾個字明明是別人寫的，他一定説是他寫的．(T)

36.0. 原文 **yuánwén** original text

36.1. 請你把原文翻成漢語拼音．

36.2. 先生讓一個學生走出來把原文念給我們聽．(T)

37.0. 分等 **fēnděng** to grade, divide into grades

37.1. 職業不分等級，不能分等．

38.0. 別處 **biéchù** other place(s), elsewhere

38.1. 這裏沒人幫你的忙．為甚麽不到別處求求人去？

39.0. 有的V **yǒu de V** have something to V, there is something to V
沒(有)的V **méi (yǒu) de V** have nothing to V, there is nothing to V

39.1. 家裏有的吃沒有？(T)

39.2. 孩子，家裏連飯都沒的吃了．還不找點兒事作？(T)

39.3. 這裏念書是好地方，可是没的玩兒. (T)

40.0. 木頭 **mùtou** wood

40.1. 那幾條船都是木頭做的.

41.0. (是)自己人 **(shì) zìjǐ rén** not be strangers

41.1. 我們自己人，你為甚麼要這樣客氣？

42.0. 往回 **wǎnghuí** back (AD)

42.1. 你往東去不對，應該往西去. 你再往回開吧. (T)

Checklist

1. 參
   參考
   參考書
   參看
2. 加
   加重
   加意
   加多
   加州
   加拿大
   參加
   更加
3. 翻
   翻車
   翻書
   翻成
   翻過來
4. 譯
   翻譯
   翻譯員
   譯音
   譯意
   譯成
5. 舉
   舉起來
   舉手
   舉行
6. 例
   例子
   作例子
   舉例句
   舉例
   例句
   例外
   例如
   定例
   前例
   先例
7. 滿
   N_1(的)N_2滿了
   滿地
   滿意
   N_1滿是N_2
   滿N_1是N_2
8. 足
   滿足
   知足
   不足
   心滿意足
   人心不足
9. 求
   求學
   求人
10. 青
   青海
   青茶

青年
青年會
11. 清
清代
清朝
清史
清華大學
12. 楚
清楚
記不清楚
楚國
13. 程
工程
工程學
工程師
課程
課程表
過程
14. 職
職業
職業學校
職員
教職員
15. 術
美術
算術
學術
術語
16. 樂
快樂
樂事
樂意
音樂
音樂家
音樂會
17. V 滿
V 够
V 足
18. 來
19. 只
只不過
只能
只有
20. 處
21. 隨 N 的便
隨 N 的意思
隨 N 好了
22. 哪兒(啊)
哪裏(呀)
哪兒的話哪！
23. 經(過)…以後
經…後
24. 生出(來)
一生
25. 談到
談起
從今
26. 高等
中等
下等
初等小學
高等小學
27. 再 SV 也沒有了
28. 有 V 的必要
意識
29. 輕易
30. 這(麽)(樣) V 法
怎(麽)(樣) V 法
算法
31. 方才
這就
講法
32. 在 N 面前
33. 來着
34. 找 N 來
35. 明明(的)
36. 原文
37. 分等
38. 別處
39. 有的 V
沒(有)的 V
40. 木頭
41. (是)自己人
42. 往回

Exercise 1. Excerpts from Actual Publications

The following excerpts are taken from the autobiography of **Guō Mòruò** (**Kuo Mo-jo**), a well-kncwn scholar and writer who after 1949 held many high posts in the mainland government.

1. 我是生在一八九二年…九月…的，日期是二十一還是二十七，我現在不記得了.
2. 我們家裏…是一個中等地主.
3. 我母親…是生在貴州.
4. 我父親…在青年的時候甚麽生意都好像做過.
5. 我的父親…當然不能生出我們現在所有的這樣的意識.
6. 我當時實在不知道應該學甚麽…「還是學實業的好，學實業吧.」
7. 小學是在一九〇六年…開學的.
8. 在第一學期中我有一個…朋友，他和我同年同月生的.
9. 我又得到了一個朋友. … 他是一位數學的天才.

10. 有許多人我現在連名字都想不起來了.

11. 年假期間在家裏做了些甚麽事情，我現在怎麽也記不清楚了.

12. 我決心不回家，我想要上成都去.

13. 先生直接寫了一封信去給父親.

14. 我…跟着父親又回到學校.

15. 我們是提前在五月畢業的，因為六月裏要考中學.

Exercise 2. Dialogues

1. 樂：程楚生你到那兒去？

程：老樂，我到青年會去看一個人.

樂：男青年會還是女青年會？

程：男青年會. 我是看我父親的朋友. 他是清華大學教授. 他從加拿大到這兒來. 我父親給我來信，讓我去看看他. 我昨天去了一次，他出去了，所以今天還得再去一次. 你到那兒去？

樂：要寫論文了．我到圖書館去找幾本參考書去．

程：我這些日子忙的不得了．我翻譯一點兒東西．

樂：你翻譯的是不是課程一方面的東西？

程：不是．我是幫別人翻書，可以得一點兒錢．

樂：把中文翻成英文，還是把英文翻成中文？

程：把英文翻成中文．

樂：翻譯東西是怎麽算哪？

程：算法大概都不一樣．我幫一位教授翻一點兒學術上的東西．他是這樣：翻滿五千個字五十塊錢．

樂：翻譯東西很不容易呀．

程：可不是嗎！有時候一句話半天也翻不過來，因為找不到一個好的中文句子跟原文的意思完全一樣．還有，遇見人名、地名要是譯音更加麻煩了．有時候找不到跟原來的聲音一樣的字來. 常常翻出來的東西, 自己越看越不滿意.… 我們説着話走路, 不知不覺的就到了.

樂: 你有工夫到我那兒去. 再見.

程: 好. 再見.

2. 李: 張青, 昨天晚上的音樂會怎麽樣? 聽的人多不多?

張: 音樂好極了, 都是有名的音樂家. 聽的人多的不得了, 大多數是青年人. 表演的前半個鐘頭人就滿了. 你跟你女朋友為甚麽不去呢?

李: 她對音樂沒興趣. 其實我有票, 她一定要看電影兒去.

張: 她將來一定去當電影兒明星去, 長的那麽好看, 對電影又那麽有興趣.

李: 要是她們家裏頭隨着她的意思, 她早就當電影兒明星去了.

張: 你的意思呢?

李: 我也不贊成.

3. 生: 老師, 清代就是清朝嗎?

師：清代就是清朝.

生：清史就是專門寫的清朝歷史嗎？

師：是的.

生：清朝前後一共有多少年哪？

師：清朝是從紀元後一千六百四十四年到一千九百一十一年，一共是二百六十七年.

生：老師，古時候的楚國是現在的甚麽地方？

師：是現在的湖南省跟湖北省.

生：老師，「從今」這個詞兒是說的嗎？

師：是說的. 我舉個例子："從今以後，我們要努力念書."

生：「意識」怎麽用？

師：我再舉例："心理學是研究人的意識的一種科學."

生：老師，「參考」跟「參看」一樣嗎？

師：一樣的.

生：「術語」怎麽用？

師：是專門學術裏頭用的詞兒. 程廣平

你舉手，有甚麽問題嗎？

生：課程表裏有很多字都不清楚．

師：課程表是不清楚．你找謝先生來我告訴他．

4．程：老張，你現在有事没有？

張：没事啊．怎麽着？

程：我有點兒事跟你研究研究．我母親前天給我來封信，讓我這學期完了放假的時候，回家定親事去，希望我早點兒結婚．

張：她老人家為甚麽讓你這麽早就結婚呢？

程：你聽着我告訴你呀．這封信她老人家寫了三大張．信上談到從我生出來不足三個月的時候我父親到青海去旅行，一直的就没有回來，而且連封信都没有．

張：一直到現在没信嗎？

程：没有．她老人家說，她只有我這麽一個兒子，在這二十年的過程裏，她很不容易. 她現在時常有病, 要是我結了婚她就心滿意足了.

張: 我看你就隨着老太太的意思, 你就回家結婚吧.

程: 説起來那麽容易, 可是我跟張小姐我們兩個人的感情很好. 他父母也很喜歡我. 你説我回我母親這封信怎麽樣寫法呢? 我跟張小姐的事情, 對她老人家説得説不得?

張: 這就要看你自己怎麽决定了.

5. 許: 老樂你説人的一生最快樂的事情是甚麽?

樂: 最快樂的事是跟談得來的朋友談談學問哪, 或者是到外面去旅行啊. 你説呢?

許: 你説的當然也是樂事了. 我認為還有比這個更樂的事.

樂: 我給你説出來得了. 跟女朋友在一塊兒談談, 聽聽音樂, 看看電影兒, 對不對?

許：不只是這個．還有呢．

樂：去喝喝茶，或者小湖裏坐小船．

許：你說喝茶我想起來了．上次在你那兒喝的青茶好極了，你在那兒買的？

樂：不是買的，是一個朋友從加州帶來的．聽說是西湖出的，是最高等的了．家裏是不是還有呢，我記不清楚了．我回去找找．要是有，我明天帶給你．

6．湯：你跟樂正青是怎麽認識的？

田：我和他認識是有一次在一個音樂會上．經過謝楚生的介紹以後，我們就認識了．

湯：他人怎麽樣？

田：人好極了．我們兩個很處得來．

湯：聽說他書念的不多．

田：他只不過是念過高等小學．只能看看報紙跟白話小說兒甚麽的．

湯：他人那麽聰明，為甚麽當初不多念點兒書呢？

田：有一天他跟我談起這個問題．他說他一生最難過的事情是高小畢業以後就不能繼續的求學了．

湯：他不念書是甚麽原因呢？

田：本來他們家裏很有錢來着．可是他父親甚麽也不做．不是喝酒，就是玩兒麻將．不上五年的工夫把房子、地都賣了．不但是念不了書了，連飯也沒的吃了．

7．生：老師，「經王先生介紹以後」跟「經王先生介紹後」有分別嗎？

師：有分別．「經王先生介紹以後」是說的，「經王先生介紹後」是寫的．

生：「高等、中等、下等」說人哪，還是說東西呢？

師：現在這樣詞兒都是說東西．要是人分等，拿職業來分呢，還是拿有錢沒錢來分別的呢．

生：「我不樂意去」就是「我不想去」的意思嗎？

師：對了．這就下課了．你們還有問題嗎？

生：沒有了．

師：好．你們一會兒考算術是不是？

生：是的．

8．李：我方才在路上遇見萬青了．他說他已經找着事了．

費：那再好也沒有了．不要天天求別人了．他找到了一個甚麽工作呀？

李：是給一個英國工程師當翻譯員．

費：他做的了嗎？

李：他英文好極了．怎麽做不了？

費：是翻譯說話呢，還是翻譯東西呢？

李：翻譯東西．是把工程一方面的中文譯英文．他說很容易，不必把每一個字都翻了，只是譯意就可以了．

9．邊：聽說從這兒到上海去的第三十六次火車，往回開的時候在半路上翻車了．

麻：是嗎？這麽多年火車還沒出過事呢，

這次真是有點兒例外了.

邊：聽説出事的火車上有中華職業學校的教職員跟學生，一共有六十多人在那個火車上.

麻：他們都到上海作甚麽去了？

邊：聽説是參加了一個甚麽大會. 其實他們沒有去的必要. 本來校長不讓他們去，他們一定要去. 為了校長不讓他們去，有人在校長面前對校長説話很不客氣. 校長一生氣説："隨你們的便好了."結果就出了事了.

10. 邊：昨天我看見謝青了. 他説他那個工作不想做了，要是別處有機會給他注意注意.

紀：怎麽他的工作不滿意嗎？

邊：他説他近來工作加重了，可是錢一點兒也沒多給. 他又説，他們幾個同樣兒學工程學的在那兒做事，別人工作少，可是拿的錢比他多.

紀：其實也對．應該有個定例．工作加多了應該加點兒錢．

邊：我認為這樣講法也不很對．謝青很年輕，對各種事情都沒甚麽經驗．一個人多作一點兒事算的了甚麽．而且現在工作是多麽不容易找．有很多人求人、找事．他應該知足．

紀：你說的很對．我說個例子．當初許練成他在一個中學當職員．因為錢少，說甚麽也不作了，到現在有一年了還沒找着事呢．本來我跟他說過，在沒找着別的事以前不能輕易的就把事情不作了．他不聽我的．

邊：其實許練成應該知足．他連中學都沒念過．能在一個中學裏當職員，還不好好兒作下去．

紀：這就叫人心不足啊．

11. 簡：老錢你到那兒去？

錢：小樂請我吃飯去．

簡：奇怪．小樂從來是不請客的．他怎

麽請你吃飯呢？

錢：是這麽一回事．昨天我到他那兒談天兒去，他家門口兒有一大塊木頭．他說："老錢，這塊木頭我們舉舉看，誰舉不起來誰請客．"小樂想我的力氣沒他大，我一定舉不起來．結果他舉了半天也舉不起來，我舉起來了．他沒法子，只好請我了．

12. 學生：先生，「舉行」是寫的嗎？我舉個例子您聽啊，「本月五日本校舉行考試」這麽用法對嗎？

先生：對，很好．

學生：「做不得」是甚麽意思？

先生：就是「不能那樣做」的意思．我拿要打人作例子："你要打他嗎？這件事你可做不得．打了他可就麻煩了．"

學生：明白了．

先生：還有一個用法，例如："那個買賣做不得．那種東西沒人買．"

學生：「前例」跟「先例」有分別嗎？

先生：沒分別．意思完全一樣．還有甚麽問題嗎？

學生：「明明的」是不是就是「很清楚」的意思啊？

先生：有時候是「很清楚」的意思．比如“功課表上，明明的寫着八點一刻上課，為甚麽八點鐘就上課了呢？”有時候也有一點兒「實在」的意思．比如“那本書我明明的還了你了，你怎麽説我沒還你呢？”還有問題嗎？

學生：沒有了．

先生：好．請你們下課以後，用今天學的生詞兒作五個例句，明天給我看看．

13. 毛：張太太，你到那兒去？

張：給我女兒買顏色去．她們學校美術這門功課是畫畫兒．

毛：是的．這裏初等小學的美術差不多都是畫畫兒．我那個孩子也是．一到了有美術的時候，你看吧，房子裏滿地是紙，滿手是顏色．真沒法子．

張：可不是嗎！我那個也是一樣．我忘了．我那個女兒要不是你介紹，這個學校這麽難考，可能進不了這個學校．應該怎麽謝謝你呢？

毛：那兒的話呢．自己人．

14\. 費：正清，天氣這麽不好路又這麽遠，你今天還是來看我來了．我真是從心裏感謝你．

湯：哪裏哪裏．老師你別這麽説．怎麽樣，您今天好點兒嗎？

費：好多了．你今天坐火車來的還是自己開車來的？

湯：我開車來的．

費：今天天氣不好，路不好走，回去的時候加意小心．

湯：您放心，我知道．

15\. 王：史太太，你為甚麽生那麽大的氣呀？

史：跟我那個先生，這個日子我過够了.

王：為甚麽呀？

史：剛才我説我那兩個孩子，他不讓我説.孩子有錯要是我一説他們，他就不高興.我怎麽着都不對.老説我用錢用的多.你比我好，王先生對你那麽好.

王：那兒啊.別提了.男人們不論太太多麽好，他們也不會滿足的.

Exercise 3. Narratives

1. 我現在正寫論文.每天都到圖書館找參考書.找參考書是一件很麻煩的事情.有時候找不到，有時候找到了看看内容，没有參考的必要.還有時候看了這一本，還得參看那一本.一天看不完第二天還得繼續看.我真不知道要費多少時間，要看多少參考書，才能完成這個論文.

2. 有一個外國學生學中文.有一天他問先生："「舉起來」這個詞兒怎麽講？" 先生

說:“舉起來就是把東西拿起來, 拿的高一點兒的意思. 例如:「大家都把酒杯舉起來.」「他舉起刀來了.」” 這個外國學生說:“我明白了, 謝謝您.”

3. 從前的人常說,人應當知足.「知足常樂」這句話的意思是因為人心不足, 所以用這句話讓人知足, 要是能知足, 就能常常的快樂了. 可是這種說法在現在這個時代就有了問題了. 現代的人對於現況不應當知足. 如果滿足了, 就不能再往前進了. 只有不滿意現況的人, 才知道努力, 才能够再往前走.

4. 研究中國文字有時候有很有趣的事. 舉個例子來說, 有一年我在中國旅行, 走到一個地方. 那個地方做的碗、茶杯甚麽的很出名. 當地人送給我一個茶杯. 在這個茶杯上有五個中國字, 這五個字在茶杯上是這樣寫的:

他們告訴我，這五個字從左往右念，隨便從那一個字念起都是一個句子，可以念出五種句子：

(1) 可以清心也

(2) 以清心也可

(3) 清心也可以

(4) 心也可以清

(5) 也可以清心

他們又告訴我上面這五個句子，第(1)(2)兩句是文言．(1)句最後的「也」字是「啊」的意思．這句話的意思是「能够清心啊」．(2)句第一個字「以」字是「用」的意思．這句話的意思是「用他清心也可以」．我看了以後覺得中國的文字真有趣呀．

5. 中國在清朝的時候，人民的職業是分等的，分成許多等級. 有幾種職業認為是下等職業. 做下等職業的人在政府舉行考試的時候，不能參加考試. 後來到了中華民國人民的職業就沒有等級的分別了.

6. 我記得我念高等小學跟初中的時候，最不喜歡看從英文譯成中文的小說. 更不喜歡看那些翻譯小說裏的地名和人名，因為那些地名和人名都是譯音的不是譯意的，記也記不住. 有一天，有人送我一本很有名的人翻譯的小說. 我拿着這本小說翻過來翻過去心裏生出一種感想來，想到要是有一天能看英文的原文本那該多麽有意思呀！

7. 老張是一個喜歡說笑話的人. 有一天我對老張說:“我們學校要請一位翻譯員專門翻書，要在一年裏頭把幾本英文書翻成中文. 最好能找一位中英文都好，而且是翻過書對翻譯東西有經驗的才好.”

老張說：“不用找別人．我是專門學英文的，我就可以．”我說：“你翻過嗎？”老張說：“我怎麽没翻過？我在去年一年裏頭，翻過了三次…”我問他：“翻過了甚麽？”他說：“翻過三次車呀．”

8．青年會時常舉行學術講演會．有一次講的是「原子」．我雖然是研究文學的，可是為了要知道一些科學的知識我也去聽講．主講的人是一位工程師．他講的話我還聽得懂，可是他一說到科學上用的術語我就不懂了．所以我聽了這次講演以後，原子是怎麽一回事我還是不大清楚．

9．張國青念初等小學的時候，就不喜歡算術．每次考試不是十分就是五分．有一次，是在他才學算術的時候，先生把他叫在先生面前問他：“三加二是多少？”他說：“是「四」．”先生聽了很生氣，就叫幾個學生走出來，做例子．先叫兩個學生站在左邊，又叫兩個學生跟張國青都站在右邊．然後就問張國青："左邊的學生加右邊的學生一共是多少？"張國青說："是四個．"先生說："你好好的看看是幾個？你是怎麽一個算法說給我聽聽．"張國青說："你叫的學生左邊是兩個右邊也是兩個，我看見的也是左邊兩個，右邊兩個一共不是四個嗎？"先生說："還有你也在右邊呀！"張國青說："您叫我來是算算術的．怎麽也把我加在算術裏頭了呢，您這麽算法對嗎？"

10. 程先生在沒錢的時候他希望有錢．他說："我要是有了錢我就心滿意足了．"後來他有錢了，他又希望在社會上有地位．他說："我要是有了地位我就心滿意足了．"不久，他果然有地位了．這時候他又有錢又有地位，大家認為他一定心滿意足了．可是有人問他，他說："我還希望活到一百歲呢！"從這裏可以看出來，人心是不足的．

11. 馬先生是出版社的經理．他說："我最樂意用職業學校畢業的學生，因為職業學校的課程都是將來在職業上要用的. 不只注重理論,也很注重實用,所以職業學校畢業的學生在工作上的表現都很好.”

12. 孔子說:“古時候的人求學是為了自己，現在的人求學是為了別人.”這句話的意思是說,古時候的人因為自己要有學識,所以求學. 現在的人為了別人要用有學識的人，所以才求學.

13. 我們學校的教職員比從前加多了. 從前只不過幾個職員，十幾個教員，現在教職員有幾十人了. 有人說:“這個學校學生不足五百人，為甚麼有這麼多的教職員呢？”有人說:“一定是有加多的必要，所以才加多的.”

14. 樂心青喜歡研究化學. 他看課程表上今天上午都是化學，他很高興. 在上課的時候，先生講「從地裏頭的油成為汽油的過程」. 先生說:“在有油的地裏頭，雖然油很多，可以說是滿地是油，但是成為汽油的過程是不簡單的，工程也是很大的．今天我給你們講一個大概情形，過幾天我們一同到附近一個有油的地方去看看.”樂心青聽了先生講的話以後，更加高興了．他說:“能去看看是再好也沒有了.”

15. 程清正喜歡美術，也喜歡音樂．有一天，有一個很有名的畫家和一個最出名的音樂家去看他，他十分高興．他們談到美術和音樂．他說:“人的一生只有能看見最美的東西，能聽見最美的聲音，才是人生的樂事.”

16. 我在美國加州念大學的時候，有一個中國同學的名字叫王楚生．我一看見他的名字就知道他是湖南人．當時有一個外國同學問我:“你怎麽知道他是甚麽地方的人呢？”我說:“他的名字叫王楚生，這不是明明的告訴人家是在楚國出生的嗎？”我剛說到這裏，還沒說完，那個外國同學說：“我這就更不明白了．聽說中國古時有一個楚國，那有楚國出生的人能活到現在呢？”後來我告訴他：“古時候的楚國就在現在的湖南，所以我說他是湖南人哪．”

17. 先生給學生講地理．先生說：“你們看看地圖，中國的東面、南面都有海，西面、北面没有海．”先生剛說完這句話，有一個學生舉起手來．先生說：“你舉手有甚麽問題要說嗎？”這個學生說：“中國西部也有海．您看地圖上中國西部不是明明寫的有青海嗎？”先生說：“你說的也有道理，但是青海是一個大湖的名字，又是中國一個省的名字．他的名字雖然是「青海」，可是不能算是海．”

18. 有一個外國人最喜歡喝茶．他說：“茶有兩種：一種是紅茶，一種是青茶．西方人多半喜歡喝紅茶，東方人多半喜歡喝青茶．我雖然是西方人，可是我喜歡喝青茶．我記得我第一次喝青茶是我在中國旅行的時候．有一天我在西湖的一個小山上，我喝的青茶．那種青茶是那個山上出的，用的水也是山上的水，所以覺得特別好喝．還有一件最有意思的事．當地的人告訴我，茶杯裏的水如果已經滿了，還能加多一些水，能叫茶杯裏的水比茶杯還高出來一點兒．我當時試一試，果然高出來了一點兒．我從這次喝青茶以後，就很喜歡喝青茶了．”

19. 先生講書，講到「例」字．他說：「例」是「樣子」的意思．「例句」就是作樣子的句子．「定例」是一定的樣子．「先例」和「前例」就是先前的樣子．還有「例外」就是在這些樣子以外的意思．”他講完以後就問學生：“方才我講的話你們都明白了嗎？”學生說：“明白了．”先生說：“那你們就用我講的這些詞作幾個句子，或者作文．可是要作短文．大家一定都要作．”有一個學生說：“我今天有病，能不能例外呢？”先生說：“你說這句話已經用「例外」作了一個句子了,而且這個句子作的很好. 你就算例外吧！不用作了."

20. 有一個音樂家要舉行一個音樂會, 可是找不到理想的地方. 後來他在一個大學借的地方開的音樂會. 開完會以後, 他去見這個大學的校長. 他説:"我知道貴校不輕易借給人用. 這次借給我了真是十分感謝. 是不是我應該給一點兒錢?" 校長接着説:"哪兒的話哪！不必客氣."

21. 老王幾個人要上山去旅行,來跟我借車. 我説:"我的車只能坐三個人. 上次我開車上山, 多坐了一個人, 車就開不上去了. 經那次以後, 我就不敢開車上山了. 這次你們的人多, 車又加重了一定上不了山."老王説:"在要上山的時候我們下來幾個人隨着車走, 那就没問題了."我説:"車我可以借給你們, 怎樣用法隨你們好了."

22. 許先生求我找工作. 我説:"前幾天有一

個朋友談起有一個外國人正研究清史，要用一個寫中國字的人．我去問問這個朋友，看看現在還有機會沒有．”許先生說：“那就求你多費心啦．”我說：“哪裏，哪裏．自己人別客氣．我應該幫你想法子的．”後來我問過這個朋友，他說：“以前有幾個人去試用，都是因為字寫的不大好所以沒用．現在可以讓這位找工作的人先寫幾個字，要加意，好好的寫．如果字寫得好，一定能成的．”我就告訴許先生，他加意的寫了幾個字．經我這個朋友拿去以後，還不到兩天就用許先生了．

23. 有一本小說是「青和藍」．內容是一個學生和他的先生的故事．開始是寫先生怎樣用心教這個學生，後來是寫這個學生的學問、事業樣樣都比先生好．有人問我：“這是一個學生和先生的故事，為甚麼叫「青和藍」呢？”我告訴他：“中國有一句成語，這句成語的意思是說「青顏色是從藍顏色裏生出來的，可是青顏色比藍顏色更好看」，所以這本小說就叫「青和藍」.”

24. 今天下課以後，我開車離開學校許多同學來坐我的車．已經坐了五個人了，後來毛小姐來了也要坐車．我說：“已經坐滿了，没法子坐了.” 毛小姐生氣了說：“你的車我已經坐够了．開的又快，又常出毛病．你以為我喜歡坐呢？”

25. 清華大學在中國的北京．是一個有名的大學．在這個大學畢業的學生，多半去美國繼續求學．我有一個弟弟從前也是在清華畢業．在他畢業以後我們家裏的人都希望他也去美國．可是他說他决不去美國，他一定要去加拿大．他為甚麽必得去加拿大呢？後來我們才知道，他是因為有一個最要好的女朋友在加拿大呢．

26. 我想找一間住的房子．有人說：“毛先生有一間房子沒有人住，你還不去問問？”又有人說：“毛先生的那間房子住不得．在那房子前面有一個小院子，天天來找毛先生的人很多，有時候滿院子是人．還有，毛先生說來着，他這間房子要看甚麽人來住，必得和他處得來的人，他才讓他住．這是實在情形，去不去住，隨你自己的便吧．”

27. 我在廣州念大學的時候，有一個同學孔達生，他因為沒有錢不能繼續念了．孔達生說，他家從前很有錢，大概從清代初年就住在廣州．他還記得他小時候家裏的情形．他父親在政府作事，家裏的人很多，老媽子就有三四個，還有其他男用人．他那時候才念小學．每天下學回家專有一位老師幫他温習功課．可是他不喜歡念書，就喜歡看電影．有時候要是有好的電影片就一天看兩三場．那位老師只好隨他的意思．後來不知道怎麽的，家裏情形和以前大不同了．現在家裏就剩下他母親和他，連書都没錢念了．我當時聽了他説的話，就有了一個感想，一個人要是有機會念書的時候，千萬專心念書，不要等到没法子念書的時候才想起來念書，那就晚了．

28. 我到張先生家，看見他的小兒子正在看書．我問他：“你看的甚麽書？”他把書拿來給我看．我一看書裏滿是畫兒．我對他説：“這本書很好看，可是没有字．你想不想認字？”他説：“我很想認字．你能教我認字嗎？”我説：“可以．從今以後我就來教你吧．”我教他没有多少天，他就認一百多字了．張先生説：“你常來教他認字，太麻煩你了．”我對張先生説：“那兒啊．”張先生又説：“我應當怎樣謝謝你呢？”我説：“教小孩子認幾個字不是甚麽大事，你不必掛在心上呀．”

29. 勞永亮是我中學的同學．那時候同學們都叫他是「老月亮」．為甚麽叫他「老月亮」呢？因為他姓勞，「勞」字的聲音和

「老」字差不多．他的名字是永亮，和「月亮」兩個字聲音也差不多．現在勞永亮已經老了．前天他來看我，他一看見我就說：“你猜我來找你有甚麽事？”我說：“我怎麽能猜得着呢？你有甚麽事就老實說吧．”他說：“從前你們叫我「老月亮」可是那個時候我還没老．現在我老了，我是來叫你看看這真正的「老月亮」呀．”

30. 許先生是一個政治家．有人問他現在一個政治上的問題，還請他舉一個例子來說明．他說：“政治本來不能從一方面來看．你提出來的問題近來有很多人發表意見．各個人的講法都有他的道理．你認為那種講法最有道理就贊成那種講法好了．”有人說：“他這種講法，簡直的跟没講一樣．”

31. 有一位小姐家裏很有錢，所以有很多用人，而且她的父母又都很喜歡她，所以在家裏甚麽事也不作．有一天她在她的房子裏大聲兒叫她的母親：“媽，快來．”

她母親馬上就來了，問她有甚麼事. 她説："我作算術用了很多紙. 您看滿地是紙，我讓您來的意思是請您找用人來收拾收拾."

32. 我好久没看見老田了，聽説他近來的生活情形更不好. 前天是一個紀念日放假，我到他家去看看他. 結果叫了半天的門没人開. 後來出來了一個老頭兒，告訴我，他們早就不在這兒住了. 那個老頭兒把他們現在住的地方告訴了我，我馬上又去了. 是在河邊兒上，和人家同住在一所兒小木頭房子裏. 我進去一看，他們一家就住了一間房子，連個客廳都没有. 心裏很難過，看情形可能連飯都没吃的了. 我拿出二十塊錢送給他，老田説甚麼也不要. 我和老田是多少年的老朋友了. 他是個好人，不論怎麼没錢，從來不求人. 我們談了一會兒，我就走了. 我一邊兒往回走着，一邊兒就想，長久這樣不成啊. 我應該想甚麼法子幫助他呢？這裏事少人多，找事不容易，不如在別處給他想想法子．昨天我去找許廣文和他談老田的問題．他說正好他父親有一個朋友，才從湖南來了一封信，求他父親在這裏給他介紹一個人要會數學的，最好對美術有一點兒興趣的．我聽了廣文的話，高興得不得了．老田正是這樣一個人才．同時廣文又告訴我，他父親這位朋友是一位大實業家，老田要是去，旅費不成問題，是他們給．如果在他沒去以前用錢，也可以先借．這真是老田的好機會．

Exercise 4. Illustrative Sentences (English)

1.4. You can take my views as a suggestion for consideration.

2.7. He was very hard-working [towards work] to begin with, and on learning that they were going to give more wages he worked even harder.

3.7. Turn the map over and look at the other [lit. that] side.

4.5. Please have the translator who has just been accepted [lit. taken the exam and entered] translate these English texts into Chinese.

5.3. When is your [honorable] school having a tea for [lit. to welcome] the parents ?

6.3. When you give examples don't give too many. One's enough.

6.7. It's a fixed habit for him to go to Dongan Market every [lit. every comes to] Sunday.

6.9. I'll give an illustration for "translate a book."

7.1. That bowl is full of water.

7.4. Everyone in the city says the [city] administration [of the city] is very bad.

7.5. What's happened, how come the road is filled with people?

8.1. His hopes are never satisfied.

9.1. One's asking people for help should be a thing of the moment. One can't always ask people to help.

12.1. He can't even speak clearly, so how can he write fiction?

13.6. Man's life is a short span of a few decades. One should take care to do a little something.

14.2. He has no profession. He stays home every day and helps his wife do the family chores.

14.4. Our school has a staff of thirty in all. This includes five non-teaching staff members. The rest are all teachers.

15.3. Please draw to Wang's attention that that school is looking for an arithmetic teacher.

15.5. Today in the arithmetic class no one else knew (how to do the work). The teacher had me come [out] (to the front of the class) and explain it for them.

15.6. Every Tuesday their school has a lecture [meeting] on some academic subject.

15.7. When I do arithmetic I don't like [other] people to talk to me.

16.7. A lot of people attended the concert yesterday. It was filled up half an hour before the performance.

17.1. An hour before the lecture, it was already all filled up.

17.2. Before finishing even one semester at this school he went to another school.

17.4. To study at that school one must get eighty on the (entrance) exam [and only then can one enter].

17.5. There's no money to see a doctor, no money to buy food. I've had enough of this life.

17.6. At our school you can graduate after completing 135 credits.

18.1. I can't speak Cantonese.

18.2. I enjoy eating Chinese food but not drinking Chinese wine.

18.3. Of all my friends, I enjoy most talking to Cheng Chusheng.

19.3. I can attend the university only if I work at night and earn a little money.

19.4. If one hopes to master Chinese, one must work hard.

19.5. I can finish that task only if you help me.

21.1. If he doesn't want to attend the meeting we're holding let him do as he pleases.

21.3. As to whether to go on a trip or to see a movie, we'll do what he wants.

21.4. If he won't fall in with your views, let him do as he pleases.

22.2. What little I know was all learned from you. ··· Not at all.

23.3. After train No. 96 overturned that time, he refuses regardless of what anyone says to take a train any more.

24.1. After he was born, his family became impoverished. Afterwards his whole life was spent in penury [lit. moneyless life].

29.1. If it weren't to make a living, how could I lightly leave home?

30.2. Zheng, do you know how to do the fifth arithmetic problem?

30.3. What's your view on this [present] political problem?

31.1. Just a moment ago everyone said for you to make the decision. This then depends on what [lit. how] you say.

31.2. Don't be in such a hurry, I'm coming right away.

33.1. What were you doing yesterday when I called? ··· I was drawing up a curriculum.

35.1. Those characters were obviously written by someone else, but he insists he wrote them.

36.2. The teacher had a student come before the class and read the original text for us [to listen to].

39.1. Is there anything to eat in the house?

39.2. Child, there's not even any food to eat in the house. Why don't you find some work?

39.3. This place is a nice place for study, but there's nothing to amuse oneself with.

42.1. (Driving towards the) east is wrong, you should go west. Back up.

Notes

1. 來 occurs as a potential complement in the positive and negative forms of resultative verbs. It has two uses:

   (a) It serves as a dummy complement (much like **liǎo**) with no special meaning:

   我就會做中國飯, 外國飯我做不來. "I can only make Chinese food."

   (b) In some cases it indicates ability to find pleasure in an activity:

   談得來 "can talk, enjoy talking (with someone)"
   說得來 "can talk, enjoy talking (with someone)"
   吃得來 "able to eat, enjoy eating"
   喝得來 "able to drink, enjoy drinking"

2. The expressions **nǎr** and **nǎlǐ** "where?" besides having their ordinary function as question words are also used in rhetorical questions and (together with **nǎrde huà ne!**) as polite rejoinders to compliments and expressions of thanks:

   Nèisuǒr fángzi tài guì le. Nǎr yǒu qián mǎi ne? "That house is too expensive. How would I have the money to buy it?"

   Nín tài bàng wǒde mángle.... Nǎr a, nǎr a! "You've helped me tremendously.... Not at all!"

3. The unsuccessful attempt to perform an action is sometimes expressed by using the ordinary form of the verb, followed by the same verb in another form indicating final success or failure:

   Zhèige dōngxi tài zhòngle. Wǒ nále bàntiān yě nábuqǐlái. "This thing is too heavy. I (tried) for a long time to lift [lit. take] it but couldn't lift it up."

4. After a phrase like **suí nǐde biàn** "do what you please" the addition of **hǎole** adds a very slight note of resignation or displeasure.

5. Item Number 4 in Exercise 3 has an example of a favorite Chinese character game, namely arranging a series of characters in a circle so that they make sense whatever the starting point in reading the characters. The example given there includes the following special usages:

   清心 **qīng xīn** "to soothe [lit. cleanse the heart]"

   也 **yě** (literary final particle)

   以 **yǐ** (literary expression for "take")

   These terms need not be memorized. The last two will be taken up later in greater detail.

第九課

1	2	3	4	5	6	7	8
組	織	度	制	解	包	劃	復

9	10	11	12	13	14	15	16
優	秀	範	圍	庭	相	非	此

1.0. 組 **zǔ** (1) group, unit, section, series (M); (2) organize

組成 **zǔchéng** accomplish, achieve, constitute, establish, organize

1.1. 這十二個人可以分成三組,每組四個人. (T)

1.2. 那個學術研究會是幾個大學教授組成的. (T)

2.0. 織 **zhī** to weave

組織 **zǔzhī** (1) organize, form; (2) organization

(在)組織上 **(zài) zǔzhishang** organizationally, in organization

2.1. 研究中文的學生要組織一個中文學會.

2.2. 中國的大學在組織上跟外國的大學不同.

3.0. 度 **dù*** (1) standard, measure; (2) a degree (M)

程度 **chéngdu** (1) extent, degree; (2) degree of advancement

温度 **wēndù** temperature

温度表 **wēndubiǎo** thermometer

3.1. 我看他的程度不像大學畢業的.

3.2. 給他試試溫度表看他的溫度是多少度. (T)

3.3. 我弟弟老玩兒溫度表. 我好幾次的告訴他不能玩兒, 他老不聽. (T)

4.0. 制 **zhì*** system, institution

制度 **zhìdu** system, institution

4.1. 日本大學是甚麽制度我不知道.

5.0. 解 **jiě** (1) untie, unfasten; (2) emancipate

解决 **jiějué** solve, decide

解放 **jiěfàng** (1) liberate, emancipate; (2) liberation, emancipation

解放前 **jiěfàngqián** before Liberation (i.e. before 1949), preliberation

解放後 **jiěfànghòu** after Liberation (i.e. after 1949), post-liberation

見解 **jiànjiě** viewpoint, understanding

了解 **liǎojiě** understand, comprehend

講解 **jiǎngjiě** (1) explain; (2) explanation

理解 **lǐjiě** (1) understand, comprehend; (2) understanding, comprehension

5.1. 他有了工作, 生活問題就解决了.

5.2. 中國人民政府説, 現在中國人民解放了.

5.3. 他是在北京解放前離開的, 我是在解放後才走的.

5.4. 他在政治上的見解比我好.(T)

5.5. 這個句子要不是你給我講解,我不會了解的.

5.6. 這個問題你理解的比我快.

5.7. 在這短短的日子裏解決不了那個問題.(T)

6.0. 包 **bāo** (1) to wrap; (2) include; (3) guarantee; (4) package (M)

包子 **bāozi** steamed stuffed dumpling

包上 **bāoshang** wrap up

包起來 **bāoqilai** wrap up

包在裏面 **bāo zài lǐmian** (1) wrap in; (2) include(d) in

手提包 **shǒutíbāo** briefcase, suitcase

紙包(兒) **zhǐbāo(r)** parcel, package

6.1. 這兩個紙包裏都是甚麽?…一包是書一包是本子.

6.2. 這個包子是豬肉白菜的.

6.3. 你把這本書用紙包上. 包起來以後,送給張教授去.

6.4. 你吃了飯再走,我包你不會晚.

6.5. 你包書的時候,怎麽把我的書包在裏面了呢?

6.6. 我每個月用一百塊錢，連吃飯住房子都包在裏面了.

6.7. 我這個手提包太重了，我簡直的拿不了了.

6.8. 我弟弟跟妹妹兩個人，為了玩父親的手提包打起來了. (T)

6.9. 老謝真喜歡旅行. 他把旅行當作家常飯. 拿起手提包就走. (T)

7.0. 劃 **huà** (1) to draw; (2) strokes (in writing characters) (M)

劃分 **huàfēn** demarcate

筆劃 **bǐhuà, bǐhuá** stroke (N) (see lesson 3, no. 1)

7.1. 中國劃分二十二省是甚麽時期劃的？(T)

7.2. 你知道「讓」字的筆劃一共是多少劃？

8.0. 復 **fù*** (1) return, recover; (2) again, anew, re-

復習 **fùxí** to review (a lesson)

復興 **fùxīng** (1) revive, recover, flourish again; (2) revival, renaissance

復古 **fùgǔ** (1) revive the old customs; (2) revival; (3) reactionary

復原 **fùyuán** restored to health

報復 **bàofù** take revenge [**bào** here means "retribution"]

8.1. 今天上課先生没講書，叫我們復習以前的功課.

8.2. 有人説那個國家一定能復興的.

8.3. 他就喜歡念古文學, 他的思想復古了.

8.4. 你打了他, 他将來一定要報復的.

8.5. 他的病是好了, 可是還没復原呢. (T)

9.0. 優 **yōu*** superior, excellent

優點 **yōudiǎn** strong point, point of excellence, advantage

優越 **yōuyuè** superior, superlative, excellent

優先 **yōuxiān** (1) precedence; (2) preferential(ly)

9.1. 在這些學生裏, 功課最優的是誰?

9.2. 他的優點是會説話.

9.3. 有些人以為自己比別人優越, 看不起別人.

9.4. 如果有機會一定優先用你.

10.0. 秀 **xiù*** refined, elegant

秀才 **xiùcái** pre-Republic scholastic degree, about equal to Bachelor of Arts

秀氣 **xiùqi** refined, elegant

優秀 **yōuxiù** superior, first-rate

10.1. 念大學的多半是優秀分子.

10.2. 張老先生在清朝的時候, 考上秀才就當縣長了. (T)

10.3. 那個女孩子跟他母親一樣那麽秀氣.

11.0. 範 **fàn*** model, norm

師範 **shīfàn** normal (school)

師範學校 **shīfàn xuéxiào** normal school

師範大學 **shīfàn dàxué** teachers' college, normal school

師大 **shīdà** (short for **shīfàn dàxué**)

11.1. 王先生在初中畢業以後没念高中，念了師範.

11.2. 在初中畢業的可以考師範學校，在高中畢業的才可以考師範大學.

11.3. 在師大念書的時候，我們兩個人相處的很好.

12.0. 圍 **wéi** to surround

圍住 **wéizhù** to surround

範圍 **fànwéi** scope, sphere, jurisdiction, field, category

12.1. 張先生很會説故事. 他一來小孩子就把他給圍住了.

12.2. 這次考試的範圍是從第十三課到二十課.

13.0. 庭 **tíng*** courtyard

家庭 **jiātíng** family, home

大家庭制度 **dà jiātíng zhìdu** big-family system

13.1. 人人都想有一個快樂的家庭.

13.2. 中國的大家庭制度是以前的一種制度.

13.3. 這一帶我還沒聽說誰家是大家庭呢.(T)

14.0. 相 **xiāng*** each other, mutually, reciprocally

相當(的) **xiāngdāng(de)** (1) corresponding; (2) somewhat, fairly

相處 **xiāngchǔ** live together

相信 **xiāngxìn** believe

相同 **xiāngtóng** like, alike, similar

相左 **xiāngzuǒ** differ, be at variance, be at odds

相遠 **xiāngyuǎn** (1) far apart, very different; (2) distant, estranged

14.1. 那個外國人中國話說的相當好.

14.2. 我和田先生相處三年我們的感情相當的好.

14.3. 我相信我們的目的是相同的.

14.4. 我們兩個人的意見相左.

14.5. 不知怎麽的, 他近來和我相遠了, 不像以前跟我那麽好了.

15.0. 非 **fēi** not, non (W)

非得V **fēiděi V** have to V, insist on V-ing

非(得)要V **fēi(děi) yào V** have to V, insist on V-ing

非(得)V(不可) **fēi(děi) V (bùkě)** have to V, insist on V-ing, won't do unless V

非N不可 **fēi N bùkě** only N will do, require N, N is indespensible

非常 **fēicháng** (1) extraordinary, unusual; (2) very, unusually

非但 **fēidàn** not only

是非 **shìfēi** (1) right and wrong, pro and con; (2) fuss, trouble

除非V_1不V_2 **chúfēi V_1 bù V_2** not V_2 unless V_1

除非V_1才V_2 **chúfēi V_1 cái V_2** V_2 only if V_1

15.1. 你為甚麽不叫我去呢？我非去不可.

15.2. 他寫的那本解放前後非常好.

15.3. 我説那本書不要包，他非得要包起來.

15.4. 田太太這個人，你要是跟他見了面，他老是説人家的是非.(T)

15.5. 我不喜歡幫他作事因為他是非不明.(T)

15.6. 家庭裏面要是人多了，我相信一定天天有是非.

15.7. 他非但研究古代史而且也研究近代史.

15.8. 王先生住的地方只有他知道，要去找王先生，非他不可.

15.9. 除非他對我認錯，要不然我以後是不理他了.

16.0. 此 **cǐ** this (W)

此地 **cǐdì** this place, here

此外 **cǐwài** apart from this, beyond this, in addition to this

此後 **cǐhòu** after this, hereafter, thereafter

因此 **yīncǐ** because of this, hence, therefore

從此 **cóngcǐ** from this time on, henceforth

16.1. 此地没有我可以做的工作，我只好到别的地方去了.

16.2. 他就喜歡喝酒，此外他甚麽都不喜歡.

16.3. 考大學的學生越來越多，此後考大學更不容易了.

16.4. 他講書的時候學生都喜歡聽，因此他越講越高興.

16.5. 有一次他開車出了事，從此他就不開車了.

17.0. 地 **de** (variant form of 的 used specifically for pre-verbal modifying phrases

一一(地/的) **yīyī(de)** one by one (W)

17.1. 他慢慢地走過來了.

17.2. 我叫他早早地吃飯，吃完飯好上學.

17.3. 我把我的兒女都叫來了，一一的給他介紹.(W)

17.4. 他父親生氣了，大聲地説:"你不能再去看電影."

18.0. 要有 **yào yǒu** (1) if have; (2) must have

如果要有 **rúguǒ yào yǒu** if have

18.1. 如果要有一個相當的工作，我就不離開這兒了.(T)

18.2. 明天晚飯以後要有時間我一定來.

18.3. 要有高中畢業的程度，才能考那個專科學校.(T)

19.0. 歷史書 **lìshǐ shū** history book

古代史 **gǔdàishǐ** ancient history

近代史 **jìndàishǐ** modern history

19.1. 他在圖書館多半是看歷史書.

19.2. 我已經把古代史看完了. 現在正看近代史呢.

20.0. 帶子 **dàizi** belt

錄音帶 **lùyīndài** recording tape

20.1. 這條帶子是手工做的嗎？

20.2. 這種錄音帶錄的音多半不大清楚.

21.0. 學年 **xuénián** school year (M)

學制 **xuézhì** educational system

學分制 **xuéfēnzhì** system based on academic credits

學年制 **xuéniánzhì** system based on school years

分數(兒) **fēnshù(r)** score, (academic) grade

21.1. 所有大學的學制都是念了四學年就可以畢業.

21.2. 有的大學是學年制,有的大學是學分制.

21.3. 這次考國語,我的分數兒是九十五分兒.(T)

21.4. 在那個大學,如果分數兒念的好,就不必參加大考.(T)

22.0. 重 **chóng** again, re-

重寫 **chóngxiě** rewrite

再重V **zàichóng V** again, re- (followed by a verb)

22.1. 你把字都寫錯了,請你重寫一次.

22.2. 他念大學的時候有三門功課都没念好,都得再重念.

22.3. 我寫的字,先生説寫的不好,叫我再重寫一次.

23.0. 省 **shěng** save (on)

省事 **shěngshì** save work (VO)

省時候 **shěng shíhou** save time

省錢 **shěng qián** save money

省力 **shěnglì** save effort (VO)

23.1. 我手裏没有多少錢了,所以我要省一點兒用.(T)

23.2. 我為了省事去吃飯館兒去,可是不省錢了.

23.3. 坐飛機比坐船雖然費錢，可是可以省時間.

23.4. 我上山的時候甚麽東西也不拿，為的是省力.

24.0. 大前天 **dà qiántiān** day before day before yesterday, three days ago

大前年 **dà qiánnián** year before year before last year, three years ago

大後天 **dà hòutiān** day after day after tomorrow, three days from now

大後年 **dà hòunián** year after year after next year, three years from now

24.1. 我不是在昨天看見他的，也不是在前天看見他的，我是在大前天看見他的.

24.2. 今年我在這裏，去年我在湖北，前年我在山東，大前年我在我的老家呢.

24.3. 今天是星期四，大後天才是星期天呢.

24.4. 我今年是大學一年級. 大後年就是四年級可以畢業了.

25.0. 少見 **shǎojiàn** (1) see little of; (2) seldom seen, rare

25.1. 包先生少見.…少見少見. 近來怎麽樣，好嗎？

25.2. 一歲的小孩子會走路真是少見哪！

26.0. 古文 **gǔwén** ancient text, classical style

26.1. 中國古文很難懂，必得經過先生講解.(T)

27.0. 不是A而是B **búshi A érshi B** be not A but B

27.1. 王先生說他一定來. 後來，來的不是王先生而是王太太.

28.0. 還好 **hái hǎo** okay, passable

28.1. 我問老張近來怎麼樣？老張說："還好."

29.0. 當年 **dāngnián** the year(s) mentioned, that year, those years

當前 **dāngqián** at present, now

(正)當V的時候 **(zhèng)dāng V de shíhou** when, while, just as V

N_1拿/把N_2當(作)N_3 V **N_1 ná/bǎ N_2 dāng(zuò) N_3 V** N_1 V's N_2 as N_3

N_1拿/把N_2當(作)N_3(一樣) **N_1 ná/bǎ N_2 dāng(zuò) N_3 (yíyàng)** N_1 considers N_2 as N_3

29.1. 馬先生老是喜歡說他當年得意的事情.

29.2. 人民怎樣才可以有飯吃？這是當前最要緊的問題.

29.3. 我上了飛機，正當要開的時候，飛機出了毛病.(T)

29.4. 李先生時常拿酒當作水喝.(T)

29.5. 包先生對我真好，把我當作他弟弟一樣．(T)

30.0. 如同 **rútóng** (1) be like, resemble; (2) such as

同歲 **tóngsuì** be of the same age

30.1. 老方和我弟弟同歲．我對老方如同對我弟弟一樣．

31.0. 再也不/沒 V **zài yě bù/méi V** never V again

31.1. 我昨天開車差一點兒出了事，從今以後我再也不開了．

32.0. 計畫 **jìhua** plan (N/V)

計劃 **jìhua** plan (N/V)

32.1. 「計劃」有時候也可以寫成「計畫」．意思是相同的．

32.2. 他們那個五年計劃成功了嗎？(T)

33.0. 人們 **rénmen** people

33.1. 人們都說民主國家好，可是有的民主國家給了人們的好處是甚麼？

34.0. V作/為 **V zuò/wéi** V as, V into

34.1. 我已經念師範大學了，我母親還把我看作小孩子一樣．到那兒去他都不放心．(T)

34.2. 昨天考試我寫錯了一個詞兒，我把「計劃」寫為「筆劃」了.

35.0. 上學 **shàngxué** go to school (VO)

下學 **xiàxué** leave school (VO)

35.1. 我每天上學下學，為了省時候都是坐公共汽車.

36.0. 等於 **děngyú** equal to, equivalent to

36.1. 三百六十五加三百六十六等於多少？

36.2. 你這樣做等於沒做. (T)

37.0. 天下 **tiānxià** (1) under heaven; (2) the empire; (3) the world

37.1. 一到了山海關，遠遠兒地就看見五個大字「天下第一關」. (T)

38.0. 好話 **hǎohuà** (1) well-intentioned remark; (2) compliment; (3) conciliatory remark

說好話 **shuō hǎohuà** put in a good word (for), intercede (for)

38.1. 他告訴你的是好話，你要聽他的. (T)

38.2. 你要是再不好好地念書，父親打你，我可不給你說好話了.

38.3. 王太太人又聰明又有本事，可是有一樣不好，老喜歡說別人的短處. 從來不說別人的好話. (T)

Checklist

1. 組
   組成
2. 織
   組織
   (在)組織上
3. 度
   程度
   温度
   温度表
4. 制
   制度
5. 解
   解决
   解放
   解放前
   解放後
   見解
   了解
   講解
   理解
6. 包
   包子
   包上
   包起來
   包在裏面
   手提包
   紙包(兒)
7. 劃
   劃分
   筆劃
8. 復
   復習
   復興
   復古
   復原
   報復
9. 優
   優點
   優越
   優先
10. 秀
    優秀
    秀才
    秀氣
11. 範
    師範
    師範學校
    師範大學
    師大
12. 圍
    圍住
    範圍
13. 庭
    家庭
    大家庭制度
14. 相
    相當(的)
    相處
    相信
    相同
    相左
    相遠
15. 非
    非得 V
    非(得)要 V
    非(得) V不可
    非 N不可
    非常
    非但
    是非
    除非V_1不V_2
    除非V_1才V_2
16. 此
    此地
    此外
    此後
    因此
    從此

17. 地
一一(地/的)
18. 要有
如果要有
19. 歷史書
古代史
近代史
20. 帶子
錄音帶
21. 學年
學制
學分制
學年制
分數(兒)
22. 重
再重
重寫
23. 省
省事
省時候
省錢
省力
24. 大前天
大前年
大後天
大後年
25. 少見
26. 古文
27. 不是 A 而是 B
28. 還好
29. 當年
當前
(正)當 V 的時候
N_1拿/把N_2
當(作)N_3 V
N_1拿/把N_2當(作)N_3(一樣)
30. 如同
同歲
31. 再也不/沒 V
32. 計畫
計劃
33. 人們
34. V 作/為
35. 上學
下學
36. 等於
37. 天下
38. 好話
說好話

Exercise 1. Excerpts from Actual Publications: Practice in Reading Stage Directions

The following excerpts, all taken from **Cáo Yú's** play Metamorphosis, consist of parenthetical stage directions. The style is terse, as in English: "walks to the door on the left," "loudly," "sits." Use your imagination in giving appropriate English equivalents for these items.

1. (大聲)
2. (笑着)
3. (站起來)
4. (看了一看)
5. (不理他)
6. (同時)
7. (大叫)
8. (走來走去)
9. (走到門)

10. (笑)
11. (對孔)
12. (吃完了)
13. (放下心)
14. (在外面)
15. (回頭)
16. (大笑)
17. (高聲)
18. (慢慢過去)
19. (沒想到)
20. (又走)
21. (關心地)
22. (放下水杯)
23. (走過來笑)
24. (笑起來)
25. (說不出來)
26. (也笑着)
27. (大喜)
28. (看表)
29. (又大聲)
30. (得意)
31. (這才明白)
32. (找着機會)
33. (孔太太下)
34. (溫笑着)
35. (笑問)
36. (跑着笑着)
37. (高興見他)
38. (忙說)
39. (走到右門)
40. (不明白)
41. (慢慢地)
42. (又坐下)
43. (近前)
44. (看看他)
45. (奇怪)
46. (跑上前)
47. (不相信)
48. (大高興)
49. (更忙)
50. (客氣地)
51. (回到中門)
52. (不好意思)
53. (對他們)
54. (才看見)
55. (不高興)
56. (高興大聲)
57. (不好意思起來)
58. (孔才回過頭來)
59. (大家笑起來)
60. (對孔得意地)
61. (跑到孔面前)
62. (回來一句話不說)
63. (從心裏說出)
64. (走到中門口笑着)
65. (十分自然的)
66. (不覺放下筆)
67. (一字一字的)
68. (想起自己的事)
69. (同時回頭講)
70. (走去接電話)
71. (知道他話最多)
72. (回頭又大聲)
73. (一面走一面對孔講)
74. (跑到她面前)
75. (跑去接電話同時對謝)

Exercise 2. Dialogues

1. 包：我姓包，我叫包學範．請問貴姓？

程：我姓程，我叫程秀山．我在遠大念書．

包：我在文華大學念書．你到此地多久了？

程：我來了五年了．你呢？

包：我來了有七年了．

程：回過家沒有？

包：大前年回去一次．你回去過沒有？

程：我老是想放假的時候回去一次，可是老也沒回去過．

包：請問遠大是學分制，還是學年制？

程：學分制．文華呢？

包：也是學分制．我想現在的學制多數是學分制了．我們文華有一樣不好．如果分數念的不好不能念下去了．

程：我們遠大可以再念下去．你們學校數學很有名，數學程度很高．

包：我們學校注重數學．

程：所以文華畢業的，各大機關都優先請他們．他們都有最好的工作．

包：有的人雖然畢業了，也不一定有很好的工作．別的機關跟學校要人都是要最優秀的分子．

2．温：謝先生病好點兒了没有？

謝：温太太，謝謝你關心．這兩天好的多了．今天早晨試試温度表，不到一百度了．

温：温度不很高了．

謝：是．他這次的病真不輕啊．我想最少得一個月才能復原．

温：謝先生一時不能出去．要有甚麽事，就打電話告訴我們温先生．千萬別客氣．要是客氣可就相遠了．

謝：好的．我常聽謝先生説，在幾個朋友當中温先生和他相處的最好，簡直拿他當弟弟一樣．

温：所以我説別客氣呢．

謝：將來有甚麽事，我們還是非麻煩兩位不可．我不好意思去麻煩別人．

温：我明後天不來，大後天我和我先生

一塊兒來看謝先生.

謝：謝謝你. 再見.

3. 生：老師. 我看別人寫的東西有時候不用「的」用「地」. 在甚麽時候用「地」呢？

師：我舉幾個例子：今天跟昨天一樣地暖和. 張先生很客氣地說：“中文雖然很難，要是你用功慢慢地就會了.”

生：「意見相左」就是「意見不相同」嗎？

師：對了.

生：「一一地」就是口語「一個一個地」是不是？

師：是.

生：老師，「報復」我不大懂.

師：要是別人打了我，我老想找個機會打他就是「報復」.

生：「理解」是甚麽意思？

師：別人寫的東西，你看了以後，非常了解，知道了意思是甚麽，就是理解了. 都明白了嗎？

生：明白了．老師下星期考歷史．古代史跟近代史都考麽？

師：不．只考近代史．不過古代史最好你們也復習一次．

4．包：老田，我想我們應該組織一個課外研究會．

田：組織這個會，研究的範圍是甚麽？

包：我們是學師範的．我們常常大家在一塊兒談談，我們在師範學校畢業以後，在教學這一方面應當提高水準，要有一個相當的水準．以前的人們都不注重師範，都不喜歡念師範，很多人叫「師範大學」是「吃飯大學」．

田：那是甚麽意思呢？

包：就是説，念師範又省時候又省錢，畢了業馬上去教書就有飯吃．

5．謝：文復，聽説你要考師範大學了．

文：誰告訴你的？

謝：我是「秀才不出門，能知天下事」．

文：說真的，你怎麽知道的？

謝：老邊告訴我的．

文：你甚麽時候看見老邊了？

謝：大前天．

文：我才告訴他，他就告訴你了．因為我感覺到教書很有意思，所以我想念師範．考師大的人很多，也許我考不上．

謝：我想不會的，你一定能考上．

文：你怎麽樣，你打算考那兒？

謝：我打算先作一年事再念書．

文：我們中學畢業的，找事很不容易呀．

謝：是不容易．有一天我求湯老師給我找事．湯老師說讓我幫他作一點兒事．

文：湯老師大概又要寫書了．

謝：是的．他計畫着寫一部歷史書．

文：你這個機會好極了．幫着老師作事可以得學問．

謝：目前找事不容易．我有這個機會很

難得.

文：湯老師的歷史要寫多少時候？

謝：他説大概要寫一年左右. 他是從古代史寫到近代史.

文：他要寫的是教科書，還是參考書？

謝：他要寫初中跟高中的歷史課本兒. 此外大概還要寫一點兒别的東西.

文：他是史學家，他寫的一定都是關於歷史的.

謝：湯老師也研究過方言. 有一天他很高興地對我説:“文復，雖然你只有高中的程度，可是你很有天才. 我相信你能幫助我. 當年我就是念完了高中給老師作事. 我的方言就是給我老師作事的期間學的. 我現在想起來很有意思. 不是給老師作事而是跟老師學.”

6. 王：聽説你府上原來是一個大家庭.

應：是. 我從我們那個大家庭解放出來還不到十年呢.

王：聽你的口氣好像你不滿意大家庭制度.

應：我不喜歡那種制度.難道你喜歡嗎？

王：這是每一個人的見解各有不同. 我認為大家庭也有它的優點.

應：你没在大家庭裏生活過，你不了解大家庭裏面的情形. 你聽我説説我們那個大家庭.因為我父親是老大，家裏頭不論甚麽事情都是我父親作主. 開始還好，等到都結了婚，問題就發生了. 天天有是非.

王：都有甚麽是非呢？

應：不是老二説老三錢用的太多了，就是老三説老四把家裏東西都送人了. 我記得我在八九歲的時候，我是家裏孩子裏面最聰明的一個，所以父親把我送到一個比較好一點兒的學校去上學. 家裏別人就不高興了. 天天有人在我母親面前説很不好聽的話，説錢在誰手裏，誰的兒子就能念好學校. 這明明是説我父親呢. 可是我母親還得跟他們説好話.

王：你甚麽時候離開你們那個大家庭的？

應：正當我念中學的時候日本人來了, 就是七七了, 我就離開那個大家庭, 到内地去了. 我再也不想回到那個大家庭裏去了.

7. 學生：先生早.

先生：同學早. 昨天的功課你們都會了嗎？

學生：有的會，有的不會.

先生：好. 我先説幾個詞兒，請你們説幾個簡單句子. 包子清，你用「非但、此後」兩個詞兒説一個簡單的句子.

學生："像張少奇那種人真少見. 上次我幫他那麽大的忙, 他非但不感謝我, 還常對別人説我不好. 此後我可不幫朋友忙了."

先生：好. 許立夫，你用「從此、如同」

說一句話.

學生:"我們從此如同好朋友一樣."

先生:對.李心清,你用「因此、圍住」說個句子.

學生:"因為他給我們講的那個問題不大清楚,因此大家都把他圍住了,請他再講解一次."

先生:很好.現在該你們問我了.

學生:先生,「秀氣」跟「劃分」這兩個詞兒我不大會用.

先生:「秀氣」是形容詞,是形容一個女人很好看.單講一個「秀」字就是「美」的意思.「劃分」,"那兩個國家是用那條大河來劃分."

學生:「劃分」的「劃」也是「計劃」的「劃」嗎?

先生:是.「筆劃」也是這個「劃」.

學生:我看有的書「計劃」的「劃」也用「畫畫兒」的「畫」.

先生:兩個都可以,不過正寫是「畫畫

兒」的「畫」.

學生：先生，還有「當前」跟「目前」都是一樣的意思嗎？

先生：一樣．都是「現在」的意思．

學生：是不是一學年分為兩學期？

先生：是的．

學生：「組成」跟「組織」一樣嗎？「組成」等於「組織」嗎？

先生：有點不一樣．「組織」是正在組織，「組成」是已經組織成了的．

8．費：小王，你還有幾年畢業呀？

王：我大後年才畢業呢．

費：那不是你就成了老王了嗎？學大夫時間可真長啊．

王：人家學別的學科，四年就畢業了．我得兩個四年．

費：可是將來你當了大夫，是一種最優越的職業呀．

王：我是數學不好，要不然我才不學呢．你作別的工作一天做八小時就可以了．一當大夫一天二十四小時甚麽時候有病人都得去，除非是大夫本人也病了．

費：我們這兒學大夫是八年，聽説有的國家要十幾年呢．

王：那是每一個國家學校制度上跟組織上的不同．

9．麻：文先生，你有這麽多錄音帶怎麽没有錄音機呀？

文：我的錄音機還没到呢．因為我從英國來的時候是坐飛機，我就拿了一個手提包．有一個朋友他坐船，我為了省事、省力也省點兒錢，所以讓那位朋友給我帶來．

麻：你錄音都錄甚麽？

文：我多半兒是練習説中國話．要是有好音樂我也把它錄下來．我錄了好多中國音樂，那是當初我在北京的時候錄的．

麻：你甚麽時候到過北京？

文：好幾年了，那是在解放前的事情了．

麻：解放後你去過没有？

文：没有．

10. 簡：你的問題解决了嗎？

常：没有．我父親還是一定讓我先念二年古文再說．

簡：大概你父親贊成中國文學復古，不喜歡近代的文學．

常：他老人家說，學校裏面現在都是用白話文，古文一點兒也不懂．還有，我將來一念了科學，更没機會念古文了．

簡：那麽你怎麽决定呢？

常：我當然希望今年考大學了，可是我們這個家庭，不論甚麽事情都是我父親作主．為了這個問題，還跟我說了半天的治國的道理．他說："中國現在這種情形都是大家對我們原有的文化太不注重了．要想復興中國，必得提高研究中國文化的水準，要注重中國古文學."

11. 紀: 老謝, 今天下學以後, 我請你到華北飯店吃包子去.
謝: 為甚麽今天要請客呢?
紀: 今天是我生日,一個人吃飯没意思.
謝: 生日不是吃麵嗎?
紀: 我最喜歡吃包子.
謝: 你今年多大了?
紀: 我二十二了.
謝: 你跟我同歲, 我以為你比我小的多呢.
紀: 怪不得你拿我當小孩子看呢. 我們現在就走吧.
謝: 時候還早吧?
紀: 我得先去買幾條帶子去.
謝: 你買帶子做甚麽?
紀: 是我母親來信讓我給他買的.

12. 應: 請你把那幾本書都包起來.
許: 那兩本算術課本也包在裏面嗎?
應: 不. 就把那幾本小説包上. 别的不

必包.

許：你這些小說是不是包上送給別人?

應：我送到圖書館去.

Exercise 3. Narratives

1. 中國有的地方有師範學校. 師範學校和師範大學不同.師範大學是大學的程度,畢業以後可以當中學教員. 師範學校是中學的程度,畢業以後只能當小學教員.我在初中畢業以後, 因為家裏沒有錢不能念高中就去念師範. 念師範和念高中大不相同. 念師範用不着學費, 可以省錢, 而且畢業以後就可以有職業當小學教員. 念高中非但要用很多錢, 而且畢業以後除非考大學就沒有相當的出路了.因此初中畢業的學生要是將來能念大學就先去念高中, 如果將來沒錢念大學, 就不去念高中, 去念師範了.

2. 有一個外國人在北京住了十幾年. 正當他要回國的時候, 北京解放了. 後來他在解放後才回國．有人問他解放後的北京和解放前有甚麽不同．他說他在解放後十幾天就離開了北京，在那短短的日子裏，他没法子比較．

3．在清朝的時候有一個種田的．他有一個男孩子才十一二歲，他就讓他學種田．那個孩子不喜歡種田，他喜歡念書．那個種田的就對他的兒子說：“我們是種田的，從來没有人念過書，你要是能把書念好，我也很樂意．”這個孩子聽了他父親這句話以後很高興，更加努力念書了．從此就專心念書．過了幾年，書念了不少就去參加考試．考試的結果，他考上了秀才．這件事真把他們全家老少都樂的不得了．種田的對他兒子說：“考上了秀才真不容易．不但我們家裏從來没有秀才，就是我們附近幾十里以內，也没聽說誰家有過秀才呀．”這個秀才後來就是清朝一個很有名的人．

4．中國有一本有名的小說「家」．這本小說寫的是中國一個大家庭的故事.從前中國人的家庭多半是大家庭制度.這種制度對於家庭裏的每個人都没有多大的好處,也就是説它的優點很少,所以後來這種制度的家庭越來越少了.現在我們要想了解大家庭制度的實在情形,可以看一看「家」這本小説就知道了.

5. 我是在大前年考上的大學.今年就要畢業了.前幾天我父親問我畢業以後希望作甚麽.我説:"我想明年到外國繼續求學.在外國兩年或者是三年,要在後年或者是大後年回國."我父親説:"你這個計劃很好,我非常贊成."

6. 我們念書的時候,第一要能記住,第二要能理解.記住就是忘不了,理解就是了解了那個道理.念書如果記不住,當然是念不好.可是只能記住,不能了解那個道理,也是没有多大用處,因為記住只能把已經學過的記住,理解是可以從已經學過的道理想出來還没有學過的.

所以理解比記住更重要.

7. 許多學生圍住了先生，請先生説説明天考試的範圍. 先生説:“所有我講過的都要考，這就是我告訴你們的範圍.”學生説:“這個範圍太大了，等於没告訴我們範圍呀.”先生説:“我再重説一次：明天要考的都是你們現在的程度應該知道的. 你們一定考的很好. 這麽樣説法你們放心了吧？”學生説:“放心是放心，可是您説來説去也没説出考試的範圍呀.”

8. 許復亮和他弟弟長的都秀氣，而且長的樣子都一樣. 兩個人都喜歡和別人開玩笑. 有一天他們家的門口來了一個賣包子的. 他弟弟和賣包子的説:“你猜我一個人能吃多少包子？”賣包子的説:“我看你最多能吃十個.”他弟弟説:“我能吃二十個你相信嗎？”賣包子的説:“我不信. 你要是能吃二十個我不跟你要錢.”他弟弟説:“可是我吃到十個的時候，我必得回家喝一點兒水然後再接着吃十個.

這樣吃法你同意嗎？”賣包子的想了一想說：“我同意.”他弟弟先吃了十個包子，然後就回去喝水．喝完水從家裏出來又吃了十個包子，一共吃了二十個．賣包子的看見他真把二十個包子吃完了就說：“一個人能吃二十個包子，真是少見，你不必給錢了.”這時候許復亮大聲的笑起來了說：“我和你實說了吧．這二十個包子，不是我一個人吃的.”賣包子的聽了覺着更奇怪了，明明的看見是一個人吃的，為甚麽說不是一個人吃的呢？許復亮告訴他說：“我說實在的吧．喝水以後這十個包子是我吃的，喝水以前那十個包子是我弟弟吃的．我和我弟弟同歲，我們長的樣子如同一個人一樣，所以你看不出來我們是兩個人.”

9．昨天晚上的天氣報告說今天的溫度二十多度，可是今天早晨我看溫度表是四十二度．不知道是溫度表不好用了呢，還是天氣報告的不準了呢？有人說：“這是天氣報告不準了.不過這也是常有的事,此後不要太相信天氣報告了."

10. 這個地方有一個學生會是當地幾個大學的學生組織的. 他們多半是大學裏的優秀分子. 當年才組織這個會的時候, 他們對於組織上的意見很多, 各有各的見解. 後來經過多少次的研究才解决了, 因此就組成了這個會.

11. 湯文遠拿些不常用的字去問謝先生. 謝先生給他一一地講解以後就問他:"你問的這些字是不是在古文上看來的?他說:"是." 謝先生說:"學習現代語文, 要多注意常用的字. 如果專去研究古書上的字, 那就是要往復古的路上走了."

12. 老王有一個兒子叫小二黑. 小二黑最喜歡吃飯館做的包子. 有一天他跟他父親去吃包子, 他父親問他能吃多少. 他說能吃十個.他父親說:"這裏的包子很大, 我相信你吃不了十個."他說:"我在這裏先吃一些，剩下的包起來拿回家裏再吃.”

13. 有一個外國人想要了解中國學校的制度. 有人告訴他，中國的學制分為小學、中學、大學. 小學有初小和高小，一共是六學年. 中學有初中和高中，一共也是六學年. 小學、中學都是學年制，如果念滿了六學年，而且各門功課的分數兒要有六十分以上，才可以畢業. 大學雖然也是學年制，四年畢業，可是也用學分制，各門功課都有學分，必得有了一百多個學分才能畢業. 如果有一門功課念的不好，就得再重念. 這就是中國學制的大概情形.

14. 大前天我在書店買了很多書，又買了些信紙、信封. 買完了以後，書店裏的人說:“把這些書都給您包上，叫人給您送到府上去吧？”我說:“好吧.”我又說:“把這些信紙、信封也包在裏面，一塊兒送去吧.”書店裏的人說:“好吧！”我就給了錢，回到家裏，等着書店把書送來.

可是一直等到今天才送來. 我問這個送書的人, 為甚麽這麽晚才送來呢? 他說: "您是大前天晚上買的. 前天是星期, 昨天又是放假的日子, 我們都不作生意, 所以今天才給您送來."

15. 有一個國家從前在各國裏可以說是一個一等國家. 後來因為國內國外發生了不少的問題, 慢慢地就成為二三等的國家了. 近來這個國家的人民和政府都很努力. 有人說: "這個國家正在復興, 又要成為一等國家了."

16. 中國從前劃分為十八個省, 每個省裏劃分為十幾個或幾十個縣. 後來又劃分為二十二個省. 有人問我目前中國有多少省? 一共多少縣? 我告訴他看看最近的中國地圖就知道了.

17. 王先生從前在一個圖書館裏工作. 他做了十幾年, 做的很好. 後來他因為有病不做了, 就回到了他的老家. 最近他的病好了，他又想做事．有人告訴他：“此地也有圖書館正要用人，他們要有經驗的人．你在圖書館工作十幾年，這是一個非常優越的條件，他們也許能優先用你．”王先生就到當地的圖書館去了，果然就優先用他了．

18. 張先生要在大後天請我到他的家裏去吃晚飯．我說：“我每次在府上吃飯，你太太都是做了很多菜，我覺得太麻煩你們了，所以我再也不敢去麻煩了．”張先生說：“我們是老朋友了，不必客氣，你非來不可．你要是不來就是和我相遠了．”我說：“好，我一定來，一定來．”

19. 高先生最喜歡一個人旅行．有的時候他自己拿着一個手提包坐上飛機就去旅行．有一次，他太太和孩子都要跟他去旅行，而且要大家一塊兒坐船去．他說：“人多了非常麻煩，坐船也太費時間了．我還是一個人坐飛機去，又省事又省時間．”

20. 我和弟弟念中學的時候，因為家離學校很遠，所以每天上學都是坐車去．坐車又省力又省時間．但是每天下學的時候，我們就走路回家．有人問我們，為甚麼下學的時候不坐車呢？我們說：“為的是省錢，要不然我們上學、下學都坐車，費的錢更多了．”

21. 有人問我師大是不是師範大學？我說是的，我又告訴他，師大的畢業生有的是當中學教員，有的是到外國去研究，他們都是有決心老在教學方面工作的．

22. 我在念中學的時候，我們學校附近有一個師範學校．這兩個學校的學生在平常的時候相處的還好．有一天師範學校的學生把我們中學的學生打了．我們中學的學生都說非去報復不可，就有很多人都到師範學校的門前去了．那個時候我也參加了．我們大聲地說，叫那個打人的人出來．後來師範學校有一個職員出來了．他對我們說：“打了人的人是錯了，可是為了報復要打人的，也是錯了．現在叫打了人的出來先認個錯，你們就不必報復了，也就是你們也不會錯了.”我們認為他說的很有道理，就叫打人的人認個錯，這件事情就這樣解決了.

23. 有一個外國學生正在家裏復習以前學過的國語，學校裏教他國語的簡先生來了.簡先生一看見他就說：“怪不得你學國語學的最好，原來是你常常自己復習呀.”簡先生又說：“我本來早就要來看看你，可是我一天老有事，老沒工夫.我今天一來是來看你，二來是送給你一個錄音帶.這個錄音帶上錄的不是國語課文而是用國語說的笑話和故事.此外還有我講的中國當前最緊要的幾個問題.你有工夫可以聽聽，也許比復習課本更有意思，更有好處.”

24. 程先生和他太太雖然感情很好，可是有的時候他們的意見相左.比方說，前幾天他們的兩個孩子為了玩兒一條帶子打起來了.程太太也不分是非，把兩個孩子都打了．正當這個時候程先生回家來了，看見家裏這樣情形，就問是怎麽一回事．他問清楚以後就對他太太說：“我從來不主張打孩子，你把打孩子當作家常飯．”他太太說：“孩子有錯我就要打．”他們兩個人各說各的理．後來程先生看他太太真生氣了，就對他太太說好話了．他說：“天下的父母没有不喜歡孩子的，你打他們也為的是他們好啊！”

25. 我有一個外國朋友，昨天給我來信，求我給他買書．他的信是用中文這樣寫的：

王先生：

許久没給你寫信了．你近來好吧？我現在想求你給我買幾本中國歷史書，因為我要把中國的古代史和近代史譯成英文．我的翻譯計畫是要在最短的期間翻譯完成．如果你能够早一點兒給我買來，我是非常感謝的．祝

近好！　　　費文遠上　三月九日

26. 我念中學的時候有一個同學我們相處的

很好.他把我當作弟弟一樣.有一次我病了,他非常難過.他對我說:“你病了如同我病了一樣,我馬上就去找大夫來.”我說:“我這是小病,不要緊,過幾天就會好的.”過了幾天果然好了.他看見我病好了,他樂了.他給我做了一碗鷄湯叫我喝.他說:“你的病好是好了,可是還是没復原哪.你多喝些鷄湯就復原了.”

27. 王小姐是青年會的職員.他說:“我在青年會工作我很滿足.為甚麽滿足呢?因為我從前找不到工作,也不認識甚麽人.要不是青年會用我做職員,很可能一直到現在還没有工作呢.還有,人要是知足才有快樂.”

28. 張大文會木刻.如果你給他一個樣子讓他去刻,他刻出來的東西和原來的樣子一點兒也不會錯的.前些日子我父親寫的小字,讓他刻在木頭上,他刻的筆劃和我父親寫的完全一樣.

29. 張楚小的時候最不喜歡學算術. 有一次先生給他講算術, 他説他聽不明白. 先生給他舉一個例子, 他還是不明白. 後來又舉幾個例子, 他也是不懂. 先生説: “你將來最好念别的, 不能念數學了.”

30. 高太太對李太太説: “近來吃的東西越來越貴. 就拿豬肉來説吧, 比從前貴多了. 我現在告訴你一個地方賣豬肉還是老價錢, 不算貴. 你可以去買.” 李太太聽了以後就跟李先生開車去買. 那個地方的豬肉果然不貴. 買回來以後, 李太太很高興地説: “買肉省了四五毛錢.” 李先生説: “買肉省了四五毛錢, 可是我開車用的汽油要用八九毛錢.”

Exercise 4. Illustrative Sentences (English)

1.1. These twelve people can be divided into three groups, four persons to the group.

1.2. This learned research institute was organized by professors from several universities.

3.2. Take his temperature [lit. try the thermometer for him and see how many degrees his temperature is].

3.3. My younger brother is always playing with the thermometer. I told him many times he shouldn't play (with it), but he never listens.

5.4. His understanding of [lit. on] politics is greater than mine.

5.7. In this short period it won't be possible to settle that problem.

6.8. My younger brother and younger sister got into a fight over [playing with] father's briefcase.

6.9. Xie certainly likes to travel. He looks upon travel as a routine matter [lit. home-cooking]. He picks up his suitcase and off he goes.

7.1. In what period was the division of China into twenty-two provinces effected?

8.5. He's gotten over his illness, to be sure, but he still hasn't (completely) recovered.

10.2. In the Ch'ing dynasty old Mr. Chang became a district magistrate after passing the examinations for the **xiùcái** degree.

13.3. In this area, I haven't heard of any family that is a big family.

15.4. This Mrs. Tian when [lit. if] you see her she always talks about other people's good and bad points.

15.5. I don't like to help him [do things] because he can't tell right from wrong.

18.1. If I had an appropriate job I wouldn't leave here.

18.3. You must be a higher middle school graduate [lit. have the standing of graduating from higher middle school] before you can take the exams for that specialized school.

21.3. In this exam on the National Language my grade was 95.

21.4. In that university, if your grades are good you don't need to take the final exam.

23.1. I don't have much money left [in hand], so I must economize a bit.

26.1. The Chinese classical style is hard to understand. It must be explained by a teacher.

29.3. I got on the plane but just as it was about to take off it developed some trouble.

29.4. Mr. Li [constantly] drinks wine like water.

29.5. Mr. Bao is very nice to me. He treats me like a younger brother.

32.2. Was their five-year plan a success?

34.1. I'm already studying at teachers college, but mother still looks upon me as a child. No matter where I go, she worries.

36.2. Your doing it this way is equal to not having done it at all.

37.1. Immediately on arriving at Shanhaikuan, from a distance one sees [the five big characters] World's Number One Pass.

38.1. What he told you was well-intentioned [remarks]. You should listen to him [lit. his].

38.3. Mrs. Wang [as a person] is clever and has ability, but there is one thing bad about her. She always likes to speak of other people's shortcomings. She never has a good word for others.

第 十 課

1	2	3	4	5	6	7	8
倒	育	濟	盡	細	詳	良	係

9	10	11	12	13	14	15	16
總	任	獎	金	務	系	室	物

1.0. 倒 **dǎo** (1) topple, collapse; (2) over, upside-down (RV ending)

dào (1) pour; (2) inverted*; (3) on the contrary*

倒不如 **dào bùrú** would be best if, can't do better than

倒(是) **dào(shi)** (1) contrary to expectation, yet, nevertheless; (2) after all, yes of course but …, to V all right but

倒茶 **dào chá** pour tea

倒車 **dào chē** back up a vehicle

倒過(來) **dàoguo(lai)** to reverse, turn upside down, back up

開倒車 **kāi dào chē** (1) back up, turn a vehicle around; (2) go in reverse, retrogress (fig.)

倒像 **dào xiàng** but seems, on the contrary it seems that

打倒 **dǎdǎo** (1) knock down, overturn; (2) Down with …!

1.1. 寫了半天你都寫錯了. 倒不如我自己寫了.

1.2. 讓你給我倒茶你怎麽不去呀? 你倒是倒

不倒啊？(T)

1.3. 王媽，來客了．倒茶來．(T)

1.4. 老許倒車去了．把車倒過來他就進來．(T)

1.5. 在這個原子時代，你讓孩子念古書簡直是開倒車．

1.6. 其實是我幫他的忙，可是倒像我去求他一樣．(T)

1.7. 他那個學說很多人不贊成，大家都說應該打倒．

2.0. 育 **yù*** nurture

生育 **shēngyù** bear offspring, give birth to a child

教育 **jiàoyu** education

教育部 **Jiàoyu Bù** Ministry of Education

教育部長 **Jiàoyu Bùzhǎng** Minister of Education

2.1. 我太太跟我結婚十年了也沒生育．

2.2. 包先生是研究教育的．

2.3. 昨天教育部長在教育部接見各中學的校長．

3.0. 濟 **jì*** aid

經濟 **jīngji** (1) economical; (2) economy; (3) economics

經濟學 **jīngjixué** economics (as a subject of study)

計劃經濟 **jìhua jīngji** planned economy

濟南(府) **Jìnán(fǔ)** Tsinan(fǔ) (in Shantung Province)

3.1. 許一文是一位很有名的經濟學教授.

3.2. 計劃經濟就是有計劃的一種經濟.

3.3. 濟南在山東省, 從前叫作濟南府.

3.4. 昨天省長在開會的時候説:"社會經濟發達, 人民生活才能提高."(T)

3.5. 他寫的那個論文對於現在的經濟情況很有見解.(T)

4.0. 盡 **jìn*** (1) exhaust; (2) exhaustive; (3) exhaustively; (4) (RV ending)

盡力 **jìnlì** expend much effort, exhaust one's efforts (VO)

盡心 **jìnxīn** diligent in doing the best that one can (SV)

盡意(的) **jìnyì(de)** whole-heartedly, single-mindely (AD)

盡職 **jìnzhí** diligent in doing one's duty (SV)

盡是 **jìnshi** (1) is nothing but, always is (EV); (2) always, merely (AD)

用盡 **yòngjìn** use up (RV)

盡可能(的) **jìn kěnéng(de)** to the fullest extent possible (AD)

4.1. 我盡了很多力才把他的忙幫成了.(T)

4.2. 我是盡力的幫助你, 我盡可能的想法子去.(T)

4.3. 王先生作事非常盡職, 不論你叫他作甚麽他總是盡心盡意的去作.

4.4. 怎麽他的錢又用盡了?…可不是嗎!他盡是這樣.(T)

4.5. 他盡是說,不去做.(T)

4.6. 你的事等於我的事,沒有甚麽兩樣.我一定盡力地想法子讓它成功.(T)

5.0. 細 **xì** (1) fine; (2) minutely, carefully

細想 **xì xiǎng** think carefully, give careful thought (to)

細說 **xì shuō** talk in detail

細問 **xì wèn** make a detailed inquiry

細心 **xìxīn** attentive, careful

細情 **xìqíng** minute detail, detailed situation

5.1. 這條帶子很細,沒甚麽用處.

5.2. 在對人說話以前要細心的細想一想再說.(T)

5.3. 請你對我細說那件事情經過的細情.(T)

5.4. 他那天走?你怎麽不細問問呢?

5.5. 請你再細細地看一看.(T)

5.6. 作買賣房子的生意很不容易.你要細細地想好了再決定.(T)

6.0. 詳 **xiáng*** detailed

詳細 **xiángxi** detailed, minute, careful

6.1. 那件事情的經過你說的太簡單了. 請你詳細講.

6.2. 請你詳細看一看有錯字沒有?

7.0. 良 **liáng*** good

良心 **liángxin** conscience

7.1. 一個人不論作事或是對人, 都要有良心. (T)

8.0. 係 **xì*** (Cantonese word for "is"=是)

關係 **guānxi** (1) connection, relationship; (2) relevance, importance; (3) involve

沒關係 **méi guānxi** (1) not have any connection with; (2) (it) doesn't matter

因為A的關係 **yīnwei A de guānxi** because of A

N_1對/跟N_2(的)關係 **N_1 duì/gēn N_2 (de) guānxi** relationship of N_1 to N_2

8.1. 昨天我看廣東日報上說:"那塊土地以前係中國的國土." (T)

8.2. 孔教授講解的, 都是對我們研究經濟學有關係的.

8.3. 對不起, 你那本書我找不到了. … 沒關係.

8.4. 因為程先生的關係, 所以我能夠在師範學校當職員.

8.5. 許先生跟湯先生的關係相當好.

8.6. 你跟我的關係, 別說客氣話. (T)

9.0. 總 **zǒng*** (1) general; (2) unify; (3) in every case, invariably; (4) all the time, keep on (doing something)

總共 **zǒnggòng** in all (AD)

總不 **zǒngbù** never

總是 **zǒngshi** (1) always is (EV); (2) always, invariably (AD)

總要 **zǒngyào** must (more emphatic than just **yào**)

總得 **zǒngděi** (1) must (before a verb); (2) require (before a noun)

總結 **zǒngjié** (1) bring together; (2) summarize, conclude; (3) summary, summation, conclusion

總會 **zǒnghuì** (1) very likely to, bound to (AV); (2) head office

總理 **zǒnglǐ** premier, prime minister

總名 **zǒngmíng** general term (for), generic name

總有 **zǒngyǒu** always have, bound to have

總算 **zǒngsuàn** finally, at any rate

總計 **zǒngjì** to total up, figure the total

總數 **zǒngshù** sum, total amount

總機關 **zǒng jīguān** headquarters

總代表 **zǒng dàibiǎo** chief delegate

總經理 **zǒng jīnglǐ** general manager

總代理 **zǒng dàilǐ** general agent

9.1. 那個汽車總代理把今年賣出的汽車總結起來. 總共賣了一千五百部汽車. (T)

9.2. 那件事情他總不告訴我．其實早晚我總會知道的．

9.3. 我們經理在這兒，總經理不在這兒，在國外呢．

9.4. 我總是這樣，每天飯前總得喝點兒酒．

9.5. 你不論多忙，總要先把今天收進來錢的總數總計一次．(T)

9.6. 中山先生我們有時也叫他「總理」．(T)

9.7. 上古史、中古史、近古史總名叫作古代史．

9.8. 我老早就想總有一天我非得到中國去，現在總算達到目的了．

9.9. 參加這次大會，我們學校學生總代表是誰？

10.0. 任 **rèn** (1) duty, responsibility; (2) allow, tolerate; (3) (a surname)

任用 **rènyòng** engage, employ

任意(的) **rènyì(de)** arbitrarily, capriciously, as one pleases, at will

任期 **rènqī** term of office

任滿 **rènmǎn** term of office expires

主任 **zhǔrèn** director, person in charge, chairman

上任 **shàngrèn** assume a post, take over the duties of a position

接任 **jiērèn** assume office (from someone else), take over

現任 **xiànrèn** incumbent, present (AT)

前任 **qiánrèn** former (incumbent) (AT)

10.1. 現任部長從上任到現在已經五年了. 現在任期已經滿了. 下個月張大同來接任部長了.

10.2. 王縣長任用自己人. 他把前任的主任跟職員都不用了, 完全用他自己的人.

10.3. 任部長任滿了以後, 有一個大學請他教書去呢.

10.4. 你以後做事要細細的想過了再決定. 不要任意的去做.

10.5. 現任的市長比前任的市長也好不了多少. (T)

11.0. 獎 **jiǎng** (1) a prize, a reward; (2) to encourage

得獎 **déjiǎng** get a reward, win a prize (VO)

過獎 **guòjiǎng** you flatter me

11.1. 你們猜我手裏有甚麽? 猜着了有獎. (T)

11.2. 今天晚上老張請客因為他跑馬得了獎了, 得了五十塊錢.

11.3. 你這麽年輕，有這麽好的學識. … 過獎過獎.（T）

12.0. 金 **jīn** (1) gold; (2) metal*; (3) Chin Dynasty (1115-1234); (4) (a surname)

金子 **jīnzi** gold

金錢 **jīnqián** money (W)

金文 **jīnwén** inscription on bronzes

金朝 **Jīn Cháo** Chin Dynasty (1115-1234)

白金 **báijīn** white gold, platinum

奬金 **jiǎngjīn** reward, prize

奬學金 **jiǎngxuéjīn** scholarship, fellowship

12.1. 我長這麽大没看見過金子.

12.2. 有人說「金錢萬能」. 你相信這句話嗎？（T）

12.3. 金文在學術上是很重要的.

12.4. 金朝是從公元一千一百一十五年到一千二百三十四年.

12.5. 張小姐的手表價錢很貴，是白金的.

12.6. 老金的工作能力好. 他今年一定得奬金.

12.7. 我那兩個孩子今年都得到奬學金了. 我不必給他們拿學費了.

12.8. 那個學校，考奬學金的人太多了，所以

我沒考上，不能得到獎學金. (T)

12.9. 想得獎學金總得用心念書啊. (T)

13.0. 務 **wù*** affair, business

教務 **jiàowù** school matters

教務長 **jiàowuzhǎng** dean

教務處 **jiàowuchù** dean's office

職務 **zhíwù** post, function, duty

事務 **shìwu** (non-teaching) task, work, business

特務 **tèwu** secret agent, secret service

公務 **gōngwu** public affairs, public service

公務員 **gōngwuyuán** government worker

任務 **rènwu** duty, mission, task, assignment

13.1. 昨天下課以後，教務長和教職員在教務處開會. 聽説談的都是關於教務這一方面的問題.

13.2. 特務的任務是給政府做一種特別的公務.

13.3. 我是一個公務員，我的職務是事務方面的.

14.0. 系 **xì*** (1) a system; (2) a college department

系主任 **xì zhǔrèn** department chairman

學系 **xuéxì** course, department (in college)

本系 **běnxì** this department

全系 **quánxì** the entire department

院系 **yuàn-xì** division and department

14.1. 我們歷史系的系主任是最有名的史學家.

14.2. 你們學校有多少院系？…我們有三院二十幾個學系.

14.3. 別的系我不知道，我們本系全系還不到六十人呢.

15.0. 室 **shì,shǐ*** a room

課室 **kèshǐ** classroom (now used less often than the next item)

教室 **jiàoshǐ** classroom

會客室 **huìkèshǐ** reception room

錄音室 **lùyīnshǐ** recording laboratory, language lab

15.1. 我們學校除了課室以外，還有錄音室跟會客室.

15.2. 我們平常考試都是在教室裏頭舉行的.

16.0. 物 **wù*** thing, object, article

物理 **wùlǐ** physics

物理學 **wùlǐxué** physics (as a school subject)

物理學家 **wùlǐxuéjiā** physicist

物價 **wùjià** commodity prices, prices of goods

生物(學) **shēngwù(xué)** biology

人物 **rénwu** (1) a personage, a person of standing; (2) personal

古物 **gǔwù** (1) ancient object; (2) relic, antiques

16.1. 你將來念生物學還是念物理學？

16.2. 去年那個得獎的物理學家叫甚麽名字？

16.3. 這裏物價很高，生活很不容易.

16.4. 現在李良也是個大人物了.

16.5. 我對物理學很有興趣，我將來一定念物理.

16.6. 王教授本來是物理學家，現在又考起古來了.(T)

16.7. 我們政府不讓把古物賣到外國去.(T)

17.0. 工會 **gōnghuì** labor union

總工會 **zǒng gōnghuì** general labor union, central labor council

17.1. 火車工人最近組織了一個工會.

17.2. 今天的工人大會在總工會開.(T)

18.0. 信用 **xìnyong** trust, credit (N)

信任 **xìnren** trust (V)

18.1. 任良總是很有信用的，所以大家都信任他.

19.0. 理學院 **lǐxuéyuàn** college of science (other than engineering)

工學院 **gōngxuéyuàn** college of engineering, engineering school

理工學院 **lǐgōngxuéyuàn** college of science and engineering, technological institute

麻省理工學院 **Máshěng Lǐgōngxuéyuàn** Massachusetts Institute of Technology, MIT

19.1. 我們學校有理學院，沒有工學院.

19.2. 我們學校正在計劃成立理工學院.

19.3. 那個孩子很有天才. 高中還沒畢業呢，就到麻省理工學院念物理去了.

20.0. 跟N(要)好 **gēn N (yào) hǎo** be friends with N

20.1. 你跟湯先生是要好的朋友，那件事情相信湯先生一定幫你的忙.

20.2. 我才發現老李跟張小姐很好. 昨天老李給張小姐打電話，談了有兩個鐘頭.

21.0. 大人 **dàrén** (1) an adult, a grown-up (2) (your) excellency, (his) excellency

21.1. 我那個男孩子昨天把人家的孩子給打了. 我對人家大人說了半天的好話，這件事情才算完了.

21.2. 我現在給我父親寫信，還是寫「父親大人」.

22.0. 本題 **běntí** this topic, today's topic, the topic in question

22.1. 我們談了半天還沒談到本題呢.

23.0. 一頭(兒)V_1一頭(兒)V_2 **yìtóu(r) V_1, yìtóu(r) V_2** V_2 while V_1

23.1. 我父親昨天和我在路上一頭兒走着一頭兒對我說："你都三十六了還不定親嗎？"

24.0. 公正 **gōngzhèng** just, impartial, fair, equitable

24.1. 人做事要公正，不論對於甚麽事情都要公平處理.

25.0. 本着 **běnzhe** (1) accord with; (2) according to, in accordance with

25.1. 他說他一生作事都是本着良心去作.

26.0. 家 **jiā** (measure for homes, families, stores, etc.)

本錢 **běnqián** capital

26.1. 張大文在一家書店工作. 因為工錢少，想作小買賣，又沒本錢. (T)

26.2. 那家人家，父親兒子都是當公務員的. (T)

27.0. 文學院 **wénxuéyuàn** college of liberal arts

27.1. 我們文學院的院長是程良，程教授. (T)

28.0. 看(N的)樣子 **kàn (Nde) yàngzi** from appearances (of N)

28.1. 他實在多大了我不清楚. 看樣子好像不到三十歲.

29.0. 實驗 **shíyàn** experiment (N/V)

實驗室 **shíyànshì** laboratory

29.1. 我在實驗室作實驗的時候，不小心把一

個杯子給打了.(T)

Checklist

1. 倒
   倒不如
   倒(是)
   倒茶
   倒車
   倒過來
   開倒車
   倒像
   打倒
2. 育
   生育
   教育
   教育部
   教育部長
3. 濟
   經濟
   經濟學
   計劃經濟
   濟南(府)
4. 盡
   盡力
   盡心
   盡意(的)
   盡職
   盡是
   盡可能(的)
   用盡
5. 細
   細想
   細說
   細問
   細心
   細情
6. 詳
   詳細
7. 良
   良心
8. 係
   關係
   沒關係
   因為A的關係
   N_1對/跟N_2的關係
9. 總
   總共
   總不
   總是
   總要
   總得
   總結
   總會
   總理
   總名
   總有
   總算
   總計
   總數
   總機關
   總代表
   總經理
   總代理
10. 任
    任用
    任意(的)
    任期
    任滿
    主任
    上任
    接任
    現任
    前任
11. 獎
    得獎
    過獎
12. 金
    金子
    金錢
    金文
    金朝
    白金
    獎金
    獎學金
13. 務
    教務
    教務長
    教務處
    職務
    事務
    特務
    公務
    公務員

任務

14. 系

系主任

學系

本系

全系

院系

15. 室

課室

教室

會客室

錄音室

16. 物

物理

物理學

物理學家

物價

生物(學)

人物

古物

17. 工會

總工會

18. 信用

信任

19. 理學院

工學院

理工學院

麻省理工學院

20. 跟N(要)好

21. 大人

22. 本題

23. 一頭(兒)V_1一頭(兒)V_2

24. 公正

25. 本着

26. 家

本錢

27. 文學院

28. 看樣子

29. 實驗

實驗室

Exercise 1. Excerpts from Actual Publications

The following excerpts are taken from Metamorphosis, by Cáo Yú, a play about wartime China.

1. 我不怪你, 我怕…全國的公正國民要怪你的.

2. 公路是不好走的, 天上有日本的飛機.

3. 馬先生, 你飯可以不吃麽? 水可以不喝麽?

4．不過，在我離開以前，我一定要把離開此地的原因…說清楚．… 好，我們再見．(走)

5．你們怕她，我不怕她．你…跟我找房子，今天不是我走，就是她走．

6．「我們要走了…」
「上哪兒？」
「華北——山西」．
「走那麽遠？」

7．你們大夫只懂得開刀．… 不明白我們…的難處．

8．你母親從早上工作到現在，還没有吃午飯呢．回頭他來，你最好——

9．「媽，你不吃一點東西？」
「我現在吃不下」．
「可是—…你不喝杯水？」
「好…這次你一定到山西去了麽？…(放下水杯)你為甚麽不早些來看我？」
「我…簡直没有一點工夫…」

「我上次給你的錢，你還有多少？」
「還有——」
「問你還有多少？」
(說不出來)「我，我——」
「又都送了人了吧？」
「沒有.」
「那麼——」
「這次沒有.」

10.「你覺得我們這個國家真沒有希望了麼？」
「當然不！」

11. 謝謝你，老先生，這次你幫了我很多忙.
…兩分鐘的工夫，你做了我們在此地四
個月的事情！

12. 我們老百姓真好，你幫他一次，他謝你
十次.

13.「你接到了我的信了麼？」
「看見了.我以為你等不了，早回家了.」
「沒見着你，我怎麼能够回去呢？你老多
了，我簡直不認識你了.」

14. 「他也要找事？」
「年青人總得做事…」
「好的很，他要多少錢一個月？」
「我看八十塊錢一個月就差不多了.」
「他要的倒不多…」
「人家告訴我，你手裏一個月出進幾百萬！」

15. 「有一個人要會您.」
「誰？」
「馬…」
「讓他快走，我不見這種人！」
「不，不，他說這次是，是想求您看看病．…」
「那麽——就請他進來吧.」

16. 我要從頭說起，實在太多；不從頭說起，怕您…不明白.

17. 「您覺得我，我老了麽？…」
「你有多大歲數？」
「不小了，五十四了.」

「那你還是我的老弟，我比你大六歲.」

「甚麽，您已經六十了！」

「我覺得我很年青呢！」

「是，您是看不出來.…」

「你聽：人永遠不會老，只要你自己不覺得老，懂麽？（笑出來）

「懂！懂！」

18. 你們回去吧，病人開刀.

19. 現在已經有完全好的希望了.

20. 這幾分鐘，我覺得比一年還要長.

Exercise 2. Dialogues

1. 金：任先生，我真為你高興．你兒子真有天才．聽說這次考試又考第一．

任：過獎過獎．他倒是很用功．

金：他在工學院一定得到了獎學金了．

任：是的．這個孩子從念中學起，一直的都得獎學金．

金：他念那一系？

任：念物理.

金：這樣好孩子真難得.

2. 程：昨天我從實驗室作完了實驗出來的時候，我看見老張和湯小姐在會客室呢.

許：老張跟湯小姐很好，你不知道嗎？

程：我不知道. 我今天是頭一次看見他們兩個人在一塊兒.

許：他們兩個人沒有一天不見面的. 要是不見面哪，一打電話總得打兩個鐘頭. 雖然他們的感情很好，可是看樣子他們兩個人結婚的希望不大.

程：為甚麽？

許：因為湯小姐的父母不贊成.

程：他父母為甚麽不贊成？

許：因為老張是學美術的. 他父母喜歡念物理、化學或是念工科的.

程：其實老張從前在理工學院書念的不錯，不知道為甚麽他又去學美術去了.

許：這是各人的興趣.

3. 樂：物價越來越高. 我們當公務員的每月拿這點兒錢簡直不够生活的.

畢：你比我還好啊. 你太太在教育部作事，而且你們又沒有孩子. 你看我一家六口，我內人不識字，不能作事，所以每月總是不够用.

樂：我比你好不了多少. 雖然是兩個人工作，一個月總共也拿不到五百塊錢，家裏還得用個老媽子，她等於沒作事. 要是有了孩子生活還不如你哪.

畢：當公務員真沒意思，想有錢總得去作買賣去.

樂：作買賣總要有本錢. 要是給人家作，就算是當了總經理，跟當公務員也沒甚麽兩樣.

畢：我想起來了. 我聽說英國有一家賣酒的，要在此地找總代理. 我們兩個人組織起來，作他們的代理好不好？

樂：好啊．我認識那家的總代表．那位英國老先生很好．明天我們和他談談去．這是没本錢的生意．

4．高：美英，這一個星期賣出去的書總共有多少本？

美：總計起來大概是四百三十五本．

高：錢的總數是多少？

美：我没算．

高：你每天到這兒，第一件事應該把賣書的錢總結一次，要是每天有一個總數，一個星期的，很容易的就算出來了．你這個孩子真不盡職．

美：我每天盡心盡意的，您怎麽還説我不盡職？

高：我跟你説笑話兒呢．你一頭兒念書一頭兒還幫助我作事，很不容易．別生氣．我和你開玩笑呢．有你這麽一個好女兒，我還不滿足嗎？

5．謝：你看小金多麽没信用．

費：怎麽了？

謝：他昨天讓我在理學院門口兒等着他，一塊兒到教務處去．我等了他兩個鐘頭，他也沒去．

費：他盡是這樣兒．有一次他和我說好了，下午六點鐘我在一個飯館兒等着他．結果他沒去．原來他去教他女朋友生物去了．到他女朋友那兒去也沒關係，可是應該給我往飯館兒打個電話呀！

6．萬：老方你現在有工夫嗎？我和你說幾句話．

方：有工夫．甚麼事啊？

萬：我們事務主任要走了．別人來當主任，我這個職務不會太長了．所以我得先找工作，求你給我在別處注意注意．

方：好的．我一定盡力給你想法子．我想起來了，前幾天我們教務長說過，現在教務這一方面，事太多人不够用，要加一個人，一會兒他來了我和他説説看.

萬： 那好極了. 要是成功了，我好好兒的謝謝你.

方： 你跟我的關係別説這個.

7. 華： 這個大房子是政府機關嗎？

史： 這是一個特務機關.

華： 特務機關不是在南京嗎？

史： 南京是總機關.

華： 特務的任務都是甚麽？

史： 我就知道他們是為政府作一種特別的工作. 作甚麽，我知道的不很詳細.

8. 邊： 文育才，我高中快畢業了，快要考大學了. 關於大學的組織我不大清楚，請你給我説一説.

文： 大學的組織是這樣兒. 一個大學最少有三院，每一院裏分幾個學系. 比如文學院有國文系、歷史系、語言學系. 理學院吧，有物理學系、生物系、化學系. 説了半天，你將來要考那一系呀？

邊：我想念物理．你説我考那個大學好？

文：遠東大學的理學院很好．物理系的系主任是現在很有名的物理學家．上次的物理學獎金他就得獎了．

邊：是啊！你説我考遠大考得上嗎？

文：考獎學金當然很難．我不敢説．如果你不考獎學金，我相信你一定考得上．

9. 許：老金，你近來怎麽樣？忙吧？

金：很忙．因為王縣長的任期已經滿了，天天忙着處理公務．

許：是啊．他是那年上任的？任期是幾年？

金：任期三年．

許：是誰接任縣長呢？

金：張達本接任．

許：張達本不是前任縣長的兒子嗎？

金：是啊．

許：他不是學教育的嗎？

金：原來是學教育的，後來又念政治去了.

許：他當縣長，我看也是因為他父親的關係.

金：那倒不是．張達本這個人倒是很有本事的，人也聰明．在政治系的時候，書念的很好．畢業的時候，全系二十二個人他考第一.

10. 畢：昨天我在路上遇見金良了．他說明年他到麻省理工學院念書去.

包：我也聽說了．不知道是不是得到了獎學金？

畢：因為在路上沒機會多說話，他也沒細說，我也沒細問．他說星期六來找我們，再細細的告訴我們.

包：他在這兒有獎學金．我相信他到麻省去也是一樣.

11. 邊：昨天我看見方先生了．他說讓我給他想法子在別處找工作.

簡：他在市政府很多年了，怎麼不想作

了呢？

邊：他說現任這位市長，不論作甚麽事從來不細想，任意去作，而且任用他自己人．市政府裏的職員，盡是他的朋友．對人一點兒也不公正．

簡：我也聽別人說過，他最信任的那位張主任就是跟他要好的朋友．

邊：其實那個主任應該讓方先生作．方先生經驗够，而且工作能力又好．

簡：這個年代作事，主要的是關係，次要的才是本事．

邊：是啊．這位市長就是以前總理的好朋友．

12. 金：聽說教育部長要作我們的校長了．

許：是．我也聽說了．我們現在的校長任滿了就出國，到外國去研究經濟學．

金：他怎麽不去研究教育呢？

許：我們校長不是學教育的，他是學經濟的．

金：說不定將來校長回國以後，就是個大人物了.

許：校長關係很多. 他回來一定有好事情作的.

13. 學生：先生，計劃經濟跟經濟計劃一樣嗎？

先生：不一樣. 有的國家已經實行計劃經濟了. 它是一種經濟制度. 你們對經濟問題有興趣的同學，下課以後，你們到錄音室去聽聽經濟系的錄音帶，講的很詳細.

學生：我們前幾天在教室聽過一次，是經濟系王教授講演的錄音帶. 我們聽不懂.

先生：王教授是山東濟南人，所以他的話你們不大懂. 不過你們要是細心聽，總會聽出來.

學生：先生，「打倒」的「倒」是第三聲嗎？

先生：對了.

學生：「倒車」的「倒」跟「把車倒過來」的

「倒」都是第四聲了，是不是？

先生：是的.

學生：先生，「關係」的「係」有時候也當「是」字用嗎？

先生：是．我說個例子："張教授係中山大學文學院院長."

學生：「教室」跟「課室」是不是一個意思？

先生：是一個意思，可是「教室」這個詞兒比較常用.

14. 文：聽說中國人從前如果結了婚，女人不生育就有離婚的可能.

連：是．中國人以前的思想是，結婚為的是生孩子．你聽我告訴你我父母的故事．當初我父親和母親結了婚三年了，我母親也沒生孩子．家裏的別人就說了，這個女人不會生育了，就讓我父親跟我母親離婚．可是我父親跟我母親的感情好，所以沒離婚．後來沒有好久就生了我.

15. 簡：李太太，聽說孔太太近來跟你有了意見.

李：我正想到你那兒,和你説這件事呢.

簡：甚麽原因呢？

李：上星期六，他們大文來找我們少奇玩兒來了．玩兒着玩兒着，不知為了甚麽兩個孩子打起來了．結果我那個孩子把大文給打倒了．大文起來就跑回家去了．我馬上也到了孔家説這件事．孔先生、孔太太很不高興.

簡：為了小孩子大人不要有意見.

李：我也是這麽想啊.

簡：也許過些日子，把這件事就忘了.

李：我是盡可能的想法子，不要為了這件事情大人們不和氣.

簡：這麽多年的朋友了，總有一天他們會跟你們和好了的.

李：我希望是這樣.

16. 湯：甚麽叫二十四史？

麻：就是二十四個朝代的歷史．比如漢書、後漢書，還有金朝的金史和元史、明史等等的．總名就叫作二十四史．

湯：二十四史裏沒有清史嗎？

麻：没有．因為二十四史是清初編定的．

17. 費：老張，我這幾天太累了．

張：你雖然累點兒，總算把王會長的忙幫了，工會也組織成了．

費：成了是成了，可是還有很多別的問題．

張：為了組織工會，老王自己也用盡了力．我不明白為甚麽總會原來不許可組織地方工會呢？

費：其實這裏有好幾千工人，應該有地方工會．開始為甚麽不讓組織，細情我們不知道．

18. 邊：萬思聰來了請坐．王媽！倒茶！我們下星期又開學了．

萬：可不是．日子過的真快，兩個星期

很快就過去了．聽説從這學期起，我們學校所有的院系，每次小考都八十分以上就不必參加大考了．

邊：我們本系裏多數是八十分以上的．

19\. 畢：我好久没看見王教授了．

應：他現在不出門兒，在家研究金文呢．

畢：王教授開倒車呢．

應：這句話我不懂．

畢：王教授本來是學科學的．又考起古來了．這不是開倒車嗎？

應：王教授長的樣子倒像個考古學家．他應該研究古文化．

20\. 田：昨天你們看的電影兒有意思嗎？

史：没意思．倒不如在家談談了．你没出去嗎？

田：没有．昨天老王來了．

史：他來找你一定有事了？

田：没事．來找我談天兒來了．跟他在一塊兒談天兒真没意思．先説人得有朋友，朋友是金錢買不到的．又說人作事得本着良心. 還說聽說政府把古物要送到外國去了. 談天兒說這個多麽沒意思.

21\. 李: 張子奇來了.

張: 李教授您好.

李: 好. 田媽倒茶來!

張: 您別客氣.

李: 沒別的. 茶得喝一杯呀. 論文寫多少了?

張: 沒寫多少. 我寫了一點兒自己看看簡直的離開本題了.

李: 你才寫了一點兒不見得是離開本題了.

張: 李教授, 第二十五期的經濟學報您收到了沒有? 我想借來看一看.

李: 可以. 我昨天收到的.

張: 您看了嗎?

李: 看過了. 你拿去不必還我了. 這期有謝大為寫的關於白金的論文很有看的必要.

張：我就是要看他寫的那個論文．謝大為先生老是寫關於金子的問題．第二十四期的經濟學報，他寫的是金子出口問題．

李：對了．

22. 王：張太太，張先生做甚麼事啊？

張：他是一個公務員，在教育部作事．王先生呢？

王：他教書．在第一中學教歷史．

張：作教員比當公務員大概還好一點兒．你看我那個兒子中學快畢業了，將來就沒法子念大學．

王：我那個孩子得了獎學金．要不然也上不了大學．

Exercise 3. Narratives

1. 有一個國家經濟情形很不好．他們政府用盡了法子，經濟情形還是不好．後來他們政府實行計劃經濟，經濟情形就越來越好了．

2. 母親對孩子說:“如果我們家裏有客人來，我們應當給客人倒茶. 如果我們到了別人的家裏，人家要是給我們倒茶來，我們應該說「謝謝.」”

3. 有一個人是研究教育的. 他對現在的教育很不滿意，有很多意見，常在報紙上發表. 有一次他在報紙上說:“今日教育，係在開倒車.”有一天，他遇見了教育部長，教育部長說:“你在報紙上發表的意見我都看過了. 都很好，很有見解. 歡迎你能到教育部來詳細的談談. 希望能聽到你更多更好的意見.”

4. 有一個人許久沒有工作了. 他各處求人找工作，也沒找到. 他說:“從前我有工作的時候，不知道好好兒地作，作甚麽事也不認真，都是任意的作，所以人家不用我了. 此後如果再有工作，我決定盡心盡意努力去作.”他說過這話以後沒有多久，就找到了工作. 可是他有了工作就忘了他以前說過的話，又不認真工作，人家又不用他了．有人告訴他：“你有了工作總是不認真去作．到了沒有工作，才想起來應當好好的作．你這樣作法，永久不會有長久工作的．”

5. 濟南是山東省一個有名的城市．從前叫濟南府．這個地方的人所說的話是山東話．山東話和北京話不同，可是濟南人能聽懂北京話，北京人也能聽懂濟南人所說的話，因為他們說的都是北方話．甚麽叫北方話呢？北方話是中國北方像山東、山西、河南、河北…還有北京各地方話的總名．

6. 今天講經濟學的時候，先生講「生育和經濟的關係」．先生說：「不論是國家方面，或者是家庭方面，如果是生育的太多了，人口也一定太多了，在經濟上總要發生問題的．”

7. 我不會開車．我的女兒會開車．我讓她教我開車．她告訴我學開車很容易，就是倒車相當的難，一定要回過頭來看．有時候看不清楚，就容易出事了．

8．有一個有錢的人，他本來不認識字，但是他不樂意人家知道他不認識字．有一天，他和一個人對面坐着．他手裏拿着一張報，好像是在看報．這時候又有一個人來，看見他拿的那張報紙是倒過來拿着呢．這個人說：“你怎麽把報紙倒過來看呢？他說：“我剛看完，現在要給坐在我對面的人看呢．”

9．我弟弟要去考大學．他本來想考理工學院的工程學系．我告訴他：“遠東大學的工學院相當的好，不但功課認真，而且在學術研究方面和美國的麻省理工學院很有關係．你應當去考這個工學院．”弟弟說：“好．我就去考這個工學院．”

10．高子元是一個大學的教務長．有一天，有一個外國人跟他談到中國大學的制度和組織．他說：“中國的大學制度必得有三個或者是三個以上的學院,才能叫做大學. 如果只有一兩個學院,就不能叫大學,只能叫學院. 比方說研究物理、化學的就叫理學院. 研究文學的就叫文學院. 關於大學裏的組織,多半分為教務和事務兩大部分. 教務處是最主要的部分."

11. 王縣長的任期就要滿了. 他的計劃是任滿以後再也不想當縣長了. 他說:"我還記得我才上任的時候,前任的包縣長對我說:「縣長這個職務太麻煩了. 你做了以後總會知道的.」當時我還有一點兒不信. 我說:「縣長是公務員,所做的事都是公務. 各種公務都有一定的範圍,只要盡力去做就可以盡職,怎能說太麻煩呢?」等到我接任以後沒有多久,我才知道前任包縣長說的話是對的. 現在我雖然還是一個現任縣長,可是任期只有幾個月了. 此後我決定不再當縣長了."

12. 有人問我,金文是不是金朝的文字. 我說:"不是的,「金文」的「金」字不是朝代的名字.

13. 許式言本來在大學念生物學, 後來他不念生物學念物理學了. 他說, 他們物理系全系總共十二個學生,多半有獎學金. 他們每天在課室的時間少, 在實驗室的時間多. 他們的系主任是一位物理學家. 他也常在實驗室裏一頭兒幫學生作實驗一頭兒給學生講解. 系主任說, 研究物理不要常在教室, 要常在實驗室.

14. 王良才對別人說他在政府裏作事, 看他的樣子地位很高. 他和社會上有名的人物常有來往, 他對朋友也很有信用, 人們都很信任他. 他是一個很細心的人, 遇見甚麽事情都要細問,希望別人細說, 他要知道細情. 有人說,他是做特務的, 雖然不知道他的任務, 可是他是特務總機關裏的一個主任. 也有人說, 他不是做特務的, 他和特務機關沒關係. 因為他遇見事情, 喜歡細細的問, 倒像一個特務，所以有人說他是做特務的.

15. 高學範是工人裏的優秀分子. 他參加了當地的工會. 有一次，當地工會接到總工會來信說，要和政府談談工錢和獎金的問題，請各地工會舉代表先到總工會開會. 當地工會就舉高學範做代表，到總工會去開會. 在開會的時候，高學範說明了工錢和獎金對工人家庭生活的關係，又說明了工錢和獎金對社會經濟的關係. 他說應該本着良心作公正的主張. 當時很多代表贊成他的說法. 又因為他有這種說法的關係，就舉他做總代表跟政府去談. 談的結果總算把問題解決了. 工人和政府都很滿意. 所以大家都說高學範實在是工人裏的一個優秀分子.

16. 有一位大學的校長是有名的學者. 這個大學的院系很多，總共有七個學院三十多個學系. 他對每個學系都很注意，可是有人說他對國文系、歷史系、政治系特別注意. 有一次我跟他打電話提到了這個問題．我問他：“為甚麼特別注意這幾系呢？”他說：“只要是大學範圍以內的院系，我都注意，怎麼能只注重那幾系呢？”

17. 孔良是買賣人，因為他的本錢多，他的生意很發達．他是總經理，他想在當地做日本汽車的總代理．可是他想到當地買賣汽車的情況，他感覺到很多人喜歡買美國汽車．他說：“要做日本汽車的總代理，倒不如做美國汽車的總代理了．”後來他就做了美國汽車的總代理．

18. 中國在五四時期有的人主張用白話文，打倒文言文．也有人主張還用文言文，非打倒白話文不可．後來在事實上倒是誰打倒了誰呢．有人說，誰也沒打倒誰．

19. 白先生是一個外國人．他有一個中國朋友姓高，很喜歡古物，所以家裏有很多古代的東西．有一天白先生到高先生家裏去，在高先生的會客室裏看見一張畫兒．白先生以為是古畫兒呢．他就問高先生：“這是古畫兒嗎？”高先生說：“不是．是我女兒畫的．”白先生說：“畫的太好了，我以為是古畫兒呢．”高先生說：“你真過奬了．”

20. 毛太太對毛先生說：“現在的物價越來越貴，我們每天要盡可能的少用錢了．”毛先生說：“我們兩個大人錢倒是可以少用一點兒，孩子們用錢都是非用不可的．沒法子少用呀．”

21. 有人告訴我，常聽錄音是復習國語最好的法子．有一天我要復習國語，想到錄音室去聽聽錄音．可是我忘記了到錄音室應該從那條路走．有人告訴我，從圖書館往右邊走，就看見錄音室了．我說：“我連圖書館也找不着啊．”後來他又給我詳細的講，我才找到了．

22. 温先生有一個兒子是一個好學生，在學校考試盡是考第一，還時常得奬．温先生說：“這個孩子才上學的時候，本來不知道用功，我用盡了方法，他還是不用功．我就和學校的先生研究．學校的先生說：「你天天盡是叫孩子用功，他不一定就知道用功．要想孩子能用功，最好先叫孩子對念書發生興趣．有了興趣以後，他自然就用功了．怎樣就發生興趣了呢？這要從學校和家庭兩方面想法子．」我說：「好．你這個方法很好．我們就這樣做吧．」後來這個孩子果然用功了，成了一個好學生．”

23. 有一個人，從前做過總理．他說：“做總理最難的問題是用人．政府用人當然是要任用人才．可是有的人總是說的很好，到了做的時候就不好了．還有一種人他盡是說不去做．這兩種人都只是會說的人．如果用的盡是這樣的人，工作簡直沒法子作好了．”

24. 有人問我白金有甚麼用？我說：“我就知道白金的價錢很貴，有甚麼用處我就不大清楚了．”他說：“聽說很多女人都喜歡有白金的東西，是不是真的呢？”我說：“總得有錢的女人才能有金子的東西呀.”

25. 我們系主任對我們本系的同學都很好. 有一次要考試了，大家就對系主任說：“這次的功課太多了，多半要考不好. 請您說說考的範圍.”他說：“你們要多注意最近發明的東西. 這次我們就考一道題.”大家說：“請你再詳細講一講.”他說：“我差不多把本題都告訴你們了，你們還不知足嗎？”

26. 張先生、李先生都是王小姐的好朋友. 有人問王小姐：“你跟李先生好呢，還是跟張先生好？”王小姐說：“等我細想一想.”她想了一會兒說：“他們兩個人對我都很好. 我對他們兩個人也一樣的都很好.”

27. 我有一個朋友在火車站做賣票員. 有一天，他來找我，希望我給他在一家書店裏介紹工作. 我說：“你做賣票員已經一年了．一個月的工錢總有二三百塊錢．書店裏的職員，每月的工錢只有一百多塊錢，比較賣票員少多了．你為甚麽要在書店找工作呢？”他說：“在金錢上雖然比較少，可是在知識上，一定能學的多，因為在書店裏能有機會看書呀．所以我要在書店裏找工作．”

28. 田小姐從前是跟我妹妹很要好的同學．前幾天從北京來，昨天妹妹打電話給她，說我們星期天早上八九點鐘去看她．她說她要先到我們家裏來拜訪，叫我們在家裏等她．我們等到九點多鐘她才來．她剛一進門就說：“我來晚了，因為路上車多，我坐的車走的很慢．我真想下了車，自己走來，也許比車走的還快呢．”

29. 校長和幾位教漢語的先生開會，研究漢語教學問題．有人說，應當先從說話學起，有人主張應當學習漢字．大家研究很久，也沒有結論．校長說：“關於這個問題，我們今天研究的已經很詳細了．

我們把今天的談話作一個總結，是一頭兒學說話，一頭兒學漢字.”

30. 我在外國念書已經兩年了. 在這兩年裏，家裏給我的錢總計不到五百塊錢. 為甚麼給我這麼少呢？因為我除了念書以外還去工作. 工錢的總數就有一千多塊錢.

Exercise 4. Illustrative Sentences (English)

1.2. Why don't you go pour me some tea as I asked you to? Are you going to pour it or not [after all]?

1.3. Wang Ma, some guests have come. Come pour the tea (and hand it around).

1.4. Xu has gone to back up the car. After he's backed it up he'll come in.

1.6. Actually it's I who am helping him, though it seems on the contrary as if I'm asking his help.

3.4. At the time of the meeting yesterday the provincial governor said: "The livelihood of the people can be raised only if the economy [of society] is expanded."

3.5. That essay he's written has some penetrating views [lit. very much has views] on the current economic situation.

4.1. I expended a great deal of effort before I succeeded in helping him.

4.2. I'm helping you all I can. I'm doing all possible to think of a way (to take care of your problem).

4.4. How come his money is all used up again?… (Isn't that so!) It's always like this with him.

4.5. He just talks, but doesn't do (what he says he will).

4.6. Your business is like mine, it's no different. I'll certainly do all I can to think of a way for it to succeed.

5.2. Before speaking [to people] one should think carefully [and then speak].

5.3. Please tell me [in detail] the detailed situation regarding the course of that matter.

5.5. Please look at it again carefully.

5.6. The business of buying and selling houses is not at all easy. One must think through everything in the minutest detail before making a decision.

7.1. Whether in doing things or in one's relationship to people, one should always act in good conscience [lit. have conscience].

8.1. I read in the Canton Daily yesterday: "That piece of land was formerly Chinese territory."

8.6. Since we're so close [lit. your relationship with me] don't stand on ceremony [lit. talk polite talk].

9.1. The general agent for that car made a total reckoning of the cars sold this year. In all 1500 cars were sold.

9.5. No matter how busy you are, you must first total up [the total amount of] the money taken in today.

9.6. Sometimes we also call Sun Yatsen "The Premier" (of the Party).

10.5. The incumbent mayor can't be much better than the previous one.

11.1. Guess what I have in my hand. If you guess right you'll get a reward.

11.3. You're so young (and yet) have so much knowledge.... You flatter me.

12.2. Some people say "Money will do anything." Do you believe this?

12.8. There are too many people taking the scholarship exam at that school, so I didn't succeed in the exam and can't get a scholarship.

12.9. If you hope to get a scholarship you must study hard.

16.6. Professor Wang originally was a physicist. Now he's begun to do work in archaeology.

16.7. Our government does not permit antiques to be sold abroad.

17.2. Today's big workers' meeting will be held at the central labor council.

26.1. Zhang Dawen works in a bookstore. He would like to have a small business but lacks capital because his wages are low.

26.2. In that family, father and sons all are government workers.

27.1. The dean of our liberal arts college is Cheng Liang, Professor Cheng.

29.1. When I was doing an experiment in the laboratory, I was careless and broke a glass.

第十一課

1	2	3	4	5	6	7	8
凡	留	辦	根	據	修	合	均

9	10	11	12	13	14	15	16
醫	困	及	格	農	樓	博	士

1.0. 凡 **fán*** whatever, whoever, etc.

凡是 **fánshi** whatever, whoever, etc.

1.1. 凡是在那個大學畢業的，都能找到一個比較好的工作．

2.0. 留 **liú** (1) retain, keep; (2) leave (e.g. a message)

留住 **liúzhu** detain (RV)

留在 **N** (1) leave at N; (2) stay at N

留聲機 **liúshēngjī** phonograph

留下 **liúxia** put by

留學 **liúxué** study abroad (VO)

留學生 **liúxuéshēng** a student abroad, a returned student

留美 **liú Měi** study (abroad) in America

留英 **liú Yīng** study (abroad) in England

留法 **liú Fǎ** study (abroad) in France

留心 **liúxīn** be careful, pay attention, look out (VO)

留意 **liúyì** pay attention (to), take note (of)

留着 **liúzhe** put aside, leave

2.1. 我是一個留美的留學生. 我在美國留了五年學.

2.2. 他是留英的, 還是留法的?

2.3. 我那個留聲機留在張先生那兒了.

2.4. 他一定要走. 我怎麽留也留不住他. (T)

2.5. 弟弟, 媽出去的時候給你留下了五塊錢.

2.6. 你作實驗的時候, 千萬要留心.

2.7. 把那幾個包子留着給父親吃.

2.8. 要是那裏找教數學的, 請你給我留意. (T)

3.0. 辦 **bàn** manage, transact, carry out

辦到 **bàndào** accomplish

辦法 **bànfǎ** way to manage

辦好 **bànhǎo** do, manage, finish (a job) (RV)

辦公 **bàngōng** transact official business (VO)

辦公室 **bàngōngshǐ** office

辦公處 **bàngōngchù** office

辦公廳 **bàngōngtīng** office

辦事 **bànshì** manage an affair (VO)

辦事員 **bànshìyuán** clerk, office worker

辦事處 **bànshìchù** office

代辦 **dàibàn** (1) act in place of; (2) agent, agency; (3) chargé d'affaires

怎麽辦？ **zěnmo bàn？** (1) how manage？ (2) what can be done about it？

3.1. 你在那兒辦公？你的辦事處在那兒？

3.2. 我們教務處那幾個辦事員，工作真努力．每天天都黑了，他們才離開辦公處．

3.3. 我們先去辦事．把事情辦好再去吃飯．

3.4. 那件事情很難辦．你說怎麽辦？有辦法沒有？

3.5. 那個英國人的地位很高．他是英國代辦．

3.6. 那件事情你放心，我一定給你辦到．

3.7. 辦公室就是辦公廳．

3.8. 學校裏所有的事情，我都給他代辦了．

4.0. 根 **gēn** (1) root； (2) (measure for string, belts, sticks, etc.)

根本 **gēnběn** (1) foundation, basis； (2) fundamentally, originally, thoroughly, to start with； (3) fundamental, basic

(在)根本上 **(zài) gēnběnshang** in fundamentals, fundamental(ly), basic(ally), radical(ly)

4.1. 這根帶子是在路口兒東北角兒上那個市場買的．(T)

4.2. 昨天王老師出的那道數學題目，我們根本沒學過．

4.3. 那件事情很不容易解决，那是根本上的問題.

4.4. 他老說別人作事要科學化. 其實他自己作事根本不科學. (T)

5.0. 據 **jù*** (1) to hold as a base, to base; (2) basis; (3) evidence, proof; (4) according to

據說 **jùshuō** it is said, people say, according to (what they) say

據N說 **jù N shuō** according to what N says

據N看 **jù N kàn** from N's viewpoint, in N's opinion

收據 **shōujù** receipt

根據 **gēnju** (1) to base (on), according to; (2) basis

根據地 **gēnjudì** (military) base

有根據 **yǒu gēnju** (1) have a basis (for some idea); (2) well-supported

5.1. 據教務長說, 我們學校下學期的學生有二萬多人.

5.2. 你根據甚麽說的? 這種說法有根據没有?

5.3. 據我所知道的, 在那個學校念工程學是相當難. (T)

5.4. 據我看那個地方很重要, 可以說是他們的根據地. 他們不能隨便地就不要了. (T)

5.5. 據說老王辦事根本不行. 他收學費的時候, 時常忘了給人家寫收據.

6.0. 修 **xiū** (1) build (house, etc.); (2) repair; (3) self-improvement; (4) study, take (courses)

修理 **xiūlǐ** repair

修好 **xiūhǎo** fix, succeed in fixing (RV)

修業 **xiūyè** study at school (W)

修詞(學) **xiūcí (xué)** rhetoric

主修 **zhǔxiū** (1) a major (in reference to academic studies); (2) to major in

主修科 **zhǔxiūkē** a major (subject in college)

必修 **bìxiū** (1) require to study; (2) required

必修科 **bìxiūkē** required subject, compulsory subject

自修 **zìxiū** (1) to study on one's own; (2) scheduled study hour in school

6.1. 昨天我的車走在半路上不走了. 我修理了半天也沒修好. (T)

6.2. 我念大一, 念的是文科. 第一學期我念的是修詞學跟文字學.

6.3. 凡是在本校求學的, 不論主修那一科, 第一學年必修數學一年. (T)

6.4. 生物是我的主修科, 還修一門英文, 因為英文是必修科.

6.5. 在那個大學念書是學年制. 修業四年就可以畢業. (W)

6.6. 那個有名的學者, 他沒念過大學, 他是自修的.

6.7. 我們每天早上八點十分到九點鐘是自修的時間.

7.0. 合 **hé** (1) come together; (2) fit, suitable; (3) jointly

合編 **hébiān** (1) jointly write, write collaboratively; (2) (jointly) by (used on spines and title-pages of books after names of two or more authors)

合住 **hézhù** live together (in)

合買 **hémǎi** buy jointly

合用 **héyòng** (1) use jointly; (2) suited to use

合作 **hézuò** (1) cooperate; (2) cooperation

合作社 **hézuòshè** cooperative (store), Co-op

合作事業 **hézuò shìyè** cooperative enterprise

合意 **héyì** agreeable, in accord with one's wishes (VO)

合家 **héjiā** the whole family

合得來 **hédelái** able to get along together

合起來 **héqilai** (bring) all together, (put) together

合在一塊兒 **hézài yíkuàr** put together (in one place), unite

合理 **hélǐ** be fitting, in accordance with what's right

合力 **hélì** with united effort

同心合力 **tóngxīnhélì** united in thought and effort

結合 **jiéhé** (1) unite, combine, associate, marry; (2) union, combination, association

場合 **chǎnghé** occasion, circumstance

7.1. 這本大辭典, 我們兩個人合用, 因為是我們兩個人合買的.

7.2. 合作社是一種合作事業.

7.3. 要想一件事情成功，必得大家同心合力的去合作.

7.4. 像音樂會那種場合，我從來不喜歡去. (T)

7.5. 他們兩個人很合得來，在一塊兒合住了八年，從來沒發生過意見. (T)

7.6. 張先生和湯小姐，雖然感情很好，可是沒有結合的可能.

7.7. 這不是很合理的嗎？你合意就買，不合意就算了. (T)

7.8. 張先生和他的兒女，合家合起來合編了一本歷史小說.

7.9. 比如一個東西，你一個人拿不起來，大家把氣力合在一塊兒，合力去拿，一定拿的起來.

8.0. 均 **jūn*** uniform, even

平均 **píngjūn** (1) average, mean; (2) on the average; (3) equally

8.1. 五十塊錢四個人分，平均每人分多少？ (T)

8.2. 那個錄音機一個人買不起. 我們三個人

平均每人拿出多少錢來去買？(T)

9.0. 醫 **yī*** (1) medicine (as a science); (2) to treat; (3) medical

醫生 **yīsheng** physician, doctor

醫科 **yīkē** medical course

醫院 **yīyuàn** hospital, dispensary

醫學 **yīxué** science of medicine

醫學院 **yīxuéyuàn** medical school

名醫 **míngyī** a famous doctor

行醫 **xíngyī** to practice medicine

9.1. 這裏的醫生很少，平均每八千人才有一個醫生.

9.2. 學醫科很難. 你看每年考醫學院的學生沒有多少.

9.3. 醫學院的毛教授在這二十年裏教出不少最優秀的醫學人才. (T)

9.4. 張先生是研究醫學的. 他是一個名醫，在這裏行醫有四十多年了.

9.5. 一會兒我得到醫院去看朋友的病. (T)

9.6. 我弟弟在遠東大學醫學院學醫. (T)

10.0. 困 **kùn*** distress

困難 **kùnnán** (1) distress, quandary; (2) difficult, distressful

10.1. 那件事情很困難. 我已經盡了最大的努

力了，成功不成功很難說．

10.2. 我近來没有工作，所以生活非常困難．

11.0. 及 jí* (1) reach, attain; (2) together with, and (W)

來得及 láidejí able to arrive on time, can be in time (to) (RV)

以及 yǐjí and, as well as (W)

11.1. 王大為先生最近編寫了一本近十年來中國政治及經濟．

11.2. 要是坐四點鐘的火車，我三點半走，來得及來不及？

11.3. 我們學校教務處的工作相當認真．從校長以及職員，每天八點半以前都得到學校．(W)

12.0. 格 gé (1) frame, compartment; (2) category

格子 gézi grating, lattice, ruled square

格子紙 gézi zhǐ squared paper

格外 géwài exceptionally

合格 hègé be up to standard, qualified

及格 jígé (1) be up to standard, qualified; (2) pass an examination

人格(兒)réngé(r) character, personality

有人格(兒) yǒu réngé(r) be of good character

12.1. 寫大字，最好用帶格子的格子紙寫．

12.2. 張老師喜歡女學生．他對那些女同學格外地好.

12.3. 我考遠大没考上. 我甚麽都合格, 就是數學考的不及格, 所以没考上.

12.4. 雖然他没本事, 可是他的人格兒好.

12.5. 一個人, 最主要的是要有人格兒. (T)

13.0. 農 **nóng*** agriculture

農業 **nóngyè** agriculture

農業合作社 **nóngyè hézuòshè** agricultural cooperative

農工業 **nónggōngyè** agriculture and industry

農人 **nóngren** farmer, peasant

農民 **nóngmín** farmers, peasants

農田 **nóngtián** agricultural field, agricultural land

農學院 **nóngxuéyuàn** college of agriculture

13.1. 我們的農工業都不很發達. 我們農人跟工人應該對工業和農田加多努力.

13.2. 中國以前是一個農業國家. 人民們多數是農民.

13.3. 我們農學院自己要組織一個農業合作社.

14.0. 樓 **lóu** (1) building of two or more stories; (2) (used in names of restaurants and other buildings); (3) floor, story

樓上 **lóushàng** upstairs

樓下 **lóuxià** down stairs

酒樓 **jiǔlóu** restaurant (used mainly in South China)

茶樓 **chálóu** tea-house (used mainly in South China)

14.1. 在大華樓吃飯的，多一半兒是留學生. (T)

14.2. 我們家來了很多客人. 樓上樓下人都滿了. (T)

14.3. 酒樓就是飯館兒，是吃飯的. 茶樓是吃點心喝茶的地方.

14.4. 五年以前，這裏是一片土地，現在都是大樓了. (T)

15.0. 博 **bó*** (1) learned, well-read; (2) extensive, ample

博物院 **bówùyuàn** museum

博物館 **bówùguǎn** museum

地大物博 **dì-dà-wù-bó** large in territory and rich in natural products

15.1. 昨天我們五個人到博物館去看古物去了.

15.2. 我們學校從博物院借來了一個漢朝的酒杯，為的是讓我們參考.

15.3. 中國「地大物博」這句話一點兒也不假.

16.0. 士 **shì*** scholar

女士 **nǚshì** Miss

學士 **xuéshì** Bachelor of Arts, B.A.

博士 **bóshi** Ph.D., Doctor

博士論文 **bóshi lùnwén** Ph.D. thesis

念博士 **niàn bóshi** study for the Ph.D.

16.1. 田士達是一個外科的醫學博士. (T)

16.2. 王女士是遠大文學系畢業的. 是學士, 不是博士.

16.3. 費士達念博士的時候寫的博士論文, 對於現在的經濟很有見解.

16.4. 念博士和作學問是兩樣的. (T)

17.0. 學位 **xuéwèi** academic degree

一天到晚 **yìtiān dào wǎn** all day until late

沒有好久 **méi yǒu hǎo jiǔ** (1) before long; (2) not long after (used after a verbal expression)

17.1. 他一天到晚都是在寫論文, 所以他到研究院沒有好久就得了博士學位了.

18.0. 舉人 **jǔrén** (Ch'ing dynasty degree, about equal to M.A.)

18.1. 我們的文字學教授是清朝的舉人.

19.0. 要V_1不V_2 **yào V_1buV_2** will be unable to V_1V_2(RV)

19.1. 辦那件事情, 有很多困難. 我看一年以內要辦不完.

20.0. 算得(是) **suànde (shi)** be regarded as

就(有) **jiù (yǒu)** only have, have only

20.1. 他念中文算得是最快的了. 他到中國就一年, 說的那麼好.

21.0. 比得上 **bǐdeshàng** able to compare (favorably) with (RV)

21.1. 你雖然比不上他，也是最優秀的分子.

21.2. 許良念書雖然比不上張希達那麽好，可是他也得到奬學金了.(T)

22.0. 要件 **yàojiàn** important item

22.1. 這封信是要件. 你拿着它，在路上要多加小心.(T)

23.0. 你VS **nǐ VS** (see note at end of lesson)

手工業 **shǒugongyè** handicraft industry

23.1. 你説手工業現在是多麽的要緊哪!(T)

Checklist

1. 凡
凡是
2. 留
留住
留在N
留聲機
留下
留學
留學生
留美
留英
留法
留心
留意
留着
3. 辦
辦到
辦法
辦好
辦公
辦公室
辦公處
辦公廳
辦事
辦事員
辦事處
代辦
怎麽辦
4. 根
根本
(在)根本上
5. 據
據説
據N説
據N看
收據
根據
根據地
有根據
6. 修
修理
修好
修業
修詞(學)
主修
主修科
必修
必修科

自修

7. 合

合編

合住

合買

合用

合作

合作社

合作事業

合意

合家

合得來

合起來

合在一塊兒

合理

合力

同心合力

結合

場合

8. 均

平均

9. 醫

醫生

醫科

醫院

醫學

醫學院

名醫

行醫

10. 困

困難

11. 及

來得及

以及

12. 格

格子

格子紙

格外

合格

及格

人格(兒)

有人格(兒)

13. 農

農業

農業合作社

農工業

農人

農民

農田

農學院

14. 樓

樓上

樓下

酒樓

茶樓

15. 博

博物館

博物院

地大物博

16. 士

女士

學士

博士

博士論文

念博士

17. 學位

一天到晚

沒有好久

18. 舉人

19. 要 R 不 V

20. 算得(是)

就(有)

21. 比得上

22. 要件

23. 你 V S

手工業

Exercise 1. Excerpts from Actual Publications

The following excerpts are taken from Volume I of the collected works of Hú Shì (Hu Shih). They occur in his early essays advocating literary reform.

1. 一，要有話說，方才說話．…

二，有甚麽話，說甚麽話；話怎麽說，

就怎麽說.…

三, 要說我自己的話,別說別人的話.…

四, 是甚麽時代的人,說甚麽時代的話.

2. 有了國語的文學,方才可有文學的國語.有了文學的國語, 我們的國語才可算得真正國語. 國語沒有文學,… 便不能發達.

3. 上文所說「國語的文學, 文學的國語」…是我們的根本主張.

4. 我所主張的「文學的國語」…是中國今日…的白話. 這種國語的語法文法, 全用白話的語法文法.

5. 我們希望—注意, 我們現在不過希望—將來能有一種拼音的文字, 把我們所用的國語拼成字母的語言.

6. 文學有三個要件: 第一要明白清楚, 第二要有力…, 第三要美.

7. 我是沒有中學國文教授的經驗的, 雖然做過兩年中學學生, 但是那是十幾年前的經驗.

8. 這種研究法叫做「歷史的研究法」. 為甚麽要用歷史的研究法呢?

9. 後來語言和文字分開.

10. 有人說, 思想是一件事, 文學又是一件事.

11. 我們中國人學英文, 和英國、美國的小孩子學英文, 是兩樣的.

12. 工作的時間太多, — 每人七時以上, 十時以下, —只有工作的時間, 沒有做學問的機會.

Exercise 2. Dialogues

1. 許: 你最近看見張一凡了嗎?
湯: 上星期我到醫學院去, 看見他了.
許: 他甚麽時候到美國去?
湯: 他不是到美國去, 他是到英國去.
許: 現在多數都是到美國去留學, 他為甚麽到英國去呢?

湯：因為他父親是個老留學生，是留英的，所以贊成他兒子到英國去．

許：聽說他母親是留法的．

湯：是．他母親當初在法國一個大學裏學畫兒．

許：怪不得他母親畫的那麽好呢．有一次一凡帶我到他父親的辦公室，看見一張畫兒，他說是他父親和他母親兩個人合畫的．畫的好極了．據一凡說，他父親當初念醫學的時候，也喜歡畫畫兒．

湯：可是他沒學過，是自修的．近來也不大畫了，因為行醫太忙了．

許：他父親是個名醫是不是？

湯：是．他是有名的小兒科醫學博士．

2．謝：老邊，請你留意這一帶有沒有賣房子的．

邊：誰要買？你要買房子嗎？

謝：我跟老金，我們兩個人想合買一所房子，兩個人合住．

邊：兩個人合買房子我還沒有聽説過呢．這不是個好辦法．

謝：我們住人家房子也是合住，如果買一所兒房子住就不必每月給人家房錢了．你認為合理嗎？

邊：我的意思是將來你們兩個人萬一處的不好了，房子怎麽辦？

謝：我相信不會的．我們兩個人很合得來．老金對我好極了，拿我當弟弟一樣．

邊：好．房子是甚麽條件你們才買？

謝：主要的條件是離農學院近一點兒，上課去方便一點兒，也要價錢不很貴的．

邊：這兩個條件我想能辦到．

3．王：老李，你那兒有格子紙嗎？

李：有．你要大格子的，是要小格子的？

王：我要小格子的．溫省長讓我根據去年每一省的人口總數畫一張人口比較表．

李：據說每一省的人口都是越來越多.

王：我們中國是地大物博人口多呀.

李：你說人口多，我想起來了. 老張的太太前幾天又生了個兒子.

王：老張不得了. 結婚十二年，生了九個孩子. 聽說生活很困難.

李：合家大小十一口. 就老張在農業合作社裏當個辦事員，每月拿那點兒錢來生活，怎麽不困難呢？

王：他太太是師大畢業的.

李：可是没教過書. 結婚没有好久就有孩子了，没法子出去作事，一天到晚就在家裏.

4. 文：聽說這裏每八千人平均才有一個醫生.

田：是. 因為學醫很難，所以醫生不多.

文：醫院也少. 如果有病人要住醫院，非等不可，根本不能馬上就進去.

田：我們這裏有五十萬人口，就有三個醫院.

文：所以每天我跟我內人說，要格外地加小心，別生病.

田：關於醫院這是個根本上的問題．一來省政府没有這筆錢，二來没有人去辦這種事.

5. 應：你這個留聲機不錯呀．甚麽時候買的？

畢：不是我的，是老湯在出國的時候没帶走，也没賣出去，就留在我這兒了．我不想留着．要是有人買，還是賣了，把錢想法子給他.

應：他到美國去已經有半年了啊.

畢：是啊．日子過得多麽的快呀.

應：近來留美的學生越來越多了.

畢：因為美國是科學發達的國家，所以差不多學科學的都是到美國去.

應：老湯得甚麽時候回來呢？

畢：他說得三年．他是去念博士．他說他得到了博士學位就回國給國家作事.

6. 費：李老師，您好.

李：費一凡，你來了. 有甚麽事嗎？

費：没事. 我是來看看您.

李：謝謝你. 你這次考試都及格嗎？

費：都及格. 都在八十分以上.

李：好極了. 平常多用功，考試的時候留心，没有考不好的. 你將來念大學想主修那門？

費：我想念醫科. 我念大一的時候我想主修生物，所以生物就是我的主修科.

李：據我看，你最好學工程，因為你的數學很好.

費：我對工程學没多大的興趣.

李：學醫很不容易. 據我知道的，遠大醫學院每年考進去的總有一百人左右. 等到畢業的時候，最多不過十幾個人. 要是你念的不好，畢不了業你說怎麽辦？

費：我努力用功啊.

李：這是我的看法．你對醫學有興趣，當然是念醫科了．走，我們到南華茶樓吃點心喝茶去．

費：去是去，可是我請老師．

李：你別請我．那是我常去的地方．在放假的時候，南華茶樓就是我的辦公處．我天天在樓上一個角兒上坐着，一邊兒喝茶，一邊兒寫東西．

7. 麻：我要寫博士論文了，今天下午我想到歷史博物院去看看，你去不去？

溫：去．我還沒去過呢．你甚麼時候去？

麻：我想兩點鐘去，你說怎麼樣？

溫：好．

麻：你在那兒等我？

溫：中午有人在大華酒樓請我吃飯，我兩點鐘在大華樓下等你．

麻：好的．

溫：這兒博物院的辦公時間是從幾點鐘到幾點鐘？

麻：大概是上午九點到下午五點．

温：那麽我們五點鐘就得出來了！

麻：我想用不了三個鐘頭.

温：聽說還有一個博物院.

麻：是. 那個叫博物館. 這個博物院比不上那個博物館那麽大. 所有的博物館, 那算得是最大的了.

温：是嗎？將來有機會得去看看.

麻：好. 我吃了中飯, 到合作社去買一個筆記本兒.然後我到大華去找你.

温：好的. 回頭見.

麻：回頭見.

8. 許：你這幾本經濟學的參考書大概很貴吧？

方：你猜猜看.

許：十塊錢一本.

方：這幾本合起來也不到十塊錢.

許：大概不是在本地買的吧？

方：是在本地買的.

許：我不信.

方：誰跟你說假話呀. 你看我有買書的

收據.

許：在那兒買的？我也想買一部.

方：我實在地告訴你吧，是在我女朋友父親的書店裏買的.

許：怪不得.

方：他們那兒就有一部了. 要是你要，我馬上打電話，讓他們不要賣，給你留下.

許：要是他們已經賣出去了怎麼辦？

方：那你就跟我合用我這一部得了.

9. 常：請問連女士，是那兒的人？

連：我是廣東中山人.

常：你到這兒多久了？

連：我才來了不到兩個星期.

常：關於學校課程的事情，都辦好了嗎？

連：都辦好了. 我一來了，就去看教務長. 教務長把課程的事情都很詳細地告訴我了.

常：你打算念那一系呢？

連：本來我想念文學. 可是學校裏凡是

一年級的學生，數學是必修科，頭一年必得修一年數學.

常：是. 學校歷來是這樣. 將來有甚麽事，要我幫忙的，我都可以代辦.

連：謝謝你. 我才到這兒，學校很多事情都不了解，將來一定麻煩你.

10. 簡：老張，你的車修理好了嗎？

張：早就修好了. 你要用嗎？

簡：我明天得到城外頭去接我父親的一位老朋友. 路太遠了，所以得借你的車用.

張：可以. 是不是你常提的那位方覺農先生？

簡：是. 他是我父親的同學，也是學農的. 當初和我父親都是北京農業專門學校畢業的.

張：我看過他寫的一本農業經濟學.

簡：他有很多關於農業的著作. 同時也教出來不少的最優秀的農業人才.

張：他到這兒來是不是講學？

簡：他可能就是到我們農學院來講一次演．他這幾年不講學了，除了寫書以外多數的時間都是用在跟農民們談談關於農田的一些常識．他常對農人們説，中國是一個農業國家，我們是農業社會，對於農業上大家應該合作，看它是一種合作事業想法子把農業發展起來．

11. 湯：你説金士達有人格没人格？

包：怎麽了？

湯：他把我的手工業及輕工業借去好久了．昨天在張先生那兒我看見他，我讓他還我，他説："誰借你書了？你這話有根據嗎？"在很多人的場合，他對我説這樣兒話．

包：他不但没人格，也没良心．當初他没錢的時候，王老先生在經濟上時常幫助他．現在王老先生生病了，他連看都不去看看．

湯：聽説他在市政府辦公廳當辦事員也

是王老先生介紹的.

包：辦事處裏的職員，他誰也看不起.

12. 生：老師，甚麽叫修詞學？

師：就是研究寫作，怎麽樣兒能把句子寫好的一種技術. 從前在西方國家的教育裏是一種很重要的課程. 中國學校裏,在大學一年要是念文學，就有這門功課.

生：「修業」就是「念書」嗎？

師：是的. 學生在大學裏念書叫作「修業」. 是寫的.

生：「留意」跟「留心」一樣嗎？

師：差不多.

生：「士」是「念書的」是不是？

師：「士」就是「念書的人」.

生：老師，「合意」跟「合格」有甚麽不同？

師：「合意」是「很合我的意思」. 「合格」呢，要是一個初中學生去考大學，根本不合格.

生：老師,「農工業」這個詞兒我常看見,請您說一說？

師：「農工業」就是「農業、工業」合在一塊兒說的. 比如說「那個國家農工業都不很發達」就是說農業、工業都不發達.

生：「根據地」怎麽用啊？

師：我舉個例子:"他們都要拿那個地方作根據地."

生：「以及」我不會用.

師：我舉個例子:"近來那個國家的經濟情形不好, 原因是不論農工業以及手工業都不理想."

生：「要件」是「要緊的東西」是不是？

師：是. 如果你有一封很要緊的信, 讓別人送給人家, 信封上往往寫「要件」兩個字. 意思是, 讓收信的人注意這封信. 還有問題嗎？

生：没了. 老師, 我們這次考試那天考啊？

師：星期五考.

生：後天就考啊. 來不及温習.

師：來得及. 你們不要怕.

生：我們功課太多了,可能要温習不完. 下星期一考好不好？

師：最好是星期五考. 要是下星期考, 功課又加多了.

13. 史：湯士剛要到這兒來了.

田：是嗎！他甚麽時候來？

史：兩個星期以後.

田：他在這兒住多久？

史：他信上説, 住兩三個星期就回去. 他來買參考書來了. 我打算把他留住, 我跟他合編一本國語詞典.

田：那好極了. 你們兩位, 一位是文學家, 一位是語言學家. 兩位合力來編一本國語詞典自然是一本最好的字典了.

史：好不好不敢説, 不過我很早就希望有機會跟他合作一次.

14. 謝：老先生，您跟我說說您和您太太一個是中國人一個是外國人你們怎麽結合的？
溫：你聽我告訴你啊．當初我在美國念書的時候，我們兩個人是同學．她跟我學中國話，慢慢兒的我們兩個人的感情就很好了．以後呢就結了婚了．
謝：在您念書那個時期，您跟外國人結婚，家裏人贊成嗎？
溫：開始我父親很不贊成，因為我父親是一個舉人，他的思想很古老．等到結了婚了，他也没法子了．

15. 應：你今天怎麽没到學校去呀？
連：我今天没課，在家寫論文，所以没到學校去．今天來演講的是誰？
應：是教務主任給講的．
連：講的甚麽題目？
應：題目是談合作．大意是說，人跟人要合作．不論甚麽事情，同心合力去作是一定成功的．講的不錯．

連：今天晚上有事嗎？

應：沒事．怎麽着？

連：我有兩張音樂會的票，你要不要？

應：謝謝你，我不要．那種場合我從來不去．

Exercise 3. Narratives

1. 中國政府開始送留學生到外國留學是在清朝的時候．當時是一八七二年七月．第一次送三十個人留美．後來在一八七六年十二月又送十二個人留英，還送幾個人留法．從此以後每年都有留學生出國了．

2. 有一個外國人問我，中國人對於辦事的地方有時候叫辦公處，有時候叫辦事處，還有時候叫辦公室，或者叫辦公廳，是不是有甚麽分別呢？我告訴他，政府機關辦公的地方可以叫辦公處、辦公廳、辦公室．如果不是政府機關而是幾個人辦事的地方，就只能叫辦事處不能叫辦公處了．

3．馬良才是一個醫生，他在廣州行醫有二十多年了．他說：“我當初在醫學院念醫科的時候，主修的是外科．學外科離不開開刀，因為開刀是必修科．我第一次看見別人開刀，我怕的不得了．看過幾次以後我不但不怕，而且也學會開刀了．”有人說這位醫生每次給人家開刀，總是成功的，所以他現在成了一個名醫了．

4．我在博物院裏看見一個留聲機，樣子很古老．據博物院裏的人說，這是開始發明的那個留聲機，所以這個算得是最早的留聲機了．我問他：“像這個樣的留聲機，發出來的聲音能清楚嗎？”他說：“當然比不上現在的留聲機那麽清楚了．”

5．凡是一個國家，第一要注重農業，農業發達人民才容易生活，社會才可以安定，國家就越來越好了．所以說農業是國家的根本．第二要注重工業．工業發達才可以做出來很多日用的東西，人民的生活就可以提高．所以現代的國家都很注重工業．

6．有一個國王有六個兒子．這六個兒子都很有本事，就是大家不知道合作．有一天，這個國王把這六個兒子都叫到面前，對他們說：“我這房子裏有一樣很重的東西，你們誰能把他舉起來？”他說完這話以後，就叫他的大兒子先去舉．大兒子沒舉起來，又叫二兒子去舉，也沒舉起來．叫三兒子，四兒子…也都沒舉起來．國王說：“現在你們六個人合力去舉，看看能不能舉起來．”這六個兒子大家合力一舉，把這個很重的東西很容易就舉起來了．國王說：“現在你們明白了吧，一個人做不了的事情，大家合起來就可以做得了．今後你們應該大家合作．”

7．有一個學生問先生，「留在」和「留着」這兩個詞有甚麽分別．先生說：“我舉一個例子來說吧:「他把錢留在家裏了, 留着買書呢.」學生說:“我明白了. 現在我也用這兩個詞兒說一個故事, 請您聽聽對不對. 有一個學生, 在上課的時候看小說. 先生不許他看, 先生把這本小說拿去留在辦公室了. 到了下課的時候, 這個學生把書都收拾了以後, 就到辦公室要把這本小說拿回家去, 可是先生不給他. 他心裏想也許先生留着自己看呢.”先生說:“你在這個故事裏用的這兩個詞兒都很對, 說這個故事的意思我更明白. 你真是一個聰明的學生. 等一會兒下了課, 你就把小說拿去吧.”原來就是這個學生的小說叫這個先生拿去了.

8. 今天中午我去看王先生, 他不在家. 他太太說:“王先生上茶樓喝茶去了.”我就到茶樓去找他. 在茶樓的樓上樓下我都找了, 也没看見王先生. 有人說, 王先生才走了没有好久, 也許回家去了. 我只好又到王先生家, 可是王先生没回家.

王太太說:“我們這位先生甚麽事也不做,一天到晚不是在茶樓就是在酒樓.你可以到酒樓去看看,也許他在酒樓吃飯呢.”我說:“我不去找他了.”我留下一張我的名片我就走了.

9. 王一凡是博物館的辦事員.他說:“年輕的人在博物館裏工作沒意思極了.一天到晚只是留心看着一些古老的東西.我又不是考古的,對這些古物越看越沒興趣.有一天我就想,目前的工作又不費心,又不費力,倒不如在這個時候,自己自修學習一點兒本事.可是學甚麽好呢?想來想去就想起學習寫作來了.我就買了筆、本子還有帶小格子的格子紙,都買來了.我還買了一些名著和修辭學甚麽的.天天不是看書,就是練習寫作.這樣一來,從前認為沒意思的工作,現在覺得格外有意思了.”

10. 我和一個朋友合買一部汽車.他上午用,我下午用,晚上誰要有事誰就用.有一天晚上我們兩個人都有事，都要用車. 我說:“我去的地方不太遠,如果走路去,在時間上也來得及，我不用車.”他說:“那太不好意思了. 要不然，我先開車送你去,然後我再到我要去的地方.”我說:“好吧.”

11. 王覺農是農學院的教授. 最近他寫了一本書，很多人都說寫的很好. 有人說那本書不是王覺農一個人寫的，是他和農學院的幾個教授合編的. 又有人說:“據我看，也不能算合編的. 根本是從一本英文書上翻譯過來的.”我說:“這話是有根據的，因為我看過那本英文的原文.”

12. 我從念大學到念博士這五六年裏，都是學校給我的獎學金. 現在我寫完了博士論文，有一位教授對我說:“你的論文寫的很詳細很有見解，很可能就要得到博士學位了.”我心裏想，就是得了博士學位我還不滿足,我還是應當繼續的研究,因為我是為了學問求學，不是為了學位求學.

13. 有一個外國人，中國話說的很好. 有一次他到了中國，很多中國人開了一個歡迎會歡迎他. 他在歡迎會上對大家講話. 他說:"各位女士、先生. 今天我有機會參加這個會，能够和大家見面，我很高興. …" 他講了很多話，大家都說他講話的意思很好. 又說他講的中國話更好. 可是有一個人說，在這種場合，他講的中國話多少有一點兒問題，因為他所說的「各位女士、先生」這句話是外國話翻成的中國話，不是中國人常說的一種自然的中國話.

14. 白先生來找李先生想求李先生給他辦一件事情. 他對李先生說:"我有一件事情，自己怎麽想也想不出辦法了. 我希望你幫我想一想，還求你給我辦好." 李先生說:"你有甚麽事情叫我辦，只要我能辦到的我都可以代辦. 可是你叫我想辦法，恐怕我也是想不出來好辦法的."

15. 張先生最喜歡說笑話．他有一部藍顏色的車．有一天，我去找他，要借他的車．他說："你要借我的車嗎？我的車在醫院呢．"我心裏想，也許有人借他的車到醫院去了．我問他甚麽時候可以回來，他說："病治好了就回來了．"我心裏想這一定是有人借他的車去治病去了．後來他告訴我："這部車總是出毛病．昨天剛修好，今天又不能走了，又去修理去了．這真像一個病人得天天上醫院哪．"

16. 張先生給我來了一封掛號信，信裏有一百塊錢．他在信裏寫，收到這筆錢以後，讓我寫一個收據．我就找了一張紙，寫了一張收據．這張收據是這樣寫的：

> 今收到
> 張先生送來一百元
> 王士達 一九六七年八月七日

17. 王先生結婚以後，和他太太時常發生意見．有人說他們兩個人根本上不應當結婚．他們的結合，主要的是王先生看王太太家裏有錢．這種結合怎會有好結果呢？

18. 勞永亮在外國研究醫學的時候，他和兩個外國學生合住一間房子，合用一部汽車．他們三個人很合得來．每月用的房錢、飯錢以及汽油錢都合在一塊兒計算，他們三個人平均拿出錢來．勞先生說：“這個辦法很合理，很方便．我們三個人都很滿意．”

19. 根據中國近代教育史上說，中國在清朝開始辦大學的時候，凡是在大學修業四年的，經過考試及格以後就等於從前的舉人．後來凡是大學畢業的就可以得到學士學位．

20. 中國的大學很注重國文，凡是一年級的學生，不論將來的主修科是研究甚麽，國文這一門功課是必修的．有人說：“大學學生在念小學、中學的時候念過國文了，到了大學為甚麽還要念呢？還有，大學教育是學習專門學問的，應當學的功課本來就很多啦．那兒有時間念國文呢？我不贊成這種辦法．"

21. 有一個人很久没有工作了．他心裏想："我用盡了方法也没找到工作．我家的人口多，媽媽又有病，經濟情形本來就不好．要是長久没有工作，合家的生活怎麽辦．"他越想越難過．有人告訴他，應當天天留意報紙上請人的廣告．後來果然看報紙上的廣告找到工作了．

22. 張士英在一個合作社裏工作．有一天，我去看他，他説："你看我多麽忙．在我們這裏工作的，都是這麽忙．可是我們都喜歡這種工作，因為這是一種合作事業．必得大家都努力，這才可以表現出來大家合作呀．"

23. 中國農人在不種田的時候多半喜歡自己做一些日用的東西．這些東西都是用手工做的．最初是為了自己用，後來做的太多了，就拿出去賣給別人．別人看這個生意不錯，也就學着做起來了．做的人和做的東西越來越多，越做越好，這就形成了一種手工業了．

24. 父親給兒子講做人的道理．他說：“做人就是做一個好人的意思．一個人要想做一個好人，必得有兩個要件．第一個要件是有學問，第二個要件是有人格．在這兩個要件裏，人格比學問還要重要．人格不好，不能做人．”

25. 文英：

我到這裏已經一個星期了．本來應該回去了，可是中山中學教生物的先生病了，一時找不到人，所以李校長把我給留住了，非讓我在這兒教四個星期不可．沒法子，只好多住四個星期了．我大概下月二十左右才能回去．回去的時候，還是坐飛機．現在先告訴你，在我沒回去以前，我最少要寫五六封信給你．祝

近好　　　　　　張青　四月三日

26. 張紀良是一條大船的水手. 他說:"我們這條船走的很快, 平均每小時走三十多里. 我們常年在海上來往, 把中國的上海作為根據地. 為甚麽說上海是根據地呢? 因為這條船每兩年總要到上海去修理一次, 所以就把上海當作根據地了."

27. 有一個學生才念高中二就想考大學物理系. 有人告訴他:"考大學必得在高中畢業的才合格. 你高中沒畢業怎能考大學呢?" 他說:"聽說自修的學生只要程度相當也可以考呀. 我自己研究物理已經有五年了, 我想我不但能考上物理系, 我還要考奬學金呢."

28. 我有一個好朋友, 在政府機關裏做主任. 他讓我去做辦事員. 我說:"我們兩個人的關係是好朋友. 如果我去當了辦事員, 我想到我們的關係, 我在職務上一定要盡心盡力的去做. 可是我的職務是甚麽,請你先詳細地說一說，看看我做得了做不了，合意不合意.”他說:“職務很簡單，就是在主任室裏辦事. 除了公務以外，還要幫我計劃這個機關裏經濟上的事情. 不論你的意思怎麽樣，我倒是樂意你能來幫我的忙.”

29. 中國地大物博，歷來是一個農業國家. 全國的土地，農田最多. 當然大多數的人民是農民了. 以前中國農人種田根本不知道用科學的方法. 近幾年來他們在農業上也用科學的方法，同時也組織了農業合作社. 組織合作社的目的是讓農民大家同心合力地合作. 據說他們這種辦法對農業上比以前好多了. 但是我想中國土地那麽大，人口那麽多，在組織上一定有很多的困難.

30. 各位同學：今天是遠東大學開學的第一天. 我代表全校教職員跟所有中國同學說幾句話歡迎你們大家. 你們是從很多不同的國家來到這裏的. 你們大家來到

這裏都有一個相同的目的,就是求學.我們學校有外國學生來求學,已經有二十多年的歷史了.根據我們過去的經驗,外國學生對於學習上都非常有興趣,而且在學習的能力上也比較高.可是在學校裏學習的時間很短.因此學校就想法子怎麽能够讓你們在這很短的學習時間可以多得一點兒學識,所以今年我們在課程一方面有專題講話.專題講話的內容都是關於中國各方面的,像歷史、地理、文學、語言、教育等等.從今天起你們每一個人都是遠東大學一分子,希望大家努力學習.

Exercise 4. Illustrative Sentences (English)

2.4. He insisted on leaving. I couldn't get him to stay no matter how I tried.

2.8. Please keep an ear open for me [lit. take note for me] as to whether they're looking for someone to teach mathematics there.

4.1. This belt was bought at that market on the northeast corner of the intersection.

4.4. He's always telling other people to be scientific in [lit. to scientificize] their work, but actually he himself is basically unscientific.

5.3. From what I know, studying engineering at that school is rather hard.

5.4. In my opinion that locality is very important (to them). One might say it's their base. They can't give it up easily [lit. as one pleases].

6.1. Yesterday my car broke down after I'd gone half way. I tried fixing it for a long time but didn't succeed [in fixing it].

6.3. All those studying at this school, regardless of what they're majoring in, must take a year of math in the first year.

7.4. I never like to go to affairs such as concerts.

7.5. The two of them [are able to] get along very well together. They've lived together for eight years and have never had a quarrel.

7.7. Wouldn't this be quite logical: buy it if it suits you, don't buy it if it doesn't.

8.1. If $50 is divided (equally) among four persons, [on the average] how much would each person get ?

8.2. That tape recorder (is so expensive that) one person can't buy it. How much shall the three of us contribute equally to buy it ?

9.3. Professor Mao of the medical school has trained [lit. taught out] quite a few very distinguished [talented] men of medicine in the past twenty years.

9.5. In a little while I have to go to the hospital to see a sick friend [lit. a friend's sickness].

9.6. My younger brother is studying medicine at the Far Eastern University Medical School.

12.5. The most important thing for a person is to have (a good) character.

14.1. Most of those eating at the Great China Restaurant are returned students.

14.2. A lot of guests have come to our home. Upstairs and downstairs it's all filled up.

14.4. Five years ago this [lit. here] was a stretch of (empty) land, and now it's all big buildings.

16.1. Tian Shida is a medical Ph.D. in surgery.

16.4. Studying for the Ph.D. and acquiring knowledge are two (different) things.

21.2. Although Xu Liang isn't as good as Zhang Xida in his studies, he's also gotten a scholarship.

22.1. This letter is important. Hold on to it and be additionally careful on the road.

23.1. How important the handicraft industry is now!

Notes

As mentioned in Intermediate Chinese (see page 155, note 3), in addition to their literal meanings, **nǐ shuō** "you say," **nǐ kàn** "you see," and **nǐ xiǎng** "you think" are used as rhetorical exhortations. They occur especially often with **duó(mo) (de)** "so" plus a stative verb, or with **zěnmo bàn,** lit. "how manage?" in the following patterns:

Nǐ shuō / **Nǐ kàn** / **Nǐ xiǎng**	(N) **duó(mo)** SV	"How SV N is!"
Nǐ shuō / **Nǐ kàn** / **Nǐ xiǎng**	+ [sentence] + **zěnmo bàn**?	"What if + [sentence]?"
[Sentence] + **nǐ shuō** / **nǐ kàn** / **nǐ xiǎng**	+ **zěnmo bàn**?	"What if + [sentence]?"

The following examples illustrate these patterns:

Nǐ shuō tā duó cōngming! "[You say] how clever he is!"

Nǐ kàn tā duóma yònggōng! "[You see] how diligent he is!"

Nǐ xiǎng tā bù lái zěnmo bàn? "[You think] what if he doesn't come?"

Tā bù tóngyì nǐ shuō zěnmo bàn? "If he doesn't agree, [you say] what then?"

第十二課

Exercise 1. Review of Single Characters

1. 倒	11. 良	21. 育	31. 感	41. 楚	51. 程	61. 務	71. 農
2. 庭	12. 細	22. 系	32. 續	42. 贊	52. 况	62. 非	72. 金
3. 此	13. 物	23. 留	33. 努	43. 各	53. 盡	63. 加	73. 復
4. 組	14. 辦	24. 博	34. 形	44. 室	54. 樓	64. 許	74. 孔
5. 度	15. 士	25. 凡	35. 青	45. 織	55. 翻	65. 專	75. 包
6. 解	16. 修	26. 相	36. 舉	46. 例	56. 溫	66. 清	76. 濟
7. 劃	17. 均	27. 參	37. 術	47. 足	57. 係	67. 譯	77. 樂
8. 秀	18. 困	28. 决	38. 根	48. 範	58. 據	68. 制	78. 職
9. 滿	19. 格	29. 成	39. 合	49. 任	59. 講	69. 及	79. 獎
10. 求	20. 詳	30. 達	40. 圍	50. 醫	60. 優	70. 繼	80. 總

Exercise 2. Distinguishing Partially Similar Combinations

A. Same Character in Initial Position

1	2	3	4	5	6	7
總代表	要人	成年	同樣	省城	生病	清代
總機關	要飯	成人	同歲	省錢	生詞	清楚
總經理	要看	成見	同姓	省長	生育	清朝
總工會	要好	成了	同音	省事	生物	清史
總代理	要件	成語				

8	9	10	11	12	13	14
農人	例子	復習	當天	總共	大前天	有表現
農業	例句	復興	當年	總要	大後天	有道理
農民	例外	復古	當前	總會	大前年	有根據
農田	例如	復原	當然	總名	大後年	有人格

15	16	17	18	19	20	21
主人	學年	相信	温書	收回	青茶	平民
主任	學制	相左	温度	收據	青年	平等
主修	學識	相遠	温習	收工	青海	平均

22	23	24	25	26	27	28
名字	舉手	金錢	結婚	講話	合編	各國
名醫	舉行	金文	結合	講演	合買	各樣
名冊	舉人	金朝	結果	講解	合作	各個

29	30	31	32	33	34	35
翻車	從前	參考	必得	本人	白話	總有
翻書	從今	參看	必修	本校	白金	總算
翻譯	從來	參加	必定	本事	白字	總計

36	37	38	39	40	41	42
說好話	辦公室	組成	只能	知識	優越	應該
說大話	辦公處	組織	只好	知足	優先	應許
說不定	辦公廳					

43	44	45	46	47	48	49
以外	行政	信紙	現代	下學	談天	少見
以及	行醫	信任	現況	下等	談起	少年

50	51	52	53	54	55	56
上學	人數	輕看	情形	滿地	留下	酒杯
上任	人們	輕易	情况	滿足	留英	酒樓

57	58	59	60	61	62	63
經過	教授	見面	加多	家長	過路	關門
經濟	教育	見解	加州	家庭	過奬	關係

64	65	66	67	68	69	70
公正	根據	概念	分開	方言	發音	單子
公務	根本	概况	分數	方才	發達	單字

71	72	73	74	75	76	77
帶子	大人	茶會	筆劃	報名	包子	怎麽着
帶錢	大聲	茶樓	筆畫	報復	包上	怎麽辦

78	79	80	81	82	83	84
下半天	念大學	歷史書	錄音機	開快車	解放前	教務處
下决心	念博士	歷史家	錄音帶	開倒車	解放後	教務長

85	86
工程學	辦事員
工程師	辦事處

B. Same Character in Final Position

1	2	3	4	5	6	7
滿意	成人	上學	教務	大事	人力	還好
加意	求人	求學	職務	樂事	努力	要好
决意	別人	下學	事務	本事	省力	講好
樂意	大人	留學	特務	喜事	盡力	修好
譯意	舉人	科學	任務	辦事	合力	辦好

8	9	10	11	12	13	14
工程學	小心	要有	專用	學系	完成	例子
物理學	决心	只有	任用	本系	不成	分子
經濟學	關心	專有	合用	全系	組成	格子
生物學	專心	就有	信用	院系	形成	孔子
修詞學						

15	16	17	18	19	20	21
任意	問題	學說	良心	事情	翻成	農民
合意	講題	小說	盡心	人情	譯成	國民
盡意	專題	專說	細心	感情	贊成	人民
留意	本題	據說	留心	細情	達成	三民

22	23	24	25	26	27	28
合家	講法	談到	開車	總是	人才	音樂家
專家	算法	達到	倒車	倒是	方才	科學家
成家	留法	感到	汽車	凡是	秀才	出版家
人家	辦法	辦到	翻車	盡是	口才	老人家

29	30	31	32	33	34	35
音樂會	輕工業	生字表	賣票員	理學院	明明地	滿足
茶話會	農工業	溫度表	翻譯員	考試院	一一地	知足
總工會	手工業	生詞表	教職員	工學院	好好地	不足
青年會	重工業	課程表	公務員	文學院	根據地	

36	37	38	39	40	41	42
留住	生字	錄音	農業	感想	樓下	請問
合住	單字	聲音	修業	思想	留下	細問
圍住	認字	譯音	職業	細想	天下	學問

43	44	45	46	47	48	49
短文	學位	此外	女士	贊同	美術	翻書
古文	各位	例外	學士	如同	算術	温書
原文	坐位	格外	博士	相同	學術	講書

50	51	52	53	54	55	56
學識	一生	接任	事前	説明	定例	修理
知識	出生	現任	當前	講明	前例	物理
意識	醫生	前任	目前	文明	先例	合理

57	58	59	60	61	62	63
外科	來着	不久	聽講	茶會	筆畫	好話
醫科	留着	好久	主講	工會	計畫	問話
專科	本着	許久	演講	不會	畫畫	講話

64	65	66	67	68	69	70
以後	國都	温度	必得	師大	各處	過程
此後	全都	程度	非得	中大	別處	課程
前後	成都	制度	總得	高大	相處	工程

71	72	73	74	75	76	77
合格	實驗室	内政部	小學生	根本上	舉起來	博物院
人格	會客室	教育部	留學生	比不上	包起來	醫學院
及格	錄音室	工業部	大學生	組織上	合起來	農學院

78	79	80	81	82	83	84
感謝	學院	教員	成語	接續	好像	人物
多謝	醫院	職員	術語	繼續	形像	生物

85	86	87	88	89	90	91
成為	木頭	算術	老師	教室	而且	任期
認為	一頭	學術	講師	課室	况且	星期

92	93	94	95	96	97	98
安南	專門	贊美	快樂	成就	定價	計劃
濟南	大門	留美	音樂	這就	物價	筆劃

99	100	101	102	103	104	105
成分	講定	應當	主編	學分制	主修科	古時候
畫分	决定	相當	合編	學年制	必修科	省時候

106	107	108	109	110	111	112
出版社	一方面	作例子	錄音機	翻過來	演講詞	古代史
合作社	各方面	舉例子	留聲機	倒過來	形容詞	近代史

113	114	115	116	117	118
盡可能	博物館	職業學校	畢業論文	初等小學	工業部長
原子能	吃飯館	師範學校	博士論文	高等小學	教育部長

119
師範大學
清華大學

C. Same Character in Different Positions

1	2	3	4	5	6	7
近况	温暖	清楚	成功	續假	形容	根本
况且	暖和	楚國	功課	假話	容易	本錢

8	9	10	11	12	13	14
分等	平安	用盡	詳細	非得	各種	成了
等於	安南	盡職	細說	得獎	種地	了解

15	16	17	18	19	20	21
温帶	許可	温水	温和	來往	中等	也許
帶有	可見	水平	和氣	往回	等級	許多

22	23	24	25	26	27	28
加重	舉例	解决	紙包	優點	優秀	師範
重寫	例如	决不	包上	點名	秀氣	範圍

29	30	31	32	33	34	35
是非	從此	原因	再重	總理	古物	以及
非常	此地	因此	重要	理解	物理	及格

36	37	38	39	40	41	42
醫生	感覺	專一	高等	更加	解放	非但
生病	覺着	一生	等到	加州	放假	但是

43	44	45	46	47	48	49
打倒	盡職	總結	任滿	得獎	辦公	朝代
倒像	職員	結婚	滿足	獎金	公理	代辦

50	51	52	53	54	55
市場	困難	樓上	表演	其實	金子
場合	難看	上月	演說	實驗	子音

D. Reversals

1	2	3
出生	分成	演講
生出	成分	講演

Exercise 3. Narratives and Dialogues

1. 温：對不起，你來了半天了吧？
費：没有好久．我才來了一會兒．你到那兒去了？
温：我到圖書館找參考書去了．找了半天只找到了兩本書．
費：你找關於那種的書？
温：物理學的．
費：我倒有幾本．是毛有良去年走的時候留在我那兒的．不知道對你有用没有？
温：是誰寫的？
費：是現在最有名的物理學家張大文博士寫的．
温：再好也没有了．我就是要找張博士寫的書．
費：你來拿好了．
温：我用完了再還給你．
費：除非他回來我不用那種書．就放在你這兒好了．等着他回來再説了．

2. 程：據説老金那所兒房子要賣．

湯：是嗎？

程：你跟他那麽要好你不知道嗎？

湯：他從來没跟我説過．就是賣價錢也很貴．他那所兒房子除非有錢才能買呢．他以前説過，那所兒房子要賣的時候一定得賣一個相當的價錢．

程：他那所兒房子看樣子有幾十年了．

湯：是．是一所兒老房子了．説了半天是不是你想買房子？

程：我現在的房子因為人多不够住，所以打聽打聽．

湯：我説你倒不如問問別處的房子．他那所兒房子就是買了也有很多地方要重修．

3．許：昨天正當我吃中飯的時候，老王給我送來一封信，信封上寫着「要件」兩個字．我打開一看原來是張美英小姐給我寫的．你猜猜甚麽事？

田：我可猜不着．

許：讓我教他數學．她信上寫着，別人

教她，她不明白．除非我教她她才會．你說天下還有這樣事？

田：這是她對你好的意思．你教不教她呢？

許：我哪兒有工夫啊．我這學期念了六門功課．這學期必得把學分念足了．

田：小姐求你事情，你不好意思說不成吧？

許：要是不教她當然不好意思了．可是我得細想一想在甚麽時間．

田：張小姐很喜歡玩兒．教完了數學就會請你看電影去．

許：那可不成．我得先跟她講明白，要想跟我學東西就不能玩兒，必得把功課學得好．

田：你這個老師可不得了．

4. 應：昨天小萬才有意思呢．他拿論文拿錯了．他拿給他女朋友寫的信當了論文了，他就給了教務長了．教務長一看笑了．

簡：他盡是這樣.有一次上的是地理課，他拿一本書就往課室跑.到了課室一看是一本小說.

應：他還有個毛病，他跟誰也合不來.

簡：是.我初次看見他的時候常去找他，希望能跟他在一塊兒.後來我看他的樣子好像不喜歡我的樣子，所以後來我再也不理他了.

5. 王：今天早上我去看金教授去了.

邊：金教授的病怎麽樣？

王：跟前兩天差不多.溫度還是102度.看情形得找別的大夫.

邊：還找那個大夫呢？

王：最好我們問問金教授自己.隨他的意思.

邊：同時我們也得給金師母寫信告訴她金教授病的情形.

王：這封信寫得嗎？怎麽寫法呢？

邊：我們就說金教授有點兒小病，最好請師母到這裏來.

王：對了．就這樣兒寫．

6．史：謝小姐來過了沒有？

畢：來了一會兒就走了．

史：怎麽！她才來就走了？沒留她嗎？

畢：留她了．她説她有別的事不等你啦．

史：奇怪．她説在這兒吃了飯才走呢．為甚麽才來了就走了？一定是看我不在這兒生氣了．

畢：你要是早回來十分鐘就遇見她了．

史：我在辦公室等張先生來着．她手裏拿着甚麽東西沒有？

畢：她手裏拿着很多格子紙．

史：對了．她是説找我來畫圖表來．

7．方：怎麽，九點了我們還不走嗎？

許：等一會兒張達文，他跟我們一塊兒走．吃的東西你都包起來了嗎？

方：包起來了．我把昨天晚上剩的紅燒牛肉也包在裏面了．多帶點兒，萬一吃的不夠了，山上沒有賣的．

許：這次旅行我甚麽也沒做．就你一個

人忙了.

方：哪裏.

8. 金：昨天晚上田太太累了吧？我們也沒幫忙就走了.

田：客氣客氣.回到府上已經很晚了吧？

金：不晚，還不到十一點鐘呢. 田太太菜做的太好了,而且做的也太多了.

田：哪兒啊.你昨天先送老張回去了嗎？

金：是的.

田：我看老張好像有甚麽心事.

金：是有點兒心事.他在車上跟我説了.他説近來手工業的生意都不大理想.他那個小買賣不想作下去了.

田：説實在的，老張作那種生意不行.他是一個知識分子,不應該作生意.

金：他是師大畢業的，是學教育的.

田：那麽他應該作一點兒關於教育的工作.

金：誰説不是呢.

9. 今天早上學校的專題講話主講人是經濟

系的系主任樂士達教授給我們講的．題目是「中國近五十年來的經濟跟農業」．他先說中國和西方國家的經濟情形各有不同．他說我們中國歷來是農業國家，可以說是一種農業經濟社會．因為這個，我們必得注重農業，用科學方法讓農業發達．要想農業發達應該怎麼辦呢？最主要的是要組織農業合作社，大家同心合力在農業上去努力．農業發達經濟才能够發達．他舉了一個例子說，有一個國家本來經濟農業都不行，所以人民的生活非常困難．自從有一個國家幫助他們把農業科學化了以後，不過十年的樣子，現在已經成了一個農業和經濟非常發達的國家了．本來那個國家人民的生活多半是困難的，現在每一個人民的生活水準都提高了．

10. 老錢：

我現在在加拿大呢．你一定想："怎麼也不告訴我就走了呢？"現在我把詳細的經過告訴你．上星期晚上，我父親對我說，因為加拿大那邊生意的關係，得到加拿大去，他讓我跟他去．没想到第二天，他老人家就帶着我走了，所以來不及告訴你．我大概在這兒最多住兩個星期．我們中國是地大物博，加拿大也可以用這四個字來形容．這裏的中國人也不少．走在路上常常遇見中國人．我還遇見一個在中學時候的同學．多年不見了，在這裏遇見了，非常高興．他在加拿大一個大學裏念工程學．他說明年他到美國麻省理工學院去念書．這位同學當初在中學念書永遠是考第一．他念麻省理工學院，我想他一定念獎學金．這裏的公園很大．我們下了飛機以後，我父親的朋友就帶我們到公園去了．是坐着車在裏面走了有兩個多鐘頭，我們才出來．這裏的中國飯館兒價錢都不貴．我和父親兩個人吃了兩個菜、一個湯，只三塊錢．希望你將來有機會到這裏來

旅行一次．没的寫了．下次再談． 祝
好！ 許博九 三月九日

11. 孔夫子是山東人．他生在紀元前五百五十一年．孔夫子一生的事業是政治、講學跟編書．因為那個時候中國分成很多國，當時他不滿意他本國的政治，一生氣他就到別的國家去了．他在別的國家前後有十三年的時間．他所到的地方，都不能實行他的主張，和他的思想都相左．他很不得意，又回到了山東講學．孔夫子在三十歲的時候就開始教學生．孔夫子的學生有三千多人．他説甚麽人都可以教．他實行一種平民教育．孔夫子的思想，對政治、教育及人生各方面都有他特有的主張，所以一直到現在，中國有的學者還是把孔夫子的思想看作治國最好的學説．在五四時代，有很多人主張打倒孔夫子的學説．近來又有一些學者認為，如果想要中國復興，非得用孔夫子的學説治國不可．

12. 士達：

你們放假了嗎？我們從下星期起就開始放了. 我有一個問題, 總想和你研究, 今天專為了這個問題給你寫這封信. 有人說計劃經濟是很好的一種經濟計劃. 如果事前計劃得準, 這個辦法是非常好. 要是計算錯了, 怎麽辦呢？計劃經濟是不是最好的方法呢？我認為很有研究的必要. 你認為怎麽樣？ 祝

好！ 士其 一月二日

13. 我們文學院中文系和語言學系合在一塊兒組織了一個語文研究會, 參加的人數相當多. 昨天晚上在205教室開會. 本來說是晚上八點鐘開會. 還沒到七點半呢, 教室的人已經滿了. 據張先生說, 這個教室能坐六十人, 可是今天晚上坐滿了.

14. 昨天老王不知道為甚麽和他太太發生意見了. 太太是誰說甚麽也不行, 非要離婚不可. 老王呢, 氣也很大, 說："要離婚的不是我而是你. 隨你好了." 太太一

聽老王這兩句話，氣更大了．拿起一個手提包往外就走．我是來給他們說和的，哪兒能讓她走哪．我跟王太太說："在男人裏老王算得是好的．你這次看我的面子，算了吧．"我跟王太太說了半天的好話，又加上滿院子是人都在看他們，她的氣好像才没有那麽大了．老王一看太太氣小了，當然更没氣了．我就走了．

15. 中國從前是一種大家庭制度．比如我母親，他們家裏有五十多口人．有一年我記不清楚是在甚麽時候了，我母親帶我到她家裏去．他們的房子很大，有好幾個院子．我一進去看見男男女女、大大小小人多得不得了，母親一一地給我介紹：這個是大姐，那個是二弟⋯．他們很有意思．要是到了吃飯的時候大家就各到各的房子裏等着吃飯．如果要有喜事，人更多了．結了婚的小姐，帶着孩子們都回來了．我記得又有一年，他們家裏有人結婚．父母帶着我全家都去了．

因為人多，吃飯是在院子裏．還沒到吃飯的時候，院子滿是人．吃飯的時候，都讓老年人們先坐下．孩子、大人們都坐好了以後，大人們一頭兒喝酒一頭兒說話，孩子們都吃菜．有意思極了．從這次去過以後，再也沒去過那個大家庭了．

16. 合作事業有很多種．我舉個例子來說．合作社，就是合作事業．學校有合作社，工人有合作社，農人也有農業合作社．學校組織的合作社是，凡是學生都是社員．在合作社買東西比在外面買省很多錢．有一次我要買一個留聲機，有一個賣留聲機的地方要價一百塊錢，我到合作社一問只不過八十五塊錢．

17. 人心都是不足的．一個人不論甚麼事情沒有心滿意足的．我用錢舉個例子．如果有了一千，想有一萬．有了一萬，想有五萬．人的希望永遠是滿足不了的．

18. 我弟弟很聰明，可是不用功念書. 一天到晚就是玩兒，所以各門功課考試的結果都不很好. 母親是一個不輕易打孩子的人，氣得打過他好幾次. 因為父親在別的地方作事，不常回家. 父親如果回來的時候，她在父親面前不敢說弟弟不用功，怕父親生氣. 有一次父親回來了，父親和母親說，找弟弟學校的張老師來吃飯，因為張老師和父親是老朋友. 等到吃飯的時候，張老師和父親談着談着就談到我弟弟了. 張老師說:"我們是自己人. 不客氣地說，這個孩子聰明是很聰明，就是不用功. 有時候連應該作的功課他都不作. 以後這樣不行，非得要用功了."父親當時沒說甚麽. 等張老師走了以後，父親把弟弟叫來，告訴他，以後的功課，老師打完了分兒留着，父親回來給父親看. 經過這次以後弟弟很不喜歡張老師. 在上課的時候，老是跟張老師找麻煩. 常問張老師課程以外的題目．有一次上課的時候，張老師說：“有一種人專門喜歡說人家不喜歡聽的話．這種人你們說叫甚麼人？”弟弟馬上站起來說：“這種人叫「老師」．”

19. 謝良已經離開這裏五年了．我時常想念他．他在這裏的時候，雖然我們兩個人不在一系，他念物理學，我念生物學，可是我們兩個人同住在一所兒房子裏．他住在樓下，我住在樓上．我們吃飯也在一塊兒吃．謝良拿我當弟弟一樣．比方說吃飯吧，要是我回來的晚了，他一定等着我回來才吃．讓我永遠忘不了的是，有一次我病了．學校正在考試．他天天得念書還得做飯往醫院給我送．我很不好意思．我說：“這樣你一定考不好的．”他說：“沒關係．”後來病好了以後，我買了一個金手表送給他，意思是感謝他．說甚麼他也不要．他說：“哪兒的話呢！我跟你的關係還來這個嗎？”

20. 今天是三月二十九日．早上六點鐘起來，往外面看看，天氣很好．吃了早點，走到學校還不到八點鐘呢．八點半上課．因為歷史老師生病了，我們在上歷史課的時間自修．九點半校長講話，大意是說，我們上課已經有兩三個星期了，要是我們對於學習方面感覺到有甚麽不滿意的，比如教學方面，大家認為教授法不很好，請同學們有甚麽意見都不客氣地說出來，學校會盡可能的想法子．校長又說，同學在意識上一定認為學校方面不會讓學生隨便發表意見的．他說這就錯了．今天經校長講完了以後，我覺得我們校長真是民主．最後是教務長報告下學期的課程等．今天下午我沒有功課，十一點半我就回家温習功課．下午三點鐘老金來找我，說晚上請我吃飯，問我到哪兒去吃．我說："是你請客，隨你的便哪．"他就帶我到一個小館子吃的，然後我們到書店看見了一本中國五十年來的經濟及政治，我買了一本就回家了．

UNIT III

Lesson 13

1	2	3	4	5	6	7	8
變	取	造	律	設	立	身	體

9	10	11	12	13	14	15	16
團	新	舊	式	境	世	界	聞

1.0. 變 **biàn** change, transform, alter

變成 **biànchéng** change into, become

變為 **biànwéi** change into, become

變化 **biànhuà** (1) transform, undergo a change; (2) transformation, change

變更 **biàngēng** change (N/V) (**gēng** 'change' — note tone)

變法 **biànfǎ** reform (N)

事變 **shìbiàn** incident

演變 **yǎnbiàn** (1) develop, unfold; (2) development, unfolding

政變 **zhèngbiàn** (1) political upheaval, coup d'état; (2) undergo a political upheaval

1.1. 我記得你以前不喜歡説話. 現在話怎麽這麽多呀? 你比以前變多了.

1.2. 這孩子幾年不見變成個大人了.

1.3. 政府計劃要把這裏變為一個大城市.

1.4. 得看情形. 如果他的病没有甚麽變化, 一個星期可以好. (T)

1.5. 現在他又變更計劃了. 以前他説的辦法, 又不算了. (T)

1.6. 那個國家從變法以後, 没有好久就復興了.

1.7. 七七事變是在九一八以後才發生的.

1.8. 昨天王教授講的是「中國文字的演變」.

1.9. 那個國家政變了以後在政治方面是不是要比以前好一點兒?

2.0. 取 **qǔ** (1) take, fetch; (2) accept, admit

取得 **qǔdé** acquire, gain, obtain

取回 **qǔhuí** take back, get back, recover

考取 **kǎoqǔ** admit following an examination, accept

2.1. 我在這兒等着你. 你去取行李去.

2.2. 他在外國念書. 取得博士學位以後, 馬上就回國了.

2.3. 我的書忘在飯館兒了. 我得去取回來.

2.4. 你考麻省理工學院, 考取了没有? (T)

3.0. 造 **zào** build, manufacture, make

造成 **zàochéng** finish building, complete

造就 **zàojiù** to train

3.1. 這一帶這幾年造了不少現代化的大樓. (T)

3.2. 那個醫院要三年才能造成. (T)

3.3. 理工學院造就了不少的專門人才.

4.0. 律 **lǜ*** law

律師 **lǜshi** lawyer

法律 **fǎlǜ** law

一律 **yílǜ** (1) uniform, all of one kind; (2) uniformly, without exception, in all cases

4.1. 謝律師, 好久不見了, 我來看看你. (T)

4.2. 律師都是法律系畢業的.

4.3. 在民主國家裏, 所有的人民一律平等.

5.0. 設 **shè*** establish, found

設法 **shèfǎ** devise means, think of some way (to do something), try to

設計 **shèjì** design, plan (N/V)

設想 **shèxiǎng** (1) imagine, suppose, think; (2) supposing

假設 **jiǎshè** (1) if, supposing; (2) feign

5.1. 工人問題必得馬上設法解決.

5.2. 這個大樓的圖是王工程師設計的.

5.3. 我為你設想, 最好你還是不要離開這兒. (T)

5.4. 假設政治上有了變化，你作甚麽打算？(T)

6.0. 立 **lì** set up, erect, establish, found

立場 **lìchǎng** stand, standpoint, position, point of view

立刻 **lìkè** at once, immediately

立法院 **Lìfǎ Yuàn** Legislative Branch (of the Republic of China)

設立 **shèlì** establish

成立 **chénglì** establish

國立 **guólì** state-established, national, federal

省立 **shěnglì** province-established, provincial

縣立 **xiànlì** district-established

市立 **shìlì** city-established, municipal

自立 **zìlì** (1) be independent; (2) independency

對立 **duìlì** (1) be opposite; (2) antagonistic, incompatible; (3) opposition

中立 **zhōnglì** (1) be neutral; (2) neutrality

中立國 **zhōnglì guó** a neutral country

6.1. 市政府計劃我們這一市每年要設立一個小學校.

6.2. 站在那個國家的立場，他們只有中立. (T)

6.3. 國民政府設立五院. 立法院就是其中的一個.

6.4. 國民政府成立，是在南京還是在北京？

6.5. 國立、省立、縣立、市立學校都是政府設立的.

6.6. 要是我現在能夠自立了, 我立刻就離開我那個大家庭.

6.7. 那個國家是個中立國. 別的國發生了甚麽問題, 都跟它不發生關係. (T)

6.8. 他們兩個人對立起來了. 我們得給他們説和説和. (T)

7.0. 身 **shēn*** (1) body; (2) position, quality

身子 **shēnzi** (1) body; (2) health

身心 **shēnxīn** body and mind

身分 **shēnfen** rank, position, status, quality

身邊 **shēnbiān** by the side of a person, with a person

本身 **běnshēn** (the thing) itself, (the person) himself

起身 **qǐshēn** (1) start on a journey; (2) get up (Southern)(VO)

7.1. 我母親的身子不好極了, 時常生病.

7.2. 小學教育注意的是學生的身心.

7.3. 我的身分問題解决了以後, 我就起身到中東去. (T)

7.4. 我們現任市長本身原來是個平民, 所以他知道老百姓的困難.

7.5. 那個老太太全家人都在老家呢. 身邊只有一個女兒.

8.0. 體 tǐ* (1) body; (2) style

體會 **tǐhuì** (1) to experience, learn personally, take in, realize, comprehend; (2) understanding, comprehension

體育 **tǐyù** physical culture, athletics, gymnastics

體育場 **tǐyuchǎng** athletic field

體育館 **tǐyuguǎn** gymnasium

體育會 **tǐyuhuì** athletic club

身體 **shēntǐ** (1) body; (2) health

全體 **quántǐ** the whole body (of)

大體 **dàtǐ** (1) essence, main outline; (2) in general

大體上 **dàtǐshang** in essence, in the main, mainly, roughly speaking, speaking generally

主體 **zhǔtǐ** (1) subject, theme; (2) main person, main thing

字體 **zìtǐ** style of writing Chinese characters

8.1. 我說了半天白說了. 他根本就沒體會到我的意思.

8.2. 近幾年來, 青年的身體多數不好. 學校方面應該多注重體育.

8.3. 市立第一小學的學生今天全體都到南華體育會去了. (T)

8.4. 我們學校體育場右邊兒那個樓就是體育館.

8.5. 那件事情一定可以成功. 大體沒有甚麽問題了.

8.6. 你的工作大體上是沒甚麽了，只是一些小的問題了.(T)

8.7. 老張這次講演，是拿農業經濟作主體.(T)

8.8. 我的身體不好，時常發燒. 昨天又燒了一天.(T)

8.9. 看那封信的字體，不像王先生寫的.

8.10. 我們學校很注重體育. 每星期要上五次體育.(T)

9.0. 團 **tuán** (1) a group, a lump, a mass (M); (2) a regiment

團長 **tuánzhǎng** (1) head of a delegation; (2) regimental commander

團體 **tuántǐ** a united body, group, organization

團員 **tuányuán** member of a group

團結 **tuánjié** to cohere, join together, unite

旅行團 **lǚxíngtuán** travel club, travel group

代表團 **dàibiǎotuán** delegation

9.1. 文化代表團的團員當然都是知識分子了.

9.2. 組織一個旅行團去旅行，買團體票比較省錢.(T)

9.3. 全國的人民要團結起來.

9.4. 組織代表團倒不難，可是你看我們這幾個人裏頭誰能當團長啊？

10.0. 新 **xīn** (1) new; (2) newly, recently

新年 **xīnnián** (1) New Year's; (2) the new year

新生 **xīnshēng** (1) new student(s); (2) new life (short for **xīnshēnghuó**)

<u>新生晚報</u> <u>**Xīnshēng Wǎnbào**</u> <u>New Life Evening Post</u> (a Hong Kong daily)

新華 **Xīnhuá** New China (in institutional names)

新華社 **Xīnhuáshè** New China News Agency

新近 **xīnjìn** recently

新奇 **xīnqí** novel, extraordinary

新名詞 **xīnmíngcí** new terminology

重新 **chóngxīn** again, anew

10.1. 你這本字典是新買的嗎？

10.2. 在新年的時候小孩子們是最高興了．

10.3. 這個地方的人，從來没看見過外國人．要是看見一個外國人，他們覺得很新奇．

10.4. 這裏新近又成立了一個小學校．

10.5. 昨天我看<u>新生晚報</u>上說，新華社要在這裏成立辦事處．

10.6. 明天的歡迎新生晚會是在下午幾點鐘？

10.7. 這本詞典上有很多新名詞．

10.8. 這些字你都寫錯了．你再重新寫一次．

10.9. 新華酒樓是一個廣東飯館兒.

10.10. 這個東西很新奇.多兩塊錢少兩塊錢没關係，一定要買.(T)

11.0. 舊 jiù (1) old; (2) old-fashioned

舊有的 jiùyǒude previously possessed, previously existing (AT)

11.1. 我有很多舊書，我想賣出去.

11.2. 這本字典是舊有的，不是新買的.(T)

12.0. 式 shì* form, style, model, pattern

中式 Zhōngshì Chinese style

西式 Xīshì Western style

新式 xīnshì modern style, modern fashion

舊式 jiùshì old style, old fashion

形式 xíngshì type, form

方式 fāngshì method

正式 zhèngshì formal(ly)

合式 héshì suitable, appropriate

各式 gèshì all kinds, all sorts

各式各樣 gèshì gèyàng all sorts and kinds

樣式 yàngshi pattern, model, style

12.1. 你喜歡中式的房子，還是喜歡西式的房子？

12.2. 要是用這種方式去解决那個問題，和本來的要解决這事的目的就不對了.(T)

12.3. 張小姐那部汽車是最新式的.

12.4. 舊式家庭不許女孩子和男孩子作朋友. 現在不然, 男孩子、女孩子可以隨便作朋友了. (T)

12.5. 你看山上那些房子的形式有各式各樣的.

12.6. 你跟他研究這件事情, 用這種方式不大合式. (T)

12.7. 王市長雖然已經辦公了, 可是還沒正式上任呢. (T)

12.8. 他喜歡買酒杯. 各式的酒杯他家裏都有.

12.9. 要是你出去, 給我帶十個酒杯來, 樣式要一律的.

13.0. 境 **jìng*** boundary

境况 **jìngkuàng** situation, circumstances, condition

邊境 **biānjìng** frontier, boundary

境內 **jìngnèi** within the territory (of)

13.1. 他的境况雖然那麽不好, 可是他天天還是很快樂的.

13.2. 那兩國的邊境上近來非常緊張.

13.3. 七七事變那年北京境內有錢的都跑了.

14.0. 世 **shì*** (1) world; (2) age, time; (3) a generation, a lifetime (M)

世面 **shìmiàn** the world, society

世紀 **shìjì** century

去世 **qùshì** die

過世 **guòshì** die

14.1. 他甚麽也不懂, 他根本没見過世面.

14.2. 我們二十世紀的新青年應該注重體育.

14.3. 我母親是大前年去世的.

14.4. 我告訴你一件不好的事情. 張教授昨天晚上過世了.

15.0. 界 **jiè*** (1) realm, sphere, scope; (2) boundary

世界 **shìjiè** the world, life, society

世界語 **shìjièyǔ** (1) a world language; (2) Esperanto

邊界 **biānjiè** border, frontier

文學界 **wénxuéjiè** the world of letters, literary world

文化界 **wénhuàjiè** cultural circles

學界 **xuéjiè** student world

報界 **bàojiè** newspaper world

政(治)界 **zhèng(zhì)jiè** official circles, government circles

農業界 **nóngyèjiè** agricultural world

工業界 **gōngyèjiè** industrial world

農工界 **nónggōngjiè** world of agriculture and industry

教育界 **jiàoyujiè** educational circles

學術界 **xuéshùjiè** learned world

15.1. 世界上很多國有人懂英文, 所以有人説英文是世界語.

15.2. 昨天有文化界、報界、工業界、教育界、農業界等開歡迎大會歡迎新市長.

15.3. 那兩國的邊界時常發生問題.

15.4. 昨天參加那個演講會的都是文學界的.

15.5. 這個會，政界跟農工界都有代表參加，就是學術界沒參加.

15.6. 那個電影院門口寫着四個大字，「歡迎學界」.

15.7. 現在體育界有的團體把體育職業化了.
(T)

16.0. 聞 **wén** (1) sniff at, smell; (2) hear*; (3) information*; (4) (a surname)

聞見 **wénjian** to smell (something)

新聞 **xīnwén** news, tidings

新聞學 **xīnwénxué** journalism

新聞界 **xīnwénjiè** the press, world of journalism

(新聞)記者 **(xīnwén) jìzhě** news reporter, journalist

16.1. 誰喝酒了？…你怎麽知道？…我聞見了.

16.2. 我每天看報紙就是看看新聞.

16.3. 那些新聞記者是不是都是念過新聞學的？

16.4. 昨天聞縣長對新聞界發表談話.

17.0. 人造(的) **rénzào(de)** artificial

天然(的) **tiānrán(de)** natural

17.1. 天然的山水比人造的山水好看.

18.0. 簡化 **jiǎnhuà** simplify

簡化漢字 **jiǎnhuà Hànzì** simplified Chinese characters

簡體字 **jiǎntǐzì** simplified characters

18.1. 現在出國的辦法比以前簡化的多了.

18.2. 簡化漢字就是簡體字嗎?…是, 就是簡體字.

19.0. 多 Q N **duō Q N** to increase by such-and-such amount of N, have such-and-such amount more of N

少 Q N **shǎo Q N** to decrease by such-and-such amount of N, be short such-and-such amount of N

19.1. 奇怪!我本來有二十塊錢, 今天一數, 多了兩塊錢. (T)

19.2. 中心小學這學期比上學期多了一百多學生.

19.3. 我明明給了你六本書, 怎麽會少兩本呢?

20.0. 事件 **shìjiàn** incident, event

20.1. 九一八事件發生在東北. (T)

21.0. 法學 **fǎxué** law (as a study)

法學院 **fǎxuéyuàn** college of law, law school

公報 **gōngbào** bulletin, official communiqué

21.1. 據政府公報說, 從明年起凡法學院畢業

的必得參加政府的高等考試．合格後才能作律師．(T)

21.2. 我們學校法學院出版的法學月報內容很好．

22.0. 開頭 **kāitóu** (at) the beginning

自然而然(的) **zìrán'érrán (de)** natural(ly), spontaneous(ly), of course

學科 **xuékē** course, subject (of study)

22.1. 不論學那種學科，開頭都是很難．以後自然而然的就比較容易了．

23.0. 房間 **fángjiān** room, apartment

隨意 **suíyì** as one likes, as one pleases

23.1. 華東大旅館的房間每天十塊錢，小費隨意．(T)

24.0. 科舉 **kējǔ** selected by examination (in imperial examination system)

24.1. 聞老先生參加過清朝的科舉考試，所以他常給我們講科舉時代的故事．

25.0. 處在 **chǔzai** (situated) in (usually with words for "situation, position", etc.)

25.1. 處在你的立場，那件事情只能那麽辦．(T)

26.0. 完事 **wánshì** finish a matter, bring a matter to an end (VO)

26.1. 老張，完了事我們到那兒吃飯去？吃了飯，再去看一場電影兒好不好？

27.0. 病房 **bìngfáng** hospital room, ward

27.1. 張太太在醫院，住的是二等病房.

28.0. 就是V的N **jiùshi V de N** (1) only N V'd; (2) only N was V'd

28.1. 這次大會各界都參加了嗎？…没有，就是來的學界跟報界. (T)

29.0. 這等事 **zhèiděng shì** this sort of activity, such activities

29.1. 像喝酒玩兒麻將這等事我是從來不參加的.

30.0. 有意 **yǒuyì** have the intention to

和平 **hépíng** (1) peace; (2) be at peace; (3) be good-natured

30.1. 那兩個國家都有意和平. 我想最近的將來，和平一定能夠實現.

30.2. 我看世界上永遠是和平不了. 你說呢？(T)

Checklist

1. 變	變化	事變	2. 取
變成	變更	演變	取得
變為	變法	政變	取回

考取
3. 造
造成
造就
4. 律
律師
法律
一律
5. 設
設法
設想
假設
6. 立
立場
立刻
立法院
設立
成立
國立
省立
縣立
市立
自立
對立
中立
中立國
7. 身
身子
身心
身分
身邊
本身
起身
8. 體
體會
體育
體育場
體育館
體育會
身體
全體
實體
實體上
主體
字體
9. 團
團長
團體
團員
團結
旅行團
代表團
10. 新
新年
新生
新生晚報
新華
新華社
新近
新奇
新名詞
重新
11. 舊
舊有的
12. 式
中式
西式
新式
舊式
形式
方式
正式
合式
各式
各式各樣
樣式
13. 境
境況
邊境
境內
14. 世
世面
世紀
去世
過世
15. 界
世界
世界語
邊界
文學界
文化界
學界
報界
政(治)界
農業界
工業界
農工界
教育界
學術界
16. 聞
聞見
新聞
新聞學
新聞界
(新聞)記者
17. 人造(的)

天然(的)

18. 簡化

簡化漢字

簡體字

19. 多QN

少QN

20. 事件

21. 法學

法學院

公報

22. 開頭

自然而然(的)

學科

23. 房間

隨意

24. 科舉

25. 處在

26. 完事

27. 病房

28. 就是V的N

29. 這等事

30. 有意

和平

Exercise 1. Excerpts from Actual Publications

The following excerpts are taken from a collection of short stories by Yè Shèngtáo (Yeh Shengt'ao)

1. 上課的鐘聲叫他隨着許多同學走進教室裏.

2. 在三年以前，本地一個高等小學的校長別處去了，他就接任了校長的職務.…他想了許多的法子…才得到這個地位.

3. 本來是隨意玩玩的.… 現在…我們知道這件事是不該隨意玩的. 從此以後，我們再也不做這等不該做的事了.

4. 「你看見了今天的地方公報麽？」
「没有看見. 有甚麽緊要的事件麽？」

「原來你沒有看見. … 沒有甚麽.」

5.「找房間麽？」
「是找房間, 這裏還有麽？」
「有是有一間…」
「那一間就是我們住好了.」… 這房間就在樓下.

6. 永遠是這樣的情形. 三十年來, 就只多了那些…人力車. 走路的人永遠是這樣的慢.

7.「我們幾個朋友計劃在這裏開一個中學校.」
「那是很好的事情.」

8. 我進去時, 校長是一位方先生, 方先生後是李先生.

9. 我沒有甚麽對你說的, 只有一個字, 難！…真是難！

10. 我們中間還有東北人, 我就是一個.

11. 他…笑着説:「明華, 想不到是你呀！你弟弟也在這裏！」

12.「我們聽了你的演說…從開頭聽起，也聽了你那位同學的演說.」
「你覺得怎樣？」
「同剛才許多人說的一樣，覺得你們的話不錯.」

13.「誰這樣想起的？」
「就是我，我這樣想起的.」
「將就些，不要出甚麽主張吧！」
「為甚麽？」
「我不相信這樣會有好處.」
「怎麽沒有好處？」

14.「我不贊成你這樣做.」
「你懂得甚麽！」
「我不懂麽？」

15.「下學期我不是你們的先生了！」
「下學期誰來教我們了呢？」
「自然是一位新先生，我不知道是誰，所以不能告訴你們.」

Exercise 2. Dialogues

1. 聞：張聞天最近到越南去了？他一個人去的嗎？
   金：他們一共有五六個人呢．都是報界的，都是新聞記者的身分去的．他們像是旅行團．
   聞：當然老張是團長了．
   金：不是．他是團員．
   聞：他們去多少日子？
   金：大概兩個星期吧．
   聞：老張也不會越南話，也不會法文，多麽没意思啊．
   金：老張會英文哪．現在的英文好像成了世界語了，不論到那兒去，會英文就成．

2. 謝：聞一新，你考法學院，考取了嗎？
   聞：考取了．法學月報八月號有這次考取新生的名字．
   謝：你得在這兒幾年？
   聞：我現在不敢决定，得看情形．我是

希望快一點兒把論文寫完取得學位以後我就回去.
謝：你回去當律師,還是在政府作事呢？
聞：我打算回去教書，教法律去.
謝：那麽你是在教育界作事了？
聞：對了. 我認為造就人才比甚麽事情都有意思.

3. 毛：昨天會開的怎麽樣？
田：很好. 大體上還不錯.
毛：是不是有很多新聞界的人參加？
田：沒有幾個人. 多數是學術界的團體.
毛：據說有新華社的記者？
田：不會吧. 我想他們不會來的.
毛：學生多不多？
田：就是幾個國立大學的學生參加了.
毛：大學的學生，是每一個學校全體都去了嗎？
田：沒有. 就是去的代表.

4. 温：老湯，我告訴你一件不好的事情. 簡新民的父親，昨天去世了.

湯：是嗎？簡先生的身體很好啊，而且他的年紀也不很老.

温：是啊．上星期我在中華體育會還看見他了呢．他老人家有意過了新年旅行全世界去．想不到没有幾天就過世了.

湯：他是甚麽病你知道嗎？

温：新民說，開頭的時候就是不想吃東西，不到三天人就不行了.

湯：聽說簡先生在政界很多年.

温：可是從來是不得意．新近聽說有了一個比較好的職務，還没上任，他老人家就過去了.

5．許：老王，好久不見，你近來怎麽樣？

王：別提了．自從我父親去世以後，我的境况非常不好．你看我在文化界作事，每月得不到很多錢．我不但有父母還有個弟弟在市立中學念書，還不能自立呢.

許：你讓他作點事啊．我聽說才設立的

那個體育館裏要請一個人，是每天晚上工作的.

王：我弟弟今年才十五歲，這種工作合式嗎？

許：我想可以．他們就是要一個年紀在十四五歲的.

6. 師：昨天我介紹給你們的那本中國文字的演變你們看了嗎？

生：看了．有的不懂．先生，簡化漢字就是簡體字嗎？

師：是的.

生：「字體」是甚麼意思？

師：「字體」就是字的樣子．每一個人寫的字，樣子都不同，各有各的字體.

生：「新名詞」是甚麼意思？

師：「新名詞」就是新的名詞.

生：「設法」就是「想法子」嗎？

師：「設法」就是「想法子」.

生：「文化界」跟「文學界」有甚麼不同？

師：文學界只是文學一方面的．新聞、

美術、音樂跟文學都是文化界的.

生：「科舉」是甚麽？

師：是以前的一種考試制度.

生：老師,「變法」是甚麽意思？

師：「變法」就是把方法變更了. 我舉一個例子:“那個國家從變法以後沒有好久就變為一個第一等的國家了.”

生：「事件」跟「事變」、「政變」都怎麽用？

師：“日本人在東北境内, 造成九一八事件. 七七事變也是日本人在中國造成的”. “那個國家從政變以後, 經濟情形比較好了.”

生：「身心」就是「身體跟心」嗎？

師：是的. 他的用法是這樣:“小學的教育要注重學生的身心.”

生：老師,「身邊」呢？

師：“那個老頭兒, 雖然兒女很多, 可是過世的時候身邊連一個兒女都沒有.”時間到了. 有問題我們明天再研究. 還有, 昨天你們寫的那幾個漢字, 你們都寫的不怎麽好, 請你們再重新寫一次, 明天給我.

生: 那幾個字很難寫, 怎麽寫也寫不好.

師: 你們多寫幾次, 自然而然的就會寫好了.

生: 好的. 老師明天見.

師: 明天見.

7. 費: 老麻, 新聞學這種學科難不難?

麻: 學甚麽也不容易. 學新聞的畢了業以後, 在新聞界作事, 天天為了新聞跑來跑去, 有時候連吃飯的工夫都沒有.

費: 那麽你為甚麽要學呢?

麻: 這是個人的興趣.

費: 聽說王世平也是學新聞的.

麻: 是啊. 可是他現在在體育界作事了.

費: 這兩天放假沒報紙看. 這幾天邊境上還那麽緊張嗎?

麻: 緊張倒是不那麽緊張了. 可是邊界

問題一時解决不了.

費: 我看新生晚報上説兩國的關係越來越不好.

麻: 是的.

費: 我忘了説了,你要買的那本大字典,現在十五塊錢書店不賣了. 現在要十八塊, 少了不賣.

麻: 多兩塊錢少兩塊錢没關係. 你買來得了.

8. 包: 昨天我在省政府看見政府公報上説,政府計劃着要設立省立第三中學.

金: 是. 我也聽説了. 説教育部已經請王工程師設計了. 聽説學校房子的樣式是最新式的, 而且要造一個最大的體育場.

包: 據説將來在教育一方面大體是和第一、第二兩個中學差不多, 實體上他們注重體育.

金: 是不是要造就體育人才?

包: 不是. 原因是他們體會到近來的青

年只注重功課，不注重身體，所以學界的人很關心這個問題．

金：我也覺得我們二十世紀的青年應該有一個好的身體．

9．邊：老張，聽説程先生不久要到這兒來了，不知道起身了没有？

張：我昨天接到他的信，説下月十五號起身．他讓我在旅館給他定個房間．你説那個旅館好呢？

邊：你給他定新華大旅館吧．那兒房間的價錢不貴，而且小費隨意．他這次來，是不是跟工業界代表團來呀？

張：他是跟代表團坐同一個飛機，他跟代表團沒關係．

邊：他這次到這兒來的目的是甚麼？

張：他要旅行全世界．他説他要多見見世面．

10．畢：聽説你新買了房子了？

連：是．因為人口多，原來的房子不够住了，自己買了一所兒比較大一點兒的.

畢：是中式的還是西式的？

連：是一所兒舊的中式房子. 這所兒房子，本身的形式是舊式的，可是附近的四面兒的房子都是最現代化的西式房子. 要是站在門口兒，四面兒一看，各式各樣兒的房子真好看.

畢：幾時到你那兒去看看去.

連：等我收拾好了，請你們去. 這所兒房子還有一樣好處，院子特別大，院子裏有人造的假山. 要是天氣暖和的時候，請幾個朋友在院子坐一坐大家談談很有意思.

11. 溫：田世英的病不輕啊.

應：可不是嗎！昨天燒了一天，連一點兒東西都沒吃.

溫：要不要送他到醫院去？

應：看情形. 假設有甚麽變化，我們立刻送他到醫院. 這件事很麻煩. 他家連一個人也不在這兒，沒親人給他拿主意．要是送他到醫院，你說到那個醫院好呢？

温：最好送他去縣立醫院．那裏病房是一律的不分等級．

12. 張：老李你來了．

李：好久不見了，來看看你．是不是做紅燒肉了．

張：你怎麽知道？

李：我聞見了．

張：你晚飯在這兒吃紅燒肉好不好？

李：够吃嗎？

張：够．我做了很多呢．

李：昨天你們那個大會開的怎麽樣？

張：開會的情形很好．參加的是農業界的人數最多．

李：是不是工業界的也參加了？

張：是．雖然這次參加的是農工業界，可是還是拿農業作主體．談的都是注重農業一方面的．昨天講到中國農業不發達主要原因是農民種田不知道用科學方法．以後還談到不久的將來，這裏要成立一個農業專門學校，造就農業專門人才．

13. 學生：先生早．

先生：同學早．昨天你們去旅行，玩兒的高興嗎？

學生：我們高興極了．先生您為甚麽不去呢？

先生：我很想去的，可是家裏有很要緊的事，所以不能去了．好，你們先把書收起來．我問你們問題．温新元請你用「天然」這個詞兒説個句子．

學生：“山、水、湖、海是天然的，不是人造的．”

先生：對了．許思聰，用「對立」説個句子．

學生：“我看和平不了了．那兩個國家已經成了對立的情形．雖然那個中立國給他們説和，但是兩國和好的希望也不大．”

先生：你坐下. 謝一良, 你知道不知道立法院是甚麽？

學生：國民政府的組織裏有五院, 立法院就是那五院裏的一個.

先生：對. 不過你説的太長了, 你把它再簡化一點兒説一説.

學生：國民政府有五院, 立法院是其中的一個.

先生：好. 湯一良, 你用「中立」説個句子.

學生："處在我們這個國家的立場, 只有中立."

先生：好. 請你再用「新奇」説個句子.

學生："一個外國人初次到中國去, 他看見各式各樣的東西都很新奇."

先生：好. 現在你們看書. 要是有問題, 快問, 然後我們講新的.

14. 程：金開文把我的字典給借去了. 好幾個月也不還我. 他也不為我設想, 他不還我我用甚麽？

包：有這等事！你不會自己到他那兒取回來嗎？

程：我不好意思.

包：難道你就不要了？

程：要是要．過兩天再說．他以前不是這樣人，他最不喜歡借別人的東西.

包：我覺得他有點兒變了.

程：是啊．他老跟人家借東西．變成這種樣子，跟以前好像兩個人了.

15. 應：昨天新市長正式接任，你們市政府裏面很忙吧？

聞：可不是！從上午十點起一直到下午兩點才完事.

應：新市長、前任市長都要演講了？

聞：都離不了這種方式．演說的內容也都一樣，"希望大家團結起來，同心合力地合作."這些話聽都聽够了.

Exercise 3. Narratives

1. 在一八九八年的時候，正是中國的清朝，當時中國在政治上有一個很大的變更，叫做變法．變法是把舊的法子不用了，變為新的法子．這些新的法子，對於國家和人民都是很有好處的．可是那次變法只實行了幾天，就發生了變化．結果是變法沒成功．有人說，假設那次的政變成功了，中國也許早就成了一個很理想的國家了．

2. 中國從前在科舉時代，念書的人只知道念書，不知道注重體育，所以很多人的身子都不大好．自從設立學校以後，把體育當作必修的一種學科．在小學、中學裏，如果體育不及格就不能畢業，所以學生的身體都比從前好的多了．

3. 張士良是在大學教新聞學．他對學生說，寫新聞第一要寫真的，第二要快．社會上每天發生各式各樣的新聞，新聞記者的職務是「有聞必錄」．「有聞必錄」的意思就是聽見的事情就立刻寫出來．現在新聞界有幾個有名的新聞記者，他們就是有聞必錄，寫的又是事實而且又快．

4．據體育界的人說，有人要組織一個體育團體．這個團體的團員拿學界、文化界作主體．我說：“現在不是已經有了一個體育會嗎？體育會裏各界的人都有，教育界和報界的更多．為甚麽還要重新組織一個團體呢？那不是要跟體育會對立嗎？”他說：“體育會當初才成立的時候，倒是很好．新近有一些人參加以後，他們把體育當作一種職業．每次他們都賣票，拿體育當作生意，和本來的體育目的就不對了．體育是為了身體好，怎可以職業化呢？所以有人要重新組織一個團體，目的是為了身體才注重體育．”

5．我小的時候，家住在縣城裏頭，我在縣立小學念書．小學畢業以後，因為父親到省城一個體育館去做事，我就隨着父親到了省城，在一個省立中學念書．這就是說，我念小學、中學的時候，都没離開過父親．後來念大學了，這個大學是一個國立大學，離我家和省城都很遠，我當然離開我父親了．每天我在大學上課完事以後，時常想起父親，就給父親寫信．父親回信說：“你已經是大學生了，也能自立了，父親怎麽能常在你的身邊呢？”

6．我看法學半月報上說我們法律系前年畢業的學生許式言去年在立法院做事．現在他一面做律師，一面又在法學院教法律，所以他的身分有兩種，一種身分是律師，一種身分是大學教授．

7．世界上有一個最有名的獎金，凡是在學術上有重要發明，或者是特別盡力的，不論是那一個國家的人都可以得到這個獎金．這個獎金分為七種：物理、化學、醫學、生理，經濟，文學和努力世界和平工作的．據學術界的人說，美國的加州大學有八個人得過這種獎金，所以這個大學在學術上算是很有地位的．

8. 有一個外國學生,從前在中國念過大學.他說:“我在中國念書的時候，最喜歡看中文的報紙，更喜歡看新華日報.後來我回到本國，不常看中文報紙了.有一天,有一位朋友給我送來一張中文報紙,是新生晚報.我細看内容又有新聞又有小說，大體很好，我真高興極了.”

9. 我在中國住過的旅館可以分為兩種.一種是舊式的,房間裏的東西都是中式的.一種是新式的,房間裏的東西有中式的,也有西式的.我最喜歡住舊式旅館，因為我喜歡用那些中國的東西.

10. 農業界和工業界組織一個旅行團到外國去旅行.他們起身的時候，農工界都有人來送他們.等到他們全體都上了船,送他們的人才回去.有人說:“今天來送旅行團的人，工業界的人最多，農業界就是來的代表.”

11. 有一個國家發表公報，大意是：我們從十九世紀以來就是一個中立國．最近在我們西邊兒的邊境上時常發生一些緊張事件．此後還不知道要怎麽樣的演變．現在我們正式説明，我們的中立是永久不變的．

12. 學生問先生：“七七事變是不是發生在中國和日本的邊界上？”先生説：“不是的．發生的地點是在中國北京的附近．有了這次事變，處在中國的立場不能不起來要打倒日本了．”

13. 有一個留學生到了外國，沒有多久，就希望取得博士學位．他請一位教授給他設法．這位教授説：“應當你自己本身在學術上努力，才可以取得博士學位．”

14. 有一個文學家在文學界是最有名的．他最不贊成簡體字．他説：“漢字有幾千年的歷史，為甚麽要簡化漢字？簡化的目的是甚麽？如果是為了省時間，寫一個漢字多寫幾筆和少寫幾筆時間上差不了很多. 我舉個例子, 比如「看見」的「見」吧, 少兩筆. 你說能省多少時候呢? 現在把漢字的字體變成種種很奇怪的形式. 真是不對.”

15. 有一個男孩子最喜歡聽故事, 天天讓他母親給他講故事. 有一天是過新年的前一天, 在這天晚上十一點多鐘這個孩子又讓他母親講故事. 他母親說:“今天給你講一個故事是最短的也是最長的.”這個孩子說:“哪有一個故事又是最短的又是最長的呢.”他母親說:“我先問你, 現在是幾點鐘了?”這個孩子去看看表說:“現在差一分鐘就是十二點.”他母親說:“好. 現在我就給你講.”他母親就開始給他講故事, 講了一會兒講完了. 他母親說:“你再去看看表, 現在是甚麽時候了?”孩子看看表, 回來說:“現在是十二點過了一分鐘.”他母親說:“我講的這個故事算是最短的, 又算是最長的吧!”孩子說:“短是算最短的了, 才講了兩分鐘，可是怎能算是最長的呀？”他母親說：“你細想想看．”這個孩子想了一會兒說：“我明白了．你這個故事開頭講的時候是一九六六年，講完的時候是一九六七年，講了兩年，可算是最長的了．”

16. 有一個人在外國很多年，最近回到本國．他說：“我在外國的時候有人告訴我本國最近的境況．他說最近的情形比從前變多了．可是我這次回來，一到了本國的境內就覺得大體上是和從前差不多．後來到市場一帶看看，都是新的馬路，多了幾個大樓，是比從前不同了．可是我想這種變化都是工程上的，都是人造的，多半是表面上的．”

17. 王先生的父親去世了．他心裏想，我用甚麽方式可以給父親留一個永久紀念？後來他想到用他父親的名字設立一個圖書館，他就找人設計．他對設計的人說：“這個圖書館的樣式要新奇一點，在時間上，最好能在三年以內就造成．”

18. 有一個代表團代表本國到外國去開會. 團員、團長都是政界有名的人. 在沒開會以前, 團長問團員:“在開會的時候我們是不是應該用本國的語言?” 有的團員說:“世界各國在一塊兒開會, 多半是用英文, 現在英文差不多成了世界語了, 所以我們應當用英文.”有的團員說:“我們是代表本國, 所以應當用本國語言.”

19. 旅行對於人的身心都有好處. 有時候有甚麽心事或者是身體不大好, 就去旅行, 出去看看山水, 就把心事忘了, 身體也自然而然的好起來了.

20. 有一個從外國回來的留學生, 在本國一個中學教書. 有人問, 這個留學生的學問怎麽樣? 有人說:“他的學問怎麽樣還看不出來, 可是他說話的時候, 常說一些新名詞, 所以學生給他一個外號, 叫他是「新名詞先生」.

21. 王先生是一個體育教員. 他有一個用人,

樣子很老實, 其實很不老實. 有一天, 王先生買來的酒和紅燒鷄, 他對着酒跟用人說:"這是一種有顏色的水, 是喝不得的, 千萬不能喝. 如果喝了就一定活不了啦. 還有, 這些紅燒鷄, 你給我收起來. 我現在到體育場給學生上體育課去, 等一會兒我回來吃." 這個用人說: "好." 這個用人在王先生走了以後, 聞見了酒和紅燒鷄, 高興的不得了, 就把酒喝了, 鷄也吃了. 過了一會兒, 王先生回來了, 一看酒和鷄都不見了, 就問鷄怎麽不見了呢? 這個用人說:"鷄飛了." 王先生說:"紅燒鷄會飛? 有這等事? 那麽那些有顏色的水呢?" 這個用人說: "我老實説了吧, 你走以後, 不知道是怎麽的紅燒鷄就不見了. 我心裏想, 主人叫我收這一點兒東西, 我都不能盡職, 我太對不起主人啦, 也太沒用啦, 像我這樣沒用的人還活着做甚麽? 我就想起來主人說的話, 那種有顏色的水, 要是喝了就活不了啦. 我就把它喝啦. 可是我不明白為甚麽喝了那種有顏色的水,我還活着呢?”

22. 有兩個國家邊界的問題很久没法子解决. 有人說:“在這兩個國的中間有一道河, 是天然的邊界, 為甚麽還發生邊界問題呢?” 有人說:“問題就發生在這道河. 兩國都說這道河從來就是在本國國土範圍内,所以這個邊界問題不容易解决.”

23. 許世平病了, 住在醫院裏. 我要去看他. 有人告訴我, 到這個醫院去看病人有一定的時間. 要是不到時間, 或者是過了時間, 不論是誰, 一律不能進到病房, 去看病人.

24. 王先生的家是一個大家庭, 人口很多. 自從他父親過世以後, 他家裏的事都是他拿主意. 他對別人很好, 常常給別人設想. 他說:“如果只知道注重自己,不知道本身以外還有別人,這種人不論在家、在社會、在國家都是沒法子相處的.”

25. 有一個人，第一次到了外國看見了各式各樣從來沒看見過的東西. 他說:“我真像一個沒見過世面的孩子，看見甚麽都覺着新奇.”

26. 田先生想買房子. 我說:“我有一個朋友，前幾天給我來信說要賣房子. 在這封信裏，他把房子的情形說的很詳細，還把這所房子畫了一張圖. 你如果有意買這所房子，我把這封信給你送來看看.”田先生說:“好. 就請你先把信送來吧.”我把這封信送去了以後，田先生給我來電話了. 他說:“這封信和房子的圖我都看過了. 這所房子是舊式的，我認為不大合式. 這封信是你取回去呢，還是我給你送去呢？”

27. 老張問我:“我們大學裏的歷史系主任跟校長是甚麽關係，你知道嗎？”我說:“我知道他是校長的舊同學.”老張說:

"怪不得他總在校長室和校長隨便説説笑笑呢."

28. 在二十世紀新發明的東西太多了. 原子能就是一個重要的發明. 有人説發明原子能對於人們没有甚麽好處, 可是自從發明原子能以後很多大船甚麽的都用原子能了. 所以發明原子能對於人們是有好處.

29. 先生對學生講, 在一個國家裏人民應當團結. 要是人民能團結, 大家同心合力, 國家一定越來越好. 如果人民不知道團結, 自己為自己打算, 國家怎麽能够好起來呢.

30. 中國自從民國八年以來, 有些學者主張打倒舊的文學, 注重新文化. 可是也有些學者不贊成. 後來事實告訴人們, 新文化是合時的, 是有用的, 贊成的人就越來越多了.

31. 我是學新聞學的. 畢業以後希望作一個

新聞記者. 朋友告訴我，新聞記者這種工作很不容易，工作是沒有時間性的，不論白天晚上都得出去，連飯都沒法子好好兒吃. 他說，在新聞界作事倒可以，最好不要做新聞記者. 他還說了一句笑話兒. 他說："如果作新聞記者將來結了婚，可能你太太要和你離婚."

32. 同學們：這個時間應該是專題講話，我現在借着這個時間說一說本校的概況，讓外國同學們了解了解本校的情形. 我現在先給大家介紹介紹我自己. 我叫張友真. 我在學校的工作就是幫助外國留學生的. 如果大家有甚麼問題，可以隨時去找我. 我每天都在總辦公樓二百六十一號. 有的同學也許看見學校出的一本小册子，裏面有本校的歷史和組織等等. 我現在再詳細的把跟大家有關係的一些問題說一說. 我先把本校的院系說一說：本校有大學，有研究院，一共有六個學院. 有文學院、法學院、理學院、工學院、農學院還有醫學院．醫學院是最近才有的．學校計劃着明年還要辦一個教育學院．根據教務處的記錄，本校的外國留學生文學院的最多，法學院跟理學院最少．別的學院没有外國學生．我現在就說一說文學院、法學院、理學院這三個學院的學系．文學院有中文系、外文系、歷史系、新聞系、語言學系．法學院有法律系、政治系、經濟系、社會系．理學院有數學系、生物系、心理學系．我再說說本校的學制．我們學校是學分制．要是大學念滿了一百二十個學分，並且還要作畢業論文才能够畢業，得到學士學位．研究院要在得了學士學位之後，如果再想繼續的研究就入本校的研究院．我再說一說怎麽可以得獎學金．不論是在大學或是在研究院，凡是各門功課分數都在八十分以上的就可以請獎學金．學校大概的情形都介紹給大家了．我們還有圖書館、合作社、錄音室等等的都在那本小冊子上寫的很清楚.我很希望大家時常找我談談.我天天都在總辦公樓.

Exercise 4. Illustrative Sentences (English)

1.4. We have to see how things go. If there is no change in his illness, he'll recover in a week.

1.5. Now he's changed his plans again. The procedure that he spoke of before is no longer being considered.

2.4. Were you accepted when you took the exam for M.I.T.?

3.1. During the past few years quite a few modern [lit. modernized] big buildings have been built in this area.

3.2. That hospital will require three years for completion.

4.1. Lawyer Xie, I haven't seen you for some time. [I've come to see you.]

5.3. In my opinion [lit. I think for you], it would be best if you [still] didn't leave here.

5.4. Supposing there's a political change, what plans would you make?

6.2. In that country's situation it [lit. they] can only be neutral.

6.7. That country is a neutral country. Whenever differences arise among other countries, it is never involved.

6.8. The two of them have had a falling out. We must make peace for them.

7.3. After the problem of my status has been resolved, I'll start for the Middle East.

8.3. Today the students at Metropolitan Elementary School No. 1 all went in a body to the South China Athletic Club.

8.6. Your work in general is O.K. There are just a few small problems.

8.7. When Zhang lectured this time he had as his main topic "Agricultural

Economy."

8.8. My health is poor. I'm always getting a fever. Yesterday I was again feverish all day.

8.10. Our school places a lot of emphasis on athletics. We have athletics five times a week.

9.2. In organizing a travel group for a trip, it is [comparatively] economical to buy group tickets.

10.10. This thing is very new. It doesn't matter whether it's a few dollars more or less, (you) must certainly buy one.

11.2. I've had this dictionary for some time. I didn't buy it recently.

12.2. If we use this approach in solving that problem, it will not be in line with our original aim in resolving this matter.

12.4. Old-style families did not permit girls and boys to be friends. It's otherwise now. Boys and girls can be friends as they please.

12.6. It wouldn't be very appropriate to use this approach in dealing with this matter with him.

12.7. Although Mayor Wang has already taken up his duties, he has still not yet formally assumed office.

15.7. Now some groups in the athletic world have professionalized athletics.

19.1. Strange! I originally had twenty dollars. When I counted it today I had two dollars more.

20.1. The September 18 Incident took place in Manchuria.

21.1. According to a government bulletin, beginning next year all law school graduates must take the government's advanced examination. Only after qualifying (on the exam) is it possible to become a lawyer.

23.1. The East China Hotel rooms are ten dollars a day, (plus) tips as you please.

25.1. In your position you can only handle that matter in that way.

28.1. Did people from all walks of life participate in this big meeting? … No. Only people from the student and newspaper world came.

30.2. I think there can never be peace in the world. What do you think?

Lesson 14

1	2	3	4	5	6	7	8
展	落	流	推	選	消	稱	需

9	10	11	12	13	14	15	16
增	趕	深	漸	勢	標	堂	似

1.0. 展 **zhǎn** (1) open out, unfold*; (2) extend, postpone

展期 **zhǎnqī** postpone, defer, put off until later

發展 **fāzhǎn** (1) develop, expand; (2) development, expansion

1.1. 學術演講會聽説再展兩個星期才開呢. (T)

1.2. 許先生寫的那本中國近代史展期出版了. (T)

1.3. 辦教育的應該注重學生的身心發展.

2.0. 落 **luò** (1) fall, drop; (2) alight

落後 **luòhòu** be backward, undeveloped

落價 **luòjià** fall in price (N/V) (VO)

落下來 **luòxialai** drop down, land

2.1. 經濟落後的國家各方面都不容易發展.

2.2. 據説這幾天各種東西都落價了.

2.3. 昨天我到飛機場去接朋友, 去晚了. 飛機已經落下來了我才到的.

3.0. 流 **liú** to flow

流行 **liúxíng** (1) be prevalent, popular; (2) become prevalent, spread

流行病 **liúxíngbìng** an epidemic, widespread illness

河流 **héliú** a stream

3.1. 近來流行的這種音樂我可不喜歡聽.

3.2. 這一帶有一種流行病, 所有的小孩子差不多都病了.

3.3. 中國境内有兩條大河流. 一條在中部, 一條在北部.

4.0. 推 **tuī** (1) push; (2) refuse responsibility; (3) elect, select; (4) deduce, reason

推開 **tuīkai** push open, push away

推翻 **tuīfān** overthrow, upset

推進 **tuījìn** to promote, advance

推行 **tuīxíng** carry into operation, carry out

推舉 **tuījǔ** recommend (by a group), elect

推定 **tuīdìng** decide (on)

推想 **tuīxiǎng** (1) infer, deduce; (2) deduction, opinion

推算 **tuīsuàn** (1) calculate; (2) calculation

推廣 **tuīguǎng** promote, expand

推讓 **tuīràng** (1) yield; (2) decline honors

4.1. 誰從外面把大門給推開了?

4.2. 把清朝政府推翻了以後，中華民國就成立了.

4.3. 在這裏要推行那種學説，恐怕一時推進不了.

4.4. 我的推想，你們推舉他當代表團團長，他一定不做.(T)

4.5. 大家已經推定温思聽作我們學生代表了.

4.6. 你看漢語拼音容易不容易推廣？

4.7. 我的推算，張先生跟李先生兩個人一定要推讓的.

5.0. 選 **xuǎn** select, elect, vote for

選取 **xuǎnqǔ** select

選出 **xuǎnchu** pick out, select

選舉 **xuǎnjǔ** (1) elect; (2) election

選上 **xuǎnshang** be elected

選課 **xuǎnkè** elect courses (of study) (VO)

推選 **tuīxuǎn** elect, choose

5.1. 這次選世界小姐，昨天已經選出來了.中國小姐選上了.(T)

5.2. 將來選舉的時候，你心目中要推選誰？

5.3. 聽説市政府考翻譯員，從六十五個人裏就選取了四個人.(T)

5.4. 選課是很麻煩的一件事. 不知道選哪門好.

5.5. 中國人結婚的那天, 一定要先選個好日子. (T)

5.6. 上次選舉的時候, 把張先生忙的不得了. (T)

6.0. 消 **xiāo** (1) diminish, subside; (2) consume; (3) be necessary, require

消氣 **xiāoqì** get over one's anger

消化 **xiāohuà** (1) melt; (2) digest; (3) digestion

消路 **xiāolù** market for goods

消費 **xiāofèi** (1) consume; (2) consumption

消費的 **xiāofèide** consumers, purchasers

消費合作社 **xiāofèi hézuòshè** consumer's cooperative

取消 **qǔxiāo** cancel, annul, rescind

不消說 **bùxiāo shuō** need not say, needless to say

6.1. 從北京到張家口只消幾個鐘頭的時間.

6.2. 你看他氣還沒消呢, 先別跟他說那件事情. 等他消了氣我們再跟他研究. (T)

6.3. 小孩子不能吃那種東西, 因為不容易消化.

6.4. 我想中文書在美國沒有甚麼消路.

6.5. 我們計算計算, 這裏水果和生菜每天要消費多少？

6.6. 這裏消費合作社的範圍很大.

6.7. 學校這個星期六晚上的那個音樂晚會聽說取消了.

6.8. 老張，今天的晚飯不消說是你請客了.(T)

6.9. 在那個市場裏消費的多半是女人.(T)

6.10. 不消說，他說的跟他做的完全不是一回事兒.(T)

7.0. 稱 **chēng** to address

稱贊 **chēngzàn** to praise

名稱 **míngchēng** name, appellation, designation

簡稱(叫) **jiǎnchēng (jiào)** (1) be called in abbreviated form; (2) abbreviated name

總名(稱) **zǒngmíng(chēng)** (1) general term, inclusive term; (2) full name

7.1. 王律師雖然很年輕，可是很有本事，人人都稱他是大律師.

7.2. 湯先生在學術界很有表現，所以大家都稱贊他.

7.3. 這個東西你們知道他的名稱嗎？

7.4. 師範大學簡稱師大.

7.5. 那些歷史書的總名稱是二十四史.(T)

8.0. 需 **xū** to need

需要 **xūyào** (1) to need, require; (2) necessity, demand, need

8.1. 現在我們感到最需要的是在經濟方面的幫助.

9.0. 增 **zēng** to increase

增加 **zēngjiā** increase (N/V)

增進 **zēngjìn** (1) advance; (2) advancement

9.1. 這裏的人口已經增加到三千萬了.

9.2. 為了增進兩國的關係, 所以這個國家組織了一個代表團到那個國家去訪問.

10.0. 趕 **gǎn** (1) rush to do something; (2) catch (plane, etc.); (3) drive away; (4) by the time

趕緊(的) **gǎnjǐn(de)** quickly, immediately, without delay

趕快(的) **gǎnkuài (de)** quickly, immediately, without delay

趕上 **gǎnshang** (1) catch up with, pursue and overtake (RV); (2) just when, by the time that

趕去 **gǎnqu** pursue hurriedly, go hurriedly

趕出來/去 **gǎnchulai/qu** (1) drive out, drive away, expel; (2) rush out, rush to completion (RV)

趕回來/去 **gǎnhuilai/qu** hurry back

趕V_1再V_2 **gǎn V_1 zài V_2** V_2 by the time V_1, wait until V_1 and then V_2

正趕上 **zhèng gǎnshang** just when, by the time that

V (的) 正趕上時候 **(V) de zhèng gǎnshang shíhou** V at just the right time

10.1. 我這些日子忙的不得了，趕我的博士論文呢. (T)

10.2. 我們趕快的去推行那種計劃，要不然就落後了.

10.3. 我們趕緊地走吧，要不然趕不上火車了.

10.4. 我們雖然是比較落後的國家，但是我們努力去作，在五年以內一定趕上他們.

10.5. 昨天晚上的音樂會，因為我有事去晚了，我趕去了，已經快完了.

10.6. 他一天不是喝酒就是玩麻將，一點兒也不用功念書. 他父親一生氣把他從家裏給趕出去了.

10.7. 我是趕回來的，要不然就晚了.

10.8. 那件事情我們沒辦法. 趕謝先生從日本回來再解決吧.

10.9. 好極了，你來的正趕上時候. 你來幫我們解決這個問題吧. (T)

10.10. 我到他家去的時候，正趕上他們吃飯呢，所以我就在那兒吃的飯.

11.0. 深 **shēn** deep [lit. or fig.]

深色 **shēnsè** deep shade, deep color

高深 **gāoshēn** lofty and deep, profound

11.1. 我不要那種顏色的紙，我要深色的.

11.2. 没有高深的學問，决寫不了那樣的論文. (T)

12.0. 漸 **jiàn*** gradual(ly)

漸漸的 **jiànjiànde** gradually

12.1. 現在天氣漸漸的暖和了.

13.0. 勢 **shì*** (1) momentum; (2) tendency, situation

勢力 **shìli** strength, power, influence

大勢 **dàshì** circumstances, (general) situation

大勢已去 **dàshì yǐ qù** situation is hopeless

地勢 **dìshì** physical features (of a place)

情勢 **qíngshì** circumstances, situation, trend of affairs

形勢 **xíngshì** (1) appearance, condition; (2) topography

13.1. 這一帶都是他的勢力範圍. (T)

13.2. 看那個國家的大勢，他們是不可能再復興了.

13.3. 近來那個政府的情勢越來越不好，真是大勢已去，不久就會讓人民給推翻了. (T)

13.4. 中國地理的形勢是西北高.

13.5. 那個地勢很好．兩面是山，一面是水．

14.0.	標	**biāo***	a sign, signal
	標記	**biāojì**	sign, signal, mark, marker
	標語	**biāoyǔ**	(written) slogan
	標題	**biāotí**	heading, headline
	標本	**biāoběn**	specimen, sample, example
	標準	**biāozhǔn**	a mark to aim at, (normal) standard, example
	標準語	**biāozhǔnyǔ**	standard language
	標準音	**biāozhǔnyīn**	standard pronunciation
	目標	**mùbiāo**	goal, objective
	音標(兒)	**yīnbiāo(r)**	phonetic notation, phonetic symbol

14.1. 這個地方的河水不够深．河中間有一個標記讓船經過的時候要從左邊走．

14.2. 那些學生為了甚麽又拿着標語各處走？(T)

14.3. 今天報紙上社論的標題是「怎樣發展社會經濟」．

14.4. 今天下課以後我們得到城外頭去找生物標本．

14.5. 學國語應該用張小姐説的話作標準．他的話是標準音．

14.6. 他們用甚麽方言作標準語？

14.7. 老謝，我們下星期去旅行的目標倒是那兒啊？

14.8. 你看看這是甚麽音標啊？我不懂.

14.9.「標本」的「標」字是「木」字邊加上「票子」的「票」字.(T)

15.0. 堂 **táng*** (1) hall; (2) (measure for classes and lessons)

堂上 **tángshang** in class

上堂 **shàngtáng** go to class (VO) (now used less often than **shàng kè**)

課堂 **kètáng** classroom (now used less often than **jiàoshì**)

講堂 **jiǎngtáng** classroom (now used less often than **jiàoshì**)

學堂 **xuétáng** (pre-modern) school

15.1. 你今天有幾堂課？

15.2. 今天在堂上，張老師根本沒講書，就說故事了.

15.3. 課堂就是講堂.

16.0. 似 **sì, shì** resembling

相似 **xiāngsì** resemble, be similar (to), be alike

似是而非 **sì shì ér fēi** look like the real thing but not be so, seemingly

(好)像…似的 **(hǎo) xiàng…shide** seem as if …, be like …

16.1. 這兩本字典，外表看起來很相似，但是內容大不相同.

16.2. 那個飯館兒做的中國飯似是而非的，又不是中國飯，又不是外國飯.

16.3. 今天好像比昨天暖和似的.

17.0. 好像(是)…(似)的樣子 **hǎoxiang (shi) … (shi) de yàngzi** seems to be …

看着好像 **kànzhe hǎoxiang** seems as if

N_1也像N_2一樣 **N_1 yě xiàng N_2 yíyàng** N_1, like N_2, …

S_1好像S_2(一樣) **S_1 hǎoxiang S_2 (yíyàng)** S_1 as if S_2

17.1. 昨天晚上我看他好像是不高興的樣子. (T)

17.2. 你們兩個人，看着好像他比你大.

17.3. 我也像你一樣，對這件事想不出甚麽好主意來. (T)

17.4. 他真能喝酒. 他喝酒好像喝水一樣.

18.0. 拿A來説 **ná A lái shuō** speak of A, speaking of A, in regard to A (see Advanced Chinese, lesson 3, note 3)

對A來説 **duì A lái shuō** speak of A, regarding A, as far as A is concerned

從A來説 **cóng A lái shuō** speaking from A

簡單的來説 **jiǎndānde lái shuō** speaking simply, in brief

用A來説 **yòng A lái shuō** speak of A, speaking of A

A用B來定 **A yòng B lái dìng** A is determined by B

18.1. 你的中文比我好的多. 拿寫字來説吧，我寫的就没有你寫的那麽好. (T)

18.2. 白金跟金子對日常生活來説是一點兒用

處也沒有.

18.3. 從理論這一方面來說那是對的.

18.4. 這個問題簡單的來說不是沒辦法解決的.

18.5. 念書有的學科比較難一點兒. 用念醫科來說就比念別的學科難.

18.6. 念博士的, 得的到得不到博士學位是得用他的論文來定. (T)

19.0. 經 **jīng** a classic of literature

經書 **jīngshū** the Confucian classics

五經 **Wǔ Jīng** Five Classics

茶經 **Chá Jīng** Tea Classic

三字經 **Sān Zì Jīng** Three Character Classic

四書五經 **Sì Shū Wǔ Jīng** Four Books and Five Classics

19.1. 經書裏, 五經我都念過了.

19.2. 茶經是書的名子, 是古時候一位最喜歡喝茶的人寫的, 專門講怎樣喝茶的一部書.

19.3. 以前中國小孩子在開始念書的時候先念三字經, 然後再念四書五經.

20.0. 短期 **duǎnqī** short period, short-term

長期 **chángqī** long period, long-term

假期 **jiàqī** holiday, holiday season, vacation, vacation period

20.1. 你在立法院的工作是短期的還是長期的？

20.2. 我們那個機關裏頭假期很少.

21.0. 太差了 **tài chàle** too awful, too inferior

差得遠 **chàde yuǎn** very different, quite unlike, far inferior

差得多 **chàde duō** quite different, quite inferior

21.1. 我的中國話發音太差了. 比你可差得遠了.

21.2. 張先生的中文程度比李先生可差得多.

22.0. 剛剛 **gānggāng** just (now), just recently

剛好 **gānghǎo** (1) just right; (2) just now

22.1. 你等我好久了？…你來的剛好, 我也剛剛到這兒.

23.0. 因而 **yīn'ér** hence, therefore

23.1. 老溫和老費為了上次選舉兩個人不合作, 因而就誰也不理誰了. (T)

24.0. 對於 A 上 **duìyu A shàng** with respect to A

24.1. 這幾本書, 對於我的論文寫作上很有幫助.

25.0. 地形 **dìxíng** topography, terrain, ground form

25.1. 在地圖上看, 美國有幾省的地形是四方的.

26.0. 發問 **fāwèn** to question, ask a question

26.1. 好學生在堂上是時常發問的.

27.0. 自主 **zìzhǔ** be independent, decide matters by oneself

27.1. 因為現在我還不能自立，所以甚麽事情我都不能自主.

28.0. N_1當N_2講 **N_1 dāng N_2 jiǎng** N_1 is to be explained as N_2, N_1 means N_2.

N_1把/拿N_2當N_3講 **N_1 bǎ/ná N_2 dāng N_3 jiǎng** N_1 explains N_2 as N_3, N_1 treats N_2 like N_3

28.1. 這個「漸」字當「一點兒一點兒地」講. (T)

28.2. 你看李良真不應該，他拿我那件事情當故事講. (T)

29.0. 相當於 **xiāngdāngyú** (1) correspond to; (2) corresponding to

29.1. 這裏的錢，五塊七毛錢相當於美國錢一塊錢.

30.0. 短語 **duányǔ** phrase

30.1. 「我的事」、「五塊錢」不是句子，都是短語.

31.0. 行為 **xíngwéi** behavior, action

沒想到 **méi xiǎngdào** (1) didn't think that, didn't expect; (2) unexpectedly

31.1. 表面上看，他人很不錯，沒想到他有那

種行為. (T)

32.0. 看作 **kànzuo** look upon as

32.1. 他把我看作自己人一樣，甚麽事情他都告訴我.

33.0. V(個)第…名 **V (ge) dì…míng** rank…in V

33.1. 我弟弟書念的很不好. 他這次考試考了個第三十八名. (T)

34.0. 辭 **cí** (1) resign; (2) cashier, fire, dismiss

辭行 **cíxíng** bid farewell

辭職 **cízhí** resign a post

推辭 **tuīcí** refuse a post, refuse an assignment

34.1. 我下星期五要到南美去了. 我今天來跟您辭行來了. (T)

34.2. 校長和教務長為了課程的問題發生了意見，教務長要辭職了. (T)

34.3. 這件事你一定得幫我的忙，你千萬不要推辭.

34.4. 工業部的事情太累了，我做不了. 我已經辭了. (T)

34.5. 張太太為了想辭那個用人，時常跟張先生發生意見. (T)

35.0. V起來 **Vqǐlai** (1) start V-ing; (2) become (after SV) (RV ending)

35.1. 父親還没回來呢．怎麽你們就先吃起來了?!

35.2. 這幾天所有的東西都貴起來了．大概就是吃的東西貴不起來．(T)

36.0. N_1那兒來的N_2? **N_1 nǎr láide N_2?** where would N_1 get N_2?

36.1. 誰説的?我那兒來的女朋友啊? (T)

37.0. 辦學(校) **bànxué (xiào)** run a school (VO)

37.1. 馬先生一生都是辦學．他辦學校已經有五十年了．

38.0. 目的是好V **mùdì shi hǎo V** the aim is to facilitate V-ing

38.1. 我學中文的目的是好看中國書報．

39.0. 定理 **dìnglǐ** theorem, axiom

李政道 **Lǐ Zhèngdào** Tsung Dao Lee, Nobel Prize winner in physics, 1957

39.1. 李政道把物理學上的一個定理給推翻了，所以得到了一筆獎金．

40.0. 意氣 **yìqi** emotion, feelings

意氣用事 **yìqi yòngshì** act on the basis of one's emotions

40.1. 「意氣」多半是用在成語裏，例如「意氣用事」．

41.0. 語音 **yǔyīn** phone, phonology, phonetics

語音學 **yǔyīnxué** (study of) phonology, phonetics

41.1. 如果想學中國的語音，你得先在大學裡念語音學.

Checklist

1. 展
   展期
   發展
2. 落
   落後
   落價
   落下來
3. 流
   流行
   流行病
   河流
4. 推
   推開
   推翻
   推進
   推行
   推舉
   推定
   推想
   推算
   推廣
   推讓
5. 選
   選取
   選出
   選舉
   選上
   選課
   推選
6. 消
   消氣
   消化
   消路
   消費
   消費的
   消費合作社
   取消
   不消說
7. 稱
   稱贊
   名稱
   簡稱(叫)
   總名稱
8. 需
   需要
9. 增
   增加
   增進
10. 趕
    趕緊(的)
    趕快(的)
    趕上
    趕去
    趕出來/去
    趕回來/去
    趕V_1再V_2
    V(的)正趕上時候
11. 深
    深色
    高深

12. 漸
漸漸的
13. 勢
勢力
大勢
大勢已去
地勢
情勢
形勢
14. 標
標記
標語
標題
標本
標準
標準語
標準音
目標
音標(兒)
15. 堂
堂上
上堂
課堂
講堂
學堂
16. 似
相似
似是而非
好像…似的
17. 好像(是)(似)的樣子
看着好像
N_1也像N_2一樣
S_1好像S_2(一樣)
18. 拿A來説
對A來説
從A來説
簡單的來説
用A來説
A用B來定
19. 經
經書
五經
茶經
三字經
四書五經
20. 短期
長期
假期
21. 太差了
差的遠
差的多
22. 剛剛
剛好
23. 因而
24. 對於A上
25. 地形
26. 發問
27. 自主
28. N_1當N_2講
N_1把/拿N_2當N_3講
29. 相當於
30. 短語
31. 行為
沒想到
32. 看作
33. V(個)第…名
34. 辭
辭行
辭職
推辭
35. V起來
36. N_1那兒來的N_2
37. 辦學(校)
38. 目的是好V
39. 定理
李政道
40. 意氣
意氣用事
41. 語音
語音學

Exercise 1. Excerpts from Actual Publications

The following excerpts are taken from **Yŭyán Wèntí** (Language Problems), a series of lectures by Zhào Yuánrèn (Chao Yuan Ren), a leading Chinese linguist.

1. 今天的講題是："語言學跟跟語言學有關係的些問題."

2. 語言…是一種自主的、有意識的行為.

3. 我講一講以後幾次的題目跟各題的内容的大概.

4. 第七講, 講方言跟標準語；這是除了四聲以外講…方言跟標準語的問題.

5. 第十一講…講一點外國語言的學習跟教學的問題. 在這裏多數人注意的問題當然是中國人學外國語的問題, 但是因為我近年來對於教外國人學中國語言…有一點經驗, 所以對這方面也…提一提.

6. 平常講的時候, 如果有的字我没説清楚, 請各位隨時舉手發問. 我希望每次最後留個十分鐘左右…問問對於多數人有興趣的問題.

7. 我二十多年來沒機會用中國話演說，沒有機會用中國話演講，… 我現在想要說中國話，其實是從外國話—我心裏頭想的外國話—說出來的，不像中國話．我希望大家對於了解上不發生太大的困難，可是我很高興有機會用中文講…語言學．

8. 今天講語音學跟語音的音標．… 講語言學就得先講語音學了．

9. 近年來學術界的研究漸漸注重到語言的本身的研究，因而語法這個詞，就漸漸的用得多了，所以就有書的名字叫“文言語法．”也有書叫“國文法．”

10. 「美」是不是一個詞？好，你要是翻成別國文，相當於「美」的你要是說英文 beautiful，是一個詞，你要說 good to look at，也是「美」的意思，那變了一個短語了．

11. 方言這個名詞，在中國是很久就有的名詞．從前是當各處地方不同的語言講．

12. 世界上有少數的國家…會有很不同的語

言. … 這就發生標準語的問題.

13. 語言的變化跟文字的變化不是一回事兒.

14. 你要是研究文字學本身，當然不能不寫你所研究的文字. 就是研究中國文學史跟中國歷史，當然也非用中國漢字不可.

15. 為甚麽要學外國語文？這有種種的用處：第一，想要跟外國人說話，到外國去旅行，或者當外國語口語的翻譯，要學外國語. 第二，就注重文字方面，看外國書，學外國文學，翻譯外國書去學外國語. 那麽第三，也是必要的，就是外國語要是必修科，你得學外國語，好得學分兒.

Exercise 2. Dialogues

1. 温：天氣漸漸的暖和起來了，假期到那兒玩兒去嗎？

謝：我不打算到那兒去了. 前幾天生病. 很多天沒上課. 我得在放假的期間

把功課趕出來.要不然差得太遠了.你們作甚麽打算？

温：我們生物系是在放假期間王教授帶着我們到西山去找標本.

謝：到西山去很遠了.相當於從這兒到漢口那麽遠了.

温：是啊.坐火車要坐三個多鐘頭.

2. 田：老邊，聽説你古書念的很多.四書五經你都念過嗎？

邊：那兒啊.我就念過一部四書.經書我没念過.聽説你念過五經.

田：没有.我就是在六歲那年念過三字經.後來在中學念國文的時候，又念了一點兒.

邊：你説念古文對於白話文的寫作上有幫助没有？

田：我説有幫助.拿田教授來説吧，他原來是學古文學的，你看他白話文寫的有多麽好.

邊：我可不喜歡田教授寫的白話文，又

不文又不白似是而非的那種白話文.

3. 張: 剛才簡老師在堂上講書的時候, 看着好像很生氣似的.

費: 大概是和他太太, 要不然就是跟他兒子.

張: 從他家跑到學校來, 也該消了氣了.

費: 是啊. 據我知道的, 簡老師常為了他兒子和師母發生意見. 有一次簡師母不在家, 簡老師不知為了甚麽, 把他兒子從家裏趕出去了, 簡師母又把兒子給找回來了. 他們那個家庭真有意思.

張: 簡老師為甚麽對他兒子這樣兒?

費: 簡老師的學問那麽高深, 他兒子啊, 書念的太差了. 他們高中一, 一共四十二個人, 他大考的時候, 考第四十二名.

張: 他考最後一名?

費: 是啊. 我弟弟跟他同學. 我弟弟說, 他在課堂上才有意思呢. 他怕老師問他問題，每次一上堂老師一進來還没坐下他就發問，問的都是課外的，而且問的都是没道理的問題.

4. 聞：你這幾天是不是有甚麽心事？
湯：你怎麽知道？
聞：我看你好像是有心事的樣子.
湯：我對你實説吧. 昨天接到我弟弟一封信，説需要二百塊錢，讓我趕快給他想法子. 二百塊錢對我來説是一個相當大的數目.
聞：你有辦法没有？
湯：目前我是没辦法. 現在正趕上我没錢，要是三月就可以了.
聞：要是短期的，我先借給你.
湯：不論長期短期，你那兒來的錢借給我呀？
聞：昨天我父親才讓別人帶給我的.
湯：好極了. 你錢來的正趕上時候. 要不然，我簡直的没辦法.

5. 程：李小姐病了你知道嗎？

金： 怪不得那天開會選舉會長她没參加呢. 甚麽病？是不是流行病？

程： 昨天我去看她, 她説開始是有一點兒發燒, 吃東西不消化, 後來就起不來了.

金： 她身體不大好, 是不是？我看她老是請病假.

程： 是. 她身體比她妹妹差得多, 兩個人一點兒也不一樣. 妹妹的身體那麽好.

金： 因為她妹妹是學體育的, 所以身體好.

6. 方： 你們學校的消費合作社成立了有幾年了？

温： 大概有五六年了. 我們合作社辦的很好.

方： 消費的都是學校的學生嗎？

温： 我們全學校的學生跟教職員都是社員. 我們在合作社買東西, 合作社都在社員手册上記錄下來, 每年算一算還能得到一點兒好處.

方：合作社的經理是選出來的嗎？

溫：不是．是請的．不過當初也是我們學校經濟系畢業的．他本來在別處有很好的工作，學校讓他來幫忙，他不好意思推辭.這個人很有本事.合作社的手冊就是他設計的.

方：我看見過，是深藍色的小冊子，上面的字是金的，非常好看.

7. 謝：昨天晚上我剛剛吃完晚飯，沒想到費先生到我這兒了.

包：是不是又跟你談起地理來了？

謝：是啊．跟我談了兩個多鐘頭.

包：是不是談世界地理？

謝：沒有．給我講的中國地理．先講中國地形跟河流，又講的中國每一省的地勢．我對地理是一點兒興趣也沒有．他忘了是來談天兒，也像上課一樣那麽認真，好像在講堂上似的．我也不好意思說我要念書了.

8. 麻： 我們學校越來越有發展了.

費： 是啊. 從學生人數來說吧，上學期只有兩千五百人. 現在增加到三千二百人了.

麻： 是的. 校長上次報告不是說過了嗎？他辦學的目的是要推廣教育. 他說他有一個三年計劃，他的目標是三年以內要有四千學生.

費： 我的推想用不到三年，他這個目標就能達到.

麻： 可能. 看這個情勢，增加學生人數不難.

費： 聽說這個星期的學生晚會取消了？

麻： 我還没聽說呢.

費： 要是取消了，我們和老金去看電影兒去，好不好？

麻： 我不知道老金有事没有？最好趕老金回來我們再决定，好不好？

費： 好啊.

9. 程： 家農，如果清朝那次的變法要是成功了，不知道中國現在政治是怎麽樣一種情形？

田：也許清朝不會讓別人給推翻了.

程：後來清朝在政治上表現的很不好，所以才把它推翻.

田：這幾天新生晚報上的歷史小説，正寫到清朝變法以後辦學堂的故事，很有意思.

程：是. 我也看了.

田：你也看新生晚報啊？新生的消路非常好，聽説每天出版五萬張.

程：現在已經增到十萬張了.

田：新生每天第一版的新聞標題都是用很大的紅字.

程：目的是好讓人家注意呀.

10. 王：近來東西都落價了.

簡：這可以説是省長的經濟計劃成功了.

王：可以那麽説. 你看近來各種東西一律把價錢落下來了.

簡：他是有辦法.

王：當初大家推選他作省長，就是因為他在經濟這一方面有辦法．

簡：他作過經濟部長，是不是？

王：是．他當經濟部長的時候，發表談話．他的經濟計劃是「拿增加出口作目標」．他又說："我們國家是一個經濟落後的農業國家，應該趕緊的發展工業來解決目前的需要．"從他當經濟部長以後，經濟情形越來越好，當時人人都稱贊他．

11. 關：今天報紙上的社論談的是「中國的農業」．大意是：中國雖然是農業國家，對於農業不知道用科學的方法，因而地裏出的東西不合理想．政府應該推行一種科學方法，可以增進農業的發達．

紀：這是一種理論了，事實上我們是一個經濟落後的國家．簡單的來說，一個經濟落後的國家要想推進農業科學化，還得一個相當的時期．

12. 田：是不是下星期那個音樂會要展期了？
邊：大概是．老實説像現在流行的這種音樂，我真不喜歡．
田：現在大多數的青年人都喜歡．
邊：這個音樂團團員的行為怎麽樣？
田：還好．你看他們的外表很奇怪，可是人都是好人．我弟弟也是團員．
邊：參加那個音樂團難不難？
田：也不容易．我弟弟是選上的．當初一共五個人都要參加，就選取了我弟弟一個人．

13. 方：張小姐要結婚了．
常：是嗎！你怎麽知道的？
方：昨天我到張家去剛好他們忙着選好日子呢．
常：她跟誰結婚你知道嗎？
方：説是一位姓關的，是在政界作事的．
常：沒聽説過張小姐有這麽一位朋友．
方：哪兒是她的朋友啊．她根本就不認識那個人．她母親的思想很舊，女兒的親事不能自主,得她母親作主.
常: 她甚麽時候結婚你知道嗎?
方: 不知道. 我一看她們在選日子呢,
我就走了. 我的推算得學校考完了
試.

14. 金: 文化代表團已經選團長了嗎?
程: 還没有呢. 得開會大家推舉一位.
金: 你們想推舉誰?
程: 我想大家一定都推王先生.
金: 王先生他一定要推讓的.
程: 我想大家推定他他不會推辭的.
金: 我還不知道我們這個代表團的總名
稱是甚麽呢.
程:「中國文化代表團」.
金: 代表團這次出國的目的是甚麽?
程: 到各國去訪問各國的學術團體跟各
大學.

15. 外國人: 這次選課我要選一門國語.
中國人: 你中國話説的很好了. 就是有
一點兒山東口音.

外國人：是啊．所以我要學一點兒標準的國語啊．

中國人：你當初為甚麽要學山東話呢？

外國人：別提了．我才到中國的時候，朋友就給我介紹了一位山東老先生，教我學中國話．我也不知道中國有很多的方言，甚麽是標準音，甚麽是標準語．我還認為是中國人説的話都是國語呢．

16\. 湯：昨天上課的時候我把詞兒給看錯了．我把短語裏的「標語」看作「標記」了，所以把「標語」當「標記」講了．

畢：你為甚麽不看清楚了呢？

湯：看的時候很小心，可是「語」字跟「記」字的左邊兒都有「言」字邊兒，所以我就看錯了．

17\. 邊：老張，茶經是甚麽意思？

張：是一部古人專門談茶的書．

邊：你見過這部書没有？

張：我没見過．我聽人家説過．據説那

部書把喝茶的事情說的非常詳細, 而且也是很好的一部著作.

18. 先生：昨天的詞兒你們都會了嗎？

學生：會了.

先生：好. 我現在問你們.「推開」是甚麽意思？

學生："把門推開."

先生：「趕去」怎麽用？

學生："時候太晚了. 就是我趕去也來不及."

先生：「音標」是甚麽意思？

學生："在那本字典裏用的音標是注音字母."

先生：請你說說「語音學」跟「語言學」有甚麽分別.

學生：「語音學」是專門研究語音的, 可是「語言學」的範圍比較大.

先生：「勢力、大勢、形勢」有分別嗎？

學生：有分別.

先生：請你用這三個詞兒, 各說一個句子.

學生:"他們的勢力很大, 這一帶地方都是在他們勢力範圍以內的." "那個國家大勢已去, 要想復興是不可能的." "我們中國土地的形勢是西北比東南高."

先生: 很好, 還有甚麽問題嗎?

學生: 請問您, 「意氣」跟「意氣用事」怎麽用?

先生:「意氣」這個詞兒多半用在成語裏, 例如 "對這件事你不要意氣用事."

學生: 先生, 「定理」就是物理學和數學上那個「定理」是不是?

先生: 是的.

Exercise 3. Narratives

1. 三月四號的日記

今天星期一. 天氣很暖和. 早晨七點半鐘我才起來. 恐怕上課要晚了, 在家裏只喝了一杯茶就趕緊的到學校去. 教務長説過了凡是還沒選課的學生必得在三天以內一律選好，不能展期．我本來想要選金先生講的那門功課．老孔告訴我，那位先生在上堂的時候常生氣，有的時候把學生從課堂裏趕出去．看他那種行為，不像是一個有高深學問的人．我說："學問是學問，行為是行為．你怎麽能從他的行為推想他的學問呢？"老孔說："我說這話是有根據的．中國有一句成語,「學問深時意氣平」．這句話的意思是說，一個人要是到了學問高深的時候，也就很少意氣用事了．他的心裏是很平的，不會常生氣的．"我聽老孔說的很有道理，因而没選那門功課．

2. 有一個地方，近來發生了一種流行病．開始有這種病的都是小孩子，後來漸漸的連大人也有這種病了．有一個醫生說近來流行這種病是因為天氣的關係．天氣暖和了，這種病自然而然的就少了．

3. 從前中國人念書先從三字經念起，以後再念四書和經書．經書有五種所以叫做五經. 四書五經都念過了就可以去參加考試. 第一次的考試如果及格了, 就是秀才. 考取秀才以後再去參加考試, 如果及格了就是舉人. 這種考試制度叫做「科舉」. 「秀才」和「舉人」都是科舉時代的一種名稱. 從清朝辦了學堂這些名稱就取消了.

4. 我們學校裏有一個消費合作社, 所有的學生都是社員. 我們買日常用的東西, 都是在這個合作社. 在合作社買東西可以有兩種好處. 第一是東西的價錢不比外邊賣的貴. 第二是他們每年算一算, 我們還可以得一點兒錢. 誰消費的多, 也就是誰在這裏買的東西多, 誰就可以多得一些錢. 有時候, 在一年裏頭賣剩了的東西, 我們用很少的錢就可以買到, 所以我們買東西都在這裏買, 把合作社看作好像是自己的買賣似的.

5. 有一個小的國家, 從前文化經濟都很落後. 當時有一個大國, 在世界上的勢力很大．這個小國在這個大國的勢力範圍以內，甚麽也不能自主．後來這個小國的人民把原來的政府推翻了，用選舉的法子選出有能力的人組織新政府，推行民主政治．辦教育，設學校，發展農業、工業．國內的情勢越來越好．現在在世界上已經是一個完全自主的國家了．

6．茶經是中國古時候的人寫的．寫這本書的人對於喝茶很有研究．這本書裏寫的都是關於喝茶的事．比方說，那種茶要用多少水，要用多大的火，要用多少時間燒，要用甚麽茶杯喝，都寫的很詳細．有人說，只有根據茶經上的法子來喝茶，才覺得喝茶是很有意思的．要不然，那不是喝茶，那簡直像牛喝水似的，有甚麽意思呢？

7．近來日常用的東西都落價了．有人說，物價落下來以後生活就不困難了．又有人說，物價雖然落下來了，可是要是手裏沒有錢，還是沒有法子買，生活還是不容易呀.

8. 有一個地方的工會接到全國總工會來信，請各地工會推舉代表去開會，研究增加工人工錢的問題. 這個地方的工會就推選代表. 本來已經推定王先生了，可是王先推辭了，又推舉了李先生. 李先生說，還是應該請王先生做代表. 後來大家對王先生說:"請你不要推讓了." 王先生就做了代表去開會去了.

9. 張先生在講堂上給小學生講中國地理. 他說，中國全國的地勢是西邊比東邊高，所以中國境內最大的河流都是從西邊往東邊流.

10. 張先生正在家裏看書，有人把門推開就進來了. 張先生一看是他的兒子從外國回來了. 張先生說:"沒想到是你回來了. 你來信不是說下個月才回來嗎?" 他的兒子說:"我本來是想在下月回來的. 後來我想起來了，後天是您的生日，我就趕回來了.”

11. 昨天我和老張都接到王小姐的信. 她在信裏說，明天上午九點鐘坐火車到這裏來. 我們看完了信就說好了在明天早上八點半我先到老張家裏，然後一塊兒到火車站去接王小姐. 今天早上我開車到了老張那兒已經過了八點半了，老張已經走了. 他太太說：“老張剛剛走了幾分鐘. 他是走路去的. 你趕快開車趕去，一定可以趕得上.” 可是路上我沒趕上他，等我到火車站的時候，正趕上老張跟王小姐從車站出來.

12. 金先生問我：“前幾年有一個物理學的博士研究出來一個新的定理，把從前舊的定理推翻了. 這個人的名字你知道嗎？” 我問：“是中國人是外國人？” 金先生說：“是中國人.” 我說：“是不是李政道？” 金先生說：“是的. 你一說我也想起來了. 聽說他在中國念大學的時候，先生都很稱贊他，說他是一個可以造就的人才.

後來他果然成了一個世界上最有名的物理學家了.”

13. 王先生想請幾個朋友來玩兒麻將. 王太太聽說了, 很生氣. 她對王先生說:“玩兒麻將又費時間又費錢. 再說, 你的病剛好, 吃東西都不能消化, 身體還不怎麼好, 現在從那一方面來說都不應當玩兒麻將.”後來王先生把玩兒麻將的意思取消了. 王太太才消了氣.

14. 這幾天天氣暖和起來了. 很多人都去旅行. 有人問我為甚麼不去旅行呢? 我說:“我的工作是沒有假期的, 我哪兒來的工夫去旅行呢?” 他又問我:“那麼星期天呢?” 我說:“星期天也像平常一樣還是要工作的.”

15. 弟弟問我, 報紙上重要新聞的標題為甚麼要用很大的字? 我告訴他:“標題用大字, 目的是好讓看報的人注意.”弟弟說:“怪不得有的時候看見標語上面的字都是很大的，為的是讓人家注意呀．”

16. 從前中國人結婚或者是出外都是選日子的．選日子就是選一個好日子．怎樣才算一個好日子呢？怎樣選呢？拿甚麽作標準呢？有人說，結婚選日子要用男女兩個人的八字來推算．出外也是一樣要選好日子．

17. 有一個科學落後的國家為了推進科學教育就想在國內選一些聰明優秀的學生送到外國去研究科學．後來選取了不少人．有人說，選上的人不一定都是聰明的，真正聰明的人也許沒選上．

18. 有一個國家因為在行政上太不行了，所以人民都不喜歡那個政府，因而就要發生政變．因為大勢已去，沒有好久，就讓人推翻了，成立了新政府．據說，這次政變和上次政變相似，對於人民來說是沒有甚麽好處的．有人說，拿這次政變以後的情勢來說，這個新政府也許又是一個短期的．現在這個國家最需要的是要有一個長期安定的政府，要不然，看這個國家的大勢就越來越没希望了．

19. 有一個外國人會說中國話．他說：“常用的中國話我都會說，就是對於發音上太差了．我也知道學中國話應當注意發音，我更知道北京話是標準音，可是我當初學的是山東話．山東話和北京話差得多了．所以我說我對於發音上太差了．”

20. 我們家裏每天都是在晚上八點鐘吃晚飯．今天晚上八點鐘我們正要吃晚飯的時候，老王來了．我母親對老王說：“你來的正趕上時候，就在這裏一塊兒吃晚飯吧．”老王正要說話，我說：“他大概已經吃過了．”母親說：“你怎麽知道呢？”我說：“您看！老王的身上還有標記呢．”老王往自己身上一看，原來有兩條麵條還在身上呢．

21. 張校長是山東人，在北京做中學校長已經有二十多年了. 昨天他來看我. 他說:"我已經辭職了, 就要回山東去, 今天是來辭行."我說:"你辦學辦了二十多年, 在北京的中學校長裏可以說你是第一名, 為甚麽要辭職呢?" 他說:"我從來把這個學校都看成好像是家似的. 現在我老了,我要離開這個家,回山東老家去了."

22. 祝少堂是一個中學的教員. 他說:"我們學校裏近來新用的教員比從前差得遠了. 從前的教員一定是大學畢業的, 或者是相當於大學畢業的程度. 現在新的教員用關係來定. 誰和校長有關係, 誰就可以當教員. 有的教員在堂上講些似是而非的理論. 有的教員為了取得學生的歡喜把笑話當功課講. 如果有人對校長說, 校長把没道理當有道理講, 還説他們是好教員. 簡單的來説, 就没有一個像教員的."

23. 王先生自己做了一些生物的標本. 他為了推廣消路, 就到各地方去賣. 有人對他說:“你不要到各處去賣，小心有人把你趕出來.”他說:“我賣標本的目標是學校和博物館. 他們為了增進學生和人們的學識多半需要標本，怎麽會把我趕出來呢？”

24. 先生對小學生說，有一塊水田，地形是四方的. 有人從這塊水田的東邊走到西邊，用了半小時的時間. 如果從南邊走到北邊需要多少時間？要用甚麽方法才可以知道呢？有一個小學生舉起手來說:“我知道. 最好的法子是叫那個人從南邊到北邊再走一次，就可以知道了.”

25. 世界上有很多地方都有紅十字會. 最初設立的紅十字會是在一七九三年. 後來各國都設立了. 現在這個會的總名稱是萬國紅十字會，簡稱紅十字會.

26. 有的國家歡迎外國人來旅行，因為他們認為旅行是消費的，對於經濟上來說是有好處的. 可是有的國家不歡迎外國人去旅行. 為甚麽不歡迎呢？也許是政治上的原因吧.

27. 我和弟弟的身體都不大好. 父親叫我們參加一個體育團體. 這個體育團體在一所舊樓的樓上. 有人説，那所舊樓快要倒了. 我們每次去練習體育的時候，也覺着這所舊樓的形勢太可怕，所以我們後來就不去了.

28. 老王要買車. 我問他要買甚麽樣式的？他説："甚麽樣式都可以，可是車的顏色我不要深色的，最好是白色的，因為我平常用的東西一律不用深色的."

29. 今天報紙上有一條新聞是邊境上發生問題了. 邊境上有了甚麽問題呢？新聞裏也没詳細的説明. 有人説，可能又是因為邊界的問題. 為了這個問題已經發生了不少次的事情了.

30. 我和張先生合編了一部字典，不到一年的工夫就出版了. 有人問我："你們的字典怎麽這麽快就出版了呢？" 我說:"我們是趕出來的. 我們兩個人每天平均要編五百字左右, 所以很快就出版了."

Exercise 4. Illustrative Sentences (English)

1.1. I hear the [learned] lecture [meeting] is being postponed two weeks.

1.2. The publication of Modern Chinese History that Mr. Xu wrote is being put off till later.

4.4. In my opinion, if you recommend him to be head of the delegation he will certainly refuse [lit. not do].

5.1. (In connection with) this (year's) choosing of Miss Universe, the selections were [already] made yesterday. Miss China was chosen (as Miss Universe).

5.3. I hear that the municipal government in the examinations for interpreters selected only four men out of sixty-five.

5.5. Chinese insist on [first] selecting an auspicious day for a wedding day.

5.6. In the last election Mr. Zhang was awfully busy (i.e. the election made Mr. Zhang very busy).

6.2. You see that his anger hasn't abated yet, so for the time being [lit. beforehand] don't talk to him about that matter. Wait until he's over his anger and then we'll take it up [lit. investigate] with him.

6.8. Zhang, needless to say this evening's dinner is on you.

6.9. The shoppers [lit. consumers] in that market are mostly women.

6.10. Needless to say, what he says and what he does are two completely different things [lit. completely not one thing].

7.5. The inclusive term for those history books is The Twenty-Four Histories.

10.1. I'm terribly busy these days. I'm rushing my Ph.D. thesis.

10.9. Swell, you've come at just the right time. Come help us solve this problem.

11.2. Without profound learning it would certainly be impossible to write such an essay.

13.1. This whole area is within his sphere of influence.

13.3. Recently the government's position has deteriorated more and more. The situation is indeed hopeless, and before long (the government) is likely to be overthrown by the people.

14.2. Why are those students parading around everywhere again with [lit. holding] slogans ?

14.9. The character **biāo** in "specimen" consists of the side character "tree" with the addition of the **piào** of "paper bill."

17.1. Yesterday evening he seemed to me to be unhappy.

17.3. I, like you, can't come up with a good idea about this matter.

18.1. Your Chinese is a lot better than mine. Take writing characters, I don't write as well as you do.

18.6. Whether someone studying for the doctorate gets a degree or not is [lit. must be] determined by the thesis.

23.1. Wen and Fei, because they didn't see eye to eye [lit. cooperate] in the last election, [therefore] don't speak [lit. pay attention] to each other now.

28.1. This character **jiàn** is to be explained as "little by little."

28.2. [You see] Li Liang really shouldn't (behave so). He treats that matter of mine like a story.

31.1. Superficially he's not at all bad as a person. I didn't think he would behave thus [lit. have such behavior].

33.1. My younger brother does terribly in his studies. He ranked 38th in this examination.

34.1. I'm going to South America next Friday. I've come to say goodbye to you now.

34.2. The president and the dean clashed over the curriculum, so the dean intends to resign.

34.4. The duties [lit. affairs] in the Ministry of Industry are too exhausting. I can't stand it. I've already resigned.

34.5. Because Mrs. Zhang wants to fire that servant, she often quarrels with Mr. Zhang.

35.2. The past few days everything has become more expensive. Only food most likely won't [lit. can't] become higher.

36.1. Who says so? Where would I get a girl friend?

Lesson 15

1	2	3	4	5	6	7	8
使	受	充	普	遍	響	屬	般

9	10	11	12	13	14	15	16
基	限	末	私	規	章	唐	之

1.0. 使 **shǐ** (1) use (V); (2) make, cause; (3) with (CV); (4) envoy*

使用 **shǐyòng** employ, use, make use of

使得 **shǐde** (1) be all right, OK (Peking dialect); (2) can use, can be used (RV); (3) make, cause, have the result that (W)

使不得 **shǐbude** (1) can't use; (2) can't be used, useless

大使 **dàshǐ** ambassador

公使 **gōngshǐ** minister (i.e. representative of one country in another)

使館 **shǐguǎn** embassy, legation, diplomatic quarters

大使館 **dàshǐguǎn** embassy

公使館 **gōngshǐguǎn** legation

1.1. 那個外國人能使毛筆寫漢字.

1.2. 那本字典是學校的，人人都可以使用.

1.3. 你那本字典再讓我用兩天好不好？…使

得使得. (T)

1.4. 你的錄音機還使得使不得了? (T)

1.5. 因為那個國家的經濟落後, 所以使得農工業都不能够發展. (T)

1.6. 以前外國在中國的大使跟公使的使館都在北京的東城. (T)

1.7. 昨天晚上在法國的中國大使館有一個晚會. 各國的大使、公使都到了.

1.8. 下星期一各國公使都在英國公使館開會.

2.0. 受 **shòu** (1) receive, take; (2) undergo, endure; (3) by (agent) (CV)

受氣 **shòuqì** suffer indignity, be the object of a person's anger, be ill-treated, be abused (VO)

受累 **shòulèi** endure fatigue, be troubled, be bothered (VO)

受不得 **shòubude** hard to bear

難受 **nánshòu** depressed, saddened, unhappy

接受 **jiēshòu** receive, accept

受…歡迎 **shòu…huānyíng** (well) received by …, (well) liked by …

2.1. 我不想再給他作事了. 天天受他的氣, 我真受不了了. (T)

2.2. 你說你受氣我可不信. 王先生是好人, 他不會給人氣受的. (T)

2.3. 張先生，您才到這兒就麻煩您去給我拿行李，真是讓您受累了.

2.4. 隨便怎麼累的工作我都受的了，要是受氣我可受不得.(T)

2.5. 作教員的，大家都希望教學能受學生們的歡迎.(T)

2.6. 我父親去世了，我心裏非常難受.

2.7. 他提出的那幾個條件，我們一個也不能接受.

3.0. 充 **chōng** (1) pretend; (2) fill*

充數 **chōngshù** complete a number, fill out a number, take up a place, fill a spot (without really filling the role)

充實 **chōngshí** fulfill, round out, fill full

3.1. 老王連一個錢也沒有,可是他老充有錢.

3.2. 研究那種學問的都是優秀分子，可是我這個沒本事的人也充數參加了.(T)

3.3. 他根本就不念書,上課不過是充充數去.(T)

3.4. 我感到自己的學識不夠,所以得多看書,充實充實自己.

4.0. 普 **pǔ*** universal, general

普及 **pǔjí** make universal, make common, popularize

4.1. 普及教育是當前最需要的.

5.0. 遍 **biàn** (1) (measure for occurrences); (2) throughout, everywhere (RV ending); (3) all of, the whole of

piàn throughout, everywhere (RV ending)

遍地 **biàndì, piàndi** the whole earth, everywhere

普遍 **pǔbiàn, pǔpiàn** universal, widespread

一遍 **yíbiàn** once, one time

V一遍又一遍 **V yíbiàn yòu yíbiàn** V over and over again (similarly with other measures of occurrences)

5.1. 人家說美國遍地是金子, 怎麽我走遍了美國也沒看見一塊金子呢.

5.2. 這種流行病很普遍, 我們這一城裏的人差不多都病了.

5.3. 我沒聽清楚, 請你再說一遍.

5.4. 從前念古書的時候, 老師都是一遍一遍地讓你大聲兒的念. (T)

5.5. 我還差着三本書沒買呢. 各書店都買遍了, 我也沒買到. (T)

5.6. 那幾個字他念了一遍又一遍的, 怎麽念也念不會. (T)

6.0. 響 **xiǎng** (1) to sound, ring; (2) make a sound

響聲 **xiǎngshēng** a sound, a noise

影響 **yǐngxiǎng** influence, affect

受…影響 **shòu…yǐngxiǎng** be influenced by

6.1. 你聽聽外頭甚麽響？(T)

6.2. 昨天我們家門口汽車出事了，響聲很大.

6.3. 我國語說的好，是受了我老師的影響，因為他說的是最標準的國語.(T)

6.4. 這裏物價這麽高，都是事變的影響.

6.5. 我本來是學生物的．我學文學完全是受了馬教授的影響.(T)

7.0. 屬 **shǔ** (1) belong to, be part of, be under the control of, pertain to; (2) subordinate*; (3) be born under the zodiacal sign of; (4) family, genus*

屬於 **shǔyú** belong to, be subordinate to

屬地 **shǔdì** a dependency

屬員 **shǔyuán** subordinate official, a subordinate

屬下 **shǔxià** subordinate(s)

金屬 **jīnshǔ** metals

7.1. 那個縣是屬哪一省啊？

7.2. 我屬牛的．你屬甚麽的？…我屬豬.(T)

7.3. 以前越南屬於中國，是中國的屬地.

7.4. 他以前是我的一個屬員，現在他的地位比我高得多.

7.5. 我們是他的屬下．他的主意，我們怎麽敢說不對呢？

7.6. 白金也是屬於金屬的一種.

8.0. 般 **bān*** (1) sort; (2) average, common; (3) alike

一般 **yìbān** (1) alike, like; (2) the average; (3) general

一般的 **yìbānde** (1) the average (AT); (2) general (AT); (3) generally, in general (AD)

一般人 **yìbān rén** the average person, people in general

一般 SV **yìbān SV** equally SV

一般的說 **yìbānde shuō** generally speaking

8.1. 現在一般的青年多數都喜歡那種奇怪的音樂.

8.2. 姐姐和妹妹長的一般高. (T)

8.3. 現在一般有錢的人都喜歡旅行全世界.

8.4. 一般的說，這種病得的機會很少. (T)

8.5. 在民國初年，一般人因為受了五四的影響都要寫白話文.

8.6. 一般的說，政府推行普及教育算是相當成功了.

9.0. 基 **jī*** foundation, base

基本 **jīběn** root, foundation

基地 **jīdì** a base

9.1. 你要從基本上了解不成功的原因. (T)

9.2. 在世界上各處都有他們的基地.

10.0. 限 **xiàn** (1) limit (N/V); (2) limit to

限於 **xiànyú** limited to, limited by

限期 **xiànqī** (1) a set period, a time limit; (2) to set a period of, limit to a period of

限定 **xiàndìng** fix a limit to

限度 **xiàndu** a standard, a limit

限制 **xiànzhi** (1) to restrict, limit; (2) restriction, fixed measure

有限 **yǒuxiàn** there is a limit, be limited

界限 **jièxiàn** (1) boundary; (2) (fixed) limit

年限 **niánxiàn** a limit in years

10.1. 造那所房子他限我兩個月就造好. 限期這麽近我没法子造.

10.2. 我在圖書館借的那本書還没看完呢, 可是限期到了. 我昨天到圖書館去, 他們限我兩個星期以後再還. (T)

10.3. 那個國家很想發展工業, 但是限於經濟的條件目前是不可能的. (T)

10.4. 他們想要發展農業, 但是限於地理的關係是不可能的. (T)

10.5. 我作事不喜歡人家限定我時間. (T)

10.6. 人求人幫忙應該有一個限度, 不應該甚麽事情都求人.

10.7. 到美國來旅行, 美國政府限制六個月就要離開.

10.8. 我們學校選課程不能隨便選, 可是外國留學生就不必受限制. (T)

10.9. 你限我幾天就把這事做完. 那怎麽能够辦得到呢? (T)

10.10. 你看他寫的東西就知道他的學問有限.

10.11. 那兩國的邊界用那條河作界限.

10.12. 他們借那個國家的土地作基地是有年限的, 借用的限期是六十年. (T)

11.0. 末 **mò*** (1) last of a series (ordinalizer); (2) end

末年 **mònián** last years, closing years

末後 **mòhòu** afterwards (MA)

末末了(兒) **mòmoliǎo(r)** (1) the very last, the very end; (2) finally

末了(兒) **mòliǎo(r)** (1) last (of a series) (ordinalizer); (2) the very last, the very end (TW)

11.1. 謝先生要寫一本歷史, 專寫明朝的事情, 是從明初寫到明末. (T)

11.2. 清朝末年的變法没成功, 你知道是甚麽原因嗎?

11.3. 昨天考國文，我是最末一個考完了的. (T)

11.4. 昨天我和張先生說話太不客氣了. 末後想一想很不好意思.

11.5. 田老師上課的時候問問題，別人都問完了，到末末了兒才問我.

11.6. 王太太生了六個女兒，到了末了兒才生個兒子.

11.7. 站在那兒買電影兒票末了兒的那個人是湯先生. (T)

12.0. 私 **sī*** (1) private, personal; (2) partial, selfish; (3) illicit, contraband

私人 **sīrén** a private individual

私事 **sīshì** private affair(s)

私話 **sīhuà** private talk

私立 **sīlì** private(ly established) (AT)

私用(的) **sīyòng(de)** private(ly used) (AT)

私有(的) **sīyǒu(de)** private(ly owned) (AT)

12.1. 別聽他的，他沒真話. 那本書不是他私人的，是學校的. (T)

12.2. 我這次到英國去是為了我個人的私事.

12.3. 他們是要好的朋友，他們常常兩個人私自談私話.

12.4. 私立大學的學費比公立的貴的多.

12.5. 那部書是我個人私用的, 是我私有的.

13.0. 規 **guī*** rule, regulation

規定 **guīdìng** (1) regulate (that); (2) regulation

定規 **dìnggui** fix, decide, determine (Peking dialect)

13.1. 政府規定小孩子不能到那個博物館去.

13.2. 我定規每天早上八點鐘到學校去.

14.0. 章 **zhāng*** (1) chapter (M); (2) essay; (3) chop, stamp, seal, insignia; (4) (a surname)

章程 **zhāngcheng** regulations, by-laws

圖章 **túzhang** a seal

文章 **wénzhāng** an essay

作文章 **zuò wénzhāng** write an essay

14.1. 章思聰的文章作的非常好.

14.2. 你要知道那個學校的情形, 最好你去看看他們的章程.

14.3. 溫先生不但會作文章而且還會刻圖章.

15.0. 唐 **táng** (1) T'ang Dynasty (618-900); (2) (a surname)

唐朝 **Táng Cháo** Tang Dynasty

唐代 **Táng Dài** Tang Dynasty

唐人 **Tángrén** Chinese

15.1. 中國在唐朝的時候, 文學跟美術都非常發達.

15.2. 唐代是中國最好的時期. 那個時候在外國的中國人都説自己是唐人. 他們拿唐朝代表了中國.

15.3. 請問,「唐朝」的「唐」姓這個姓的多不多? (T)

16.0. 之 **zhī** (literary pronoun and particle. See Advanced Chinese, lesson 3 note 1)

總之 **zǒngzhī** finally, to sum up, in brief

之中 **zhīzhōng** among, within, in

之內 **zhīnèi** inside of, within, in

之間 **zhījiān** among, between, within, in

之外 **zhīwài** outside of, apart from

之前 **zhīqián** before, in front of

之後 **zhīhòu** after, behind

總而言之 **zǒngéryánzhi** finally, to sum up, in brief

NU_1分之NU_2 **NU_1 fēnzhī NU_2** $\frac{NU_2}{NU_1}$

16.1. 那個會我們必得參加. 不論是你還是我, 總之我們必得去一個人. (T)

16.2. 隨便你説唐老師的學問怎麽好, 總而言之我可不喜歡他.

16.3. 在這個大學研究語言的, 十分之八是外國學生. (T)

16.4. 這裏不久要成立一個農業機關. 據說政府正在計劃之中. (W) (T)

16.5. 那個報館讓我寫社論，他們限我兩個鐘頭之内必得給他們趕出來.

16.6. 你我之間為甚麽要這麽客氣呢？

16.7. 在我没走之前，一定把你的事情辦好.

16.8. 他除了喜歡研究音樂之外，他還喜歡畫畫兒.

17.0. 回 **huí** a time, an occurrence (M)

有一回 **yǒu yìhuí** one time, once

又一回 **yòu yìhuí** another time

17.1. 謝小姐跟簡士其在一塊兒，我看見兩回了. 有一回是在公園裏，又一回是在電影院.

18.0. 見着 **jiànzhao** see (RV)

見好 **jiànhǎo** show signs of improvement

不見SV **bújiàn SV** no evidence of being SV, no sign of becoming SV, not SV

18.1. 這幾天你見着老金没有？

18.2. 我父親的病這幾天見好.

18.3. 張先生長的真年輕. 我十年没看見他了，還不見老.

19.0. **SV 過 N** **SV guò N** be more SV than N (RV)

過活 **guòhuó** make a living

個子 **gèzi** stature

個兒 **gèr** stature

高個子 **gāo gèzi** a tall person

高個兒 **gāo gèr** a tall person

19.1. 你看湯小姐的個子高過他母親了.

19.2. 教我們生物學的章老師是個高個兒.

19.3. 我有五個孩子, 可是我没有工作. 你説我拿甚麽過活.

19.4. 張一凡的英國話好過我這個美國人. (T)

20.0. 附帶 **fùdài** attach, append

地帶 **dìdài** district, region, area

20.1. 幫助他們發展工業,那是一個附帶條件. (T)

20.2. 這是學校地帶, 開車要小心.

21.0. 起飛 **qǐfēi** start flying, take off

21.1. 今天到上海的飛機是下午三點鐘起飛.

22.0. 毛孩子 **máoháizi** little child, mere child

了不起 **liǎobuqǐ** extraordinary, unusual

22.1. 現在他是個毛孩子,都有那麽好的見解, 将來一定是了不起的人物. (T)

23.0. 分別 **fēnbié** to separate, part (see also <u>BCR</u>, lesson 38)

分別出來 **fēnbiéchulai** distinguish, tell apart (RV)

23.1. 我跟她從七七事變的時候就分別了.

23.2. 你看這些字是<u>張</u>先生寫的還是<u>唐</u>先生寫的?…我分別不出來是他們兩個人誰寫的.

24.0. 後代 **hòudài** descendant

24.1. 那位<u>孔</u>先生是<u>孔夫子</u>的後代.

25.0. 美國近代語言學會 **Měiguo Jìndài Yǔyán Xuéhuì** Modern Language Association of America, MLA

25.1. 美國近代語言學會上次開會你參加了沒有?

26.0. 遠不如 **yuǎn bùrú** far inferior to

26.1. 從前中國的工業發展遠不如別的國家那麼快.

27.0. 半真半假(的) **bànzhēnbànjiǎ (de)** half-jokingly

27.1. 那件事我不知道是不是真的, 他半真半假的那麼說的. (T)

28.0. 着 **zhuó*** to cause

着重 **zhuózhòng** emphasize, stress, place emphasis on

28.1. 近來所有的國家都非常着重重工業.

29.0. 本部 **běnbù** (1) this ministry; (2) China Proper

29.1. 昨天教育部的公報說:「凡是要考大學的請到本部報名.」

29.2. 我不知道中國本部現在一共有多少省.

30.0. 來回的 **láihuíde** (1) back and forth, to and fro; (2) round-trip; (3) repeatedly

30.1. 要是從這兒到西山去, 買來回的火車票是不是省一點兒錢?

30.2. 那件事他來回的說, 不知道他說了有幾次了.

31.0. 不了 **bùle** No (more)

31.1. 忙甚麽?再坐一會兒. … 不了, 我該回去了.

32.0. (用)一句話說 **(yòng) yíjù huà shuō** in a word, in short

沒(有)N 可 V (的) **méi (yǒu) N kě V(de)** there is no N to V

32.1. 張先生對人太好了, 用一句話說那是沒話可說的. (T)

32.2. 你好好兒的做事. 要是讓人辭了, 就沒飯可吃了.

33.0. 不安 **bù'ān** (1) uneasy, disturbed; (2) embarrassed

33.1. 您對我這麽好, 真是使我心裏不安.

34.0. 古城 **gǔchéng** ancient city

34.1. 河南有的古城,考古學家還沒研究過呢.

35.0. 公事 **gōngshì** public business, official business

35.1. 我每天忙的不得了.不是公事就是私事.

36.0. 李自成 **Lǐ Zìchéng** Li Tzu-ch'eng (1606-1645, general who overthrew the Ming Dynasty)

36.1. 明朝可以說是讓李自成給推翻的. (T)

37.0. 用經濟來V **yòng jīngji lái V** V economically

37.1. 那幾個國家用經濟來幫助落後的國家. (T)

38.0. 外人 **wàiren** outsider, bystander

38.1. 我們這裏沒有外人, 大家隨便談.

39.0. 要 **yāo*** (1) force, compel; (2) demand

要求 **yāoqiú** demand (N/V)

39.1. 他們要求用我們的土地作基地, 我們不同意.

40.0. 長大水 **zhǎng dàshuǐ** have a flood

40.1. 那一次長大水的地方太多了.

41.0. 應 **yìng*** answer, reply, respond

有求必應 **yǒu qiú bì yìng** ask and you shall receive

41.1. 謝先生人好極了. 誰求他, 他都幫忙,簡直是有求必應.

42.0. 公家 **gōngjiā** public, belonging to an organization (e.g. government, school, business concern) (AT)

42.1. 王先生真是個好公務員，他連公家的一張信紙都不用.

43.0. 廳 **tīng*** department of a provincial government

廳長 **tīngzhǎng** commissioner, head of a provincial department

43.1. 張思聰是河南省教育廳的廳長.

44.0. 起名(子)(叫) **qǐ míng(zi) (jiào)** give a name, call (**qǐ** is similarly used with **wàihào** "nickname")

44.1. 老王給他的老三起名叫王大文，可是別人給他起了個外號兒叫王太文，因為大文常常用太「文」的詞兒.

Checklist

1. 使	公使館	3. 充	一遍
使用	2. 受	充數	V 一遍又一遍
使得	受氣	充實	6. 響
使不得	受累	4. 普	響聲
大使	受不得	普及	影響
公使	難受	5. 遍	受…影響
使館	接受	遍地	7. 屬
大使館	受…歡迎	普遍	屬於

屬地
屬員
屬下
金屬
8. 般
一般
一般的
一般人
一般 SV
一般的說
9. 基
基本
基地
10. 限
限於
限期
限定
限度
限制
有限
界限
年限
11. 末
末年
末後
末末了(兒)
末了兒
12. 私
私人
私事
私話
私立
私用(的)
私有(的)
13. 規
規定
定規
14. 章
章程
圖章
文章
作文章
15. 唐
唐朝
唐代
唐人
16. 之
總之
之中
之內
之間
之外
之前
之後
總而言之
NU_1分之NU_2
17. 回
有一回
又一回
18. 見着
見好
不見 SV
19. SV過N
過活
個子
個兒
高個子
高個兒
20. 附帶
地帶
21. 起飛
22. 毛孩子
了不起
23. 分別
分別出來
24. 後代
25. 美國近代語言學會
26. 遠不如
27. 半真半假(的)
28. 着
着重

29. 本部
30. 來回的
31. 不了
32. (用)一句話説
    沒(有) N 可 V (的)
33. 不安
34. 古城
35. 公事
36. 李自成
37. 用經濟來V
38. 外人
39. 要
    要求
40. 長大水
41. 應
    有求必應
42. 公家
43. 廳
    廳長
44. 起名(子)
    (叫)

Exercise 1. Excerpts from Actual Publications

The following excerpts are taken from the autobiographical story **Wǒde Yìjiā** (My Family), by Táo Chéng, whose account of her family's participation in revolutionary activities is one of the best known examples of this sort of literature. There are several editions of this work, including one entirely in pinyin and another in both Chinese characters and pinyin transcription.

1. 我的家庭是個大家庭，合起來有十七口人. … 但是我要講的不是這個家. … 我所要講的「家」，是已經過去了的. 也可以説是這個家庭的歷史.

2. 我在家…看看孩子. 孩子們從學校回來大家…總是…要我講故事. 而且往往還有附帶條件 "…要講真的！要我們沒聽過的！" 我想…讓他們知道一點我們的過去.

3. 這是四十八年前, … 這一天, 正是我第十七個生日. … 選了這個日子叫我「過門」. …他…比我還小一歲…我們都還是毛孩子.

4. 第二年, 我們有了第一個孩子, 起名立安.

5. 一九二三年, 他…離開家, 和幾個朋友…去辦學校. 他說要出去「見見世面」. …誰知不到三年, 他又…回來.

6.「你變多了!」
「是嗎?…那麽我來看看你變了沒有」.
「你的心也變了!」我也玩笑的說.
「是變了!」他半真半假的說.

7. 告訴你, 你門門功課都得考够八十分, 少一分別來見我!

8. 天黑了, 立安還不見回來. 我有些奇怪. …這是怎麽回事?

9.「媽媽, 你怎麽知道我在這裏!」

「我怎麽能不知道！…一家人滿城找你.」

10.「我的算術不及格！」

「你以為功課不好,一跑就完了嗎？…也許你想算術有甚麽了不起，不學它，還不一樣過活！是不是？這樣説該學的東西就太少，不該學的就太多了.」

11.「甚麽事都會發生的,…你怕嗎？」

「跟你在一起，我甚麽也不怕.」

「就是你一個人，也不要怕.」

12. 我們在一起生活了十幾年，我是到現在才了解他的！可是剛剛了解,就分別了.誰知道還能不能再見？

13.「媽媽,你和弟弟先回去吧,我再等一會.」立安説.「一塊回去吧.」

14. 有一個…人説過:「誰笑到最後，誰就笑得最好.」

15.「媽媽」，立安…説,「這裏有後門，我送你出去！」

16.「怎麽了？」…他不安的説,「立安他們剛走，開會去了．你是找他嗎？」

17.「媽媽！」

我的天哪！這不是立安嗎！…立安…個子高過我一頭還多．

18.「這半年多你跑到那裏去了？找也找不到！」

「我跑的可遠！」…孩子快活的說．

「回來多久了？」

「快半個月了！」孩子說．

立安參加工作以後，這還是第一次回家，我們雖在一個城市，久不見面，… 但一見面就有說不完的話．

Exercise 2. Dialogues

1. 章：唐先生，您到這兒來是為了公事還是私事？

唐：可以說一半公事，一半私事．公事呢，是教育廳讓我訪問幾個學校．我們現在正在推行普及教育，拿它作個參考．私事呢，一來是旅行，二來是看看朋友.

章：是的.

唐：請問這裏私立學校多不多？

章：不太多. 政府很限制私人辦學校.

唐：為甚麽要受限制呢？

章：因為政府設立的學校,程度都很高. 一般的私立學校限於經濟的問題不够水準, 所以政府要有一個規定.

2. 謝：聽説連基平教授要到我們這裏來講學了.

温：是. 我也聽説了.

謝：他在中文系講學一學期, 聽説很受人們歡迎.

温：連教授不但講學受歡迎, 他的文章也是人人喜歡看的. 他真有高深的學問, 真是了不起的學者.

謝：他作的文章我沒看過.

温：我有他寫的東西, 你如果想看可以到我那兒去看.

謝：他這次到我們這兒來講甚麽？

温：教務長告訴我他講唐代文化.

謝：他講唐代文化不知道是着重那方面的？

温：他着重唐代的美術和文學.

謝：他講唐朝那一個時期的？

温：連教授要在四個星期之内把唐代文化都講完了，他是從唐初講到唐朝末年.

謝：他這幾年到處去講學，大概没甚麽寫作的時間了.

温：他過去把時間用在寫作上也太多了.也應該各處走走了.

謝：對了.聽説連教授不但學問好，圖章刻的也很有名.

温：是.他畫兒也畫的很好.

3. 田：昨天我在路上遇見唐大章了.我問他，他父親的病近來見好不見好.他説不見好，遠不如上個月了.他説着説着就難受起來了.

麻：我真為唐大章難過.他母親去年去

世了，今年他父親又病的這個樣子．要是他父親再去世了，他們這些不能自立的毛孩子怎麽過活呢？

田：總而言之，没法子可想．

4．程：<u>老湯</u>，你是不是有甚麽為難的事情？

湯：没有．

程：我們是要好的朋友，你我之間甚麽私話不可以談呢？

湯：我没甚麽大事．就是這學期我除了有了學費之外，還差着一百多塊錢呢．老實對你説，没有生活費．

程：這是小事．昨天我父親對我説過了，要是你的錢不够他幫助你．

湯：他老人家對我太好了．真使我心裏不安．

程：不要那麽説．在一般同學裏我父親最喜歡你．

5．文：昨天美國大使館有一個晚會．

田：昨天是七月四號．今天報上説各國的大使、公使都參加了．當然也請你們新聞界了.

文：是.我這個新聞記者也充數參加了.他們是下午四點鐘開始，我三點多就到了.因為日本公使館離美國大使館很近，附帶着，我還到日本公使館去訪問了一次.

田：報上說日本公使的任期滿了，已經回國了.

文：昨天使館裏人說，新公使下月就上任.

6. 邊：你中文這麽好，你一定研究了相當的時候了.你寫的文章好過我這個中國人.

文：你太客氣了，不論怎麽好，也好不過你呀.說實在的，我中文有一點兒心得.雖然是自己也用了一點兒功，可是同時受我中文老師的影響很大.

邊：大概你的老師教學很認真.

文：是的.我開始學漢字，他限定每天

我必得會寫幾十個字，還得懂得每一個字的意思．要是不會了，他相當的不客氣．天天上課之前，我緊張的不得了．有一回我感覺到這樣的老師我真受不了了，我不想念下去了．可是又一想，使不得，我應該繼續的念下去．

邊：作學生的，大家都不喜歡太認真的老師．可是老師教學認真不認真對學生的影響很大．

文：他實在是認真．比如教我們念課文兒吧，他教了一遍又一遍．非得你完全會了，他才不教了．

7．應：老金，你幾時來的？我怎麽一點兒也不知道啊？

金：我才到這兒．今天晚上就得回去．

應：我們兩個人還沒談談呢．明天再走吧．

金：王廳長讓我今天就回去，而且我買的是來回的票．

應：他讓你今天晚上回去，你明天回去有甚麽關係呢？

金：我是他的屬員．我為公家事來的，那兒能不聽他的．

應：你今天是來作甚麽來了？

金：這裏有一個農業團體開會，廳長讓我代表他參加．

應：我也聽説了．他們研究怎麽樣用科學跟經濟來幫助農民發展農業．

金：對了．

應：我還是希望你到我那兒去，明天再走．你説廳長對你很好．我想你明天回去也沒甚麽．

金：很好是很好，可是我是他的屬員．在公事上總得有個限度，不能隨自己的便哪．

應：那麽你到我那兒吃飯去？

金：不了．我沒時間了．我們兩個人用不着客氣了．下次我來先到你那兒去．我忘了説剛才我也遇見老章了，他說他要離開這兒了.

應：是真的嗎？

金：誰知道呢.他半真半假的對我說的.

應：他沒真話，你別信他的.他在這兒工作是有年限的. 他怎麽可以隨便離開這兒？簡單的一句話說，他又說假話呢.

8. 包：李正之，你那本唐代的歷史故事借我看看成不成？

李：使得，使得.

包：我還得問你一個詞兒.「唐人」是甚麽意思？

李：這個你都不懂嗎？

包：我在外國長大的，中國的事情知道的太少了.

李：你聽我告訴你. 當初唐朝是中國最好的時期. 那個時候在外國的中國人都很有面子，他們用唐朝代表了中國，所以他們都說是「唐人」. 現在的廣東人還說我們是「唐人」.

包：我得多看點兒中文書充實充實自己．我想下學期到你們學校念書好跟你學東西．

李：你要是真的想到我們學校來念書，明天我把學校章程帶來，你看看．

包：我的中文程度有限，章程是文言的，我看不懂吧？

李：我想你看得懂．如果你不懂，我告訴你．

包：我還有一個詞兒忘了問你．「本部」就是「中國本部」是不是？

李：要看上下文．在中國地理上用就是中國本部．要是在公告上就不同了．比如教育部他們用「本部」就是「我們這個部」的意思．

包：我明白了．

9．費：你這幾天見着唐之華了沒有？

溫：沒有．我好幾天沒看見他了．

費：前些日子他告訴我市政府的工作他要辭了．他說工作倒沒甚麽，就是太受氣了. 他説他錯了，不應該自己要求到市政府去，應該在內政部作下去.

温：他受誰的氣？這個時代還有給人氣受的嗎？

費：他説市政府的職員都是市長的私人，只有他是外人. 他們對他都有一個界限.

温：我認為這是他自己的一種感覺. 因為從前內政部的一般人對他太客氣了，他到市政府來，大家不像內政部的人對他那麽客氣，他就受不得了.

費：你説的不對. 從前他很喜歡説話，現在他在辦公室裏連一句話也不説. 他不理別人，別人也不理他.

温：這個他就受不了. 他是最喜歡説話的人.

費：一個人受累沒關係，就是怕受氣. 他不應該自己要求到市政府去，未末了還不是得走？

10. 金：老畢，你有沒有國語文法這本書？中國城的書店我都買遍了也沒買着.
畢：我有. 你先拿去用. 可是你得快點兒還我. 我要作論文了，很需要這本書.
金：你限我幾天的日子呢？
畢：限你看一個星期怎麽樣？
金：我用不到一個星期. 我三天之內就還你.
畢：那更好了. 聽説張教授到這兒來過了.
金：我沒見着他. 聽説他是從這兒路過. 因為美國近代語言學會開會，他去參加那個會.

11. 程：李少堂説要回家了. 甚麽時候走？
麻：他已經走了.
程：是嗎?! 我一點兒也不知道，也沒送送他.
麻：我雖然去送他去了，可是去晚了.

到了飛機場飛機已經起飛了.

程：他這次回家一定很高興. 和家裏人分別了十年了.

麻：那當然了.

程：聽說他是李自成的後代.

麻：很多人都那麽說，可是他最不喜歡人家說他是李自成的後代.

程：我們五個最要好的同學之中，倒有兩個是名人的後代.

麻：還有一個是誰？

程：孔思聰人家説他是孔夫子的後代. 李少堂這回回去,得多少時候回來？

麻：我想在開學之前,他定規要回來的.

12. 唐：章太太，你們小姐今年多大了？

章：屬鷄的，今年十六了. 唐小姐呢？

唐：跟章小姐同歲，也是屬鷄的.

章：兩個人年紀一般大，可是個子唐小姐比我們那個高多了. 有一回我在路上遇見她，簡直連我都不認識她了.

唐：有的孩子長的晚，説不定將來章小姐比我們那個還要高呢．聽説章先生又出門兒了，是不是？

章：是，又去考古去了．

唐：到那兒去考古？

章：到河南．有人發現河南省有一個地方地裏有古城．

唐：是啊．這幾天天氣很不好啊．

章：可不是！這幾天的流行病很普遍．我想跟前些日子長大水也有關係．我昨天跟我那個孩子説，我們母女兩個可別得流行病．父親不在家，誰給我們請醫生啊．

唐：我也這麽想．很多人都得了．可別末了兒讓我們也得了．

章：我們平常注意身體，得的機會總是少一點兒．

13. 先生：現在先不要看書．我先問你們幾個問題．

學生：是．

先生：以前中國和越南有甚麽關係？

學生：以前越南屬於中國．它是中國的屬地．

先生：白金是不是金屬？

學生：是，白金是金屬的一種．

先生：政府幫助農民，對國家有甚麽影響？

學生：一般的説農業是經濟的基本，農業發達經濟就發達．

先生：現在請你們用「基地」和「接受」這兩個詞兒説一句話．

學生："有一個國家要借用我們海邊地帶作基地，我們不接受．"

先生：「私有、私用」有甚麽分別？

學生：「私有」是我自己的．「私用」是我個人自己用的．

先生：「有求必應」是甚麽意思？

學生：就是凡是有人求我幫助，我都幫他們的忙．

先生：還有甚麽問題嗎？

學生：「使用」就是「用」的意思嗎？

先生：是的．好．現在拿出書來把新詞兒念一遍．

14. 連：昨天晚上外面有很大的響聲兒你聽見沒有？

文：我也聽見了．可是我分別不出來是甚麽聲音．

連：或者是汽車出事了．

15. 用人：先生，我得跟您借一個月的工錢．

主人：你借錢作甚麽？

用人：我跟地主借的錢，因為有年限的，今年必得還．可是我們那兒今年有大水，我們的地裏遍地都是水．没法子種地．

主人：你可以跟他們説明，將來能種地的時候再還嗎．

用人：説是説過了．不行啊．他們一定要．説來説去，末後地主説，今年先還他一半，剩下那一半限期明年再還．

主人：好吧，我借給你.

16. 馬：你為甚麽給老王起了個「老好人」的外號兒呢？

章：因為老王常説："做人應該説好話，做好人."所以「老好人」就變成了他的外號兒了.

Exercise 3. Narratives

1. 世界上的事可以分為兩種，一種是公事，一種是私事．世界上的人也可以分為兩種，一種是好人，一種是不好的人．好人和不好的人從甚麽上分別出來呢？可以從他們做事上分別出來，更可以從他們對公事和私事的做法上分別出來．有一種人，對公事十分着重，他先做公事後做私事，有的時候為了公事忘了私事．像這樣的人可以算第一等好人．還有一種人，在他應當做公事的時候他不但去做私人的事，而且用私人，説私話，私用公家的東西，把公家的錢想法子變為私有. 像這樣的人就是最不好的人.

2. 有一個孩子没有父親, 家裏只有他和他的母親. 母子兩個人簡直是没法子過活. 有一天, 他的母親對他說:“因為我們家裏没有錢, 不得不叫你去給別人做工. 你到了別人家裏, 要好好兒的給人家做事. 不要怕受累, 也不要怕受氣.”這個孩子說:“您放心好了. 您別看我的歲數小. 可是我的個子不小, 我不怕受累, 更不怕受氣.”他的母親聽了孩子說的話, 又加上就要和孩子分別了, 她心裏很難受. 她又對孩子說:“我從前就怕你受不得累, 受不了氣. 現在你說你能受, 我就不掛念你了.”

3. 教育部的部長讓他的屬員寫一個章程. 他對那個屬員說:“這個章程是要限制中學畢業的學生出國留學的. 出國留學為的是充實學識是可以的, 但是一般的中學畢業的學生, 他們雖然有了基本的學識, 但是他們學的外國語文當然有限.

到了外國之後，一般的説不容易受到外國學校的歡迎，他們到處都找不到相當的學校，到了末了兒也許又回國了．他們費了很多時間，費了來回的旅費，為的是甚麽呢？所以本部必得定一個章程限制他們出國．”

4．白先生叫我跟他一塊兒去旅行，他説開他那部汽車去．我説：“你那部舊汽車還能使得嗎？”他説：“怎麽使不得，我天天都使用呢．”我説：“我上次開那部車的時候，我聽見車走起來的響聲我就説，這部車太老了，使不得了．没想到你現在還在使用呢．”他説：“在你上次對我説了以後我就修理了．現在甚麽都修理好了．今天加了很多汽油．我們可以往遠一點兒的地方去．我們趕快開車走吧！”

5．妹妹問我：“大使和公使、大使館和公使館有甚麽分别？”我告訴他：“大使、公使都是國家在外國的代表．大使的地位高過公使．大使辦公的地方叫做大使館，公使辦公的地方叫做公使館．大使館和公使館都可以簡稱叫使館．有的大使館在大使之下還有公使．有的公使館只有公使，在公使之上沒有大使．”

6. 有一回我從美國一個基地坐飛機到日本東京去．飛機起飛之後，聽到日本東京飛機場的報告說，東京附近那一帶天氣很不好．飛機上的人，大家都認為那天一定會受天氣的影響，不可能三點鐘到東京了．但是飛機還是繼續的飛．結果到東京的時候連一分鐘都沒差．

7. 有一個外國人很喜歡吃中國菜．他說：“我不論走到甚麼地方，只要有中國飯館兒我就去吃．我最喜歡豬肉燒豆腐，在中國各地方吃的這個菜都做的很好，那是沒甚麼可說的．在英國和法國吃的這個菜就遠不如在日本做的好啦，因為英國和法國不容易買到好的豆腐．有的時候他們用一種好像是豆腐又不是豆腐的東西來充數，所以做出來不好吃．”

8. 清朝末年為了要普及教育，所以在國內各地方都設學校．當時政府的規定是：在各縣設小學，在各省設中學，在北京設大學．

9. 今天上午消費合作社開社員大會推選經理．開會之前，有人猜這次推選出來的人一定是包先生，要不然就是溫先生．可是到了開會的時候，因為社員來的太少，有人主張展期三天．後來就展期了，所以今天沒推選出來誰是經理．

10. 有一個朋友因為他太太病了好久也不見好，而且他的經濟情況又不好，所以時常來跟我借錢．有一回借去十塊錢，又一回借去五塊錢，還有幾回借去三塊兩塊的，我都記不清了．我內人說："你對那位朋友太好了，用一句話說簡直是有求必應．"我說："因為他太太生病，他來借錢．朋友有困難是應該幫助的．"我內人說："幫助朋友應該有限度，不能這樣有求必應啊．"

11. 越南從漢朝、唐朝以來就是中國的屬地．到了清朝末年，越南屬於法國了．到五十年代的時候，他們就是一個國家了．這個國家農田很多，人民多半是農民，也是一個農業國家．

12. 我家種的田都在河邊．我每天跟着父親去種田．有一天，父親對我說:“我們今天不能去種田了．昨天晚上河裏長大水了，遍地都是水．我們田裏的水很深．我們沒法子去種田了．”我說:“我要去看看水有多麽深．”父親說:“水太大了，不要去了．”後來我一個人自己去看了一看．河邊所有的田地果然都是水了．

13. 張先生在出國的時候，他把他的房子借給朋友了．借出的年限是兩年，在限期之內，不能收回．後來不到兩年，張先生從外國回來了．他朋友說:“我趕快找別的房子．你回來住你自己的房子吧．”張先生說:“找房子也需要很多時間呢．你不要忙．我可以先在旅館裏住些日子．”

14. 有一個中國人很喜歡開玩笑. 有一天, 有一個外國人問他貴姓. 他知道這個外國人中文很好,就開玩笑地說:“我姓「十八子」.” 這個外國人心裏想, 中國人的姓都是一個字, 或者是兩個字, 沒有三個字的呀, 這「十八子」三個字也許是拼音. 一面就拿筆把拼音字母寫出來往一塊兒拼, 拼了一遍又一遍, 也不明白是甚麽, 又不好意思再問. 他就問那個中國人:“這個姓中國古時候就有吧?” 這個中國人說:“是的. 古時候姓這個姓的在唐代最有勢力.” 這個外國人還不明白. 這個中國人說:“我給你用中文寫出來吧. 你看,我先寫一個「十」字,再把一個「八」字寫在「十」字的兩邊, 末後在下邊寫一個「子」字. 這「十、八、子」寫在一塊兒, 是甚麽字呢?” 這個外國人一看是一個「李」字, 就說:“你是姓李呀. 姓李的在唐朝的勢力最大, 唐朝在中國歷史上也最有名, 所以中國人也叫唐人, 這些我都知道. 可是我還要請問, 明朝末年有一個李自成, 你是不是他的後代?" 原來這個外國人也是喜歡開玩笑的.

15. 在一個文學研究會裏, 大家談到作文章. 有人說, 從前的文章是屬於知識分子的. 只要是一些知識分子認為做的好, 就算是好文章. 現在的文章是屬於一般人民的, 必得一般人都看得懂才是有用的文章.

16. 有一個私立學校, 近來因為學生增加太多, 需要更多的教室, 要求教育廳在經濟上給一些幫助. 教育廳長說:"很多私立學校, 因為限於經濟的問題不能發展. 我們都沒法子用經濟來幫助他們. 可是這個私立學校, 在私立學校之中是比較好的, 也可以說是最標準的. 現在這個學校的目標是增加教室, 我們一定要給這個學校想辦法."

17. 謝太太在菜市買菜的時候遇見了湯太太.

謝太太說:“這幾天的東西普遍都貴起來了. 我前幾天和今天都是買的一般大的鷄. 前幾天是一塊錢, 今天是一塊三了.” 湯太太說:“不但鷄貴了, 牛肉、豬肉、青菜、魚都貴了. 物價好像得了流行病了似的, 一樣貴, 樣樣都貴起來了.” 謝太太說:“可不是嗎! 我走遍了菜市覺着沒有一樣東西不比從前貴的. 不知道甚麽時候物價才能落下來.” 湯太太說:“只要不再貴了就是很好了. 怎能落價呢?”

18. 有一個外國學生在中國研究中國語文. 他對刻圖章也有興趣. 他有很多刻圖章的書, 也有刻圖章用的刀子和木頭等等. 他說他初學刻圖章的時候是先在木頭上練習. 漸漸的會刻了, 又在金屬的東西上刻. 他又說:“圖章也是一種美術. 我最喜歡這種美術.” 有一回, 有人求他刻一個圖章, 希望他在三天之内刻出來. 他說:“讓我刻圖章不能限定日子的. 如果限幾天刻出來, 最好找刻字的工人去刻，他們一定能刻出來的.”

19. 張先生和田先生從前是同學，現在是同事. 有人問田先生:“你跟張先生又同事又同學，你們兩個人一定也是很好的朋友了.”田先生說:“我跟張先生的關係在私人方面是很好的朋友. 在公事方面，他是主任，我是辦事員. 我是他的屬下.”

20. 老金在沒結婚之前，有人問他:“甚麽樣的女人才是你最理想的太太？”老金說：“我喜歡個子高而聰明的女人.” 後來老金結婚了，他的太太果然是一個聰明的人，就是個子不怎麽高. 有人問他，為甚麽找了一個個子不高的人呢？他說：“她很聰明，我就很滿意了. 天下的事那有完全合理想的哪？”

21. 馬先生病了，住在醫院裏. 有幾個人都要去看他. 有人說:“最好我們定規一個時間，大家一塊兒去.”後來大家就定了一個時間到了醫院，見着了馬先生. 馬先生説:“謝謝各位來看我. 我的病見好了, 最近就要回家了.”

22. 有一個孩子不喜歡上學. 有一天他没上學, 到别的地方玩兒去了. 後來他的母親知道了, 就對他説:“你時常不上學. 今天非打你不可.”她就一面打他, 一面問他:“你以後還敢不上學吧?” 這個孩子説:“不了, 不了.”

23. 山上有一所很大的房子, 從遠的地方看這所房子好像是一個古城似的. 從前這所房子除了房子的主人之外, 外人一律不能進去. 現在甚麽人都可以進去了, 因為現在是一個博物館了.

24. 在政府裏做事的人是公務員. 做了公務員就不能接受人民送的東西. 不論是吃的東西, 或者是其他日用的東西, 總而言之只要是東西都不能接受.

25. 王達之正在家裏復習物理, 有人給他來了一個電話. 他聽完電話之後樂的不得了．原來是學校第二天的物理考試取消了．他說："我正因為物理上有些專用的名詞跟一些奇怪的名稱老記不住，心裏感覺到非常的煩．現在不考了，你說我怎能不樂呢？"

26. 明天是放假的日子，老王來問我有甚麽計劃．我說："我想去旅行．離城三里多路有一條小河．河水流的很慢．河裏有小船．在船裏坐着看看山水很有意思．明天天一亮我就去，天黑了才回來．你呢？" 老王說："我没甚麽計劃．我也許到美國近代語言學會去看個朋友．也許去吃中國飯館兒．"我說："你說去吃中國飯館兒我想起來了．上次你請我吃飯末末了要了一碗肉片湯好極了．我現在還没忘記呢．"

27. 有一個先生給學生講數學．先生舉了很多例子來講，學生有的明白了，有的還是没明白．在要下課的時候，先生說："我舉了這些例子，總之是一個道理．本來要給你們詳細的再講一講,可是限於時間,没法子多講了."

28. 有一個地方有一個湖,湖水很深,從遠的地方看這個湖水是藍色的.有人說,這個湖好像是一個大海,在大海裏有的時候海天之間成了一片藍色,分不出來那裏是天,那裏是海.這個湖水有的時候也是這個樣子.

29. 有一個工業落後的國家要想發展工業,寫了一個五年發展計劃.有人說,這個計劃很好,如果根據這個計劃去做,到了五年工業一定相當的發達.可是這個國家限於經濟問題,不能根據這個計劃去做,所以雖然有了很好的計劃也是没用的.

30. 有一個工人,每天在火車上工作.有一天是九月裏的第一個星期一,有人問他:"今天是甚麼日子?"他說:"是勞工日."那個人說:"在勞工日這一天全國很多工人都放假，你為甚麽不放假呢？”他說：“我是在火車上工作，不能放假.”

Exercise 4. Illustrative Sentences (English)

1.3. Let me use your dictionary for a couple of more days, OK? ··· All right.

1.4. Can your tape recorder still be used?

1.5. Because that country's economy is backward, [therefore it has the result that] neither agriculture nor industry can develop.

1.6. Formerly the diplomatic quarters of the foreign ambassadors and ministers in China were all in the eastern part of Peking [lit. Peking's east city].

2.1. I'm not going to work for him any more. I take his abuse every day, and I can no longer put up with it.

2.2. You say you are abused but I don't believe it. Mr. Wang is a nice person, and he couldn't ill-treat people.

2.4. I can endure any sort of tiring work, but I can't put up with being ill-treated.

2.5. [Those who are] teachers all hope that they will be liked by students.

3.2. Those engaged in that academic research are all superior scholars [lit. elements], except for me [lit. but I this person without talent also participate by making up the number].

3.3. He actually doesn't do any studying. His attending classes is simply a matter of adding to the enrollment [lit. filling a number].

5.4. Formerly when studying the ancient books the teachers all had you declaim in a loud voice over and over again.

5.5. There are still three books [lit. I'm still lacking three books] that I haven't bought. I tried buying them at every bookstore, but I wasn't able to (buy them.)

5.6. He read the characters over and over again (but) no matter how he tried to read them he couldn't read them (correctly).

6.1. Listen, what's that noise outside?

6.3. The fact that I speak the National Language well is due to [having received the influence of] my teacher, for he spoke perfect [lit. most standard] Mandarin.

6.5. Originally I was a student of biology. My studying literature is entirely due to [lit. received] the influence of Professor Ma.

7.2. I was born under the zodiacal sign of the ox. What were you born under? ··· I was born under the pig.

8.2. The younger and older sister are the same in height.

8.4. Generally speaking, there's very little chance of getting this sickness.

9.1. You should understand the basic reason for the lack of success.

10.2. I hadn't yet finished reading that book I borrowed from the library, but it was due back [lit. time limit had arrived]. I went to the library yesterday and they renewed it for two weeks.

10.3. That country would like to expand industry, but owing to economic limitations [lit. limited by conditions of economy] it can't do so at present.

10.4. They would like to expand agriculture, but owing to geographical limitations this is impossible.

10.5. When I do something I don't like people to limit me in time.

10.8. At our school you can't select any courses you please. Foreign students, however, aren't limited [lit. don't have to endure restriction].

10.9. You've limited me to a few days in which to finish this job. How can I manage it?

10.12. There's a time limit on their borrowing that country's territory as a base. The time limit is sixty years.

11.1. Mr. Xie plans to write a history devoted especially to the Ming Dynasty, from the beginning of the dynasty to the end.

11.3. In the national literature exam yesterday I was the very last to finish.

11.7. The last man standing there to buy movie tickets is Mr. Tang.

12.1. Don't listen to him, there's not a bit of truth in him. That book isn't his own [lit. private individual], it's the school's.

15.3. May I ask whether there are many who have the surname "T'ang" of "T'ang Dynasty" ?

16.1. We must attend that meeting. It doesn't matter whether it's you or me, but in any case [lit. in short] one of us must go.

16.3. Eight-tenths of those studying languages at this university are foreign students.

16.4. An agricultural organization will be established here before long. They say the government is right in the midst of planning.

19.4. Zhang Yifan's English is better than mine, and here I am an American.

20.1. Helping them to develop industry is one of the conditions [lit. that is an attached condition].

22.1. Now he's a mere child, and he has such good views. In the future he will certainly be an exceptional person.

27.1. I don't know whether that [matter] is true or not, as he spoke half-jokingly.

32.1. Mr. Zhang is awfully nice to people. In a word, there isn't anything (bad) one can say (against him).

36.1. The Ming Dynasty, one can say, was overthrown by Li Tzu-ch'eng.

37.1. Those [several] states help backward countries economically.